I Myself
Am a Woman

I Myself Am a Woman

Selected Writings of Ding Ling

Edited by

TANI E. BARLOW

with

GARY J. BJORGE

Introduction by

TANI E. BARLOW

Beacon Press / Boston

BEACON PRESS
25 Beacon Street, Boston, Massachusetts 02108

Beacon Press books are published under the auspices of
the Unitarian Universalist Association of Congregations.

96 95 94 93 92 91 90 89   1 2 3 4 5 6 7 8

Text design by Ann H. Stewart

LIBRARY OF CONGRESS CATALOGING-IN-PUBLICATION DATA
Ting, Ling, 1904–85
[Selections. English. 1989]
I myself am a woman : selected writings of Ding Ling / edited by
Tani E. Barlow with Gary J. Bjorge.
p.   cm.
ISBN 0-8070-6736-9
1. Ting, Ling, 1904–85—Translations, English.   I. Barlow, Tani
E.   II. Bjorge, Gary J.   III. Title.
PL2747.P5A23   1989
895.1′35—dc19   88-43313

Dedicated to the memory of
BENJAMIN B. BJORGE
1974–1981

A man, at any rate, is free. He can explore the passions and the continents, can surmount obstacles, reach out to the most distant joys. Whereas a woman is constantly thwarted. At once inert and pliant, she has to contend with both physical weakness and legal subordination. Her will is like the veil on her bonnet, fastened by a single string and quivering at every breeze that blows. Always there is a desire that impels and a convention that restrains.

GUSTAVE FLAUBERT
Madame Bovary

Heaven is my father and Earth is my mother, and even such a small creature as I finds an intimate place in their midst.

Therefore that which fills the universe I regard as my body and that which directs the universe I consider as my nature.

All people are my brothers and sisters, and all things are my companions.

ZHANG ZAI
The Western Inscription

CONTENTS

ACKNOWLEDGMENTS

The editor wishes to thank the following for their help over a period of years. Lenore Timm and the University of California, Davis, Women's Center provided an early grant. The history department of the University of Missouri–Columbia has supported the anthology's production. In particular, Ms. Patricia Eggelston typed repeated drafts with unfailing good humor and patience. Peter Carroll advised on the development of the initial idea, as did Howard Goldblatt. Ms. Joanne Wykoff provided outstanding editorial guidance and a sustaining enthusiasm for the project.

The following individuals helped in the process of translation: Howard Goldblatt, Katie Haeger, Loretta Li, Chang Jun-mei, Wang Zheng, Yao Lan, and Bi Xiufen.

Professors Susan Benson, Dina Copelman, Irene Eber, and Donald M. Lowe enriched the Introduction. Ms. Barlow also wishes to thank the following China scholars, from whose work she has drawn: Marsten Anderson, Arif Dirlik, Y. K. Feuerwerker, Charlotte Furth, Gary Hamilton, Chad Hanson, Ted Huters, Ambrose King, Andrew Plaks, and Yuan Liangjun. Thanks are also due to the original Beacon reader, a number of whose suggested revisions have been incorporated.

Finally we thank our families and parents for all their support.

"When will it no longer be necessary to attach special weight to the word 'woman' and raise it specially?" Ding Ling wrote in 1942. The question joined Ding Ling's two paramount concerns, women and literature. When she composed the introduction to her famous essay, "Thoughts on March 8," at dawn on August 3, 1941, she had not yet determined how to locate its intended audience. Eight months later, she offered it as she "always intended, for the perusal of those people who have similar views," in the Chinese Communist Party's *Liberation Daily* and thus helped instigate Mao Zedong's decisive "Talks at the Yan'an Forum on Art and Literature." "I myself am a woman," she wrote in the essay, and on that basis she believed she had a writer's authority to represent women. "We need the critical essay," she had written in an October 1941 essay arguing that Communist Party writers had to have publication venues for material critical of the state. "Thoughts on March 8," a critical evaluation of Yan'an Communism and women was the result.

Ding Ling wrote Chinese feminist fiction as a young writer, but over the course of her life she abandoned most of feminism's component elements. Her unique significance as a twentieth-century Chinese cultural figure lies in this. No other writer in this century has conveyed better, not just what it felt like to be a modern Chinese woman, but also how impossible an imported Western-style feminism was to sustain, even for the most ambitiously experimental and internationalist cultural revolutionary.

Ding Ling's writing and her life history have far more than tangential interest for us. How we understand her work, how we translate her into our familiar categories and associations, depends on how seriously we take cultural difference and sexual coding. It requires, in other words, interrogation of some of our own assumptions and allows us critical access to questions being begged in our own feminisms. How should we regard the "we" constituted by our sympathetic connection with women outside our own culture, while we continue to shelter the old universalist pretensions so thoroughly basic to most Anglo-American feminisms? Do we really believe that all women should be liberated in the same way? If not, how do we evaluate those liberations? Ding Ling's literature and life experience pose, in other words, very contemporary, transnational questions of women's writing, feminist theory, and sexual difference.

I

Ding Ling was one of modern China's most famous writers and cultural revolutionaries. She belonged to the May Fourth generation, a group of academics, writers, politicians, and cultural revolutionaries who acted as brokers between imperial and socialist China. Many came from the disintegrating *shidaifu,* or gentry class of imperial power-holders. Many belonged to the new social category of educated people, the *zhishifenzi,* or intellectual class. In the biography of Ding Ling that follows, we will stress the significance of May Fourth as a political movement. Now we need only note that the generation remade national political culture by withdrawing their support from the religious and ethical constructs that had made the *ancien regime* seem all of one piece: in the relation of Confucian ideology to family practice, of textual knowledge to the civil service examination system, of the imperial government to the authority of the father.

By the 1930s, the May Fourth generation had made literature and politics its two signature vocations. In this regard, Ding Ling was an exemplary May Fourth figure. But she was one of the few women in the movement, and she further set herself apart by placing the problem of being a woman at the center of her fiction. We are particularly concerned here to show how Ding Ling's fiction connected to a body of literature concerned with the "woman problem," and how her concerns changed through time. To do so requires a brief comment on what being a writer in twentieth-century China meant and why the fiction the May Fourth writers produced was so important.

The nature of written Chinese is key to the whole issue of literacy for Ding Ling's generation. As late as 1919, people read and wrote in a range of styles now grouped collectively as "literary" or "classical" Chinese. Qing dynasty (1644–1911) scholarship had made it clear that the Four Books and Five Classics—the Confucian canon—were true only in a historically relative sense, so that educated people did not necessarily consider the Confucian heritage scripturally sacred. But since Confucianism was also the elite's literary repository, scholars still learned by memorizing core texts like *The Great Learning* and *The Doctrine of the Mean*. The dominant theory of the genre also held that Confucian poetry and essays were valuable because they transmitted Truths, the Dao, and since narrative fiction did not, serious people should avoid it. This position was quite deceptive on a number of counts, particularly because colloquial novels had been flourishing since the eighteenth century among the most cultivated people. Furthermore, such novels—even the magnificent eighteenth-century *Story of the Stone* (or *Dream of the Red Chamber*), often classified as a *Bildungsroman* in the West—often demanded tremendous erudition of the reader and represented a closed world of philosophic and linguistic signs. *The Story of the Stone* thus reads more like a fantastically elaborate *Alice in Wonderland* than a Chinese *Buddenbrooks*.

A number of historical factors affected the "revolution of genres" that replaced the Confucian-style essay with the foreign-style novel. European and North American Christian missionaries to China in the nineteenth century had already demonstrated how colloquial language could be used as a powerful propaganda weapon. A handful of Chinese political reformists and theorists in the 1890s, knowing that Western countries all had long traditions of colloquial fiction and used novels to circulate new ideas, made the case that Western fiction, particularly the political novel, could serve as a tool for alerting and transforming the Confucian literati, still somnolently unaware of how powerful the West really was. They encouraged translations and appropriation of new genres. By the turn of the century, narrative fiction had already gained new ground.

When the Versailles Conference handed China's Shandong Province over to the Japanese in 1919, the betrayal triggered a local response that snowballed from political street demonstrations to a revolt of young intellectuals. Educated youth subjected all received ideas (which they began for the first time to lump together as "Confucianism") to criticism. They condemned everything: texts, thinking, language, and social practices, including the poetic and "classical" written languages, the etiquette and protocol of sex, age, and class hierarchies, and the ways that heritage had subordinated certain kinds of individual expression. Their own popular tradition was rich, and in time leading intellectuals did recuperate indigenous colloquial fiction. But the hallmark of the May Fourth literatus, as with the present generation of young Chinese intellectuals, was identification with Europe and North America. A frenzy of activity ensued as young intellectuals organized literary circles devoted to promoting specific Western theories and genres. People, most of them men, translated favorite authors from Mark Twain to Mallarmé, Alexander Dumas to Flaubert, Shakespeare to Lewis Carroll. They began producing modern narratives modeled after the romanticism, realism, and impressionism of the appropriated European master texts.

That educated Chinese chose fiction—rather than journalism, essay, or philosophy—requires some explanation. Victorian fiction offered immediate moralistic categories, yet remained free of discredited Confucian dogmatism. May Fourth fiction had the virtue of seeming both new and familiar because it linked moral instruction to story telling, and that connection gratified intellectuals no matter how they felt about Confucianism. European techniques also allowed Chinese writers new means to express their alienation. When anti-Confucian thinkers attacked old-fashioned family life and ripped away the façade of surname solidarity to reveal sexual and generational oppressions, they valorized confessional literature. Western bourgeois fiction offered ready-made narrative models for expressing shock and individual panic, just as Rousseau's *Confessions* supplied new ways to define the person. Chinese writers also accepted the internationalist position then current in the United States and Western Europe, which fitted the so-called development of Chinese fiction into a larger, purportedly universal, form. In "moderninzing" fiction, they believed, they were actually making China a part of the "family of nations," and thus part of the civilized world. Another reason to choose fiction was power. Since the eighteenth century, the dominant tendency in Western-style fiction—realism—had proposed to represent not just truth but Reality. This was, of course, a complex and highly ideological claim.

Particularly since the eighteenth century, Western writers of narrative fiction had assumed that they could represent the truth of experience, both internal emotional experience and human affairs, by stringing words together in a way that decreased the distance separating language and reality. Text and reality would be linked by the hidden authority of the narrator, everywhere present but often not directly acknowledged, and by the narrator's claim to show reality as it is apprehended through our human senses. For young Chinese intellectuals ardently pursuing cultural transformation, realism had the advantage of seeming to be an essentially transparent medium. Writers of Western-style fiction could represent Chinese reality "as it was" without any special technical training. Realist fiction also magnified the importance of writers. The realist writer re-presents reality through a unique genius. Thus conceived, a writer could be simultaneously the servant of society, (laboring to represent reality correctly) and the special vehicle of truth, since by bourgeois definition writers had keener sensibilities, better sight, more "creativity," than other educated people. Finally, of course, once they developed a written language close enough to popular speech that any literate or semiliterate person could understand it, Chinese fiction writers could hope to reach a much wider audience than did Confucian scholars or even modern technocrats.

Chinese tradition, however, had its own version of how fiction was made. It had linked fictional representation to the transmission of verities. Novels belonged to the same tradition as Confucian philosophy and historiography, that of transmitting facts. Chinese historians and fiction writers expected to pass on truths that were self-evident to writer and reader. For instance, the truth of the universal power of ritual was expounded in *The Scholars,* a Qing satire that illustrated the decadence of a community no longer capable of conducting ritual. Writers of such novels were simply transmitting common knowledge or belief rather than constructing an image of the "real world" through the mediation of their individual imaginations. As a consequence of this heritage, sometimes fiction writers did not claim their own work or pretended that their stories had been inherited or even found. Other major narratives had joint authors. Still other writers of novels chose to remain anonymous. So while prerevolutionary China had a rich variety of fiction, novels remained a subgenre. The various Confucian schools did not specially privilege the producers of fiction or value their vocation.

When May Fourth writers adapted Western narrative practice to their immediate needs, they valorized the storyteller but never relinquished their belief that literature transmitted available, common, social truths. This, joined to the liberal internationalism of the May Fourth period, meant that new fiction writers assumed enormous power. Gathered in enclaves that stressed youth and experimentation, reading Western novels, watching Western movies, attending Western-style schools, adopting Western names, the Europeanized May Fourth generation glamorized the literary man and literary woman in a wholly unique way. Anyone who mastered the new narrative convention became a writer and had access to truths of experience, representing them to others. In fact, having discredited Confucianist moral discourse, the treaty port bourgeoisie had little immediately to fall back on but the imported texts of the "superior" cultures and, eventually, the syncretic political ideologies of what might be called the Chinese Enlightenment, liberalism, conservatism, anarchism, democratic socialism, and Marxism.

May Fourth writers used their powers in many ways. They deliberately confused author and protagonist and invited readers to project their sympathies beyond the story to the writer, and from them, metonymnically, to the "youth of China." Writers like the anarchist Ba Jin built faithful middle-class audiences this way. Novelists also heightened their reputations by borrowing techniques, plots, even characters from foreign novels. A good example is the way Ding Ling used Flaubert's Emma Bovary as a female type in all four of her first short stories, collected in the anthology *In Darkness*. Usually writers gave young readers ethical models in their fiction and presented themselves as personal advisors. The literate urban youth in the 1920s and 1930s circulated an entirely new literary culture. They modeled themselves on characters out of European books. They spoke a new moral language that took foreign novels as its referent. Marguerite of the Camellia's represented loyalty; Young Werther, poetic depression; Ibsen's Nora gave instruction on the female will; Mao Dun's Mei illustrated female will in a Chinese setting; Ba Jin's trilogy outlined moral response in a revolutionary world through the typology of character. Ding Ling's Miss Sophia stood for the "psychology of the modern girl."

Ding Ling belonged to this first, large, group of writers who came to prominence by producing Western-style literature for a restricted middle-class audience in a special language, a mixture of colloquial Chinese and more classical syntax. Following the first successful explorations of Western narrative in the 1920s, writers, like most intellectuals, found themselves preoccupied with China's national politics. Chinese society was in full crisis. Many writers felt they had to step beyond realist representation to active, interventionist politics. In the late twenties and early thirties, the League of Left Wing Writers, its agenda set by the Communists and Democratic Socialists, debated the notion of a revolutionary modern fiction. It was not immediately clear who the audience of such a fiction would be. Nor, on the other hand, was it clear that "good" writers were knowledgeable witnesses of the realities they felt it politically necessary to represent. Engaged writers worried about whether they should educate the masses first (many of whom were only barely, if at all, literate) or create works the masses would appreciate after the revolution, whether a revolutionary narrative could be both good and instructive, and about political ideology and fictional verisimilitude could correspond and on whose terms.

After the 1927 counterrevolution, right and left fought for the loyalties of the educated elite. Writers were key in this struggle. They had the audiences, the means to persuade. They had inherited and transformed the peculiar service ethic—part selfless, part self-aggrandizing—of their Confucian forebears. Political chaos made the literary livelihood increasingly precarious, shutting down presses, destroying publishing outlets, and Japanese encroachments made many writers into refugees. Never-

Nevertheless, as fear of retaliation from the right grew, so too did the social value of writers. With their rapidly changing narrative practices and their astonishingly generous personal commitments, writers like Ding Ling transformed fiction-reading from an act of personal liberation to a revolutionary statement. In recognition of that fact, the Communist Party (composed in the thirties of women and men who came from similar backgrounds as the writers and shared many attitudes and allegiances with them) sought both to attract and to discipline the major May Fourth literati.

When the Communists reached the far Northwest in the late thirties, set up their military base area, and began the social experiment known as Yan'an Communism, the importance of writers was enhanced once again. But the association of the May Fourth generation and the Party was not without conflict. On the one hand lay the propaganda value of a "free" corps of writers to face down charges of literary oppression leveled by the right. On the other lay the tactical need to curb the power of the writers over the Party's most valuable asset of all, the politically uncommitted educated youth. These concerns formed the backdrop to matters of ideology that Ding Ling's audacious charge in 1942 brought to the surface. Out of Mao Zedong's "Talks at the Yan'an Forum on Literature and the Arts" came, for the first time, a Party orthodoxy that required adherence to crude political guidelines and handed literature and writers over to an empowered literary bureaucracy. After 1942, approved literature made claims to represent only the realities mediated through the reigning political line.

If ideology was the parameter of literary substance after 1949, it did not always determine literary politics. The state set up cultural bureaucracies, and as diffused as power was, the bureaucrats ensconced there did exercise control, at the very least over each other. The more power at stake, the crueler the struggle to hold it became. Personal conflicts stretching back decades, vendettas held over from past campaigns, work unit incest, old love affairs, professional jealousy, and gossip all had a part in the growing viciousness of literary politics. One purge followed the next: 1956, 1957, 1962, and then, 1966. Writers of the generations after the May Fourth giants became proxies for Party officials, the voices of future orthodoxies. Networks of discreet politicians produced texts through "writers" who subtly criticized opponents or sought out allies. Upright officials sacrificed themselves on behalf of heterodox truths and expressed their visions through literary texts. Dissident writers claimed extra-bureaucratic powers, claiming the allegiance of readers.

In other words, the assumption that fiction was a transparent screen onto which specially endowed people projected their own formulations of reality sustained the claims of literature to truth even as it neatly sub-ordinated literature to social theory and political struggle. Texts and the people who produced them were as powerful as they were vulnerable to political persecution.

The problem for many left-wing May Fourth veterans in 1966, on the eve of the Great Proletarian Cultural Revolution, was that they believed the charges shortly put to them: that their literary revolution had been bourgeois and their conception of the writer's role contemptuous of the masses. While Ding Ling was always sufficiently correct politically to avoid this self-censure, the feeling was widespread among writers and intellectuals. Over the years 1942–66, many writers had attempted to invent syncretic narratives. Others like Ding Ling had largely stopped producing and waited for the proletarian writers of the future to mature. But concurring or not, May Fourth or younger, the Cultural Revolution decimated the ranks of writers and literary bureaucrats. Many commit-ted suicide, or at least suffered a literary death. Others were murdered or fell to ill-treatment, insanity, depression, untreated disease, old age. Oth-ers lost faith in reeducation camps or lived, under suspicion for a decade, in circumstances shrewdly calculated to humiliate them. Or, like Ding Ling, they languished in prison.

Writers, of course, were not the only people to suffer during the Cul-tural Revolution. Party cadres on whatever could be defined as "the other side," all intellectuals contaminated by the West, professionals, old class enemies, ordinary schoolteachers, hungry villagers denied traditional marketing outlets and forced to cultivate inappropriate crops, Red Guards robbed of education—all emerged in the late 1970s full of griev-ances. For May Fourth writers like Ding Ling, Ai Qing, and Ba Jin who had generally supported the revolution, nothing could completely ex-plain its implosion.

In 1983 the Party officially reversed the policy set forth in Mao's "Talks at the Yan'an Forum." Today the primary producers and consumers of literature are the self-educated survivors of the Cultural Revolution, the Chinese baby-boom generation now in their thirties and forties. Readers find in literature and aesthetics a counterideology to the discredited po-litical ideology. May Fourth writers who have survived seem to find their grandchildren's generation of literati contemptible. Some distrust the re-glamorization of the bourgeois writer as avatar of truth. They worry about the young writers who push the limits of Party control, not in the old generation's heroic game of advice and dissent, but with a cynicism that they, now returned to power, cannot recall feeling.

A great deal has been written about the history of fiction writers in twentieth-century China. Here it must simply provide a context. The point as it pertains to Ding Ling can be easily summarized: if the state takes the power to ratify all modes of literary representation, how can female writers and readers ensure that their felt needs will be addressed, their experiences correctly represented? Pushing the point further still, in a slightly different direction, what in Chinese literature in the relationship of gender and representation specifies the "needs" of female writers and readers and how does the notion of a Chinese feminism fit when this question is specially privileged?

2

In "Thoughts on March 8," Ding Ling was also addressing a body of theory we may call, loosely, May Fourth feminism (*nüquan zhui*) and redefining yet again what being a woman should mean in a revolutionary world. As Qing society buckled under the pressures of imperialism and internal chaos, a revolution in the relations between women and men occurred in urban areas. This was different from the family crisis that wracked village China, denying sectors of the peasantry their traditional goals of family formation. The "woman problem" led cultural revolutionaries to attack Confucian social relations and to develop a critique of inherited gender categories.

Qing China did indeed derogate women and privilege men. Yet male dominance was never enforced by a strictly binary discourse permitting only two polar perspectives, male and female. Nor did Qing social relations share the liberal Western mythology that humans had of necessity traded a "natural" condition of brutal conflict for the limiting rights of the social contract. Chinese language and social practice foreclosed several other aspects of Western thinking, including the notions that communities are composed of autonomous individuals who act out of self-interest, that the desires of individuals inevitably clash with the needs of society, and that human beings are the product of their component elements (reason, sense perception, circulatory system, sexual essence).

Under Qing inscriptions, language and social experience had a very different order. In a largely agrarian, "preindustrial" world, social life was projected as a series of relationships (*lun*) between pairs of people, all of whom participated, albeit unequally, in the three areas of experience: of the person, the family, and the group. Whereas Western logic tended to privilege metaphoric logic (individual matter, social body, heavenly bodies, for example) Confucian logic convinced through metonymic association. It understood things in terms of part to whole rather than the one and many. Thus the human subject was never autonomous and never a microcosm of atomistic society. A subject could exist only in relation to another partial element of the larger context that the two of them formed when conjoined. Subjects participated in other movements, a point I'll take up in a moment. But here I want to stress that there simply could not be an imperial subject since *ji* always define themselves in relation to other *ji*.

Male and female, Confucian subjects always appeared as part of something else, defined not by essence but by context, marked by interdependency and reciprocal obligation rather than by autonomy and contradiction. The most compelling contexts were formed out of the five *lun* of Confucian practice, father to son, monarch to minister, husband to wife, older to younger brother and older to younger friends. In the family, subjects participated in obligatory dependencies modeled after the primary and tertiary *lun* of son to father/father to son and wife to husband/husband to wife and all the varieties suggested there—daughter/father, daughter/mother, granddaughter/grandmother, and so on. Indeed, groups of people not related by kinship and not covered by the first four *lun* might form groups based on their common subdialect and home ties. Strangers constructed groups (lineages, bandit gangs, marriage-resistance sisterhoods, benevolent societies, etc.) on the model of face-to-face relations of kin, drawing on a pseudo-kinship language, within concrete parts of larger contextual wholes.

The social construction of gendered subjects followed, first, from dialectical binarisms that set poles to mark the ends of extremely wide lines of possibility (rather like bookends mark the ends of rows) concerning qualities of personality. These polarities were infinitely complex and ceaselessly changing when considered in their totality: hot/cold, soft/hard, wet/dry, still/active, north/south, male/female. Engenderment thus could not proceed purely from biology or even from principle (the "form" infesting matter) because masculine/feminine and male/female were subordinate, complementary, bipolar attributes subject to qualification and constant reassignment.

Second, engenderment relied less on the operation of masculine/feminine than on the inclusive *yin/yang*, the "Two Modes" associated with male/female. Women are in this way associated with *yin*, as men are with *yang*, but are not "composed" of it. All *lun* relations had a *yin* aspect and a *yang* aspect: father/*yang* and son/*yin*, husband/*yang* and wife/*yin*, older friend/*yang* and young friend/*yin*, master/*yang* and disciple/*yin*. *Yin/yang*, like "science" in the capitalist West, was the epistemological basis for all theorizing. It controlled and enclosed all subordinate bipolarities, thus incorporating the male/female qualities in its operation. A woman master in a vegetarian hall, for example, stood in *yang* relation to her disciples, regardless of their sex. Similarly, a pregnant woman was *yin* in relation to her embryo's *yang*, regardless of its sex.

Engenderment relied most heavily on the *li,* the ritual, governing how the parts of the *lun* should act in relation to each other. Gendered subjects were an effect of *li,* the highly graded, absolutely specific technical knowledge of proper behavior. It is quite fashionable to comment on the correspondence of current Anglo-American role theory and the Chinese notion of *fen.* But what goes unremarked is that *fen,* or role, did not constrain personality, nor (at least until the May Fourth critique) did it suppress the natural feelings of individuals. Knowledge in the late Confucian episteme, as one historian has recently noted, was "knowing how to," it was "skill-knowledge." [1] Knowing how to behave as a person in a given range of contexts was continuous with being that person. Roles like "virtuous wife, good mother" were restrictive by definition and could be quite oppressive, of course. But the rules of proper behavior were neither arbitrary nor repressive in the sense of masking a true and submerged nature.

A recent study has demonstrated empirically that in seventeenth-century China, cases of men becoming women and women becoming men were surprisingly common. [2] In each case once the physiological transformation had taken place (a man gradually became a woman when he developed breasts and began menstruating; a girl became a boy when hit suddenly by a lucky meteorite), the individuals engendered themselves quite naturally. They expressed the desire to dress in a manner appropriate to their age, marital status, and social status and began developing the natural feelings and behaviors associated with that position. Other elite cultural expressions of divergence between physiology and ritual codes included strategies for eluding restrictions. Girls commonly took their educations dressed as boys, sitting among brothers and cousins; this kind of female-to-male cross-dressing reinforced the *li* of segregation while at the same time maintaining the ritual base of engenderment. Cross-dressing and cross-role behaviors also figured prominently in utopian speculation, farce, irony, criticism, and fantasy.

Qing processes of engenderment did not lack access to contemporary Euro-North American truths. People simply constituted themselves on different grounds altogether. As in European cultures before the Enlightenment, Qing Chinese found women and men rather similar, physiologically malleable, defined more in terms of ability to procreate than through sexual acts or preferences, distinguished primarily by ritual protocols, not chromosomes or mannerisms. Qing Chinese weighted birth order and generation heavily. They also used kinship as the imaginary referent for a series of discourses that completely obscured socioeconomic associations of extra-kin nature.

The early twentieth-century critique of Chinese culture and May Fourth iconoclasts like Ding Ling attacked the hold that the Three Bonds (the first three of the five *lun*) exercised over Chinese of all orders: Father is to son, as monarch is to minister, as husband is to wife. These formulas involve sexual categories without mentioning gender. They express the social order through a rhetoric of personal relationships.

3

Historians of women and feminist theoreticians in Europe and North America today are reevaluating feminism. What seems less clear now than a decade ago is whether feminism is a series of oppositional practices, a body of theory, or a cultural habit. Theoreticians are calling into question the targets of their own practice—family, state, men—and are asking if feminism without a binary opposition has any meaning. Gender theorists suggest that there is nothing universal about women at all. Postfeminists question the need to challenge sexual division of labor and suggest that feminism might indeed be the private, local mythology of post-Enlightenment liberalism in Europe and the United States, a parasite of dominant, nineteenth-century social theory. At the very center of the controversy resides the explosive question of whether liberal and socialist feminism speaks on behalf of all women or is simply another instrument of Western imperial control.

Critics frequently call Ding Ling a feminist because of her long-term interest in the woman problem. She was indeed, briefly, a Chinese feminist, but understanding that phenomenon involves examining how feminist tropes and assumptions travel across cultural codes. The manner in which "feminist" notions that seem self-evident in one context become problematic in a borrower's context must concern us. Most important, we need to grasp why people borrow across culture and the uses to which they put what they have taken. In the case of Chinese feminism, the object was clearly to use imported Western ideology as a fulcrum to dislodge the Confucian heritage schematized so elegantly in the Three Bonds.

May Fourth feminism consisted of several elements. First, it drew on arguments about universal suffrage, legal rights, and equal access to the public domain that had unfolded after 1848 in the United States and England. Before the May Fourth movement, political rights for women was a part of general revolutionary dogma and did not always or necessarily involve its male and female proponents in a critique of Confucianism. On the contrary, the effort of leading male Confucianists like Kang Yuwei and Liang Qichao,[3] to redeem China in the eyes of the imperialists, initiated the movements to unbind feet, extend civil "rights," and develop formal educational institutions for women. This element of Chinese feminism coexisted with subsequent governments.

The more challenging strand in feminist thinking was the attempt to translate into Chinese revolutionary practice Western oppositional structures. Western social theory after the Enlightenment linked a binary discourse of gender to a long series of oppositions and thus connected sexual qualities to a general cosmology. The formulaic expression of this effort is the familiar equation of culture and man, of nature and woman. "Culture is to nature as man is to woman" surfaced in late-twentieth-century American feminist theory, a connection rooted in Rousseau, Voltaire, Diderot, and Lévi-Strauss. Critics of this connection have noted how it has naturalized and made essential the notion of sexual opposition. They have also pointed out that the equation holds true in very few cultures (since many do not theorize "nature" as natural) and is at best a highly ideological version of our own order.

All Chinese cultural revolutionaries, theorists, fiction writers, dress reformers, and so on, who borrowed narrative, sociology, political science, or media images as a means of distinguishing male and female on the basis of sexual identity contributed to Chinese feminist theorizing. The affirmation of "nature" over "culture" as the base for social theory especially attracted May Fourth thinkers because the ascendancy of nature elevated sex and physiology over *li* and *lun*. Not kinship but personal identity, not procreative fertility but sexual expression, not appropriate behavior but natural behavior should regulate human lives. People in China would naturally become masculine and feminine to the degree they liberated themselves from culture.

Feminist intellectuals charged that the Three Bonds could not be eternal or universal because they had been imposed on China by "culture" and hid a true and better world based on natural instinctive behavior. Gu Chengwu, Lo Jialun, Mao Dun, Yu Pingbo, Mao Zedong, Ye Xiaojun—all of them leading "feminists," all of them men—began their revolutionary careers with a general critique of Chinese women's oppression, arguing that Confucianism had produced a culture so inhuman that it could not exist without the derogation of women and children.

Against the patriarchal family, and for women, many cultural revolutionaries did argue for "individualism." The compelling opposition between patriarchalism (*jiazhang zhui*) and individualism (*geren zhui*) rested on the possibility that women and men would grow naturally into autonomous beings once they were liberated from their common past. Even so, advocacy made a lot of them uneasy. Ye Xiaojun voiced their ambivalence when he asked whether, after all social restriction had been removed, women would prove to have any personal being at all.

Over the course of the 1920s, feminist activity infused family reform politics, although not all issues pertaining to family reform were feminist. Since in Confucian thought family regulation had a central part to play in good government, attacks on the past often shaded off into attacks on the "traditional" family. The major family reform issues of the early twentieth-century—footbinding and concubinage, female slavery and marriage reform, female education and domestic seclusion, career autonomy and the freedom to love (*lianai ziyou*), the priority of love over obligation and of sexual desire over the desire to please parents—thus became sometimes inadvertently important issues for both the feminist and nonfeminist of the urban educated elite.

Both wings of Chinese feminism—the women's rights movement and the cultural revolutionaries' efforts to establish "woman" in dialectical opposition to "man"—had an enormous impact on the transformation of Chinese culture, though neither in the way its initial advocates had anticipated. The rights movement was absorbed into the statist politics of the contending parties by the mid-1920s. Both the right, the Nationalist Party, and the left, the tiny Chinese Communist Party, formed Women's Departments in order to mobilize the female citizenry, and as one part of the effort at cultural renovation against the claims of foreign superiority. For the duration of the Northern Expedition, Chiang Kaishek's effort to recentralize China in 1927, left and right collaborated. After 1927, politically active feminism foundered.

Activist women felt torn between the objectives of gender reform and national salvation. Patriotic women were moved by arguments that feminist objectives wasted political resources, thus damaging Chinese unity, or that they subordinated inherited tradition to foreign conventions, thus violating an essential Chineseness. It was difficult to insist on political separatism at a time when Japanese incursions threatened national sovereignty. Also, when the Northern Expedition revealed exactly how inflammable family reform issues could become, a split opened up between those who saw family reform as a means to stabilize the nation and those who hoped to alleviate the position of women in oppressive families. Both political parties pondered the choice between sexual politics (women's liberation) and family reform ("new democratic patriarchy," in the words of one recent critic).

The theorization of woman/man had a more durable career. It persists to this day, grounded in China's institutional structure as the venerable Women's Association (*Funü lianhehui*). From its earliest years, the Chinese Communist Party had adapted its women's policy directly from the writings of cultural revolutionaries like Mao in conjunction with what could be learned about sexual liberation in the revolutionary Soviet

Union. Emancipation of women became the bellwether of social revolution.

In Jiangxi Province in the late 1920s and early 1930s, the Party grafted liberation theory developed in urban areas onto its rural policy. The first experiments to mobilize women from oppressive patrilineal families resulted in a rash of murders and suicides as chaste widows were forcibly married and women were handed as booty to local "reform" cadres. The Jiangxi experience colored marriage reform and policy on sexual politics in the Party formulations ever afterward because it demonstrated both the advantages and drawbacks to organizing people on the basis of gender. Emancipating women often meant handing them from the control of fathers and abusive husbands to hostile strangers. Without Party protection, daughters and widows fell prey to men whose familistic goals had been thwarted for lack of bride price. Female solidarity came more easily in this early soviet than later, but even so, those responding to the notion of common womanhood tended to be rebellious, young, unmarried women.

In the shelter of the Northern border regions, the Party retained its commitment to separate-sex organizations in the late 1930s, but its problems intensified. Eventually the Party relied on mobilized female labor to feed its army and clothe its isolated population. But the local people were poorer than in the South, kinship obligation and economic indebtedness locked villagers into miserably oppressive forms of "feudalism," and the family enforced a filial respect for age that made it difficult to mobilize young women against even the most abusive kin. Without intensive preparation, the policy of organizing mass associations into groups defined by sex, degree of poverty, or social class did not succeed. Yet rigid sexual and economic segregation of the rural areas in the 1940s foreclosed any other possibility.

In 1942 Ding Ling's essay "Thoughts on March 8" raised some of these old contradictions in a public forum. The tension between the Party and its most literate, educated women involved policy issues. Whether to mobilize women outside the family or to retain the family as the basis of production was the most clearly defined dispute. Other differences included removing women from abuse where their labor was crucial to family survival and the question of marriage reform for young women. It was not clear who, in the long run, was more important, the accommodationist female majority or the minority of young activists, and it was no clearer in 1942 than before what alternatives to the peasant family existed. Even the policy of raising women's status inside the family through model-worker spinning and weaving campaigns and propaganda seemed to be flagging.

If Party theory persisted in "raising high the word 'woman,'" Ding Ling argued in 1942, it had to charge that word with fresh meaning. The 1942 confrontation did revitalize policy on women. The Party reworked its mass organizations and mobilized women for war production. Subsequent organizational energies were poured into the reconstruction of the New Democratic family, linking the raised status of daughters, daughters-in-law, and wives to national salvation, prosperity, and social reconstruction. When, after defeating Japan, the Party turned to civil war, it drew on the other part of its May Fourth heritage, and women's policy shifted to emphasize class struggle and sexual struggle. But by that time, women's organizations had become simply one element of the Communist subordination of all social distinctions to the dominant paradigm of class.

In other words, Maoism transformed "woman" into a subordinate ideological category. It is a rich category, infused with the "scientific socialism" of Engels, the Victorian biological reductions of Spencer and Darwin, medical models derived from nineteenth-century physiology, and Qing *yin/yang* theory. It has an iconography familiar to all of us—women driving tractors, women teaching school, women building dams—and a rhetoric, "women hold up half the sky," that makes it attractive, self-congratulatory, and accessible, from time to time, to the oppressed daughters-in-law it originally intended to represent. With some significant political interruptions, it has sustained specialized periodicals like *Chinese Women* and *Women's Literature*.

But "woman" had far less weight in the post-Liberation construction of gender than the neofamilism of the Maoist cosmology. The major consequence of New Democracy for women's policy was the government's commitment to revitalize domestic relationships. Where the rural peasant family made the father-son relationship sacrosanct, the Communist government propagandized for filial obligation to mothers and to the nation, the *guo,* through the mother-and-father. It recuperated into theory the cultural codes of filial subordination, the emphatic preference for immediate relationships, and the pattern of social construction of personal identity through participation in social dyads. If the Three Bonds schematize the relations of the Qing, the post-Liberation People's Republic of China might be represented by the following formula: Husband is to wife as parents are to children and the state is to its citizens.

The similarities between old and new China are due to rural cultural conservatism, in part, to the state's preferences. The novelties are just as obvious. Gender has entered the primary relation of state and citizen, breaking all historical precedent. Parent-to-child replaces the dominant father-to-son bond, and husbands now marry female citizens. Daughters now grow up—in rare cases—to be officials, no matter how restricted their powers may be in comparison to that exercised by male colleagues.

This new order appears on balance to be more hospitable to women than earlier regimes. Individuals say their lives are better than their grandmothers' lives. Girls no longer suffer the pain and indignity of foot-binding their grandmothers did. Fewer are subject to anonymous sale, extinction at birth, or starvation, all of which the state prohibits even as it feels compelled to put into practice birth control policies that provoke resurgent female infanticide. In spite of great burdens from the double load, many rural, urban, worker, and intellectual women endorse government policy on their emancipation within the family through work. As yet there is no indication that a Western-style women's movement would survive even if state restrictions against sexual politics were to be lifted.

4

Ding Ling was born Jiang Bingzhi on September 4, 1904. The Jiangs, a large, undisciplined gentry family, dominated the small county of Linli in Hunan Province through their patronage and examination successes in a style typical of China's late dynasty elite. Ding Ling's father, Jiang Yufeng, earned the primary *xiucai* degree in the last years of the dynasty. He also spent a year in Japan studying the new discipline of law before he retreated to his little corner of Hunan to indulge in timeworn fashion in gentry eccentricities like profligate generosity, impulsive friendship, and endless rounds of banqueting, drinking, and opium smoking. In 1909 Jiang Yufeng died leaving a widow, Jiang (née Yu) Manzhen, four-year-old Bingzhi, and a baby boy who did not survive childhood.

A generation earlier, Yu Manzhen might have suffered this loss stoically. The compound gates of the Jiang family were, even then, still ringed with arches honoring chaste widows, bestowed by successive thrones on well-behaved Jiang women. Conventional familist norms required widows to stake their futures on a son's eventual success in the civil service exams. In pre–twentieth-century China, exam degrees formed the only fully sanctioned route to government office and hence to social position and legitimate authority. Yu Manzhen's natal family had its own recent history of examination successes; her father and brother served in government posts and appear to have maintained a lively scholarly domestic culture. Neither Yu Manzhen nor her in-laws seem to have considered either suicide, which at the height of the Qing period gave the fundamentalist Confucian wife an extreme loyalist option (and the family a legitimate excuse for murder, on occasion), or remarriage, the other, more common alternative to widowhood. Since women like Yu Man-zhen frequently remained chaste, or sexually loyal to their husbands, deeply felt social norms and pressures would probably have kept Ding Ling's mother in respectable, miserable penury at the margins of her husband's greedy, thoughtless family. But Yu Manzhen made other choices. Events far away from torpid Linli County had begun changing gentry culture.

When the European imperialists turned to China in the nineteenth century, they fitted standard colonial techniques of domination to Chinese circumstances. Armed incursion, systematic use of "lawfully" imposed treaties, and Christian missionary outposts nibbled away Chinese imperial sovereignty. These and internal pressures threw the Chinese government into crisis: a devastating series of wars over the right to refuse British opium in the 1840s; massive peasant wars stimulated by overpopulation and poor government in the 1850s and 1860s; the degeneration of rural agricultural relations and institutions; the building recognition in the 1870s and 1880s among the literati of Chinese "backwardness"; debilitating indebtedness capped by the Boxer Indemnity imposed in 1900; Japanese encroachment into Chinese suzerainties; the rise of a Sino-foreign treaty port society; and by the turn of the century, the widespread, real fear that China, like India, would simply be partitioned.

Yu Manzhen's widowhood suddenly became a tactical asset. When the throne abolished the civil service examination in 1905, in a late effort to stem reform pressures from other quarters, the control and social uses of knowledge had already shifted from the dynasty to the hands of the reformist, progressive gentry, which had arisen in the new treaty ports and provincial capitals. Among those active in the politics of reform were literate gentry women. Arguing from a variety of bases, including doctrinal Confucianism, anti-imperialism, national salvation, embarrassment at European scorn for the Chinese treatment of women, and Christian-influenced notions of gender justice, they sought "Western" learning and they built an elite women's movement around their demand for valorization of their scholarship.

Of course, Yu Manzhen was already a very well educated woman. Like many women of her class, she read extensively, knew poetry and letters, and probably could recite the Confucian basic texts. When one of her brothers, a local reformist, helped sponsor a female academy in her hometown of Changde, Yu Manzhen took the unusually bold step of entering the Changde Women's Normal Academy, where she learned the new disciplines of geography, mathematics, world history and literature, political theory, constitutional law, and geopolitics. During her years as a student, Yu Manzhen met other women like herself. Xiang Jingyu, later a theoretician, revolutionary strategist, and martyr, became a close friend and sworn sister. At the academy, Yu Manzhen framed her teaching philosophy—anti-imperialism, love of homeland, revolutionary struggle, democracy, sexual equality—and after matriculating, she took positions in a series of new-style schools in the province.

Ding Ling grew up inside China's first network of girls' schools and female academies. Yu Manzhen sent her to Changde Normal's kindergarten and then on to Changsha First Girl's Normal School, Taoyuan Second Provincial Girl's Normal, and to Zhounan Girl's Middle School, where she made friends with progressive girls from all over Hunan. Women of Yu Manzhen's generation had spent their childhoods with siblings and cousins; Ding Ling's earliest relationships developed with classmates like Wang Jianhong (her closest friend and a model for many of her "modern girl" protagonists), Yang Kaihui (future wife of Mao Zedong), Xu Wenxuan (the first Hunanese woman to join the Chinese Communist Party), and Zhou Yumin (another early Party member). They were an elite formed on considerations of gender and social class unmediated by kinship. The classroom also gave Ding Ling an arena for acting out in boyish fashion, precociously challenging teachers, and in general testing limits. In between her intensely social school days came months spent alone with her slave girls and female servants, reading and playing in her uncle's courtyard while her mother taught in other towns.

Yu Manzhen's remarkable career affected Ding Ling's later life in a variety of ways and added unique tensions to their relationship. Although the senior woman had up-ended family expectation by seeking education, she also appears to have taken great care that her responsibilities to her children were met quite conventionally. As had countless other widowed gentrywomen, Yu Manzhen sought to act as her children's father as well as their mother. At the same time she was attempting to uproot she turned a face frequently identified with the paternal role, the moral pedagogue, upon her daughter. So, for example, the revolutionary teacher in her encouraged Ding Ling's interest in old Chinese stories and translated Victorian novels, while the old-fashioned mother indulged the little girl with ghost stories and local legends. But her moral lessons were not really at odds with her revolutionary ambitions. Convinced that old-fashioned moral instruction had ruined past generations of women by persuading them of their inferiority, Yu Manzhen shifted the content of her tales. She cashiered all the mawkish daughters-in-law, the strong-willed and ferociously self-denying widows, the single-mindedly chaste suicides in favor of fresh emblems—Madame Roland, martyred in the Revolution of 1789, and Qiu Jin, hero of the Revolution of 1911.

Ding Ling remembered her mother in later years as an ambivalent figure, very differently from the amused, indulgent way she framed memories of her father. When she refused to marry the man her Jiang uncles had selected, Yu Manzhen, albeit reluctantly, supported her decision; when she could not find work in the early 1920s, her mother sent her money; her mother sheltered her newborn son, Zulin, in 1930 and attended the birth of her daughter, Zuhui, in prison in late 1934. Yet for all Yu Manzhen's help over the years, Ding Ling also knew that the older woman deeply resented having sacrificed a precious chance to go to France with Xiang Jingyu, blamed the girl, in fact, for her own stunted revolutionary life. Mother and daughter also had major political disagreements throughout Ding Ling's anarchist adolescence. The adult daughter retained her own resentful memories of her mother's earliest experiments to train her into precocious independence, though she later appreciated how Manzhen had undermined the old-fashioned, dependent, guilty sense of obligation Chinese parents cultivate in their children.

As a little girl, Ding Ling was therefore thoroughly immersed in the vibrant, reformist, political and intellectual culture that had begun bubbling to the surface as elites in the provinces actively confronted Western imperialism. Her maternal uncles cut off their queues and imported subversive tracts from Shanghai. Her mother unbound her "lotus feet," agitated for the recovery of sovereign rights to China, and demonstrated for female suffrage at a regional constitutional convention after the 1911 revolution, daughter in one hand, club (for beating recalcitrant deputies) in the other. But Ding Ling's teenage years and her later intellectual life were shaped by cultural politics of a different, if related, order.

What came to be known as the May Fourth movement was ushered in by the Beijing publication, in 1915, of the intellectual journal *New Youth*, and erupted four years later in street demonstrations against the Versailles Treaty and Japanese imperialism by Chinese of every class in major cities all over the country. The May Fourth movement signaled the beginning of popular nationalism. After 1919, new-style politicians turned to the general strike, worker's turn out, popular boycott, student demonstration, and mass education to resist intervention. This surge of popular mass action eventually became the political legacy of the Chinese Communist Party. At the same time, however, the modern intelligentsia fused activist politics and anarchist theory into a syncretic cultural politics of their own.

At this level, the major players were not so much Shanghai mill workers, striking prostitutes, or chamber of commerce dignitaries (as was the case in the successful political action of the spring of 1919), but the new generation of intellectuals and, through the propaganda of the act, the young educated boys and girls who were their students and restless followers.

Ding Ling was fifteen years old when the movement broke out at Zhounan Girl's School in Changsha. She spent the next five years "in the movement." It was, as one historian has recently emphasized, a movement in the American sense: the synchronous appearance of a liberationist vision, politico-ethical strategies and tactics, multiple individual and collective social practices, and a process—a sustained, daily process continuing into the late 1920s and early 1930s—in which women and men of Ding Ling's generation tried to join utopian desire, cultural politics, and personal transformation.

The movement centered on liberation (*jiefang*): attack all authority, starting with personal authoritarian relations in daily life and extending the critique, through immediate personal acts, into all major social and cultural institutions—family, school, class, and nation. Such an attack demanded a new rhetoric. The old literary language simply foreclosed cultural revolution and was therefore discarded for a new, experimental written language proposed first by the New Culture movement *zhishi fenzi,* or intellectual class, and developed in the mushrooming periodicals aimed at young people. May Fourth language also extended utopian desire into the realm of the subject. Utopian visionaries formed ways of being what writers, readers, and activists called "free people." The free person—this was where the amorphous anarchism at the heart of their vision was most apparent—would live in a wholly invented world of disciplined, voluntary, egalitarian relationships (rather like those of the new classroom) foreshadowing New China, a China released from old, barbarous, oppressive, "Confucian" relationships. And unprecedentedly the New Culturists elevated gender, relocating masculine/feminine from the periphery to the center of cultural politics.

Theoreticians debated matters in the new journals. But in the streets of China's major cities and in the provinces, young people like Ding Ling lived the movement, convinced they were saving the nation and renovating the people by demonstrating against the old and agitating for the new.

At Taoyuan Second Provincial Girl's School, Ding Ling joined her classmates in hair bobbing, organizational work, speaking, and organizing boycotts. Months later she entered middle school at Changsha's Zhounan Girl's School, where Mao Zedong was publishing his famous essays on the oppression of women in the school newspaper *The Women's Bell* (the name reveals the anarchist flavor of the journal). At Changsha she joined provincewide protest organizations set up by the Alliance of Girl's Schools and the Progressive Association of Girl Students. Her radical teacher Chen Qimin and the emerging practices of self-liberation inspired Ding Ling to write colloquial-language poems. She rioted and demonstrated for an end to the oppression of women. She went to the lectures of Bertrand Russell, John Dewey, and the anarchist intellectual Wu Zhihui and frequented the radical bookstore. She was in Changsha when the uneducated wife of a Zhounan instructor committed suicide from shame when her husband forced her to pretend to be his servant, a case which became a national cause célèbre, a symbol of Chinese women's oppression. With her close friends, she integrated the local boy's school. In 1920, refusing the punitive marriage her Jiang uncles in Linli were planning, Ding Ling fled Hunan with Wang Jianhong.

Drawn to Shanghai's anarcho-feminist culture, where some of the movement's most innovative social experimentation was going on, Ding Ling settled into the informal collectives at radical schools like Common Girl's Middle School, a pattern she continued later in Nanjing. She and Wang Jianhong did formally join the Anarchist Party. They believed that their actions would hasten the end of government and its replacement by cooperative villages. Ding Ling edited the Common Girl's School paper, *Women's Voice,* studying Kropotkin and Bakunin, the lives of liberated women in the Soviet Revolution, Margaret Sanger's position on contraception and women's sexual pleasure. She also knew about the slightly older women at Beijing University who were molding anarchist political practice into structures for collective domestic work and child care.

The point of anarcho-feminist process was to develop independence and become a woman. Ding Ling refused to marry her cousin on the grounds that she owned her own body. Previously Chinese subscribed to the notion, enshrined in Mencius, that parents were the source of one's body and that children were obliged to look after themselves out of filial duty. May Fourth cultural revolutionaries sought a new jurisdiction over their bodies in order to take control of decisions that parents conventionally had made for children. Thus the first key to living independently was to seize control of mobility and jurisdiction over the self.

Even more difficult than achieving independence was the problem of becoming a woman. Physiology had, this argument went, a more fundamental importance to human personality than did artificial Confucian prototypes such as "virtuous wife, good mother." But the old culture had trapped female nature in such a tangled net of distorting and false expectations that transformation, or the recovery of true nature, would have to rely on imported models. So although independence for women (a de facto repudiation of the Confucian Three Bonds) was the centerpiece of movement thinking, and though the aim of liberating women was to free the repressed, biologically truthful individual trapped inside every filial daughter, because women were thought to be more burdened by past practice than men, it was difficult for (largely male) theorists to imagine what a female individual would be like. Ding Ling and Wang Jianhong's lives aimed at putting the lie to their doubt. Anarchism was the most hospitable culture available for cultivating independent personality.

Chinese anarcho-feminism had only a fleeting organizational life, although the questions of personal identity it had raised lingered on. In 1922 Ding Ling and Wang Jianhong lost control over *Women's Voice*. Marxists and labor socialists took over, playing down sexuality, individualism, and feminism in favor of a major strike of Shanghai's female mill workers. This small incident was symptomatic of a larger split between feminists and socialists over the question of organizing women.

In 1922 the Chinese women's movement bifurcated. The bourgeois feminist wing moved rapidly into reform politics (anti-concubinage, for example), professional self-help, and civil, property, and family law reform. What might be called the socialist-feminist wing merged with the Communist women's labor movement, becoming particularly active in the mid-twenties during the United Front. The hardening of political lines constricted the areas anarchist women had opened up for personal experiments and forced the undisciplined, undecided, and ambivalent onto the defensive. Unwilling to submit to the seemingly arbitrary authority of the Communists, Ding Ling and Wang Jianhong left Shanghai when the Anarchist Party dissolved, and drifted to Nanjing where they sought work as teachers, domestic servants, factory workers—anything they could find to preserve their independence. They had a difficult time because of their youth and because people mistook them for prostitutes or revolutionaries. The following year, the two women followed Qu Qiubai—who had become Wang Jianhong's lover—from Nanjing to Shanghai, where Ding Ling, seeking the very discipline she had earlier avoided, entered the new Communist Party–sponsored Shanghai University. There she met major left-wing intellectuals like Mao Dun, Tian Han, Yu Youren, and Li Da. Following Wang's death from tuberculosis in 1924 after Qu left her, Ding Ling finally abandoned movement life altogether and moved to Beijing to find new direction and recover from her disappointments.

Over the next few years, Ding Ling seemed deadlocked. She had indeed achieved a life of independent personality, but she found that freedom under those circumstances offered neither livelihood nor even a socially recognizable role. She was free. But she had nothing to do. Her daily habits placed her beyond the provincial culture she had so emphatically rejected. Her stubborn renunciation of "old" culture also made the conventional life of the insecure, careerist urban middle class an unattractive option. But she was also unfit for life after the revolution. She was unsuited for the Western-style professions—law, university teaching, medicine—then opening doors to a handful of women, since these required degrees and, in some cases, training abroad. She failed the Beijing University entrance exams, which she rationalized, saying she would never have been able to tolerate the careerism of successful students. Other possibilities, such as teaching or domestic service, did not suit her temperament. She was unwilling to compromise for still others on ideological grounds. She decided one year, for example, to use her Shanghai University connections to become a movie star, and she got as far as the screen test. But the vulgar way movie directors prostituted women's sexuality revolted her, and she abandoned that idea as well.

As she backed away from the increasingly dangerous world of direct cultural and political activism, Ding Ling fell back on the world of texts. She began reading seriously. She selected out of the many available novels in translation the works of Alexander Dumas, Tolstoi, Gorki, and especially Flaubert. She befriended young male writers. And she fell in love, not once, but repeatedly, under a number of circumstances and toward a variety of different ends. It was not an arbitrary or accidental pattern. Just as Ding Ling had quite significantly recalled being drawn to May Fourth literature when she read Guo Moruo's long poem *Goddess (Nushen)* in the French Concession park, her experience of femininity was connected to the foreign fiction she read and the Hollywood movies she loved. Ding Ling absorbed the full range of the European feminine representations. The muse, the temptress, the corrupter, the mistress, the incarnate symbol of love, the sexual force, the sign of pure absolution were all a part of the world she encountered through *La Dame aux Camélias, Anna Karenina,* and *Crime and Punishment.*

Love and literature coincided neatly in her first romance, with the impoverished, undereducated, sweet-natured worker-poet Hu Yepin. Her relationship with him began as sisterly affection and deepened into a sexual affair, and finally into a romantic, irregular, common-law marriage. Ding Ling appears to have refused all civil marriage on grounds that, as she put it in her short story "Mengke," bourgeois marriage was simply a way of legalizing prostitution. Her emotional life deepened in complexity, however, when Shen Congwen, Hu's close friend, who would become eventually one of the century's major colloquial prose stylists, began living with the couple in what outsiders took to be a ménage à trois. In 1926 or 1927, she also developed a passionate, deeply erotic attachment to a man who struck her as even more crude and rustic than Hu, the taciturn, unresponsive literary critic Feng Xuefeng, who would become her colleague and critic after she joined the Communist Party.

Ding Ling had left the homosocial milieu of the girl's school and entered the intensely masculine world of literature, or more accurately, the fringes of that world. She consorted with young male writers, edited Hu's manuscripts, and discussed literature with Shen Congwen. Yet she seems not to have considered writing herself until 1927 when, miserable, drinking heavily, dispirited by the national tragedy of political counterrevolution, and exhausted by her impoverished, often squalid life in boarding-house rooms, she produced a series of extraordinary narratives about the lives of modern women. The context of her first stories was the impossibility of female individualism in a postrevolutionary, post-Confucian society, and she conveyed the message throughout that modern Chinese women would never succeed in living a life of truly independent personality.

With the 1928 publication of "Miss Sophia's Diary," Ding Ling became a nationally recognized writer. She continued producing "bourgeois" fiction for several years, narratives with no formal political coding, focused exclusively on the matter of female subjectivity, touching the extraordinarily sensitive issues of sexual repression and expression, homoeroticism, female Don Juanism, sexual politics, and the generally "dark" quality of female consciousness. She appeared to blame women's undisciplined subjectivity in part upon male society and in part upon the victims themselves. And since she borrowed heavily from her own experience—Wang Jianhong's life in particular became an icon to what she cast in retrospect as the wasted efforts of their anarcho-feminist years—readers, especially critics, understood the short stories collected in the volumes *In Darkness, A Woman, Suicide Diary*, and the novel *Wei Hu*, to be unmediated confessional autobiography. This critical reading of her work made her angry and defensive. Even publishing in the country's leading progressive literary journal, *Short Story Monthly*, failed to reassure her that her work had intrinsic merit beyond its power to shock and her own freak value as a woman writer who had raided the "male" subject matters of sexuality, power, death, and despair.

We have selected two stories to represent the earliest period. "Miss Sophia's Diary," the most notorious, recounts the emotional life of a tubercular woman driven to near madness by erotic passion for an unworthy man. Ding Ling worked the rest of her life to prove that the work was not autobiographical, and for better or worse it remains her signature text. "A Woman and a Man" details a conflict of will between a rapacious and self-deceiving woman and a sexual profligate and bogus poet whom she seeks to enslave.

These narratives unfold in the context of a conundrum posed by Sophia's foreign name: how does the post-Confucian Chinese woman exist inside the tension between feminism and the feminine? Ding Ling gave many of her female protagonists Western names like Wendy, Mary, and Ilsa. These are marks of their universal femininity, their transcendence of parochial Chinese social restraints. "Sophia" has extra significance. In the Chinese feminist tradition, the name had an unmistakably revolutionary cachet derived from such figures as Sophia Perovskaya and Sophia Zhang—themselves perhaps decendants, through translation, of European Sophias like the Chartist pamphleteer. Ding Ling's Sophia is heir to this political tradition. She assumes without question the ethical and political correctness of unrestricted freedom of choice for women.

But the name—Shafei—that our translator renders as Sophia can also be represented as "Sophie." Ding Ling's Shafei also refers back to the Sophie of Rousseau's *Emile* and through her to the imported Enlightenment philosophy of sexual difference. Miss Sophia is cousin to Sophie, the "natural" woman whose innate "female" qualities became a textual reference in subsequent European philosophies of sexual essentialism. When "The Diary" makes claims about how women naturally act, it is to this aspect of the imported heritage that Ding Ling alludes. Sophia seeks to locate the feminine as her essential nature. Her concern throughout is with how "a woman" should act or feel, and she measures many of her actions against what "a woman" ought to do.

Ding Ling's characterizations of Sophia, of Wendy and those in other contemporary pieces, like Amao and Mengke, resolve the old May Fourth question of what modern Chinese women would be in the absence of Confucianism. All share qualities represented as universal and innate, qualities bracketed in the text as the "feminine": repressed eroticism, self-delusion, irrational and sudden mood changes, obstructed will, hyper-romanticism, childish impulsiveness, obscured vision. These are traits that, while resolutely feminine, also, as Sophia notes, chronically undermine self-respect and autonomy.

This characteristic encoding of the feminine had two sources. First, the texts draw abundantly on the author's experiences as a May Fourth woman; they are the observations of a participant. Many focus on a riddle that had absorbed social theorists since 1919, "Where do Chinese Noras go?" Nora, heroine of Ibsen's *A Doll's House,* had literally closed the door on her insulated, bourgeois life. Ding Ling's answer was a series of portraits of women. As a group, these characters accept without question the cardinal tenets of May Fourth feminism, such as the priority of autonomy, alienation from family control, the importance of willed action, sexual experimentation, the centrality of love as an effect of freedom, and so on.

Yet as the Nora issue itself makes manifest, the other major source of Ding Ling's early casting of the feminine was imported and text based. Nora is, after all, a fictional character in a script about, among other things, the oppression of middle-class women in Norway. Our three earliest stories are self-consciously literary texts that refer back to what was for Ding Ling the master text of the many European novels she had absorbed in translation. Reading Flaubert's *Madame Bovary* (according to Shen Congwen, she read it a dozen times) against her own experience, Ding Ling cast her early texts as illustrations of the same "feminine" she recognized in Emma Bovary, and in herself as "woman." These texts privilege an irony born of recognition across literary conventions.

As the stories we translate here make clear, Ding Ling adapted extensively from *Madame Bovary*. In other stories, Ding Ling adapted other elements. The plot appears in the story "Amao" in great detail, including the suicide by poisoning. The Flaubertian love triangle structures narrative action as late as the novel *Wei Hu* in 1930. Ding Ling made use of Flaubert's ironic narrative very skillfully. She infused it with the same feminine that she represented in the stories, thereby injecting into the narrative a critical tone of ambivalence. The characteristic sentence structure with its sudden reversals, its ability to reveal what surface description cannot, namely, the hidden reality of a character's illusions, all owe a huge debt to Flaubert.

Largest of all is her debt to the character Emma Bovary. Both stories offered here map out the feminine through Ding Ling's reading of Emma. It is highly significant that what Ding Ling emphasizes is Emma's eroticism. Like Emma, Ding Ling's female characters endure revery, the eroticization of memory, and fail to escape the ill effects of romantic confusion. But unlike Flaubert's rendition, Ding Ling essentializes and grounds eroticism in sexual repression. Sophia speaks of the confusion between love and lust and knows her nature is defined by repressed desire. Wendy, in "A Woman and a Man," cannot understand love at all and is driven by an aggressive libido. The feminine in these early works is not only recognizable as a bundle of emotional conditions, it is fundamentally sexual. The natural woman defines herself as sexual essence. Feminism, the demand for human equity, and femininity, the essential qualities of woman, work at cross-purposes. Sexual difference, what makes the Emma characters discursively feminine, and the politics of gender equality derived from similar sources. But they undercut each other. As Ding Ling's earliest texts make abundantly clear, the only resolutions possible under this inscription of femininity are death and repetition.

At the end of the twenties, Hu Yepin became deeply involved in Communist literary politics. Ding Ling apparently remained fixed to the demands of her own literature and continued her explorations of femininity. But her fiction took an interesting turn, which we have sought to illustrate with two key texts. "Yecao" introduces a female figure whose discipline as a writer keeps her from capitulating to the repetitive emotional crises of the Flaubertian woman. The novel *Shanghai, Spring 1930* connects the project of literature and the literary feminine in a new way. The latter piece, particularly, belongs to what contemporaries called the genre of "love and revolution." The text juxtaposes the individual's need for love against the growing, obvious, desperate need of the oppressed for political redress.

The title character of "Yecao" is the first of a line of figures who use literary praxis as a means of disciplining their unruly feminine temperaments. Significantly, "Yecao" does not rely heavily on a love triangle; the central figure is apparently a woman on her own. Further, the text unloosens the tight correspondence of the feminine with emotion and the masculine with reason encountered in "Miss Sophia's Diary" and other earlier texts. Finally, Yecao signifies a rather hopeful escape from endlessly repetitive organic femininity. "Yecao" allows the protagonist to place her destructive habits in her recent past, in memory, safely in her personal history as a woman, and identifies the demands of her writing as her salvation. For Ding Ling, a new writer, to have defined literature as potentially transformative is understandable, particularly under an inscription of femininity that undermined female aspirations.

But in fact the correspondence of literature and liberation in the literary feminine was very shortlived in Ding Ling's work. *Shanghai, Spring 1930* introjects a whole range of competing demands into the resolution "Yecao" had tentatively suggested. The Flaubertian triangle of impossible desire disappears. Replacing it, using a method she called "dialectic," Ding Ling lines up a series of oppositions between lovers, classes, and social commitments. Pairs of modern lovers—Mary and Wang Wei, Meilin and Zibin—and supporting figures outside the romantic domestic unit represent "dialectically" how impossible all personal solutions are, given the vaguely sketched, but strongly felt, "historical conditions" in 1930. In this narrative, the favored level of signification is not the internal or "subjective" interior of one or several separate protagonists but rather the nature of the relationships conjoining them.

The obvious irony of this novel is that the lovers of the two parts are mismatched. Meilin and Wang Wei should be together, not sequestered with incompatible lovers in the two opposite halves of the dialectic. The inappropriate partners underline a certain compatibility, based on associations beyond domestic romance, between Mary and Zibin. In the orderly logic of this text, Zibin forthrightly represents the deadend of literature, which is cast here as self-indulgent, masculinized, almost masturbatory. Literature has become "bourgeois literature," the writer a private and alienated figure. Mary, by this logic, becomes Zibin's natural partner. She is the hyper-feminine, tortured, essentially sexual creature of imported European literature, and he the bogus reproducer of those texts. Mary is Ding Ling's final reference to Emma Bovary and stands to Meilin as Zibin, the treaty port literary star, stands to Wang Wei. Less vividly represented are the service ethic of Wang Wei and the curious reliberation of the wifely Meilin from the modern love match back to social engagement.

In the winter of 1930, Ding Ling gave birth to a boy. On February 7, 1931, the Nationalists executed the boy's father, Hu Yepin, and twenty-three other Communist writers and activists. This horrible event speeded up changes in Ding Ling's work that had surfaced as early as *Wei Hu* (a masked account of the Wang Jianhong–Qu Qiubai romance) and that had been explicated in *Shanghai, Spring 1930*. The brutality of the murder led her to a clean break. She sent her child to her mother in Hunan, took over editorship of the Communist Front journal *Great Dipper* for the League of Left Wing Writers, a coalition of progressive writers and cultural workers. She began working undercover and, in March 1932, secretly joined the Chinese Communist Party.

The early thirties also marked a shift in the way Ding Ling represented herself. She displaced her older project of realizing herself as a woman. Over the ensuing decade, she identified herself first as a writer, and furthermore, as a certain kind of writer. Drawing on her previous experience with Hu Yepin and Shen Congwen, editing their experimental literary magazine *Red and Black* in 1928, Ding Ling used the *Dipper* assignment as a means of personal transformation, as a publishing outlet for her own explorations in critical realist narrative, and as a forum from which she discussed the need for literature and literary culture to respond to political crisis. Her grueling efforts at self-discipline she chronicled in fragmentary writings like "Not a Love Letter," "Miss Sophia's Diary, Part 2," and "From Dusk to Dawn," Her struggle to reframe her narrativity inside a referential code largely determined by revolutionary politics gave rise to "Water," a pathbreaking story that combined Qu Qiubai's insistence that writers focus on the life of the masses with an attention to panoramic representation, probably influenced by film. "Net of Law," "Flight," "Songzi," and other so-called proletarian pieces followed. In each, the representation of "objective reality" dominated the process of narrative. Ding Ling's subject was thus the present stage of history rather than any specific internal conflict of human consciousness. This breakthrough suddenly made her a leading pioneer in explicitly ideological left-wing fiction.

Ding Ling's new ability and willingness to speak authoritatively on broad literary matters had several important results. It implied a new sense of legitimacy. Speaking as a revolutionary writer, rather than as a woman, Ding Ling felt empowered to criticize the masculine world of "bourgeois" literature in stories like *Shanghai, Spring 1930*. She freely mocked the self-important, careerist *artiste* in nastily jaundiced portraits of the male writer as bourgeois and effete. Her public pronouncements no longer reflected anger at her sexual marginalization. Yet the new sense of legitimacy came linked with a rigid service ethic. Her instructional stories (one historian has called "Tianjia Ravine" and "One Day" mentor stories because they include a figure who points toward the inevitable revolutionary resolution), and her acts of personal heroism suggested that assuming the position of revolutionary intellectual required sacrifice—of career, autonomy, individual comfort, small personal pleasures, and possibly even life itself. Finally, Ding Ling's public views on the literary vocation also promoted the abrasive, doctrinaire position on language, representation, and the role of writers connected in the 1930s with Qu Qiubai and the Mass Language debates. Qu had called for an end to "literature." He had demanded a genuinely colloquial Chinese writing free of Westernisms and foreign intertextual baggage, and the literary incest anchored in the continued stranglehold of the educated elite over the means of expression.

Ding Ling did not make the transition from May Fourth Chinese feminism to Party communism easily. Before she could reinvent herself as a political writer, she had to resolve certain tensions in her own past. First, she drew on that part of what she believed to be the strongest, most disciplined, and willed part of her (female) personality. Then she needed to probe far enough into Marxism to find an argument for sexual egalitarianism. No matter how critical Ding Ling might have been of contemporary womanhood, she never stopped insisting that equality of women and men was central. Thus, although her narratives of the 1930s marked a distancing from feminism per se, it did not signify the end of her demands for gender justice and change. Particularly after her novel *Mother*, which she began in May 1932 and ended in April 1933, Ding Ling started edging toward a recuperated understanding of the female self in terms of the normative behavior categories of her mother's era.

In the 1930s Ding Ling stopped writing stories about women with "female personalities." In other words, she shifted the location of personality away from sexual essentialism, which argues that women and men differ primarily because sex determines character, that they will always remain estranged by the contradiction of gender itself. In Chinese Marxism, as in most socialist traditions, the central contradiction among people was determined by class, not gender. Ding Ling resolved the tension, inherent in most efforts to combine feminism and socialism, in a novel manner. Revolutionary praxis erases the superficial barriers of gender because women and men become sisters and brothers when they do national (not domestic) work together. And in that context, they are equally valuable because social revolution requires that you contribute what you have, not that you do the same work. This she illustrated in such stories as "News" and "For the Children," and in subsequent fables of revolutionary efficacy in which footbound, aged, or sexually traumatized women or defenseless children perform heroic, powerful acts on behalf of society.

The real question is how Ding Ling, a sexual, literary, and cultural radical, could have committed herself to the statist project of revolutionary Chinese Communism. As a female writer and as a cultural revolutionary heir to the ethical tradition of elite paternalism, as the widow of a political martyr, and perhaps most uniquely, as a woman who seemed to distrust the grounds of her femininity, Ding Ling faced the 1930s both more deracinated and more flexible than intellectuals whose stake in the status quo was higher. The national catastrophes of Japanese invasion (Manchuria in 1931, the Shanghai region in 1932), continued civil conflict between Whites and Reds, mass evacuations, escalating hydraulic and environmental disasters, and neo-warlordism overtook intellectuals as they did everyone else.

We have selected two texts to represent this period. "Net of Law" is a work of critical realism. It relies explicitly on political codes to convey its argument that contradictions in exploitative social relations of production will eventually consolidate the proletariat's resistance to oppression. *Mother* is an experimental novel about wealthy gentrywomen who develop rudimentary political consciousness in the 1911 revolution. The two selections are generically distinct, yet both exemplify how Ding Ling joined fiction and political theory. Ding Ling had always problematized gender. "Net of Law" and *Mother* do not abandon the problem but recast it.

To transform her work, Ding Ling turned to China's native canon, to nineteenth-century Russian realism, and to the theory and literature of Soviet socialist realism. Both socialist realism and dynastic narrative assign the author importance, but not as an imperial subject, the originator of unique personal truths. This fitted the belief of many left-wing writers that they had to shift the emphasis away from the person of the creative writer to the role of writers as moral servitors of a culture and people in crisis. "Net of Law" is constructed as a "critical realist" narrative. French naturalism provided models for the rough dialogue, symmetrical, tragic plot, and the violent denouement. Marxism-Leninism supplied the thematic and social referent. Russian socialist realism offered models of heavily coded political narrative. Interestingly, the text foregrounds the problem of women's oppression without making it central to the meaning of the story. That is, the plot unfolds around an oppressed female protagonist, Acui, but is "about" the problem of class consciousness. These shifts opened the possibility for a literary reconstruction of the female subject on substantially new grounds. First, Acui has no idiosyncratic female personality. She is defined by her occupation, her proletarian class background, her kinship status, and pseudo-kin networks. Narrative constructs her through enumeration of relationships and social convention.

Second, while the text obviously privileges class and explicates the culture of the urban, industrial subproletariat, it also reads as a reinterrogation of the problem of sexual oppression. It argues that in the "natural" order of things, the strong respond to oppression by oppressing the weak. Class exploitation grounds a social order that has at its apex the relation between foreign capital and the national bourgeoisie. This order is directly represented by the relation of the bourgeois managers to the labor elite, of the labor elite to the lumpen unemployed, of male itinerants to their wives and mothers, and finally, of the starving young wife Acui to the aging generation of Grandma Wang. Each link in the chain reinforces enduring hierarchies of social class, gender, and age.

Mother is less typical of the bulk of Ding Ling's work in the early thirties. The novel, excerpted here, is an invaluable record of how China's earliest female academies operated. It also complements "Summer Break" well; the schoolteachers of *Mother* are only fifteen years older than the faculty at Independent Girl's School. The detailed explication of provincial gentry life and its network of women does not subordinate female characters to the masculinist trope of the son's rebellion, as does Ba Jin's famous domestic novel *Family,* for example. Finally, since the novel is expressly autobiographic, it also is a source of material on Ding Ling's life.

Mostly, however, *Mother* illustrates how Ding Ling relied on narrative to transform the way she represented women in fiction. The novel is anomalous for several reasons. First, it is not socialist realist in form but is curiously reminiscent of Ming-Qing domestic fiction. Second, while it foregrounds Yu Manzhen's experience in the progressive school, it does not explain why Ding Ling's mother changes so radically. And third, although Ding Ling had proven skill at drawing characters, Yu Manzhen is better understood as a peculiarly formulaic stereotype. In terms of Flaubertian narrativity, Yu Manzhen is obviously "flat."

I would argue that Yu Manzhen represents a fresh model of the feminine in Ding Ling's fiction. She achieved her revolutionary female model shorn of "feminine" temperament by hybridizing her genre. *Mother* is part Western *Bildungsroman,* part recuperated Ming/Qing domestic romance. It is a *Bildungsroman* to the degree that it follows the development of a single protagonist. But it incorporates many elements of indigenous narrativity, including the ceaseless recurrence of time, the convention of the wine party, the oath of sibling solidarity, the discovery of female literary virtue, and the formation of subject identity through adherence to kinship and pseudo-kinship expectations, all of which have precedent in the dynastic canon.

In line with this externalization of causality, Manzhen's education is not so much for self-knowledge as to acquire access to revolutionary pedagogy. Manzhen never considers the question of "being" female outside the terms set by gentry society. She and her revolutionary sisters are oppressed not by the simple operations of masculine or feminine, but by a systematic discourse of *lishu* (convention) and *guiju* (rules of personal etiquette) that bind women to clichéd behavior, and by an oppressive feudal hierarchy that pivots on the double oppression—by wealth and convention—of high gentrywomen. As Manzhen puts it, "It's the rules of conduct that are the cause of our suffering and with us Chinese, the richer your family is, the harder it is to be a woman." *Mother* relocates sexual subordination outside the sexual identity of women and men and recategorizes "woman" as a social product of historically defunct habit, soon to be swept aside.

The "woman" of *Mother* and the "woman" of early pieces like "Miss Sophia's Diary" are different because in the novel female characters are linked by the notion of a political sisterhood. Manzhen acts in a world of dyadic bonds. Women form selves on the basis either of oppressive family relations or of transformative rituals associated with progress, such as the Confucius ceremony at the school opening and the oath-swearing in the flower garden. Moreover, Manzhen recognizes, not the essential differences separating women and men, but their essential similarities. By representing female characters in *Mother* as sisters rather than as women, Ding Ling had replaced the troublesome Victorian notion that women formed a category of beings whose common mentality, emotions, and human significance set them apart from men.

On May 4, 1933, Ding Ling and Feng Da, the lover she had acquired immediately after Hu Yepin's death, both disappeared, kidnapped from the French Concession by the Nationalist secret police. Their disappearance caused enormous concern in the leftist literary world. Since she had contacts with foreign reporters like Harold Isaacs, and since Feng Da had been Agnes Smedley's translator, Ding Ling's presumed death was publicized internationally. Translations of her work appeared in English. Ding Ling remained under house arrest in Nanjing, where she received her mother, gave birth to her daughter by Feng Da, and where, eventually, Feng died of tuberculosis. Ding Ling's affair with Feng had baffled long-time friends from the beginning, coming as it did so quickly after Hu Yepin's death. She seemed incapable of explaining why she stayed with him so long or how, given her political commitments, she spent the Nanjing years. Later she complicated the whole affair by suggesting that Feng Da himself had betrayed her to the police, though she never supplied any proof nor any clear reason why he should have done so. Shortly after Feng's death, Ding Ling recontacted the Communist underground and, leaving her children with their grandmother (they would join her later at Yan'an), she escaped to the Red Army's new base area in North China.

The Yan'an period (1937–47) refers to the decade that the Chinese Communist Party spent in the so-called border regions of the country during the Sino-Japanese War. From its political capital, Yan'an, in Shaanxi Province, the Party sat atop a growing jurisdictional entity that functioned as the government of vast areas of Northern China. It directed a vicious guerilla war against the Japanese and, after the breakdown of the United Front, constant warfare against it. It rebuilt the economy of surrounding cachement regions to support the war. It sent its cadres into remote villages, setting down the institutional framework for a guerilla-style local government. And it forged a state ideology, a Chinese interpretation of Marxism-Leninism that served as the legitimating ideology of the forced socioeconomic reordering following Liberation in 1949.

The Yan'an decade also formed the distinctive socialist culture of Chinese Communism. Among the intellectuals, middle-class student refugees, writers and artists, and Party theorists who spent the war years in the border regions, a moralistic service ethic developed that stressed their personal role in the pedagogy of cultural transformation. In New China, art and culture (*wenyi* and *wenhua*) would finally become the property of the masses.

The Yan'an dialectic of cultural renovation—modernize the people's lives and art, rusticate bourgeois habits and the arts—was inescapably recuperative. The major resources of the local peasantry were, after all, the patrilineal family, the loosely Confucian authority structures of dyadic kinship, and the assumption of unity between ideograph and state. The very notion of popularizing peasant habits, transmitting them into the daily practice of intellectuals, meant accommodation of postures that Ding Ling, at least, had spent the better part of her life disrupting. Thus, despite the enthusiasm Ding Ling brought to renovating the revolutionary community of bourgeois activists around her, two related questions remained unresolved. Under what formulation would modern literature be judged? And how would women be represented under such an inscription? In other words, when the state takes the power to ratify all modes of literary representation, how can female writers and readers feel sure that their needs will be addressed, their experience correctly represented? These remained contested, open questions until 1942.

Initially Ding Ling had an important hand in revolutionizing the official arts in the Soviet. After the public relations campaign celebrating her escape from the Nationalists, she organized a service-group theater that combined agit-prop, revolutionary reform of local arts, and collective self-improvement, and set off for the front with it. Traveling with her was a man in his early twenties. Chen Ming became her first official husband during the agitation for democratic family reform that accompanied the 1942 Party rectification. The year-long tour of war-torn back-country towns and villages in the company of passionately revolutionary young "culture workers" brought her into prolonged contact with peasant communities for the first time. She returned to Yan'an as one of a handful of writers who actually had met the audience that, theoretically, Party literature was to serve.

Ding Ling was also a government cadre, a bureaucrat. She taught periodically at Party universities, wrote about popularization of the arts, encouraged young writers, advised on women's policy, lobbied for family reform, and edited the literary section of the Party's official government newspaper, the *Liberation Daily*. Ding Ling's unusual authority (unlike other leading women, she was married to a man junior rather than senior to her in the Party system of official rank), her personal sympathies, and her charisma made her an informal youth leader as well. She established a record of speaking for the young middle-class women who were coming to the border regions. She composed work in various genres, ranging from reportage and didactic essays (*zawen*) to plays, statements on ethics and correct attitudes, and notes on cultural matters. Mostly she produced National Defense narratives, a genre of propaganda that Party theorists had decided best fit the current stage of the struggle.

We have chosen three stories to represent Ding Ling's Yan'an work before 1942. "Affair in East Village" is a critical realist work, while "When I Was in Xia Village" and "New Faith" are both National Defense narratives. All share two premises. First, that mobilization for war or class struggle offered a valuable moment of social chaos that might result in personal, community, and national transformation of womanhood. Second, that the Party itself held the most radical alternative to the patrilineal family structure that Ding Ling, true to her May Fourth origins, continued to identify as the major source of women's oppression. These texts and others are consistently structured around a central opposition between the state (*guo*) and the family.

All three works problematize rape. The context for these stories was a world in which the "line," the decision that leaders made on tactics and policy, consistently mandated attention to rural women. Rape in this world was both a familiar political weapon the enemy used as a tactic of terror and a crime requiring state redress. Literary narratives that examine the issue of rape either endorsed, expanded upon, illustrated, contested, or revised a real policy. But rape also posed questions of meaning and power. Who assigned meaning to loss of female chastity? Was it the rape victim? Was it the signifying system anchored in the village patriline, which joined the sexual organs of women to civic virtue? Did the two systems coincide? Also, since rape was itself a recommended trope in National Defense literature, a subject appropriate to the interests of the nation, would state control of rape's significance subordinate living women to systems of meaning over which they had no control?

Ding Ling appropriated the literary rape. She used rape narratives to redefine and focus upon the question of representation of women in statist discourses. "When I Was in Xia Village" particularly questions the conjuncture of women and literary representation—to what effect, on whose terms, under what inscription of femininity, for what eventual political good? Many of the ancillary issues raised first in these stories appeared later in balder terms with "Thoughts on March 8." They include Ding Ling's refusal to conjoin women to sexual matters, her conviction that women and men were rather similar and should be treated equally on that ground, her persistent rejection of the double standard, her anger at the injustices women suffered at the hands of the men who betrayed them, whether to community standards or the universal ethics of filial piety, and her certain knowledge that villagers, at least, did not follow National Defense literature's coded message that the rape victim stood as a metaphor of China under the Japanese occupation.

"Affair in East Village" is classified as a realist piece, although it employs the National Defense theme of rape and prefigures many themes developed later in Ding Ling's 1947 novel *The Sun Shines over the Sanggan River*, a socialist-realist master text. She plotted the story to emphasize the degree to which women act as sexual commodities in the political economy of rural society.

The text links class struggle, sexual repression, and the psychodynamics of revolt in a way that foregrounds rape as a form of tyranny and privileges the sexual love of Chen Delu and Qiqi as a cause of revolution. Qiqi's rape anchors a signifying chain linking the victim-woman to a series of victim-positions, all of them reiterating the dynamic of revolution as Ding Ling apparently understood it then, an animal-like passivity turned to bestial rage that eventually overwhelms the oppressor entirely. But the victim herself has virtually nothing to say, and after the rape she vanishes from the text.

"New Faith" advances the connection of rape and self-representation. After witnessing the murder and rape of her granddaughter and being raped herself, an old woman returns to her village. Rather than dying of shame, as her sons would prefer, she tells her shocking story as a way to recruit men into the army. "New Faith" linked enemy atrocities, rape, and national defense to a range of other plot elements. The old woman acts as an agent of transformation linking the *jia*, the Party, and the nation. Her impulse to tell other villagers her story violates family convention and loses face for her patriline, yet her selfless patriotism actually renews her family by giving it a larger focus. In the end it is she who links villagers with the transformative power of the state when she joins and recruits members for the Women's Association.

"New Faith" makes much of an irony inherent in any reduction of women to rape victim. It does successfully what the conventions of its genre call on it to do. Readers, paralleling the villagers' sympathy, are shocked and moved by the terrible details. The need to protect, even to revenge, women follows obviously. But what the story also does is call attention to the problems of the rape victim metonymy. The same narrative written by Grandma Chen's sons would have ended before it started with the old lady's dignified and face-saving death. In Ding Ling's story, however, the state's equation of rape victim–passive woman, the anticipated, masculinist appropriation of woman as a sign, does not emerge. Rather, the victim stands up and speaks: she tells her own story in her own way, embarrassing and shaming her family, derationalizing herself, and genuinely changing her community by transforming her family as well as recruiting men into the army.

The dangers of making rape a metonymy for woman took the central position in the best of Ding Ling's National Defense texts, "When I Was in Xia Village." In this work the question of how the powerful metonym would be officially represented became the major plot element. The story is told by a female Party writer, "I," who gathers material for a (presumably National Defense) narrative from a village woman whom the Japanese have raped and infected with venereal disease. Furthermore, after the rape, the woman became a prostitute behind the lines to gather intelligence. "I" never speaks explicitly of gender, though references make it clear she is female. The victim, Zhenzhen (her name is the doubled ideograph for female chastity), does more than passively supply the writer with material, however. The character's reappearance in her native village sets off a war over the meaning of unchastity. Her eventual abandonment of the village for the Communist capital's relative freedoms resolves a series of related problems.

First, the narrative refuses the solution that would reduce experience to the equation of rape victim and woman. Responding to the sympathetic reaction of others—"It's a real tragedy to be a woman, isn't it?"—Zhenzhen distinguishes between her unfortunate experiences and her self. The narrator endorses this solution. She notes that despite the repeated rapes, Zhenzhen is still a normal, eighteen-year-old girl. Second, the narrative surrounds the victim with a series of identities. Each has the power to situate her in a preexisting context of meaning. The conservative villagers call her a prostitute. Local cadres see her as a war hero. Her family bargains with her, blaming her rashness for the rape and seeking to marry her to her old sweetheart as a means of reasserting its control over a daughter. Third, the narrative allows Zhenzhen herself to assign meaning to her experience. To the victim, the question is one of the meaning of life, not the meaning of chastity. "A person's life is not just for one's father and mother," she concludes, "or even for one's self."

"Xia Village" refuses closure. No system of pre-fixed meaning supersedes the significance assigned by the woman who suffered the rape. Zhenzhen concludes that rape does not signify woman. In fact, she extends that refusal of closure to gender itself. She claims a meaning for herself that will emerge only in the context of personal political practice. She will serve the nation but not as a symbol. She will honor her parents but not at the expense of her power to recreate herself in the new society. Rape in war is a political act. Through Zhenzhen, "Xia Village" suggests that unchastity as an ethical issue is best resolved in political terms.

The distinctly political resolution achieved in "When I Was in Xia Village" resonated in the charges Ding Ling made in her "Thoughts on March 8." By this point it is no longer adequate to call Ding Ling a Chinese feminist without reducing the word's significance completely. She had backed away from the basic tenets of feminism, even under the loosest formulations—sexual essentialism, the problem of the feminine, biological reduction, the peculiar and dangerous elision of subjectivity that being designated the victim confers, and arguments for liberation based in all of these conceptions of femininity. The woman of "Thoughts on March 8" is an androgyne. Women are, as Ding Ling put in the essay, a category of beings marked by social expectations, the organic demands imposed by childbearing, and the scars of a history of derogation. Political liberation, if it means more than resubjugation under a new inscription of the feminine, must open a position for experimentation.

In late 1941, as the Party campaign to rectify its work habits unfolded, Ding Ling weighed her decision to publish "Thoughts on March 8." The choice to go ahead meant she felt she had the power as a writer to declare when, where, and how the given political line would be evaluated. Her act insinuated further that as a writer and a woman she might have access to truths of experience beyond that line. It emphasized (at least momentarily) a form of personal politics over the more abstracted concerns of military strategy, class struggle, or institutional reform, and it embarrassed men and women in high positions once the charges reached enemies of the Party in the White areas. Ding Ling chose to remain oblivious to her essay's many implications.

5

Her decision as editor to invite open discussion of personal politics in the literary column of *Liberation Daily* took place against a situation that, in hindsight, was a turning point in modern Chinese history. Rectification began in Ding Ling's area in early 1942. She used her considerable powers to encourage the public analysis of work and living style, thus opening a gap of her own, an opening where the issues of relations between the sexes could be raised. This was a literary problem, as representation, of course, always is. But it was also a concrete way to air policy problems in the Women's Department and to discuss the daily injustices younger educated women, particularly, encountered in a world short of middle-class women. Ding Ling published "Thoughts on March 8" on March 9, 1942, the day after the official celebration of Women's Day. In the days and weeks that followed, many cadres took Ding Ling's lead and debated major issues of Party life. Subsequently, in a political coup of great acuity, Mao Zedong reframed all of these issues—the proper balance between public persona and private practices among Party leaders, cultural politics versus stable structures of authority, the correct direction for marriage and divorce reform, separatist or integrationist policy on women's work—not as flexible debatable issues of cultural politics, but as inflexible matters of correct or incorrect literary representation. That is, the mass line encouraged flexibility among local cadres but refused to allow the representation of the very weaknesses and failures assumed to lie behind their debate. Literary workers would henceforth take the line as their referent. Their function was to enforce a vision of the future. In laying out an impossibly narrow doctrine for literary production in his "Talks at the Yan'an Forum on Arts and Literature," Mao laid the framework for imposing democratic centralism on the educated elite. It is not that Mao muffled debate or creativity in these matters. That would come later. Rather, he enlarged the scope of the literary and subsumed literary representation, making it the end product of political decision-making.

Ding Ling was punished for having raised embarrassing questions of personal and daily life in a public forum. She left her editorship under fire. But her strongly populist position on literary matters, including the dogmas that literature take the masses as its audience, use language colloquial enough to be understood when read aloud, and promote political ends, made it easier for her to recoup her political losses than it was for others. Mao had found the basis for his views in the same place as she had, in Qu's call for mass literature. It also apparently cost her less to make a scapegoat of the intransigent theorist Wang Shiwei (critic of Party authoritarianism, labeled a Trotskyist and executed in the 1947 evacuation) in mass struggle sessions, than it cost to keep quiet. She criticized herself for irresponsibility and for mistaken beliefs developed "over a lifetime." But she refused to admit to charges of being a "narrow feminist."

These events colored Ding Ling's subsequent career. Zhou Yang, a leading bureaucrat, was only one of the powerful figures who took offense at her behavior. The complicated politics of Party intellectuals, which had begun as early as the formation of the League of Left Wing Writers in the 1930s, became more inbred than ever after 1942. In the aftermath of the Yan'an Forum, Ding Ling spent two years in the Central Party School studying politics. Later she traveled and began writing of her encounters with model workers and local revolutionary heroes. Once again her reports began appearing in *Liberation Daily*. As the land reform program unfolded in Southern Chahar in late summer 1946, Ding Ling started work on *The Sun Shines over the Sanggan River*. Her innovative novel about the land reform process reached the press in June 1948, and in July she attended the Second Meeting of the World Democratic Women's Association, a sign that her experimental text had been approved.

This anthology does not include an excerpt from *The Sun Shines over the Sanggan River*. Translations of the novel, which won a Stalin Prize in 1951, are available in full and in part. It is a stunning achievement and to be recommended highly. But it does not do a number of things Ding Ling had done for many years. First, it does not champion individual women against the family system, or even imply that land reform ought to be the moment of transformation. *Sanggan River* presented female protagonists in a conventional village world and acknowledged the rural habit of subsuming gender into dyadic social or *lun* relationships. It displayed a high sensitivity to the specific experiences of rural women but did not point toward alternatives to village kinship relations. It foregrounded the experience that many cadres had reported, of finding village women resistant to calls for transformation of kinship. It faithfully reflected the notion that the future might indeed bring a transformation of rural sexual relations, but that such change was not an immediate priority.

What happened to gender in all this? By the late 1940s, Communist China's ideological apparatus was perpetuating a new relationship: the family is to the procreative unit (husband/wife) as the state is to civil society. Put slightly differently, the state formalized the family through its policies and bureaucracies in order to take it out of the hands of the community and patriline and open it to the interventions of "development." This extension of central power to the level of the reproductive unit cut both ways. First, it increased the degree to which state bureaucracies touched upon the lives of people in officially registered families. Second, state policy endorsed in theory the freedom of individual women and men to make marriages on the basis of personal preference. Legal marriage required that couples be licensed by the state. Since the state took over the power to ratify marriages from the community and patriline, it stood behind the new family as the agent of "modernization" and democratization.

"Women" became a product and province of state ideology. As a category and a social construct, women had no precedent in the political heritage of Chinese statecraft before the twentieth century. Liberation institutionalized women. The Women's Association (*funü lianhehui*) was formed as the arm of the state, to operate in the area between state and family. The association both represented the new social category that the revolution had finalized and intervened in the lives of women to enforce general policies. It provided the organizational anchor for the instrumental use of female labor, for the protection of women in families, for a debate over child care, the opportunity to introduce hygiene and nutritional expertise, and various interventions to form the democratic small family out of the welter of familist relations inherited from the past.

At Liberation, "women" became an effect of state rectification. What had begun as a daring use of the European discourse on sexual difference in the May Fourth revolt against the Confucianized received tradition had, through decades of use and appropriation, become a wholly political category of mobilization into national development. The category "women" was a part of the Maoist renaming of social order. It was part of the state's biopolitics, the subject and audience of literature on democratic family practices, the disciplining of procreative acts, the staging area for mobilizing women into campaigns. "Women" became a tangible, formal category of political economy.

A Party writer like Ding Ling dealt with the politics of women through the effect this final categorization had on literary representation. What it meant was formal closure, the summing up of the meaning of things. Under the strictures of Mao's policy on literature, all stories about women were stories about political subjects. Ding Ling may certainly have had personal disappointments at the form "women" had taken after 1942. Although she "studied" village women intensively as part of her rehabilitation, and thus conceivably might have changed her position on oppression, the patriline, the need for greater attention to women's affairs, the questions she had raised in 1942 were no longer open to contest. Her stories of village women after 1942 subscribe to the recategorization as strictly as one might imagine.

The two pieces we have selected to end this volume clarify the effects on Ding Ling's work of the state's hegemony over "women." The first, a report titled "People Who Will Live Forever in My Heart: Remembering Chen Man," was inspired by the land reform process that also produced *Sanggan River.* It represents Ding Ling's solution to the question of representing women and political closure. It should bring to mind the earlier "When I Was in Xia Village." The same plot structure brings the unidentified "I" into Song Village and confronts her with a woman suffering unusual oppression in a backward, rural community. The story's action concerns Chen Man's effort to understand political transformation in her own terms. Since she is a natural poet, her own terms are paeans to Chairman Mao.

"People Who Will Live Forever" makes a number of important points. First, Chen Man has no interest in being female outside the parameters set by community and political intruders. Second, she herself privileges the opposition insider/outsider as the most deeply rooted source of her suffering. Third, the narrative points out that women less disadvantaged than Chen Man are successfully brought into the land reform process as leaders. Fourth, the narrator very carefully assures readers of her inability to intervene and of the reason why (ignorance of the specific conditions, primarily). And finally, although the story is about the liberation of an old, miserable, and abused woman, gender is only ironically made the subject of the narrative. It is constantly elided in favor of the kinship relation of mother and daughter, of relative village position, and—in the person of Chen Man's late husband—of the peculiar violation of gender roles that the female impersonator signifies.

6

Ding Ling understood political power in 1949. She knew that the Party's political base was the peasantry. She had come to terms with the renovated kinship base of the polity, a product of Party accommodation of rural realities. In 1949 Ding Ling knew that she had to emphasize her position to retain power. She was an anomaly, a powerful woman. For a brief time, this strategy allowed her to become one of the country's most visible cultural leaders.

Biographers have generally been quite kind to Ding Ling and have maintained that she always had a relatively "liberal" secret agenda. This may be so. The evidence for the 1950s remains ambiguous. She did say that nothing was more important to her than writing one good book, even consistent adherence to the line. Indeed, her relations with younger writers were later termed subversive. It is more important to recall, however, that Ding Ling had been heavily implicated in the Communist Party's efforts to control all literary expression for many years, and she was equally involved in struggles for power inside the state bureaucracy, particularly as the stakes got higher and the arbitrary power of the positions increased. The reasons for her fall have not yet been fully clarified.

In any case, her position was not secure in the 1950s. In 1952 she left her editor's post at the Literary Gazette. A year later her second important position, editor of People's Literature, disappeared. By 1956 antagonisms reaching back to the Yan'an days that were not really ideologically motivated, that had in many cases developed on the basis of jealousy or personal dislike, came to the forefront. Probably under the direction of Zhou Yang, Ding Ling's enemies in the Writer's Union began to organize a campaign against her. In 1957 she lost everything: her membership in the standing committee of the All-China Federation of Literature and Art Circles, her position as vice-chair of the All-China Union of Literary Workers, her control over the Literature Bureau of the Propaganda Department, and ultimately her Party membership itself. The most damaging charge against her was her supposed "unchaste activities" during her years in Nanjing under house arrest. Critics happily conflated political loyalty and sexual ethics. The linkage signified, as well, the revival of something resembling the old Qing chastity cult and meant that Ding Ling had not made the transition from feminist insurrectionist to neutered Party powerbroker.

The first nine years of her internal exile in Manchuria did not completely subdue her. Many of the older artists purged in the 1950s and early 1960s led relatively safe, comfortable lives in remote villages. Ding

Ling was in her vigorous fifties, freed from the pressures of committee life that attend high position, a gregarious woman who apparently enjoyed her village relationships and remained in contact with her family. Nothing prevented patrons and supporters from sending in supplies of paper, special food, and medicines. So Ding Ling continued writing. In 1966 she had just completed the sequel to *Sanggan River, In the Bitter Winter,* when the Great Proletarian Cultural Revolution broke out and her patrons themselves came under attack. Ding Ling and thousands of other intellectuals fell into the hands of the Red Guard, and a decade of baffling horror began. Young revolutionary Red Guards seized her, destroyed her draft and all her notes, forced her into the ritual humiliations that were common currency then—"capping," face painting, public confession—and then placed her in solitary confinement for several years. The same woman who, as a girl of sixteen, had published a denunciation of her father's family, had attacked everything associated with inherited culture, and had declared her body her own property, found herself, a single generation later, denounced by boys and girls born in socialist China, who had no direct connection to Confucianism, yet who had been mobilized once again to renovate Chinese culture.

In 1978, two years after the end of the Cultural Revolution decade, Ding Ling reappeared in Beijing under Deng Xiaoping's sponsorship. In China and abroad, she immediately became a symbol of the unresolved guilt and horror of the government's thirty-year policy toward intellectuals. Party membership and attendant honorary positions followed. Since then a number of old rivalries between major cultural figures, some of over half a century's duration, have been publically unraveled. Ding Ling's restoration in the late 1970s and early 1980s seemed part of this reconciliation. In particular, young readers of the "lost generation" brought a fresh view to Ding Ling's case. Because her hardships in some ways mirrored their own, they expected that she, of all people, would find some way to explain their suffering. In 1983 when the Party reform faction suggested that Mao Zedong's now infamous "Talks at the Yan'an Forum" had not said everything possible about Chinese literature, Ding Ling's own position in 1942 seemed to have been vindicated.

Ding Ling surprised them. She earned the nickname "Old Shameful," one of a number of "Old Shamefuls" who have refused to make Party control of literary representation responsible for their years of suffering. In fact, she seemed increasingly authoritarian and illiberal, as the younger generation of female writers like Yu Luojin and Dai Houying took greater and greater risks to express views different from those established by Comrade Mao—and by Comrade Ding Ling. She spent the last years before her health failed circulating in the upper realms of the old literary establishment, granting interviews, writing for newspapers, researching the past record to make sure history received a "correct" representation of her. On lesser details such as her birthdate, the name of her mysterious lovers, great Communists she had known, she was forthcoming and voluble. But on the larger issues such as the "Yan'an Talks" and her house arrest, she remained evasive to the end and, in the case of literary "crimes," politically correct by some earlier measure.

The final sketch translated here, "Du Wanxiang," signifies how completely Ding Ling chose in the end to identify herself with the history of the Chinese Communist Party. In this final metonymic fable of Chinese womanhood, the protagonist of the title lives out the roles expected of women by Liberation's political inscription. Du Wanxiang does so with compliance, humility, discipline, and a moral certainty that transforms her eventually into a living model for others. Du Wanxiang's life differs from that of her female predecessors because the Party connects her thoroughly to itself through her uncomplaining service to the nation. She labors on behalf of her husband and children, her work unit and commune, of course. But the object of her toil is eventually total identification of the female citizen to the nation. Du Wanxiang's story is a parable of Chinese women's liberation. She is liberated without ever leaving the New Democratic family, the recuperative normative behavioral categories of socialist China, or the revolutionary masses. She achieves self-definition in the end through service to the Party.

In 1981 Ding Ling visited the United States. She stayed in Iowa at the University of Iowa's International Writing Program. She visited her friend Arthur Miller, who had become a champion of the memories of writers punished during the Cultural Revolution. She and Chen Ming claimed to have been baffled by the contemporary women's movement here and found American feminism indigestible. Throughout the 1980s, Ding Ling continued to write. In 1985 she died at the age of 81 of complications from diabetes and breast cancer. Her death was noted in formal eulogies in China and her obituary ran in the *New York Times,* as well as in Chinese and English-language newspapers all over the world, wherever Chinese communities existed.

Tani E. Barlow

NOTE TO THE READER

Every book has its intended audience. This anthology took shape with three readers in mind. One comes to Ding Ling out of interest or familiarity with China studies. The second, because Ding Ling was such an important female writer, arrives through women's studies or the desire to know about Chinese women's lives. And the third is attracted because of Ding Ling's literary reputation. We hope that we have not only accommodated the needs of each reading constituency but have also served to introduce them to each other.

As translators we strived to balance accuracy against elegance. Chinese and English have little in common and thus translation between them allows for even greater interpretive variety than between the major European languages. Accuracy means faithfulness to the world represented as well as to diction. Readers of both languages will find, depending on the individual translator, varying degrees of literalness in the renditions that follow. Under all circumstances, nonetheless, elegance means good English. In those cases where literal translation rendered awful English sentences, we took our liberties with the Chinese text.

In one respect we have done some violence to accepted English usage as well. To transmit the "Chineseness" of the texts, we made several choices. First, judicious use of Chinese terms for kinship relations reinforces the notion of cultural difference. Thus the reader will find occasional reference to the kin terms, like "Gonggong" and "Popo," rather than the rather flat English "parents-in-law." Second, feeling strongly that literal translations of place names exoticize translations from the Chinese, we have generally left them transliterated unless they signify obvious meaning or had a contemporary English usage, as for example,

Union Medical College, Sincerity Department Store, or Shanghai's Bund. Third, Ms. Barlow has included historical and textual annotations in the form of notes. These are aimed at both the Chinese-reading audience and the exclusively English reader. Some of the notes explain the importance of key terms. Some clarify a cultural usage. Others point to consistent use of tropes, vocabulary, and logic.

To avoid excessive noting, the following information holds true for all of the texts. Chinese names usually begin with the surname and tack onto that a one- or two-syllable given name. A person might be called by her or his full name, say Jiang Bingzhi, or more familiarly, "Lao (Old) Jiang" or "Xiao (Young) Jiang," depending upon whether the namer is junior or senior to the named. The same person would be referred to familiarly as *jiejie* (older sister) in the following ways, again assuming that the namer is junior to the named: Bing*jie,* Zhi*jie,* Bingzhi *jiejie,* and so on. (Younger sister, *meimei,* and older/younger brother are just as elastic.)

Many people of Ding Ling's generation either chose or were given two-syllable names, a surname and one given ideograph. We have transliterated, where the sense is not immediately clear, into two "words" any name that begins with a surname. Thus, Wang Wei rather than Wangwei, but Zibin not Zi Bin. Ding Ling's pseudonym, which she chose in the mid-twenties, has no great ideographic sense. As an anarchist gesture she chose a name by arbitrarily selecting syllables from an open dictionary. Not so arbitrarily perhaps, the *ding* signifies an adult human being, and *ling* is the sound of two jade pieces striking each other.

TEB

Miss Sophia's Diary

"Miss Sophia's Diary" depicts a cycle familiar to European dramas of self-knowledge. The story was published in 1927, and contemporary readers found the first-person rumination on loneliness and lust enthralling. In part they like it because both author and protagonist were female, and older Chinese literary convention had discouraged women from writing on erotic topics. In greater part, however, its popularity can be ascribed to the skillful way Ding Ling handled the Oedipal trajectory: Sophia succumbs to blind desire. She holds off the searing light of reality for as long as she can but finally submits to the torments of self-knowledge.

As a May Fourth text, "Miss Sophia's Diary" is significant not only in its description of female sexuality but in its use of Chinese and European conventions. Ding Ling invokes both canons in her depiction of love triangles. She bows to the late-eighteenth-century Chinese memoir *Six Chapters of the Floating Life* when she hints that Sophia, Ling Jishi, and Yun(je) might form a triangle. Yun, Sophia's girlfriend, is a homophonic reference (same pronunciation, different name) to Shen Fu's wife, who, he claimed in *Six Chapters*, died of love for the courtesan Han Yuan after failing to acquire the girl to be her lover and his concubine.

"Miss Sophia's Diary" ransacks Flaubert's *Madame Bovary*, as most of Ding Ling's early stories do. The primary triangle of Weidi, Ling Jishi, and Sophia is obvious. Sophia's blindness and willful femininity resound with Emma's voice. "I've a lover," Emma shouts in triumph, "a lover." "Sophia," the diary reads, "Sophia has a lover." Flaubert's influence on Ding Ling is most obvious in the story's peculiar diction. The diary is notoriously difficult to interpret because of what one critic has called its "loose" language. Ding Ling didn't use punctuation very consistently (it was new to Chinese), and she scattered semiclassical structures at will into her phrasing. Sophia's diary sounds a lot like *Madame Bovary* in Chinese translation. The diction is a period mannerism, the mark of the writer's sophisticated borrowing from Western-language sentence structure.

Both May Fourth writers and May Fourth feminists looked to Western literature for models of modern behavior. The category "woman" that Sophia transmitted to her readers contains a little Rousseau, a little Herbert Spencer, a little Maupassant. Her question "What is love?" echoes the torment of many liberated Chinese women who struggled against the contradictory claims of political rights and modern theories that made women less than men by nature. The "feminine" liberated woman is possessed by love. But to her everlasting sorrow, Sophia finds that the more feminine she becomes for Ling Jishi, the less clearly she can see herself.—TEB

December 24
The wind's up again today. The blowing woke me before day broke. Then the boy came in to start the stove. I know I'll never get back to sleep again. I also know that my head will start whirling if I don't get up. Too many strange thoughts run through my mind when I lie wrapped in the covers. The doctor's instructions are to sleep and eat a lot and not to read or think. Exactly what I find most impossible. I can never get to sleep until two or three o'clock in the morning and I'm awake again before dawn. On a windy day like today, it's impossible to keep from brooding over every little thing. I can't go outside when the wind's this strong. What else can I do but brood, cooped up in this room with nothing to read. I can't just sit vacantly by myself and wait for time to pass, can I? I endure it one day at a time, longing for winter to be over fast. When it gets warmer, my cough is bound to clear up a little. Then if I wanted to go south or back to school, I could. Oh God, this winter is endless!

As the sunlight hit the paper window, I was boiling my milk for the third time.[1] I did it four times yesterday. I'm never really sure that it suits my taste, no matter how often I do it, but it's the only thing that releases frustration on a windy day. Actually, though it gets me through an hour or so, I usually end up even more irritable than I was before. So all last week I didn't play with it. Then out of desperation, I did, relying on it, as though I was already old, just to pass time. I read the newspaper as soon as it comes. I start, systematically, with the headlines, the national news, the important foreign reports, local gossip, and then . . . when I've finished the items on education, party propaganda, economics, and the stock market, I go back to the same announcements I read so thoroughly yesterday . . . and the day before . . . the ones recruiting new students, the notices of lawsuits over division of family property. I even read stuff like ads for "606" and "Mongolian Lark" venereal tonics, cosmetics, announcements of the latest shows at the Kaiming Theater, and the Zhenguang Movie Theater listing. When I've finished everything I toss the paper away, reluctantly. Every once in a while, of course, I find a new advertisement. But what I can never get free of are the fifth- and sixth-year anniversary sales at the fabric shops, and the obituaries—with apologies to those not contacted personally.

Nothing to do after the paper except sit alone by the stove and work myself into a rage. What infuriates me is the daily routine. I get a nervous headache every day as I sit listening to the other inmates yell at the attendants. Such loud, braying, coarse, monotonous voices, "Attendant, bring hot water!" or "Wash basin, attendant!" You can imagine how ugly it sounds. And there is always somebody downstairs shouting into the telephone. Yet when the noise does let up, the silence scares me to death. Particularly inside the four whitewashed walls that stare blankly back at me no matter where I sit. If I try to escape by lying on the bed, I'm crushed by the ceiling, just as oppressively white. I can't really find a single thing here that *doesn't* disgust me: the pockmarked attendant, for example, and the food that always tastes like a filthy rag, the impossibly grimy window frame, and that mirror over the washbasin. Glancing from one side you've got a face a foot long; tilt your head slightly to the side and suddenly it gets so flat you startle yourself . . . It all infuriates me. Maybe I'm the only one affected. Still I'd really like a few fresh complaints and dissatisfactions. Novelty, for better or worse, always seems just out of reach.

Weidi came over after lunch.[2] The familiar hurried sound of his leather shoes carried all the way from the other end of the corridor and comforted me, as though I'd suddenly been released from a suffocating room. But I couldn't show it. So when he came in, I simply glanced silently at him. Weidi thought I was peeved again. He clasped my hands tightly and cried, "Sister, Elder Sister!" over and over. I smiled. Of course. Why? Oh, I know. I know what's behind those shy glowing eyes. I understand what it is that he'd rather keep from others. You've been in love with me for such a long time, Weidi. Has he captured me? That is not my responsibility. I act as women are supposed to act. Actually, I've been quite aboveboard with him. There isn't another woman alive who would have resisted toying with him, as I have. Besides, I'm genuinely sorry for him. There have been times when I couldn't stand it any longer, when I wanted so badly to say, "Look, Weidi, can't you find some better way of going about this? You're making me sick." I'd like Weidi a whole lot better if he'd wise up, but he persists with these stupid abandoned displays of affection.

Weidi was satisfied when I smiled. Rushing around to the other end of the bed, he tore off his overcoat and leather hat. If he'd turned his head and glanced at me just then, he'd have been saddened by my eyes. Why doesn't he understand me better?

I've always wanted a man who would really understand me. If he doesn't understand me and my needs, then what good are love and empathy? Father, my sisters, and all my friends end up blindly indulging me, although I never have figured out what it is in me that they love. Is it my arrogance, my temper? Or do they just pity me because I have TB? At times they infuriate me because of it, and then all their blind love and soothing words have the opposite effect. Those are the times that I wish I had someone who really understood. Even if he reviled me, I'd be proud and happy.

I think about them when they forget me. Or I get mad at them. But then when somebody finally does come, I end up harassing him without really meaning to. It's an impossible situation. Lately I've been trying to discipline myself not to say whatever jumps into my mind, so I don't accidentally hurt people's secret feelings when I'm really only joking. My resulting state of mind as I sat with Weidi can easily be imagined. If Weidi had stood up to go, I'd have hated him because of my depression and fear of loneliness. Weidi has known this for a long time, so he didn't leave me until ten o'clock. But I deceive no one, certainly not myself. The fact that Weidi waited around so long gave him no special advantage. In fact, I ended up pitying him because he's so easy to exploit and because he has such a gift for doing the wrong thing in love.

December 28
I invited Yufang and Yunlin out to the movies today. Yufang asked Jianru along, which made me so furious I almost burst into tears. Instead I started laughing. Oh, Jianru, Jianru, how you've crushed my self-respect.[3] She looks and acts so much like a girlfriend I had when I was younger, that without being aware of what I was doing, I started chasing her. Initially she encouraged my intimacies. But I met with intolerable treatment from her in the end. Whenever I think about it, I hate myself for what I did in the past, for my regrettably unscrupulous behavior. One

week I wrote her at least eight long letters, maybe more, and she didn't pay the slightest bit of attention to me. Whatever possessed Yufang to invite Jianru when she knows I don't want to dredge up my past all over again? It's as though she wanted to make me mad on purpose. I was furious.

Though there was no reason for Yufang and Yunlin to notice any change in my laugh, Jianru must have sensed something. But she can fake it—play stupid—so she went along as though there was nothing between us. I wanted to curse; the words were on the tip of my tongue, when I thought of the resolution I'd set myself. Also I felt that if I were that vehement she'd get even more stuck on herself. So I just kept my feelings to myself and went out with them.

We got to the Zhenguang Theater early and met some girls from our province at the door. Those girls and their practiced smiles make me sick. I ignored them. Then I got inexplicably angry at all the people waiting to see the movie. So I capitalized on the situation, and as Yufang talked heatedly with the girls, I slipped away from my guests and came home.

I am the only person who can excuse what I did. They all criticize me, but they don't know the feelings I endure when I am with other people. People say I am eccentric, but no one notices how often I'm willing to toady for affection and approval. No one will ever encourage me to say things that contradict my first impulses. They endure my eccentricities constantly, which gives me even more cause to reflect on my behavior, and that ends up alienating me even further from them.

It is very late and the entire residence is quiet. I've been lying here on the bed a long time. I have thought through a lot of things. Why am I still so upset?

December 29
Yufang phoned me early this morning. She's a good person and wouldn't lie, so I suppose Jianru really is sick. Yufang told me that Jianru is sick because of me and wants me to come over so she can explain herself. Yufang and Jianru couldn't be more mistaken. Sophia is not a person who likes listening to explanations. I see no need for explanations of any kind. If friends get along that's great; when you have a falling out and give someone a hard time, that's fair enough too. I think I am big enough not to require more revenge. Jianru got sick because of me. I think that's great. I'd never refuse the lovely news that somebody had gotten sick over me. Anyway, Jianru's illness eases some of the self-loathing I've been feeling.

I really don't know what to make of myself. Sometimes I can feel a kind of boundless unfathomable misery at the sight of a white cloud being blown and scattered by the wind. Yet faced with a young man of, what, about twenty-five?—Weidi is actually four years older than I—I find myself laughing with the satisfaction of a savage as his tears fall on my folded hands. Weidi came over from Dongcheng with a gift of stationery and envelopes. Because he was happy and laughing, I teased him mercilessly until he burst into tears. That cheered me up, so I said, "Please, please! Spare the tears. Don't imagine I'm so feminine and weak that I can't resist a tear. If you want to cry, go home and do it. You're bothering me." He didn't leave. He didn't make any excuses, either, or get sullen, of course . . . He just curled up in the corner of the chair, as tears from God knows where streamed openly, soundlessly, down his face. While this pleased me, I was still a little ashamed of myself. So I patted his head in a sisterly way and told him to go wash his face. He smiled through his tears.

When this honest, open man was here, I used all the cruelty of my nature to make him suffer. Yet once he'd left, there was nothing I wanted more than to snatch him back and plead with him: "I know I was wrong. Don't love a woman so undeserving of your affection as I am."

January 1
I don't know how people who like to party spent their New Year's. I just added an egg to my milk. I had the egg left over from the twenty that Weidi brought me yesterday. I've boiled seven eggs in a tea broth; the remaining thirteen are probably enough to last me for the next two weeks. If Weidi had come while I was eating lunch, I'd have had a chance to get a couple of canned things. I really hoped he'd come. In anticipation, I went out to the Danpai Building and bought four boxes of candy, two cartons of *dianxin,* and a basket of fruit to feed him when he got here.[4] I was that certain he'd be the only one to come today. But lunch came and went and Weidi hadn't arrived.

I sat and wrote five letters with the fine pen and stationery he'd brought me a few days ago. I'd been hoping I'd get some New Year's picture postcards in the mail, but I didn't. Even the few girlfriends I have who most enjoy this kind of thing forgot that they owed me. I shouldn't be surprised that I don't get postcards. Still, when they forget about me completely, it does make me mad. On the other hand, considering that I never paid anyone else a New Year's visit—forget it! I deserve it.

I was very annoyed when I had to eat dinner all by myself.

Toward evening Yufang and Yunlin did come over, bringing a tall young fellow with them. How fortunate they are. Yufang has Yunlin to love her and that satisfies them both. Happiness isn't just possessing a lover. It's two people, neither of whom wants anything more than each other, passing their days in peace and conversation. Some people might find such a pedestrian life unsatisfying, but then not everyone is like my Yufang.

She's terrific. Since she has her Yunlin, she wants "all lovers to be united." Last year she tried to arrange a love match for Marie. She wants things to work out for Weidi and me, too, so every time she comes over she asks about him. She, Yunlin, and the tall man ate up all the food I'd bought for Weidi.

That tall guy is stunning. For the first time, I found myself really attracted to masculine beauty. I'd never paid much attention before. I've always felt that it was normal for men to be glib, phony, cautious; that's about the extent of it. But today as I watched the tall one, I saw how a man could be cast in a different, a noble, mold. Yunlin looked so insignificant and clumsy by comparison . . . Pity overwhelmed me. How painful Yunlin would find his own coarse appearance and rude behavior, if he could see himself. I wonder what Yufang feels when she compares the two, one tall, the other not.

How can I describe the beauty of this strange man? His stature, pale delicate features, fine lips, and soft hair are quite dazzling enough. But there is an elegance to him, difficult to describe, an elusive quality, that shook me profoundly. When I asked his name, he handed me his name card with extraordinary grace and finesse. I raised my eyes. I looked at his soft, red, moist, deeply inset lips, and let out my breath slightly. How could I admit to anyone that I gazed at those provocative lips like a small hungry child eyeing sweets? I know very well that in this society I'm forbidden to take what I need to gratify my desires and frustrations, even when it clearly wouldn't hurt anybody. I did the only thing I could. I lowered my head patiently and quietly read the name printed on the card, "Ling Jishi, Singapore . . ."

Ling Jishi laughed and talked uninhibitedly with us as though he were with old, intimate friends; or was he flirting with me? I was so eager to avoid seduction that I didn't dare look directly at him. It made me furious when I could not bring myself to go into the lighted area in front of the table. My ragged slippers had never bothered me before, yet now I found myself ashamed of them. That made me angry at myself: how can I have been so restrained and boring. Usually I find undue attention to social form despicable. Today I found out how moronic and graceless I could seem. Mmm! he must think I'm right off the farm.

Yufang and Yunlin got the feeling that I didn't like him, I was acting so woodenly, so they kept interrupting the conversation. Before long they took him off. They meant well. I just can't find it in me to be grateful. When I saw their shadows—two short, one tall—disappearing through the downstairs courtyard, I really didn't want to return to my room, now suffused with the marks of his shoes, his sounds, the crumbs of his cake.

January 3
I've spent two full nights coughing. I've lost all faith in the medicine. Is there no relationship at all between medicine and illness? I am sick to death of the bitter medicine, but still I take it on schedule, as prescribed; if I refuse medication, how can I allow myself any hope for recovery? God arranges all sorts of pain for us before we die to make us patient and to prevent us from rushing toward death too eagerly. Me? My time is brief, so I love life with greater urgency than most. I don't fear death. I just feel that I haven't gotten any pleasure out of life. I want . . . all I want is to be happy. I spend days and nights dreaming up ways I could die without regret. I imagine myself resting on a bed in a gorgeous bedroom, my sisters nearby on a bearskin rug praying for me, and my father sighing as he gazes quietly out the window. I'll be reading long letters from those who love me, friends who will remember me with their tears. I urgently need emotional support from all these people; I long for the impossible. What do I get from them? I have been imprisoned in this residence for two full days: no one has visited me and I haven't even gotten any mail. I lie in bed and cough; I sit on the stove and cough; I go in front of the table and cough—all the time brooding over these repulsive people . . . Actually, I did receive a letter, but that just completed my total wretchedness. It was from a tough Anhui guy who was pestering me a year ago. I ripped it up before I had even finished reading it. It made my flesh crawl, reading page after page of "love, love, love, love, love." How I despise grandstand affection from people I loathe.
     But can I name what I really need?[5]

January 4
I just don't know how things went so wrong. Why did I want to move? In all the fuss and confusion I've also deceived Yunlin. The lies came so easily I felt I almost had an instinct for it. Were Yunlin to know Sophia was capable of deceiving him, how wretched he would be. Sophia is the baby sister they love so much. Of course I'm upset now, and I regret everything. But I still can't make up my mind. Should I move? Or not?
     I had to admit to myself, "You're dreaming about that tall man." And it's true: for the last few days and nights I have been enmeshed in wonderful fantasies. Why hasn't he come over on his own? He should know better than to let me languish for so long. I'd feel so much better if he'd come over and tell me that he'd been thinking of me too. If he did, I know I wouldn't have been able to control myself, and I'd have listened

to him declare his love for me and then I'd let him know what I wanted. But he didn't come. I guess fairy tales don't usually come true. Should I go looking for him? A woman that uninhibited would risk having everything blow up in her face. I still want people to respect me. Since I couldn't think of a good solution, I decided to go to Yunlin's place and see what would happen. After lunch I braved the wind and set off for Dongcheng.

Yunlin is a student at Jingdu University and rents a room in a house in Qingnian Lane near the university, between the first and second colleges. Fortunately I got there before he'd left and before Yufang had arrived. Yunlin was surprised to see me out on such a windy day, but wasn't suspicious when I told him I'd been to the German Hospital and was just stopping by on my way home. He asked about my health. I led the conversation around to the other evening. Without wasting any energy, I found out that Ling Jishi lives in Dormitory No. 4 in the second college. After a while I started to sigh and talk in vivid terms about my life at Xicheng Residence Hall, how lonely and dismal it was. And then I lied again. I said I wanted to move because I want to be near Yufang. (I already know that Yufang was going to move in with him.) When I asked Yunlin if he would come help me find a room near theirs, he seemed delighted and didn't hesitate to offer his help.

While we were looking around for a room, we just happened to run into Ling Jishi. So he joined us. I was ecstatic and the ecstasy made me bold enough to look right at him several times. He didn't notice. When he asked about my health and I told him I'd completely recovered, he just smiled, skeptically.

I settled on a small, moldy room with low ceilings in the Dayuan Apartment House next door to Yunlin. Both Ling Jishi and Yunlin said it was too damp, but nothing they said could shake my determination to move in the next day. The reason I gave was that I was tired of the other place and desperately needed to be near Yufang. There was nothing Yunlin could do, so he agreed and said that he and Yufang would be over to help me tomorrow.

How can I admit to anyone that my only reason for choosing that room was because it's located between the fourth dormitory and Yunlin's place?

He didn't say goodbye to me so I went back to Yunlin's with them, mustering all my courage to keep on chatting and laughing. Meanwhile I subjected him to the most searching scrutiny. I was possessed with a desire to mark every part of his body with my lips. Has he any idea how I'm sizing him up? Later I deliberately said that I wanted to ask Ling Jishi to help me with my English. When Yunlin laughed, Ling Jishi was taken aback and gave a vague, embarrassed reply. He can't be too much

of a bastard, I thought to myself, otherwise—a big tall man like that—
he'd never have blushed so red in the face. My passion raged with new
ferocity. But since I was concerned that the others would notice and see
through me too easily, I dismissed myself and came home early.

Now that I have time for reflection, I can't imagine my impulsiveness
driving me into any worse situation. Let me stay in this room with its
iron stove. How can I say I'm in love with this man from Singapore? I
don't know anything about him. All this stuff about his lips, his eyebrows, his eyelashes, his hands, is pure fantasy. These aren't things a
person should need. I've become obsessive if that's all I can think about
now. I refuse to move. I'm determined to stay here and recover my health.

I'm decided now. I'm so full of regret! I regret all the wrong things I
did today, things a decent woman would never do.

January 6
Everyone said I was being terribly foolish when they heard I'd moved.
And when Jin Ying from Nancheng and Jiang and Zhou from Xicheng
all came over to my damp little room to see me and I started laughing
and rolling around on the bed, they all said I was acting like a baby. That
amused me all the more and made me consider telling them what's really
on my mind. Weidi dropped by this afternoon too, miserable because I'd
moved without discussing it with him first and because now I'm even
farther from him. He looked straight through Yunlin when he saw him.
Yunlin, who couldn't figure out why he was so angry, stared right back.
Weidi's face darkened even further. I was amused. "Too bad," I said to
myself, "Weidi's blaming the wrong man."

Yufang never brings up the subject of Jianru anymore. She has decided
to move into Yunlin's room in two or three days. She knows I want to
be near her and won't leave me alone longer than that. She and Yunlin
have been even warmer than ever.

January 10
I've seen Ling Jishi every day, but I've never spoken more than a few
words to him, and I'm determined it's not going to be me who mentions
the English lessons first. It makes me laugh to see how he goes to Yunlin's
twice a day now. I'm certain he's never been this close to him before. I
haven't invited Ling Jishi over, either; and although he's asked several
times how things are going now that I've moved, I've pretended not to
get the hint and just smile back. It's like planning a battle. Now I'm
concentrating all my energy on strategy. I want something, but I'm not
willing to go and take it. I must find a tactic that gets it offered to me
voluntarily. I understand myself completely. I am a thoroughly female
woman, and women concentrate everything on the man they've got in

their sights. I want to possess him. I want unconditional surrender of his heart. I want him kneeling down in front of me, begging me to kiss him. I'm delirious. I go over and over the steps I must take to implement my scheme. I've lost my mind.

Yufang and Yunlin don't detect my excitement; they just tell me I'll be getting better soon. Actually, I don't want them to know. When they say how improved I am, I act as if I'm pleased.

January 12

Yufang already moved in, but Yunlin moved out. I can't believe the two of them; they're so afraid of her getting pregnant that they won't live together. I suppose they feel that since they can't trust themselves to make "good" decisions when they're in bed together, the best solution is to remove sexual temptation completely. According to them, necking is not too dangerous, so their list of proscriptions doesn't preclude the occasional stolen encounter. I can't help scoffing at her asceticism. Why shouldn't you embrace your lover's naked body? Why repress this part of love? How can they be so preoccupied with all the details before they've even slept together! I won't believe love is so logical and scientific.

Of course, when I tease them they never get angry. They're proud of their purity, and laugh at my childishness. I suppose I understand how they feel; it's just another one of those strange, unexplained things that happen in life.

I went to Yunlin's tonight (I guess I should call it Yufang's now) and we told ghost stories, so I didn't get back until ten o'clock. When I was a child I used to sit in my Auntie's lap and listen to Uncle tell strange tales from the *Liaozhai* all the time.[6] I loved to hear them, especially at night; but I never let anyone know how much they frightened me, because if you said you were afraid, that was the end of the stories. The children wouldn't be allowed out of bed and Uncle would have disappeared back into the study. Later, in school, I learned some rudimentary science from the teachers, and pockmarked Mr. Zhou inspired me enough to trust the books so I outgrew my terror of ghosts. Now that I'm grown up, I always deny the existence of ghosts. But you can't halt fear by simple declaration, and the thought of ghosts still makes my hair stand on end. No one grasps fully how eager I am to change the subject when the topic comes up. That's because later, when I'm sleeping alone under the covers at night, I think about my dead Auntie and Uncle and it breaks my heart.

On the way back, I felt a little jumpy when I saw the dark alley way. What would I do, I thought, if a monstrous yellow face appeared in the corner, or a pair of hairy hands reached out at me from that frozen alley. But a glance at the tall strapping man beside me—Ling Jishi—acting as my bodyguard, reassured me. So when Yufang asked me if I was frightened, I just said, "No. No, I'm not."

Yunlin left with us to go back to his new room. He went south, and we went north, so we'd only gone three or four steps when the sound of his rubber-soled shoes on the muddy boards was no longer audible. "Sophia, you must be scared," said Ling Jishi, reaching out to put his arm around my waist. I considered freeing myself, but couldn't. My head rested on his shoulder. What would I look like in the light, I thought, wrapped in the arms of a man so much taller than I am? I wriggled and slipped free of him. He let go, stood beside me, and knocked at the door.

The alley was extremely dark. But I could clearly see which way he was looking. My heart fluttered slightly as I waited for the gate to open.

"Sophia, you're frightened."

The bolt creaked open as the doorman asked who was there.

"Good ni . . ." I said, but before I'd finished, Ling Jishi was holding my hand tightly.

Seeing the large man standing beside me, the doorman looked surprised.

When the two of us were alone in my room, my bravado disappeared. I tried to conceal my discomfort with a little conventional chatter, but couldn't manage that either. "Sit down" was all that came out, and I went to wash my face. I can't remember how we got off the subject of the supernatural.

"Sophia, are you still interested in studying English?" he suddenly asked.

It was he who had come looking for me. He's the one who brought up the subject of English. He'd never sacrifice his time just to help me with my English, and no one as old as I, over twenty, could be deceived by such an offer. I smiled and said, "I'm too stupid. I probably wouldn't do very well. I'd just make a fool out of myself."

He didn't say anything, just picked up a photograph from the table and toyed with it. It was a picture of my older sister's daughter, who had just turned one.

By that time I'd finished washing my face and was sitting at the end of the table. He looked at me and then back at the little girl, then at me again. It's quite true. She does look a lot like me, so I asked him, "Cute, isn't she? Does she remind you of me?"

"Who is she?" There was unusual earnestness in his voice.

"Tell me, don't you think she's cute?"

He asked again who she was.

Suddenly I realized what he meant by the question, and I had an impulse to lie about it. "She's mine." I snatched the photograph and kissed it.

He believed me. I made a fool of him. My lie was a complete success. His seductiveness faded in the face of my triumph. Otherwise how— once he'd revealed such naiveté—how was I suddenly able to ignore the power of his eyes and become so indifferent to his lips? I had triumphed indeed, but it cast a chill over my heated passion. After he left, I was consumed with regret for all the obvious chances I'd let slip away. If I'd shown more interest when he pressed my hand, if I'd let him know I couldn't refuse him, he'd have gone a lot further. I'm convinced that if you dare to have sex with someone you find reasonably attractive, the pleasure must be like bones dissolving, flesh melting. Why was I so strict and tight with him? Why had I moved to this shabby room in the first place?

January 15
I certainly haven't been lonely recently. Every day I go next door to visit, and at night I sit and talk to my new friend. Yet my condition continues to deteriorate. That discourages me, naturally, since nothing I desire ever ends up helping me. Is this craving really love? It's all so completely absurd. Yet when I think about dying—and I think about it frequently— I'm filled with despair. Every time I see Dr. Kelly's expression I think to myself, it's true, say what you like: there's no hope left, is there? I laugh to mask the tears. No one knows how I cry my eyes out late at night.

Ling Jishi has been over several nights in a row, and he's telling everybody he's helping me with my English. Yundi asked me how it was going, but what could I say? This evening I took a copy of *Poor Folk* and put it in front of Ling Jishi, who actually began to tutor me, but then I threw the book aside. "You needn't tell people you are helping me with my English anymore," I said. "I'm sick and no one believes it anyway." "Sophia," he said hastily, "shall we wait until you're feeling better? I'll do whatever you want, Sophia."

My new friend is quite captivating. Yet for some reason I can't bring myself to pay much attention to him. Every night as I watch him leave morosely, I feel intense regret. Tonight, as he put on his overcoat I said to him, "I'm sorry. Forgive me, but I'm sick." He misunderstood what I meant, took it for convention. "It doesn't matter. I'm not afraid of infection," he said. Later I thought that over. Perhaps his comment had a double meaning. I don't dare believe people are as simple as they appear on the surface.

January 16
Today I received a letter from Yunjie in Shanghai that has plunged me into a deep depression.[7] How will I ever find the right words to comfort her? In her letter she said, "My life, my love are meaningless now."

Meaning, I suppose, that she has less need than ever for my condolences or tears shed for her. I can imagine from her letter what married life has been like even though she doesn't spell it out in detail. Why does God play tricks on people in love like her? Yunjie is a very emotional and passionate person, so it's not surprising that she finds her husband's growing indifference, his badly concealed pretense at affection unbearable . . . I'd like her to come to Beijing, but is it possible? I doubt it.

I gave Yunjie's letter to Weidi when he came over, and he was genuinely upset because the very man making Yunjie despair is, unfortunately, his own older brother. I told Weidi about my new "philosophy of life." And, true to form, he did the only thing instinct gives him leave to do— he burst into tears. I watched impassively as his eyes turned red and he dried them with his hands. Then I taunted him with a cruel running commentary on his little crying jag. It simply didn't occur to me then that he might indeed be the exception, a genuinely sincere person. Before long I slipped off quietly by myself.

In order to avoid everyone I know, I walked alone around the frigid, lonely park until very late. I don't know how I endured the time. I was obsessed with one thought: "How meaningless everything is, how I'd rather die and have done with it."

January 17
I was just thinking, maybe I'm going crazy. It's fine with me if I lose my mind. I think, once I've got to that point, life's sorrows will never touch me again . . . It's been six months since I stopped drinking because of my illness. Today I drank again, seriously. I can see that what I'm puking now as a consequence is blood-redder than wine. But my heart seemed commanded by something else, and I drank as though the liquor might ease me toward my death tonight. I'm so tired of being obsessed by these same endless complications.

January 18
Right now I'm still resting in my bed. But before long I'll be leaving this room, maybe forever. Can I be certain I'll ever have the pleasure of touching these things again—this pillow, my quilt? Yufang, Yunlin, Weidi, and Jinxia are all sitting protectively in a gloomy little circle around me, waiting anxiously for dawn when they can send me to the hospital. I was awakened by their sad whispers. Since I didn't feel much like talking, I lay back and thought carefully over what had happened yesterday morning. It wasn't until I smelled the stench of blood and wine in the room that I was overcome with agony and convulsive tears. I had a premonition of death as I lay in the heavy silence and watched their dark, an-

guished faces. Suppose I were to sleep on like this and never wake up . . . would they sit just as silently and oppressively around my cold, hard corpse? When they saw I was awake, they drew near me to ask how I felt. That's when I felt the full horror of death and separation. I grabbed at each of them and scrutinized their faces, as though to preserve the memory forever. They all wept, feeling, it seemed, that I was departing for the land of the dead. Especially Weidi; his whole face was swollen, distorted with tears. Oh! I thought, please, dear friends, cheer me up, don't make me feel worse. Then, quite unexpectedly, I started to laugh. I asked them to arrange a few things for me, so out from under my bed they dragged the big rattan box where I kept several little bundles wrapped in embroidered hankies. "Those are the ones I want with me when I go to Union Medical College," I told them. When they handed me the packages I showed them they were stuffed full of letters. I smiled again and said, "All your letters are here," which cheered them up a bit. I also had to smile when Weidi took a picture album from the drawer and pressed it on me as though he wanted me to take that along, too. It contains a half dozen or so photographs exclusively of Weidi. As a special favor I let him hold my hand, kiss it, and caress his face with it; and so, just as we'd finally dispelled the sensation that there was a corpse in the room, the pale light of day broke across the horizon. They all rushed about in an anxious flurry searching for a cab. Thus my life in the hospital began.

March 4
It was twenty days ago that I got the telegram notice of Yunjie's death. Yet for me each passing day means more hope of recovery. On the first of this month, the crowd that had brought me to the hospital moved me back to the freshly cleaned and tidied residence. Fearing I might get cold, they'd even set up a little iron coal stove. I have no idea how to convey my thanks. Especially to Weidi and Yufang. Jin and Zhou also stayed two nights before they had to go. Everyone has played nursemaid, letting me lie in bed all day feeling so comfortable it's hard to believe I'm living in a residence and not at home with my family. Yufang decided she's going to stay with me a couple more days, and then, when it warms up, she'll go to the Western Hills to find me a good place to convalesce. I am so looking forward to getting out of Beijing, but here it is March and it's still so cold! Yufang insists on staying here with me. And I can't really refuse, so the cot set up for Jin and Zhou remains for her to use.

I had a change of heart about some things during my stay in the hospital. I must credit it to the overwhelming kindness and generosity of my friends. Now the universe seems full of love. I am especially grateful to

Ling Jishi. It made me so proud when he visited me in the hospital. I thought that only a man as handsome as he should be allowed to come to the hospital to visit a sick girlfriend. Of course, I was also aware of how much the nurses envied me. One day that gorgeous Miss Yang asked me, "What's that tall man to you?[8]

"A friend." I ignored the crude implication.

"Is he from your home area?"[9]

"No, he's an overseas Chinese from Singapore."

"Then he's a classmate, right?"

"No, he isn't."

She smiled knowingly, "He's just a friend, right?"

Of course I had no reason to blush and I could have called her on her rudeness, but I was ashamed to. She watched the way I closed my eyes indecisively, pretending to be sleepy. Finally she gave a satisfied laugh and walked off. After that she always annoyed me. To avoid further trouble, I lied whenever anyone asked about Weidi. I said he was my brother. There was a little guy who was a good friend of Zhou's whom I also lied about. I told them that he was a relative or close friend of the family from my home province.

When Yufang leaves for class and I am alone in the room, I reread all the letters I've gotten in the last month or so. It makes me feel happy and satisfied to know there are so many people who still remember me. I need to be remembered. The more the better. Father, needless to say, sent me another picture of himself, hair whiter than ever. My older sisters are all fine, but too busy taking care of their children to write more often.

I hadn't yet finished rereading my letters when Ling Jishi came by again. I wanted to get up but he restrained me. When he took my hand, I could have wept for joy.

"Did you ever think I'd make it back to this room?" I asked him. He gazed, tangibly disappointed, at the spare bed shoved up against the wall. I told him that my guests were gone but that the bed was left up for Yufang. When he heard that, he told me that he was afraid of annoying Yufang and so he wouldn't return that evening. I was ecstatic. "Aren't you afraid that I'll be annoyed?" I said.

He sat on the bed and told me in detail what had happened over the past month, how he had clashed with Yunlin over a difference of opinion: Ling Jishi felt I should have left the hospital earlier, but Yunlin had steadfastly refused to allow it. Yufang had agreed with Yunlin. Ling Jishi realized he hadn't known me very long and that therefore his opinion did not carry much weight. So he gave up. When he happened to run into Yunlin at the hospital, he would leave first.

I knew what he meant, but I pretended not to understand. "You're always talking about Yunlin," I said. "If it hadn't been for Yunlin, I wouldn't have left the hospital at all, I was so much more comfortable there." I watched him turn his head silently to one side. He didn't answer.

When he thought Yufang was about to return, he told me quietly that he'd be back tomorrow. Then he left. Shortly after that Yufang came home. Yufang didn't ask and I didn't tell her anything. She doesn't like to talk too much, since with my illness I might easily exhaust myself. That was fine with me. It gave me a chance to think my own thoughts.

March 6

After Yufang went to class, leaving me alone in the room, I started thinking about weird things that go on between men and women. It's not that I love boasting, actually, it's just that my training in this regard is far greater than all of my friends' combined. Still, recently I've felt at a spectacular loss to understand what is happening. When I sit alone with Ling Jishi, my heart leaps and I'm humiliated, frightened. But he just sits there, nonchalantly, reaching over to grasp my hand from time to time, and tells stories about his past with apparent naiveté. Although he carries on with supremely natural ease, I find that my fingers cannot rest quietly in his massive hand; they burn. Yet when he rises to go, I feel an attack of anxiety as though I am about to stumble into something really horrible. So I stare at him, and I'm not really sure whether my eyes seek pity or flash with resentment. Whatever he sees there, he ignores. But he seems to understand how I feel. "Yufang will be back soon," he says. What can I say to that? He's still afraid of Yufang! Normally I wouldn't like to have anybody know what kind of private fantasies I've been having recently; on the other hand, I do feel the need to have someone understand my feelings.[10] I've tried to talk indirectly with Yufang about this, but she just covers me with the quilt loyally and fusses about my medication. It depresses me.

March 8

Yufang has moved out, and Weidi wants to take over her job. I knew I would be more comfortable with him here than I was when Yufang nursed me. If I wanted tea in the middle of the night, for instance, I wouldn't have to creep back under my quilt with disappointment, as I did when I heard Yufang snoring and I didn't think it would be fair to disturb her sleep. But I refused his kind offer, naturally. When he insisted, I told him bluntly, "If you are here I will be inconvenienced in a number of ways, and anyway I'm feeling better."

He kept insisting that the room next door was empty and he could live there. I was just at my wit's end when Ling Jishi came in. I didn't think they knew each other, but Ling Jishi shook Weidi's hand and told me they'd met twice before at the hospital. Weidi ignored him coldly.

"This is my little brother," I said with a laugh to Ling Jishi. "He's just a kid who doesn't know how to act in mixed company. Drop by more often and we'll have a great time together." With that Weidi really did turn into a child, pulling a long face as he rose and left. I was annoyed that somebody had been present when this took place, and I felt it would be best to change the subject. I also felt apologetic toward Ling Jishi. But he didn't seem to notice particularly. Instead he just asked, "Isn't his last name Bai? How can he be your younger brother?"

I laughed. "So you only let people surnamed Ling call you 'Little Brother' or 'Big Brother,' " I said to him, making him chuckle.

These days when young people get together, they love to explore the meaning of the word "love." Although I feel at times that I understand love, in the end I can never really explain it. I know all about what goes on between men and women. Perhaps what I already know about it makes love seem vague, makes it hard for me to believe in love between the sexes, makes it impossible to think of myself as someone pure enough, innocent enough to be loved. I am skeptical of what everyone calls "love." I'm just as skeptical of the love I've received.

I was just becoming aware of the realities of life when those who loved me made me suffer by allowing outsiders the chance to humiliate and slander me. Even my most intimate friends abandoned me. And it was precisely for fear of the threat of love that I left school.[11] Although I mature more each day, those previous liaisons influenced me so much that I still have doubts about love and sometimes thoroughly despise the intimacy love brings. Weidi claims he loves me. Then why does he make me so miserable all the time? He came over again this evening, for instance, and as soon as he got here, he burst into tears and sobbed his eyes out. No matter what I said—"What's wrong with you? Please talk to me" or "Weidi, say something, I beg you"—he just carried on as before. Nothing quite like this had ever happened before. I exhausted myself trying to guess what catastrophe had befallen him until I couldn't think of any other possibilities. Eventually he cried himself out. Then he started in on me.

"I don't like him."

"Who's bullying you, Weidi? Who made you cry and throw this tantrum?"

"I don't like that tall guy. The one you're so close to now."

Oh! I really hadn't realized until then that he was furious over something I had done. Without thinking, I started to chuckle. This insipid jealousy, this selfish possessiveness, this is love? I couldn't help myself. I broke into laughter. And that, of course, did nothing to calm poor Weidi's raging heart. In fact, my condescending attitude increased his fury. Watching his blazing eyes, I got the feeling that what he really wanted was to rip me to shreds. "Go ahead and do it," I thought to myself. But he just put his head down, started bawling again, and rubbing tears from his eyes, staggered out the door.

A scene like this might conceivably be considered an ardent expression of tempestuous love. Yet Weidi stages these things for me with such artless lack of forethought that he defeats himself. I'm not asking him to be false or affected in the expression of his love. It's just I feel it's futile for him to try to move me by acting like a child. Maybe I'm just hard by nature. If so, I deserve all the anxiety and heartbreak that my failure to live up to people's expectations has brought me.

As soon as Weidi left, I scrutinized my own intentions. I recalled in vivid detail someone else's tenderness, someone else's warmth, generosity, and openly passionate bearing, and I was so drunk with sweet joy that I took out a postcard, wrote a few sentences, and ordered the attendant to take it over to Dormitory No. 4.

March 9
When I see Ling Jishi sit so relaxed and casually in my room, I can't help pitying Weidi. I pray that not every woman in the world will neglect and disdain his great sincerity, as I do, thus submerging myself in a morass of guilty sorrow I cannot get free of. More than that. I hope a pure young girl comes along who will redeem Weidi's love, fill the emptiness he must feel.

March 13
I haven't written anything in days. I don't know whether it's because I'm depressed or that I just can't find the so-called right mood. All I know is that since yesterday all I've wanted is to cry. When the others see me crying, they think I'm homesick or worried about my health. When they see me smile, of course, they think I'm happy, radiant with the glow of improving health . . . but my "friends" are all the same. Who can I tell about my stupid moods, which I refuse to cry over but haven't the strength to laugh at? Since I know it's because I won't forsake my ardent, worldly expectations, and because everything I try to do ends in disappointment, even I can no longer sympathize with myself when I end up heartbroken, as I invariably do. How can I possibly take pen in hand and spell out in detail all my self-accusations and self-hatred?

Yes, I guess I'm whining again. But it's only silent suffering, the unrestrainable repetition of my own voice inside my head, so it doesn't matter. I've never had the sort of courage it takes to let people see my agony or listen to me moan, although people very early on unconditionally labeled me as "haughty" and "eccentric." Actually, I don't want to whine so much as to cry. I want someone who'll hold me close and let me sob, someone who'll listen to me cry, "I've degraded myself again!" But who will understand me? Who will embrace me and comfort me? Only laughter prevents me from crying aloud, "I've degraded myself again."

What I'm really doing is very difficult to put into words. Naturally I have never for a moment acknowledged to myself that I might be in love with Ling Jishi. But if I'm not, why do I find him vaguely present at the core of my most intimate thoughts? His tall lean body, his delicate flower-soft skin, his soft lips and provocative eyes are tempting to women susceptible to beauty, and his languid sensuality unsettles me. But how could I become infatuated with this totally foreign man just because of his unwitting seductiveness? Our most recent conversations have taught me a lot more about his really stupid ideas. All he wants is money. Money. A young wife to entertain his business associates in the living room, and several fat, fair-skinned, well-dressed little sons. What does love mean to him? Nothing more than spending money in a brothel, squandering it on a moment of carnal pleasure, or sitting on a soft sofa fondling scented flesh, a cigarette between his lips, his legs crossed casually, laughing and talking with his friends. When it's not fun anymore, never mind; he just runs home to his little wifey. He's passionate about the Debate Club, playing tennis matches, studying at Harvard, joining the foreign service, becoming an important statesman, or inheriting his father's business and becoming a rubber merchant. He wants to be a capitalist . . . that is the extent of his ambition! Aside from dissatisfaction because his father hasn't sent him enough money, there isn't anything to disturb his sleep. Were there, it would be displeasure at finding so few pretty girls in Beijing and the fact that he finds going to so many theaters, so many plays, movies, and public gardens so very, very tiresome . . . God! What else is there to say? When I think that in this precious, beautiful form I adore, there resides such a cheap, ordinary soul, and that for no apparent reason I've gotten intimate with him several times (but nothing even approaching what he gets at his brothel)! When I think about how his lips brushed my hair, I'm so overwhelmed with regret I nearly break down. Don't I offer myself to him for his pleasures the same as any whore? But what makes the whole thing so painful is that I have only myself to blame. Because if I had been able or willing to face him with determined refusal in my eyes, I dare say he would never have been this bold with me. And I dare say the reason he wouldn't is that he's never been ignited by the fires of passionate love. Oh God! How can I revile myself enough!

March 14
Is this love? Perhaps only love can influence us so powerfully; otherwise, how could my thoughts have been so easily reversed. When I fell asleep,

I despised the gorgeous man. But as soon as I woke up, opened my tired eyes, the philistine was in my thoughts at once.[12] I wondered . . . Would he come today? When? Morning? Afternoon? Evening?

Then I leapt out of bed, quickly washed my face, made the bed. I picked up the large book I'd dropped on the floor last night and stroked its spine. It was a copy of Wilson's collected speeches, which Ling Jishi had left behind the night before.[13]

March 14, evening

I've been living an illusion, an illusion which Ling Jishi created for me— and which he just destroyed. Because of him, I can drink the sweet wine of youthful love to my heart's content and spend the morning basking in the smile of love. Yet also because of him, I now appreciate this plaything "life." I've been disenchanted, think again of death; the self-loathing I feel at my own willingness to fall is the lightest punishment. Really, there are times when I wonder whether I have the strength to kill him in order to protect my romantic illusion.

I've thought it over and decided that to preserve the beautiful fantasy and prevent my vitality from ebbing away day by day it's best that I go immediately to the Western Hills. But Yufang says her friend in the Western Hills whom she'd asked to find a room hasn't answered her letter yet. I can't really make further inquiries or pressure her, can I? So I made my decision. I decided to give that bastard a taste of me when I'm not so passive, a little taste of my outrageous arrogance and sharp, derisive tongue.

March 17

The other night Weidi left in a great rage. Today he cautiously returned to make his meek peace with me, and I couldn't help chuckling at that. I found myself thinking how cute he is. If all a woman wanted was an honest man to live with, I don't think she could find anybody to match Weidi for reliability. "Weidi," I asked jokingly, "do you still hate me?" "I don't dare," he said, abashed. "You understand me, dear sister. I have no designs on you other that hoping you don't completely abandon me. I only want you to be healthy and happy. That's quite enough for me." That is true devotion! Genuinely moving! How can an ashen face and ruby lips compare to this? Then I said to him, "Weidi, you're all right. The future is sure to bring you everything you've wanted." He responded with a pained smile. "That will never happen. I only wish things could be as you say." Not again. He was making me despair all over again! If only I could kneel down in front of him and beg him to love me like a friend or brother. Out of pure selfishness, I wish I could decrease these complications and increase my own happiness. Weidi loves me. And he can mouth those lovely sounding words. But he overlooks two things: first, he really ought to cool his ardor, and second, he should learn to hide his love. I can't stand the pain of regret in the face of my own ambivalence toward this ingenuous man.

March 18
I asked Xia to go to the Western Hills and find me a place to stay.

March 19
To my amazement, Ling Jishi hasn't been by in days. Then again, I don't dress well, I'm no good at entertaining, I'm a terrible housekeeper, I've got TB, and I'm broke. So why should he? I didn't need him in the first place. Only when he doesn't come, I feel so terrible and become convinced of his fickleness. Could it really be that he's as genuine as Weidi, and when he read the note I sent him—"I'm sick. Please don't bother me anymore"—he believed it and stopped coming out of respect for my wishes? This uncertainty makes me want to see him again, if only to make sure once and for all what this strange creature sees when he looks at me.

March 20
Today I went over to Yunlin's place three times without bumping into the person I wanted to see. Yunlin suspected something and asked whether or not I had seen Ling Jishi over the past few days. I returned dispiritedly. I'm terribly worried and there's no sense deceiving myself; I've been thinking about him constantly.

   Yufang and Yunlin came by at seven to invite me to Jingdu University to an English debate at Third College. Ling Jishi is the captain of the second team. My heart began to pound when I heard that last bit of news. But I used my health as an excuse to decline their kind invitation. I'm a useless weakling. I don't have the courage to withstand that kind of excitement. I still hope I won't have to see him. Yet as they left, I asked them to send my greetings to Ling Jishi and tell him I was asking after him. Damn. How stupid can I be!

March 21
I had just finished drinking my egg and milk when I heard the familiar knock at the door and a long shadow appeared on the paper window pane. My one thought was to leap up and open the door but at the direction of an inexplicable emotion, I swallowed hard and bowed my head. "Sophia, are you up?" His voice was so gentle that the second I heard it, I nearly burst out crying.

Did he just want to know if I was out of bed and sitting in the chair? Or was it to find out if I'd be capable of rage and refuse to see him? Tentatively he pushed the door open and came into the room. I didn't dare to raise my wet eyes.

"Are you feeling better? Did you just get up?"

I said nothing.

"You're really angry with me, aren't you, Sophia. I bore you. I'd guess I'd better go." It should have suited me fine to see him leave. Suddenly I raised my head, my gaze stopping at his hand as he reached for the door.

Who says he isn't a bastard? He understood the situation perfectly and boldly grasped my hand.

"Sophia, you're playing with me. I've passed your door every day but didn't dare come in. If Yunlin hadn't assured me you wouldn't get angry, I'd never have dared come today. Sophia, are you sick of me already?"

Had he dared to embrace me, had he kissed me passionately, I'd have fallen into his arms and cried, "I love you! God! I love you!" But he was so dispassionate, so cool and dispassionate, that I hated him for it. "Come, hold me," I thought wildly, "I want to kiss your face!" Naturally, through all of this he was still holding my hands, his eyes fixed steadily on my face. I searched frantically but nowhere in his expression could I find what I wanted. Why is he only able to respond to my helplessness, my vulnerabilities? And why doesn't he understand what position he occupies in *my* heart? I wished I could kick him out, but a different kind of feeling dominated me. I shook my head, to indicate I wasn't upset at his coming over.

So once again I yielded to his shallow affection and listened while he talked animatedly about the stupid pleasures he enjoys so much, listened to him expound on his philosophy that making money and spending money sum up the meaning of life. I even acceded to his insinuation that I try acting more feminine. That made me despise him even more than before, and I cursed him and ridiculed him secretly, even as inwardly my fists struck painfully at my heart. Yet when he left me quite triumphantly, I was so upset I could barely contain myself. I'd repressed my frenzied desires. I hadn't begged him to stay.

He left.

March 21, evening

What a life I was living last year at this time! To trick Yunjie into babying me unreservedly, I'd pretend to be sick and refuse to get out of bed. I'd sit and whimper about the most trivial dissatisfactions to work on her tearful anxiety and get her to fondle me. Then there were the times when, after spending an entire day in silent meditation, the mood of desolation I'd finally achieved made me unwilling to do anything, since by that time I could derive such utter sweetness from it. It hurts even more to think about the nights I spent lying on the grass in French Park listening to Yunjie sing "Peony Pavilion." [14] If she hadn't been tricked by God into loving that ashen-faced man, she would never have died so fast and I wouldn't have wandered into Beijing alone, trying, sick as I was, to fend for myself, friendless and without family. I admit I do have some friends here. Very sympathetic friends, in fact. But how could I possibly equate my relation to them with the love Yunjie and I had. When I think of Yunjie, I want so badly to lose myself in unrestrained sobs, the way I could do when we were together. But I've gotten more self-conscious this year. Even though I'm always on the edge of tears, I choke them back out of fear people will get tired of hearing about my troubles. Recently I've struggled even harder to understand why I get so desperately anxious. I no longer seem to find the time and leisure to sit and contemplate my own actions, my thoughts, my health, my reputation, or what, good or bad, is going to happen to me in the future. All day long my tangled mind revolves around what I try not to think about. It's precisely what I want to avoid that drives me to the extreme of mental distress. Besides stating for the record that I deserve to die, what other hope is there? Can I solicit sympathy and comfort? Even now I sound like I'm just begging for pity.

Yufang and Yunlin came over after dinner. When it got to be nine, I was still unwilling to let them go. I knew that Yufang could only stay a little longer, just to save my face. Yunlin seized on the pretext that he had to prepare for tomorrow's class and left alone. So very circumspectly I mentioned to Yufang how tormented I'd been feeling lately. I really thought she'd understand. I thought she'd take the initiative and force me to change my way of life, since I'm clearly not up to doing it myself. But when she'd heard what I had to say, she took it at its opposite meaning and warned me: "Sophia, I don't think you're being honest. Naturally you don't intend anything, but you should be more careful about the way you look at men. You must realize that people like Ling Jishi are not like the guys we ran around with in Shanghai. [15] They have very little contact with women and don't understand well-intentioned friendliness. You don't want him to end up disappointed and unhappy, do you? I say this because I know you would never actually fall in love with a man like Ling." The blame, it seemed, was on me now. If I hadn't enlisted her help but had just complained, would she have said such infuriating things to me? I swallowed my anger and smiled. "Yufang, don't make me out to be so awful!"

Yufang was willing to spend the night, but I got rid of her.

When they are feeling bad, talented women these days can write poems about "how depressed I am," "Oh, the tragic sufferings of my heart," and so on. I'm not gifted that way. I find I'm incapable of exploiting a poetic situation. Or even of letting my tears act as poems to somehow express the terrible war going on in my emotions. Actually, given this feeling of inadequacy, I ought to forget everything and pack myself off again to start my life over. I should make myself good with either a pen or a gun even if its purpose is just my own vanity or to win the praise of some shallow audience.[16] I've lowered myself into a dominion of suffering worse than death. All for that man's soft hair and red lips . . .

It was the chivalric European medieval knights I was dreaming about. It's still not a bad comparison; anyone who looks at Ling Jishi can see it, though he also preserves his own special Eastern gentleness. God took all the other good qualities and lavished them on him. Why couldn't God make him intelligent? He doesn't understand what love is. If fact, he hasn't the slightest idea, though he has a wife (Yufang told me tonight), and once in Singapore he had a short affair with some woman in a rickshaw he'd chased on his bike. All those nights at the Hanjiatan brothel notwithstanding, has he ever really experienced a woman's love? Has he ever loved a woman? I dare say he has not.

A strange thought burned its way into my mind again. I think I'll teach this college boy a lesson. The universe is not as simple as he seems to think!

March 22

In my mental confusion I've managed to force myself to keep this diary. I initially started it because Yunjie wrote and asked me repeatedly to do so. Now even though Yunjie has been dead a long time, I can't bear to give it up. I suppose I'll go on forever, writing the diary in her memory as a testimonial to all the things she told me while she was alive. However much I'd rather not, I always feel I have to scrawl a page or so. I'd been dozing, but I couldn't stand seeing Yunjie's picture looking at me from its place on the wall, so I got up and started noting things down to avoid the pain of thinking about her. I have always felt I didn't want anybody but Yun reading this diary. That's because I was writing it primarily because she wanted to know about my life, which I recorded in quotidian detail, and second, because I'm afraid that another reader might turn the face of Reason on me, and I'd be devastated. It seems that I really do feel like a criminal when I violate the moral code that other people prize so highly. So for a long time, I've kept the little black leather book under the mattress below my pillow. Today, inopportunely, I disobeyed my original injunction. In retrospect it seems fated, though at the time I appeared to act without forethought. I did it because Weidi has been consistently misinterpreting me lately, using his observations to feed his chronic apprehension, then infecting me with his anxiety. I believe my behavior has always made my attitude perfectly clear. How could he possibly misunderstand me? If I told him directly, would that obliterate his love? I often think that if it weren't Weidi but someone else, I'd know how to deal with it better. But no. He's such a good person that I just can't steel my heart against him. I had no other recourse. I gave him my diary to read. It was to show him the hopelessness of his situation, how undeserving of love, how cold and inconstant a woman I am. If, of course, by reading my diary, Weidi ended up understanding me, then he'd become my intimate confidant, the friend to whom I could pour out my heart, embrace earnestly, kiss. Then I'd become the most beloved, beautiful woman in the world, the woman of his desires.

Diary, Weidi read through the pages once. Then once again. All the while he remained self-composed despite tears. I had not anticipated this. "Do you understand me," I said.

He nodded.

"Do you believe me?"

"Concerning what?"

Finally his nod made sense. A reader who really understood would know that the diary revealed only a fraction of me, and could then help me see my limitations and misery. How could I hope for understanding from a reader, when all I give him is a diary carefully crafted to convey meaning solely through writing? That's devastating enough by itself. On top of that, Weidi was afraid that I'd thought he'd not fully understood me, so he burst out, "You love him. You love him! I'm not good enough for you."

I nearly tore the diary to pieces out of spite. I'd debased it by letting Weidi see it—how could I claim otherwise?

"I want to go to sleep," was all I could think of to say. "Come back tomorrow."

We can expect nothing from other people. That's terrifying, isn't it? If Yunjie were alive and read my diary, I know that she'd hold me in her arms. "Oh, Sophia, my Sophia," she'd cry. "Why can't my valor rescue Sophia from so much suffering?" But Yunjie is dead. I cannot figure the best way to grieve with this diary.

March 23

Ling Jishi said to me, "Sophia, you really are a strange girl." This was not, I repeat, not praise based on a clear grasp of who I am. He finds strangeness in the fact that I wear tattered gloves, that I don't perfume my dresser drawers, that at times for no reason I've been known to tear my new cotton-padded jacket, that I've saved some old toys from childhood. What else? He hears me laugh from time to time. There's nothing more to it. He comprehends nothing. And I've never said anything to him that really came out of me. For instance, when he says, "I want to focus on making money from now on," I laugh. When he talks about the time he went to the park with some friends to harass women students— "Boy, that was interesting, Sophia"—I laugh. All he really means by strange, of course, are things that fall outside the scope of his ordinary life. It hurts me deeply that I'm not able to command his respect and understanding. Now all I want is to go to the Western Hills. Contemplating the absurd fantasy he used to inspire in me, I can't help laughing at myself.

March 24

When he's here alone with me, I suffer scouring torment as I stare into his face and listen to the musical sound of his voice. Why don't I crush his mouth with kisses, his temples, his . . . his whole body. The words "My lord and master! Grant me one kiss!" rise to my lips. But then reason overcomes me—no, no, I've never been reasonable. It's my self-respect that surfaces and controls my emotions allowing me to choke back the words. My God! No matter how dreadful his ideas, there is no doubt he is driving me mad with desire, so why can't I admit that I'm in love with him? Not only that, I know for certain fact that were he to hold me tightly in his arms, let me shower his body with kisses, and then throw me into the sea, or into an inferno, I would happily close my eyes and await the arrival of the death that sealed my love. God! I love him so much. Let him give me a sweet death; I'll be satisfied . . .

March 24, *midnight*

I've made up my mind. In order to save myself from being destroyed by this sexual obsession, I'm going to Xia's place tomorrow morning.[17] It's to spare myself the torment of seeing Ling Jishi, torment that has ensnarled my life for too long already.

March 26

I left because of one involvement. But I got tangled up in another, so I had to rush back again. My second day at Xia's place, Mengru arrived.[18] Although she said she'd come to see somebody else, her arrival made me feel terrible. That night she expanded at great length on some new theory of emotions she'd picked up somewhere, taunting me covertly as I lay there in silence. To deny her any further satisfaction, I closed my eyes and lay on Xia's bed until daybreak when, rage barely checked, I rushed home.

Yufang told me she'd found a place in the Western Hills and that she'd gotten hold of a good friend, also recuperating from illness, who'd stay with me. I should have been delighted by the news, but even though I forced a smile onto my face, I felt a cold mournfulness settling over me. Although I left home at an early age and have pretty much run wild since, I have always had a few friends or relatives close by. This time, even though I'm only going to the Western Hills, only a couple of miles from town, it will be the first time in my whole short life I've ever gone to a strange place by myself. If I were to die in those hills, who'd be the one to discover my corpse? Who can reassure me that I won't die out there? Other people might smile and say I'm morbid, but I really did cry over this once before. When I asked Yufang if she would be able to let me go that far, she just laughed at my infantile question and said it was such a short distance that it was hardly a matter of being able or not. Finally Yufang promised me she'd come to the hills every week. Embarrassed, I dried my eyes.

That afternoon I went over to Weidi's place and got him to promise he'd also come to the hills once a week, on a day Yufang wasn't coming.

I got back home that night and began to pack desolately. As I thought about the Beijing friends I'm leaving behind, I started to cry. When it finally struck me that they had no intention of ever weeping over me, I brushed aside the tears running down my face. I'll leave this ancient city alone.

I thought of Ling Jishi again, I was so lonely. Actually, that's not entirely accurate. With Ling Jishi it's not a matter of saying "I thought of him . . . then I thought of him again." Since I'd been thinking of him obsessively all day, it's closer to the truth to say that I wanted "to *talk about* my Ling Jishi again."

March 27

Yufang went to the Western Hills early this morning to get the room fixed up for me. She determined that I'd leave tomorrow. How can I repay her enormous kindness when I can't even put my gratitude into words? I had thought initially of staying another day in the city, but now I just can't force myself to say so.

Just when my anxiety over leaving so early was at its peak, Ling Jishi arrived. I grasped his hands tightly. "Sophia," he said. "I haven't seen you in days!"

How I longed to burst into tears and cling to him, weeping. My tears refused to flow. I was reduced to grinning. I did get a little consolation;

on hearing that I'd be leaving tomorrow for the hills, he was so surprised that he was moved to sigh. My expression became more genuine. His grip tightened in response to my smile, so tight it hurt. "You're smiling," he said resentfully. "You're smiling."

The pain this cause him flooded me with a pleasure I'd never experienced before; it felt as though something had pierced my heart. Just as I was about to fall straight into his arms, Weidi arrived. Weidi knew I hated him for coming at that moment, but he wouldn't leave. I gave Ling Jishi a sign with my eyes and said to him. "Don't you have a class now?"

Then I escorted Ling out. He asked me when I was scheduled to leave the next morning. I told him. I asked him whether or not he was going to come back before then. He said he'd be back soon. I looked at him happily, forgetting how despicable his character is, and the mirage that is his beauty, because at that moment he was a storybook lover in my eyes.[19] Hah! Sophia has a lover . . .

March 27, evening
I rushed Weidi out of here five hours ago. How can I describe those hours? Restlessly, in this cramped room, like an insect on a hot pan, I've sat, then stood, then rushed to the crack in the door to peer out. But . . . he isn't coming. He just isn't coming. Again I teetered on the edge of tears because my exit from Beijing has to be so desolate and lonely. In all Beijing will no one cry with me? I should just leave this cruel city. Why am I so loathe to renounce this hard board bed, the greasy desk, the three-legged chairs? . . . That's it. I'm leaving tomorrow. My friends in Beijing will never be burdened with Sophia's illness again. Why doesn't Sophia do her friends a huge favor and die somewhere out in the Western Hills. They're perfectly willing to let me go off to the hills lonely, desperate, friendless. On the other hand, presumably I won't die and people won't be harmed or unduly grieved . . . Oh, don't worry it to death. Don't think about it! What's there to think about, anyway? If Sophia weren't so needy that she ran around begging for an emotional fix, then she'd get some satisfaction from the looks of sympathy she does get, wouldn't she? . . .

I have nothing further to say on the subject of friends. I only know that Sophia will never find satisfaction in ordinary friendship.

But what satisfaction can I ever expect? Ling Jishi promised he'd come. It's already 9 P.M. Even if he does, will that make me happy? Can he give me what I need? . . .

I've even more reasons to hate myself now that it's clear he's not coming. In the far, far distant past, I knew how to adjust my style to suit the man, but I've gotten quite moronic about that lately. Why did I give him such a supplicating look when I asked if he'd be back? In the case of such an attractive man, I should avoid being too candid, since he'll just despise me for it . . . But I love him. So why should I use technique? Can't I express my love directly? Anyway, providing that it harms no one, why shouldn't I be allowed to kiss him as many times as I want to?

He said that he was coming back, but he's broken his promise again, so it's clear he's only playing me along. You wouldn't lose anything, beloved friend, just by humoring Sophia a little on her way out of town.

I've gone insane tonight. How useless speech and the written word seem now! My heart heels as though it were being gnawed by tiny rats, as though a fire inside it were raging out of control. How I'd love to smash everything in sight. How I'd love to rush out into the night and run wildly in desperate confusion. I can't control the surges of madness. I lie on this bed of the thorns of passion. I turn this way and feel the stabs; I turn the other way only to be pierced again. I'm in a vat of oil listening to its roaring boil, feeling its burning heat sear my entire body . . . Why don't I run away? Because I linger over a vague and meaningless wish. God! . . . When I think of those red lips, I lose my mind again. If this wish could only come true. All alone, I can't restrain my own explosive laughter as I interrogate myself compulsively: "Do I love him?" Then I break into fresh gales of laughter. Sophia could never be such a fool as to allow herself to love that man from Singapore to such extremity. Is it possible that because I refuse to admit I love him I'll never be allowed to consummate this perfectly harmless relationship?

If he doesn't come tonight, how can I just leave complacently for the Western Hills?

Damn! 9:30!

9:40!

March 28, 3:00 A.M.

In the course of my life, my desire for people to understand and sympathize with me has been too strong, which is why I've felt such bitter despair for so long. Only I know how many tears I've shed.

Rather than calling this diary a record of my life, it's more accurate to regard it as the sum of all my tears. At least that's the way it feels. But now it's time to end the diary because Sophia doesn't need it anymore, doesn't need it as a vent or consolation, since now she understands that nothing has any meaning whatever and that tears are only the most elegant proof of that lack. Yet on this last page of the diary, I ought fervently to toast the fact that suddenly from the depth of disappointment I did achieve the satisfaction that should rightly have killed me with ecstasy. I

. . . I . . . all I felt out of that satisfaction was victory. From victory came a terrible sorrow and an even profounder understanding of how pathetic and ludicrous I am. And so the "beauty" that has been the focus of my tangled dreams for months was dissolved away, revealed as nothing more than the image of a tall man's exquisite bearing.

How shall I analyze the psychology of a woman driven insane by the way a man looks? Of course I didn't love him, and the reason why is easy to explain: inside his beautiful appearance his soul is completely degraded! But I revered him. I thought about him so much that without him I'd have abandoned all that makes life meaningful. I often thought that if one day my lips touched his, I'd happily see my own body disintegrate from the force of my heart's violent laughter. In fact, for a sweet, soft caress from that knightly man, wherever his fingers deigned to touch me, I would willingly have sacrificed everything.

I ought to be mad with joy now, since all the wondrous elements of my fantasy actually happened to me as though in a dream, effortlessly. But did I get all the soul-intoxicating bliss I had imagined? No!

When he—when Ling Jishi—came in at ten and began stammering about his desire to have me, I felt my heart throbbing in my breast. The lust in his eyes scared me. I felt my self-respect revive finally as I listened to the disgusting pledges sworn out of the depths of Ling Jishi's depravity. If he'd tried the same pat, superficial, revolting come-on with some other woman, she would certainly have been fascinated and he might well have achieved his goal. But when he tried it on me, he drove me off by the very force of all those words. Stupid, pathetic man! God granted you this beauty of form but deceived you by giving you a totally incongruous soul. Did you really think that all I desire is marriage and family?[20] That all that amuses me is money? That all I'm proud of is my "position"? You have shown yourself to be an extraordinarily pathetic man! As I teetered on the edge of tears over this turn of events, he locked his eyes on my face. The lust burning in his eyes was terrible. If he'd wanted nothing more than sexual satisfaction, he might conceivably have seduced me with his sensuous beauty. But then in a tearful, trembling voice he said, "Trust me, Sophia, just trust me. I'll never fail you."

Wretched, wretched man! He still had no inkling of the disdainful pity the woman seated before him felt at his stooping to such a ridiculous affectation. Finally I burst out laughing. It's absurd to say that he knows what love is, that he's able to love me. Beyond revealing his shallow, contemptible need, those outrageous, lustful, flashing eyes made it certain that he would never understand a thing.

"Oh stop it! Get out of here! You'll find the kind of pleasure you like at Weijia brothel." Since I saw through him so clearly, I should have said that. I should have told one of the vilest beasts on the face of the earth to leave me the hell alone. Yet even as I was secretly ridiculing him, when he flung his arms around me in a reckless, bold gesture, I forgot everything. I stood poised to toss away all my self-esteem and pride. I was bewitched by this man who had only his appearance to offer. In my heart all I could think was "Tighter. Hold me longer. I'm leaving tomorrow." If I'd had a little self-control at that moment, I'd have thought beyond his beautiful form and thrown him out of my house like a rock.

God! What words, what feelings can voice my bitter regret. That disgusting creature Ling Jishi kissed me! I endured it in silence! But what did my heart feel when lips so warm and tender brushed my face? I couldn't allow myself to be like other women who faint into their lovers' arms! I screwed open my eyes wide and looked straight in his face. "I've won!" I thought "I've won!" Because when he kissed me, I finally knew the taste of the thing that had so bewitched me. At the same moment I despised myself.

Suddenly I felt deeply hurt; pushing him away with all my strength I wept.

He probably dismissed my tears. Maybe he thought that the warmth and tenderness of his lips, their smooth delicacy, had made my heart so drunk with joy that I'd just gone crazy. So he sat nearer and went on muttering the revolting nonsense that he believes expresses love.

"Why go on showing your most repellent weakness?" I thought, but I felt a surge of pity for him again. I said, "Don't be ridiculous. There's no certainty I'll be alive tomorrow."

It's hard to say what his reaction was. He tried to kiss me again. But I moved away and his lips fell to my hand . . . I decided then that as I was in full control of my mental faculties, I wanted him out. He looked peeved; he kept after me. I thought, "Why are you so incredibly stupid?" It was almost 12:30 before he'd go.

After he left, I tried to think about what had just happened. I drew on every strength remaining to me and struck my heart! Why, why had I permitted a man I despise to kiss me? I don't love him. In fact, I mock and ridicule him. Yet I permitted him to embrace me. Was it just his knightlike airs that had brought me so low as this?

In short, I caused my own ruin. The self is every person's true enemy. How in God's name will I ever avenge myself and restore what I have lost?

It's certainly fortunate that in this universe, my life is my own plaything. I've wasted more than enough of it. This one experience had me plunged into the most profound anguish. Yet I now feel as though it's been a mere trifle.

I don't want to stay in Beijing. I'm even less interested in the Western Hills. I've decided to take a train south, somewhere where no one knows me, where I can squander the remaining days of my life. The agony is gone and I feel excitement. I laugh wildly, I feel so sorry for myself.

Life sneaks on. Death too. Oh, how pathetic you are Sophia!

Translated by Tani E. Barlow

A Woman and a Man

Many of Ding Ling's early stories seem to be variations on a single theme, the struggle between men and women. Ding Ling was intent on defining what it was that made women and men different. "A Woman and a Man," written in 1928, was later collected in a famous anthology called, appropriately enough, *A Woman*. Not only was Ding Ling's emphasis on the war between the sexes new to Chinese fiction, but the way she went about depicting "woman" and "man" owed a lot to European literature and American movies.

Wendy, the main character, even has a European name. Wendy is in a literal sense a translated person. Ouwai Ou says she reminds him of the heroine of *La Dame aux Camélias*, and of the "Salome type woman." He believes that she "hasn't got the slightest idea what Reason means" and that "all she knows is crazy emotion." Wendy in fact agrees, and she acts to perfection the role of the femme fatale—French romance crossed with Greta Garbo movies. Both Wendy and Ouwai Ou are Chinese versions of the essential biological man and woman, smuggled into treaty port fiction through realist fiction and social theory. And that means they are frauds in more than one respect. They are self-invented fakes, of course. But they are also made up out of literary texts rather than human flesh. They have strung themselves together out of the little bits and pieces of borrowed images and words.

Even so Wendy is still admirable. Particularly, this story makes clear, when she appears in contrast to the "Chinese" alternative, Ajin, the passive, mercenary prostitute. Wendy's a swaggering, aggressive fake, but she's somebody Ouwai Ou has to respect. Ajin, on the other hand, is the stereotyped May Fourth female victim, that plaything, bedraggled and available for any man's use. Ouwai Ou likes showing off his masculine, predatory instincts and sex drive; in a fit of bad faith he even fantasizes about Ajin's (presumably bound) little feet. Ouwai Ou, the essence of the Chinese male, is never confused about lust. He may find the "modern girl," as women like Wendy were called, intriguing. He may even find her posturing erotic. But he turns for sex to an idea of femininity that is his own fabrication, something Wendy would never submit to. Poor Ajin supplies only the body for his fantasies.—TEB

It was the twentieth of November, a day the wind stopped blowing.

Around two or three that morning the wind started dying down, though it still could chill you to the bone. That's why the streets remained hushed and silent even though the sky was already light. Yellow dogs the size of small lions had to sleep with their heads tucked up firmly against their chests. Heavy with dust, the shutters of the shops remained tightly shut.

Just then a man wearing Western-style clothing emerged from Stone Alley. He was young, of course. The idea that one of the alley's bearded old inhabitants might show up all alone in this faint early light of dawn was ridiculous. Even the sight of a young man was rather peculiar.

He'd drawn his cap deep down over his face, revealing only what lay beneath his nose. A thin overcoat wrapped the warm body that he'd torn from a snug quilt just a moment earlier. Walking out of the alley, he stopped. Head raised slightly, eyelids swollen, his small gray pupils darted in all directions, searching for a rickshaw.

At night this street was quite lively, but in the early hours of morning few people ever came around. The strong wind had blown all night, so there wasn't a single rickshaw out. Not a person to be seen.

"Rickshaw! Rickshaw!"

He couldn't hear a sound. He shifted his feet indecisively. When he turned around to glance back, that head with the two plaited pigtails and the extraordinarily tangled hair appeared before his eyes: that small oval face, pale, so very pale, the ears partly covered by the wild hair; those slender hands rubbing sleepy eyelids; the thin, pale-red lips parted into an innocent yawn. "She really suits my taste!" the young man mused. "God, that pure oriental style, that graceful Chinese bearing!"

His eyes seemed to take in the rest. A close-set row of jadeite buttons opened halfway down over soft, supple breasts, the dimly revealed, finely arched lines of the two half-globes, and that necklace of tiny locks resting between her breasts, the lockets her hands pressed down firmly onto her bosoms . . .

At this, he started back in the direction he'd come. But a second face—that of the doorman from Lingering Fragrance Garden—brought an abrupt end to his sweet dream. Thinking back to how the guy had just let him out, with grumbles and angry looks, he decided he wasn't at all keen to see that surly face once he got him up—he couldn't pretend to be deaf—out of bed again to reopen the door. "Why go looking for trouble?" So he stopped dead in his tracks.

The lovely face lured him forward again. The thought of those small hands caressing his body, the easy feeling he got when she snuggled up under his arm, the sound of her childlike giggle made his heart pound even harder, so at last he started walking.

While he had been standing there, hesitating, he'd been fishing something out of his pocket. Unfortunately, although he'd stuck his gloved hands into his coat pockets, they'd already stiffened from the cold, without his realizing it. With a great effort he wrapped his fingers around a little object and unfolded it. It was a piece of paper, crumpled around the edges. Someone had scribbled on it in an uneven scrawl, "Tomorrow morning at seven o'clock—please wait for me at home!"

Rolling the note into a ball for the third time, he shoved it back into his pocket. Then this young man of ours heaved an enormous sigh and weakly, yet with determination, changed his direction once again, heading eastward along the empty street.

This young man frequently wrote vernacular free verse that was published in a number of magazines. He had also just recently changed his name to something very Japanese sounding—Ouwai Ou.[1] The street was made of slabstone, and two nights and a day of wind had swept it clean. The sound of his leather soles made a rhythmic racket that echoed in the distance. There wasn't a single rickshaw in the alleys on either side of the street.

With practiced sentimentality Ouwai Ou pondered his hard, drifting life. Women were the reason he'd written off all his burning hopes of a future and become a completely despondent, decadent man, leading a dissipated life in Shanghai. He had thought that by coming to Beijing he'd be able to take advantage of the calm and do some work with his mind again. Who'd have thought that his frustrations would drive him to the brothels so often or that he would contract such a terrible case of tuberculosis? His health worsened by the day, he could see, and his spirit was getting sluggish too. Now, again, for some woman—a woman—he was braving a frigid morning to keep an appointment made by someone else. This was really no way to live!

Since his melancholy was rather superficial, he kept his feet moving steadily along. When he noticed that he was actually rushing forward, he had to smile a little in spite of himself. The rhythmic sound produced by his shoes on the stones formed into a melody that caught his fancy. He started searching for rhyming words to turn it into a poem.

He hadn't quite found exactly the right words for this poem when a rickshaw he hadn't heard approaching swept past him from behind. He could only make out a net-covered basket. Someone rushing to catch a train. By this time the versifier had turned onto Qianmen Avenue. Here and there large carts loaded with coal and pulled by filthy, emaciated donkeys rumbled by. The tower over Qianmen city gate, so many meters high, was set off against the clear, bright sky. A handful of people wearing so much quilted clothing they looked like candy dolls could be seen strolling along the gray city wall.

Ouwai Ou shouted again, "Rickshaw! Rickshaw!"

Two or three passersby wrapped in heavy gray scarves and large, dog-skin coats, gave him a glance because even though he used the Beijing dialect, his pronunciation still had a Southern ring to it.

Qianmen Avenue was so very broad. It was early in the morning and there were few people out. Through the withered tree branches, the boulevard stretched far into the distance. As Ouwai Ou crossed the street, he felt a sense of joy. Once again his thoughts drifted to the girl with the big eyes.

"Hmm, she's a strange woman. It's as though she hasn't got the slightest idea what Reason means; all she knows is crazy emotion which floods everything. I've never met anyone like her. Today. Today. I really don't know what to prepare myself for . . ."

Quite unawares, Ouwai Ou reached East Station. Rickshaw men surrounded him, shouting for customers.

"Hey, rickshaw!"

"Hey, four cash, wherever you want to go!"

He got into a rickshaw. Entering Qianmen archway, they headed straight north. The wind, weak yet still cutting, blew into his face, forcing him to pull his cap down even further. He thrust his right hand under his coat and up against his chest, where he finally found some warmth. He raised his left hand to his lips and blew on it. He stared absent-mindedly at his shiny black leather shoes. Automatically he started adding up the sums of money he had spent recently.

"Forty returned to Old Cheng. Fifteen back to Old Zhao. Fifty-seven for boarding house rental—make it sixty. Twenty-four to redeem Little Xu's pawn, but hadn't I spent that money long ago? What else? I only bought this pair of black leather shoes, eight and a half yuan— The rest, the rest? What happened to it all. Can I have given her that much?"

He reached into his pocket with his right hand and dragged out all the remaining banknotes. There were three of them: two five-yuan bills and a one-yuan note. Besides these he still had two silver dollars. What could be clearer? He had gone to the trouble of sending five express letters and two telegrams to his Shanghai bookstore before they finally sent the three hundred yuan they owed him for his two manuscripts. Somehow all the money had vanished in a week, and he couldn't even figure out where it had gone. If he'd given that small woman over a hundred yuan, then why hadn't she treated him better? Once or twice she'd mentioned that she wanted to go to the German Hospital to see a doctor but didn't have the money. He'd given it to her, though he'd never actually seen her enter the hospital, not even once. That really annoyed him. It also made him feel a little sad. There were plenty of idiots who, completely unconscious of their effect, had gorgeous women falling in love with them all the time. He himself, on the other hand, had spent money on countless occasions buying love from women who were available for use by any man. (He had long forgotten all the respectful names he had once lavished on them.) He had sought love and sympathy, and what had it gotten him? All they loved was money, and he had given them every cent he had. They had wanted to pay debts, and he had paid their confounded debts, even going into debt himself to do it. What did he really spend on himself? He even bought his cigarettes one by one. Quite unbelievable, come to think of it!

The more he thought about it, the more indignant he became. He wasn't easily angered, but the cold, cruel day had made him unfair to the woman, so sick with tuberculosis, whom he really did love. If he didn't repent his unkindness, his friends would certainly reproach him for having other aspirations. In that case, the woman with whom he had vowed again and again to live and die together would have to be cast aside. Sadly enough, if he did give her up, there would be plenty of people congratulating him. But he quickly turned away from that thought.

In a flash more than two dozen so-called freely-chosen love marriages came to mind. There wasn't one where the woman had not put economic security at the top of her list of conditions. But his girl, his little treasure, goddess of beauty, diseased sprite—he had so many names for her that he couldn't even remember them all—his girl clearly wasn't made happy by his money, since she couldn't be any colder to him if he'd given her none at all. A smile appeared on his face. That graceful Chinese bearing started running through the young poet's mind again. Those sloping shoulders, that narrow waistline, the two trouser legs, out from which peeked her slippers, minutely embroidered with red flowers, gently moving up and down; and that special way of breathing, so delicate and asthmatic; the cough that sent her two earrings swaying alongside her neck . . .

Love. What was love after all? It was pleasure, yes, pleasure! Ha, that woman, that little bitch. He could spend the rest of his life just gazing at her lovely face. That energy, despite her illness! Wherever had she learned it all? The moment she started pouring out that stream of sweet words in her enchanting, melodic voice, straight into your ear, you felt more drunk than if you'd just poured wine down your throat.

When Ouwai Ou, who had actually passed quite a few sleepless nights, began thinking along lines that intoxicated his feelings, he really took on the look of someone stone drunk. He stretched out his legs and sprawled on his back, his face turned upward. The rickshaw man felt a heavy jolt and assumed that they had arrived, so he drew up to the side and stopped, nearly causing the drunken Ouwai Ou to fall out. His dreams evaporated. A glance told him they had already reached Northern Pond. The three banknotes remained in his hand.

The rickshaw needed to go further north.

Ouwai Ou's thoughts drifted away from the woman. He didn't know if it was love; he didn't need to know. He wasn't even sure he wanted what they called love, so he didn't think about it again. He considered other things that gave him pleasure.

"Hmm, what gall!" Now his hands were twisting the piece of paper in his pocket. "In front of all those people. Even her husband. To have the nerve to write a note and hand it over to me, while I was convinced she was copying down a poem for Xiao Wang![2] I didn't believe my eyes when I saw it was for me. But I don't want any trouble. Lao Zhang isn't a man to mess with either.[3] If he found out, he'd get his pistol out and challenge me to a duel. I couldn't take that. Why should I go along with that nonsense? What a strange woman. She's already got Xiao Wang; he's great looking, but she doesn't love him. She doesn't love Zili either, though he's as sharp as they come. In fact, from what I've heard, she's always been absolutely faithful. She's so devoted to Lao Zhang that she can't restrain herself from kissing him right in front of everybody. She's gone crazy. I've seen through her for quite a while now. She frightens me. But not keeping the appointment won't do either. She'd probably call me up on the phone all the time. And if I do go, she might not even show up, since Lao Zhang keeps her reined in pretty tight. Hmm, those eyes. They can be really scary when they pierce right through you! She was sitting there behind old Zhang and he didn't see a thing! Then, as if she couldn't care less about all the people there, she asks, "Ou, are you afraid of me?" When I said I was, she insisted I tell her why. What could I say? All I could do was retract my words and say I wasn't afraid of her.

Everybody laughed and asked how on earth I could be afraid of her? She made things even worse by adding that she despised people who feared her. When I heard that and understood what she meant, I nearly exploded I was so upset . . .

As he thought about the woman's unrestrained behavior, Ouwai Ou became hesitant again. What if she ran right into the boarding house, into his tiny room, and Lao Zhao next door saw her? If he talked around about it that would be quite embarrassing. He considered not going home. But what if she actually came? She'd hang around even if nobody showed up, and wait one, maybe even two hours. Lao Zhao would come by for a chat, and that woman, who was quite open about her own lack of sophistication, well, who knows what she'd say? Soon everybody'd know. And Lao Zhang was a friend. He wouldn't be able to look him in the eye, and anyway he'd hate breaking up a marriage. He wasn't enough in love with this daring woman to go through all that trouble! And yet . . . no matter how often Ouwai Ou carefully considered the pros and cons, and although he had never before felt the urge to meet this woman alone, something obvious remained, an urge every full-grown man could identify very easily. No one would ever believe that Ouwai Ou, who could be completely overcome by even a second-rate whore whom he'd transfigured into a dramatic, romantic courtesan, no one would believe him capable of resisting the advances of a woman whose noble spirit even he could recognize. And him being the sensitive poet that he was! Nothing more need be written about this. No one would ever suspect that he'd have had the heart to disappoint her.

This fellow was clever. After reaching the bridge, the rickshaw stopped. He didn't head for his lodging house but turned south, strolling along beneath large willow trees. Palish-yellow sun rays from between sparse and withered branches cast his shadow far across to the center of the avenue. It made his old felt cap take on funny-looking shapes.

He glanced at his luminous watch and figured that in all probability he would run into the woman here on this street. Still, it was nearly eight o'clock already. (The sky took so long to turn light; you had to blame Beijing winter for that.)

Indeed, toward him raced a shadow wrapped in a leather-trimmed coat, her two apparently bare legs moving in quick harmony with the sound of wooden-soled shoes. Abruptly, even from a distance away, those two large sparkling eyes, hidden under a purple cap, pierced Ouwai Ou's heart.

Immediately he started acting shifty, like someone about to commit his first crime. All his ideas and plans vanished. He stood there like an idiot.

The woman's name was—well, what was her name? She had deliberately selected more than fifty interesting names and had used them at every conceivable occasion. She mostly allowed her friends to call her Wendy. She was a woman of excessive passion, yet one who would never be able to experience real love. She lived in a constant state of perverse deviancy, in that she loathed expressions of sentiment that reminded her of the desires of the flesh, and that were therefore, to her way of thinking, lacking in sincere love. Yet she would risk everything to pursue a conversation about such invigorating matters, as though she were addicted to it. She seemed to feel that she couldn't go on living unless she was in a situation of danger and secrecy where she could toy with the heart of someone she'd managed to drive to distraction. Therefore, she wasn't afraid of her husband's tight control. Her husband was a very clever schoolteacher and did, in fact, see right through her. He said she was an utterly vicious woman who would take up with any kind of man, from bureaucrat and politician down to vagabond and villain, just for the hell of it. His vigilance never slackened. When he got back from class, he searched the clothes first, then the drawers. If he found an envelope missing, he would spend all day nagging at her. But his clever wife never lacked schemes and excuses: she got more intensely involved, though she knew quite well that carrying on the way she did would make their lives miserable. At times when she had deceived him, and the affair could no longer be denied, she would break down and kneel at his feet crying, full of grief-stricken remorse. It was, however, a big act. But her husband would look at her, feel sorry for her. He would believe her, and then would spend the rest of the day comforting her. Sometimes the man didn't know what to believe. He couldn't very well renounce her, so all that remained was suicide or murder. The man loved her very much indeed.

She had not married him for name or status, nor had it been, a case of having to get married. She had simply said that she loved him and was willing to sacrifice all her other friends, though she also liked them very much, for him. At the same time, she had put him under tremendous pressure, and when they had moved in together he was still feeling fearful and anxious. Several years had passed and even she had forgotten that at the time of her marriage she had flirted with many other men for her own cruel satisfaction and had left a trail of broken hearts. Her lips, made for deceit, which her husband had implored her not to violate wantonly, often kissed other men, even when she'd originally intended not to. Yet she insisted that she loved only her husband and that even in the face of death she would never say otherwise. So although they quarreled frequently, they stayed locked together in a marriage, fated perhaps as retribution for the sins of their previous lives.

Heaven knows what had made her husband introduce Ouwai Ou into their midst! His pale, jaundiced face was certainly nothing to attract a healthy woman. And to put it bluntly, he was actually indistinguishable from many, many others, as common as a stone in the street. In every respect, yes, in every respect he could voice nothing beyond the specific ideology of a given class. As far as his poetry was concerned, Wendy had read a lot of verse and so his shallow, weak sentimentalism shouldn't have had any effect on her. This was, however, a truly exceptional situation. She seemed like a woman obsessed, completely determined that if she couldn't get a certain something from him, she wouldn't let go. It would appear that she considered the man too enervated, and wanted to provide him with the strength to live. How could she have known it would only embarrass him?

She had endured three entire nights of aching anticipation. Normally, when an idea took hold of her, she would go ahead and act—unless she lacked the proper motivation. Whenever it was a case of something she wanted, even some little trifle, she made every sacrifice necessary to reach her goal. Apart from the fact that she respected her own impulses, she never weighed things by their degree of seriousness. For three whole nights—and here the days should be taken into account too—she had made every effort to control herself. She wanted to seize a heart she regarded as cold. She wanted to see a victory over this cold, callous man. In a very short time, his blood ought to be seething for her. He, who meant to be so decadent, would have to spend his days excited over her, and his life of happiness would be ruined all because of her. However, she shouldn't proceed too abruptly. It wasn't sufficient that he notice all of her adorable personal qualities, nor would she be satisfied if he just felt drawn a bit closer to her. It was essential that once infatuated, he be led to outright worship of her. She wanted nothing less than to act out all kinds of noble and confusing airs, to shatter the other party's soul. Only when the soul she had pierced and probed leaped onto the palm of her hand would her excitement abate, could she then drop off into a long and dreamless sleep.

This woman didn't have to say very much about her needs to have other people understand her personality. In fact, her personality stimulated enormous respect from other people. That is why Ouwai Ou, no matter how often he said he did not understand her, realized from the very first moment he saw her what an extraordinary and brilliant person she was. He immediately started raving about her astonishing intelligence. He also compared her to "La Dame aux Camélias" and found her a clear representative of the Salome type of woman.

This woman was nobody's fool, as has been noted before. She knew how to handle everything. The day before, on the twentieth, she had received a letter from a good friend, a very close friend, who was always willing to do anything for her. She missed Wendy very much, and invited her to come to her school to spend the day, imploring Wendy's husband not to be too miserly, since if he had not torn her out of their midst, the lovely Wendy would still be one of them.

When the teacher read the letter, he really felt he ought to let her go and have a good time with her friends. His wife still appeared to be reluctant, pretending she didn't feel like going. Then, as though she couldn't bear to refuse him a wish, she finally agreed, adding that because she didn't want him to have his dinner all alone, she preferred to sleep a little less in the morning and leave early. That was how the matter was decided. How could her husband know that on that very evening, as everyone was shouting "Come on, finish copying that poem," she had made an appointment to meet another man?

Tonight the teacher enjoyed the sort of tenderness that normally he didn't receive. He felt that she was terribly excited and was acting the way she had during the old days when they first moved in together. Taking his hand, she looked him directly in the eyes and said over and over again, "My love, I love you, only you! You are my happiness! I want to belong to you alone! Kiss me, my beloved."

Long experience made the man a little uneasy, and he began to stare at her. Then she broke into a hearty laugh and stroked him, leaving him no time to examine her heart. He embraced her and, because she had stirred his feelings so deeply, started to cry. His life was bitter enough to begin with, and he saw no meaning in it unless he had her. His tears set the woman at ease. "Let me go, will you, I'm tired," she said, and then turned around and lay still. Thinking that she was sad, her husband stroked and patted her to make her go to sleep. As he did so his own weary eyelids closed involuntarily, and before long he began snoring noisily.

And what do you suppose the woman did then? She opened her eyes wide and started dreaming, of course. It wasn't necessarily that she needed love, because she sometimes felt that her husband loved her too much. Rather, from time to time she wanted somebody else to love her. The more indifferent someone was, the more she would be after him. It was all right for you not to love her, but you had at least to feign a kind of exceptional admiration. That was owed her because of her status. Otherwise, her extraordinary arrogance ended up making you suffer through something you'd never in your whole life forget.

She was dreaming. It was not a sweet dream. Her dreams never really needed happy endings. She felt excited, and seeing her own excitement upset her. Yet she just couldn't see that the fault lay with her.[4] The thought of loving that miserable man only made her smile coldly inside. Should their secret rendezvous become known, she would certainly hate him for it, as though it were an insult intended to damage her proud heart. It would spoil all her future interest in ever meeting anybody again.

She had toyed with the idea of standing the man up, out of respect for her husband. When she had looked at him and said she loved him, she had hoped it might help him. But the moment he started to cry, she had changed her mind. "Why's he crying?" she had thought. "Isn't he using tears as a way of controlling me?" She had to go, even if it resulted in a terrific scandal. She wouldn't admit that she loved Ou, much less that she did not love her husband. So she would go. She had to!

Yet she was still hesitating. How she regretted passing him that note and appearing so brazen. Surely he must think that she was a terrible woman who constantly did horrible things. He would withhold the respect he normally extended. He couldn't possibly be waiting for her at home, because he'd never admire her again after that. Or maybe he really would be at home, on the chance that she was just the same as one of those women from Stone Alley with whom he slept. And who could she blame? She'd asked for it! Then she was plunged into regret. She regretted choosing an inappropriate technique. If she'd sent him a letter, a very sincere letter, that would probably have been somewhat better. She had really considered calling off the assignation. Besides, she didn't want to live with a feeling of everlasting guilt toward her husband, her beloved husband. Yes, that might serve as a sufficient reason for backing out. But then, as people do, she changed her mind once again to justify her conduct. By hook or by crook, she always found a way to excuse everything she did. She felt sympathy for herself, just as she expected everyone else to sympathize with her. She heartened herself, too. Just because she had a husband or a lover, did that mean that she should be forbidden to go to meet another man? She hadn't really fallen in love with a man, hadn't sneaked out and given herself away to some guy to play with or use, had she? How . . . ah, she didn't know what to make of this possibility. If she really fell in love with someone, and was willing to give herself to him to be trifled with and used, then nothing would ever stand in her way. But since she still loved her husband and didn't get any happiness out of quarreling with him, why should she cause him unnecessary embarrassment? It would only rebound on her later as an irredeemable feeling of regret.

She heard the clock in the next room strike three, four, five. She felt unusually anxious. The harder she tried to sleep, the more impossible she found it. Perhaps if she did drop off she'd doze fitfully, since her mind was so fatigued by the last few days, and maybe then—if it was already lunchtime when her husband finally waked her—then how could she be blamed for hesitating? It wouldn't be her fault then that she'd blown the appointment. Later, maybe later, there'd be another way, of course. Or maybe she'd just give the poor man up after all.

She remained wide awake until dawn, and then took care to slip out of bed without waking her husband. Silently she dressed, combed her hair, and made certain that her appearance was just right. Then she sat down again next to the bed. Why, the poor man was still snoring away like mad. She bent over and gave him a fervent kiss. "I love you, I love you!" she called softly to him. She also wrote a note and laid it evenly next to his pillow. In it she told him that she had not wished to disturb his beautiful dreams and therefore had not awakened him. She said that she would certainly be back very quickly and, before she set off, she might give him a call to see if he was already up and about, and whether or not he yearned for her to return quickly. She also said that she actually could not bear to part with him to go meet her friend, and she added at the very end that she had given him three kisses and was saving three more to give him when she came back. Here, naturally, she wasn't lying, because every time she or he returned home she always found new reasons, or posed in special moods, in order to kiss him, and it was never only three times.

And now she set off. She took one last look at her husband, as if she felt some deep regret, and then she silently darted out of the room. Her heart was heavy. Her only thought was to turn back and embrace and kiss that man once more, but she also feared that he would make things difficult if he woke up. So she merely halted for a step and then, without even turning her head, hurried off.

Out in the street she was thrown into turmoil by a familiar disturbing feeling. Her mind was no longer on her husband. With her heart jumping and with irregular steps, she went in a panic. It was as though this were still only her first offense. She completely forgot earlier occasions when she had hurried in the same way, during daylight or at night, to the home of some other attractive person or to other places that she had specified. Those things had long ceased to be of any concern to her. Now she was only blindly running, seemingly in joy as well as fear, with no sense of order, even leaping as she hastened toward the given place. There she would do battle with someone. She wanted her opponent to capitulate and, just like a prisoner of war, to present her his heart. Once she had accepted it, she could just as well cast it aside as keep it for a time, just so long as it belonged to her. If her every single gesture could influence him, even temporarily, she would be content. If not, then this emotion would never subside, even for an instant, and the final outcome would be too terrible to imagine.

She darted out of the alley and rushed northward along the river embankment, which was densely planted with willows and spruces. The shallow river's water had already formed a thick layer of ice that reflected the sun's early-morning rays in a soft red that was glorious to behold. Wendy could not spare any attention for such things. She was afraid that he might not be at home waiting for her, even as she hoped that she would not find him there. But if she really were stood up, then her resentment would be aroused all the more. She would be even less willing to leave him in peace, and would certainly bring an overpowering ill will to bear.

In her excitement, she had already skipped past the willow tree Ouwai Ou was standing under. In their haste, they had passed right by each other. One had rushed past without noticing the other, who, however, had long since caught sight of her but was at a loss as to how to call out a greeting. Had it been possible for him to remain speechless, this affair would have ended before it began. However, this man was not a timid person. He cast one glance at those two straight shoulders, those rounded calves, and smiled cynically to himself. Very calmly, he called out that bewitching name, "Wendy, Wendy!"

Wendy, who had not anticipated that he might be waiting for her on the street, was naturally very startled. She whirled around, her face lit up happily. She was panting a little and the wind had blown her cheeks a fiery red. Several strands of loose hair hung down from her cap and snaked vaguely around her eyebrows, making them darker and more attractive. Seeing that the young man didn't speak, she too remained silent.

To try to race along with this young woman's emotions with a pen would be a simply impossible task. No sooner had she caught a glimpse of the object of her rendezvous, than her heart felt as pained as if she'd been stabbed or grievously wounded somewhere. She felt like bursting into tears and running back the way she had come. She felt like storming up to the fellow, seizing him, and giving him a pounding. She felt like asking him why he couldn't wait for her at his house, why he had acted in such an undignified manner, waiting for her at a street corner. If he should claim that he had been too eager to see her and could not bear to wait for her in his empty room, then why hadn't he come up to greet her as soon as he saw her? It was obvious that he didn't value this affair in the least, which was to say that he did not cherish the appointment with her and did not respect her. Even if she often liked to have a good time with others behind her husband's back, she nevertheless wished that even her hidden and secret activities could be conducted without any sense of shame. But what could she say now? He regarded her as a prostitute or even worse! He could go anytime he wanted to Stone Alley or the Han Mansions and sleep there for nights on end without having to hide the truth from anyone and look ashamed.

What a pitiful young woman. As this was hardly the first time she had sought love from a man, why did she still have to take all this so seriously, as if she still lacked any understanding of male psychology where women were concerned? Wasn't it absurd always to be insisting on some sort of "respect" from a man?

Inwardly she was seething, but she was not really in any position to give free rein to her anger. Instead she put a smile on her face. "Say! Today I've got three hours—all to myself. How would you like to spend them?" She affected the manner of a person who was never given freedom and had just suddenly been liberated.

This frequent versifier, this Ouwai Ou, had already realized in his bones that waiting for her on the street was going to cause some misunderstanding. Now he sought to explain, saying that he had several reasons for it, and that he could still accompany her back to his rooming house if she wished.

Wendy smiled without answering. There was no need to reply. Didn't her smile tell him that she understood everything? She only asked him where he would like to go. Ouwai Ou, quite mortified, could only suggest, "Let's go to Beihai Park."

"Beihai again!" she thought to herself, frowning. All she wanted was—now, just what did she want? As strange as it sounds, she had an extraordinary urge to go to a hotel with him. She did not dare say so, and she wouldn't necessarily have dared do so. She had never gone off to one of those places where, all day and night, many tragedies are performed. She just thought that a park or movie could no longer satisfy her, and she believed that the special atmosphere of a hotel would certainly help them to be somewhat more intimate, somewhat bolder . . . She was on the verge of blurting out, "Let's go to Qianmen!" but she saw his gloomy face and remained silent.

"If not, then how about Central Park?"

She listened to him, and then agreed to go to Beihai Park after all. She saw nothing in his face to suggest that he might go along with any of her crazy ideas. She was sorry about this; she had chosen the wrong person.

But she smiled again, nonetheless, and seemed very pleased as she went off with him in a northerly direction.

She grew irritated again when they hired a rickshaw. It was cheap of him to stand there in front of her, bartering in order to save a few coppers. "It doesn't matter, let's go!" she exclaimed, and simply climbed into the closest one.

As for Ouwai Ou, he was greatly perplexed. This woman was simply uncanny, and even the slightest movement of her eyebrows was enough to make him cringe. He began to compare her in his mind with little Ajin, who was still dozing, and with the innkeeper's daughter with whom he had lived earlier. But only a glance, from behind, at this person perched so straight in front of him on the rickshaw was enough to tell him that she was incomparably precious and that he ought to kneel down to her in homage. He should be grateful, for she had given him so much. He threw a silent kiss to the back of the person sitting there before him.

Wendy, sitting so straight in the front of the rickshaw, was annoyed by this interval of time. It was too lengthy, and so she was likely to think of some unpleasing aspects of her conduct. Wishing to avoid such thoughts, she turned her gaze to the sides of the street. Nothing worth seeing was to be found there. Then her gaze was caught by the corner of a tower on the city wall, far off in the distance. The yellow tiles were basking in the morning sunshine, emitting a brilliant gold color. It was too dazzling, and it irritated her again. She just did not know what to do with herself. After some more time, although there was no real reason, she began to loathe the person seated behind her.

Once they arrived at Beihai, everything took on a new appearance. Wendy was inwardly rejoicing. She tried to capture his eyes with hers, because she knew that he was in a state of helplessness and panic and was trying to avoid her gaze. Wishing to enjoy this situation and prolong it, she followed along behind him in utter silence the entire time. How about the young man? He was in exactly the opposite situation. His heart was tormented by baffling feelings. Yearning to look at her out of the corner of his eye, he was also afraid she would snare him with her fiery, bold gaze. You might think that he would want to flee, but not really. He was hoping that this woman might still change and become softer, or more timid, so that he could approach her and tease her, very gently. Then, once her tender face flushed, he would seize the chance to take her in his arms, where in the warmth of his embrace, she would tremble and softly cling to him. He knew that this was impossible. The person walking beside him was certainly not little Ajin, who liked to play the weak woman, or one of those other women who all seemed unable to withstand his embraces. He had already gone to the first battle line. He could not fall back to his original position, but he was still afraid to mount an assault. He longingly watched the two shadows which now extended equally in front of their feet, as they proceeded step by step over the Great White Bridge. He fervently wished that the two long shadows would somehow draw closer together and finally become one. His new leather shoes echoed on the bridge, accompanying the clear high-low, high-low tapping of her wooden heels. But the two pairs of feet were hopelessly out of step, and the jumbled medley added to the trouble on his mind.

They had crossed the bridge, and now Wendy continued along behind him up the hill. It was an exhausting climb, in the midst of which she was thinking that it was just the situation where a handsome man, who knew how to be polite, would offer his arm and take his time in helping her up the hill. At this she halted. Lowering her head, she gazed back down along the path. The entire park was still deserted and peaceful. The criss-cross of pathways underneath pines and cypresses still showed no signs of any human presence, except in one spot, at a turning in the path, where thick black smoke was pouring steadily out of a chimney. The building had a triple front, faced east, and seemed to be a jade shop. Wendy was feeling extremely sorry for herself and only wanted to sit down alone. But her companion had already raced to the peak and was urging her on. So she summoned up her courage, which she needed for more than just climbing the hill, and soon had scurried up until she was standing in front of the young man. He asked if she was tired. She held her handkerchief over her mouth and shook her head to indicate that she wasn't; actually, she was gasping so hard that she couldn't utter a word. She was naturally somewhat annoyed. Now Ouwai Ou insisted on leading her to the steps in front of the pagoda, where she could be in the sun. He feared that her feet must be cold. Although she had no preference for any particular place, it dawned on her that he was quite eager to devote attention and concern to her feet, and she felt the icy touch of something colder than the north wind or the frozen Beihai lake as a consequence. Tremendously aggrieved, she stood there at the marble balustrade.

The vision of another man flashed before her. She was thinking back to a certain night in the past. Wasn't it in this very spot? Yes, and it was on that special night. What a night! She had completely fainted away into those two powerful arms. In that darkness their eyes had been so close, so transfixed. Their lips were never going to part. Her bosom was aflame; she feared only that it still might not be pressed as tightly as possible up against his. Her sheer India-silk scarf had been raised by the cool breeze and fluttered alongside their necks and cheeks. That fellow, that magnificent fellow. Wasn't it on that evening that he had said over and over a thousand times, "I want to possess you, I want to possess you completely!"? Hadn't she felt compelled to walk out on her husband and rush to his side? And yet afterward, for some reason, she had cast him off instead, and had told him that she loved no one but her husband. Even now that man continued to resent that he had been deceived, but he was also still too indecisive and was living in self-imposed exile overseas. Wendy recalled how his soft, short hair nestled against her cheek and the place where she had put her lips. Those unending kisses of his, raining down upon her eyelids. His lips, so delicate. His embrace, so wild. His words, oh, those words! . . . Wendy only wished she could faint away again immediately, as she had done then. She so dearly missed that intoxicating feeling. Deep down in her heart, she heaved a great sigh.

Ouwai Ou's heart, too, had unconsciously begun to wander. Although he often seemed quite unable to do without women, he was in fact really incapable of freely and genuinely loving anyone. It was simply that he had never been willing to sacrifice anything at all for a woman. Of course everyone knew that he often went off to Qianmen in the dead of night, thinly clad in an unlined topcoat suitable only for Canton, all just for little Ajin's sake. What they did not know was that he loved his melancholic state of mind far more deeply than he loved Ajin. On those cold, dreary streets, he could brim with indignation and hatred—hatred of the capitalists. At such moments he could become a revolutionary hero. Although it was certainly the fact that he lacked the money to frequent brothels or procure a concubine that brought home to him the need for revolution, he was nevertheless aware of the situation of the rickshaw men found on the streets at this same hour. They wore only shredded cotton jackets. They did not dare return home to their wives and children but continued, instead, to wander the streets searching for fares. Ouwai Ou's ideology of wanting to eradicate the monied class really originated in large part with these rickshaw men. Of course, he was not unique. There were other people who felt the same way as he, and only when he had overheard others complain of the rickshaw men's miserable conditions had he too finally caught sight of them. Soon after that, he published a vernacular poem about rickshaw men in a journal. The good thing about all this was that the rickshaw men themselves could not possibly know how magnificent they were. His feelings of depression and the senselessness of his life all came from those streets at night. In sum, everything of his—his theories, his interests, and his style of life, which is to say his entire personality—all grew out of the self-pity he loved so much. As a consequence, he also considered this play-acting ridiculous. He did not need to take this woman as his prey, nor did he feel any need to win a victory at the cost of one of his friends. If he only wanted to have a good time, then he would be just as willing to go to little Ajin. With her he could chat and banter freely. Whereas this woman, having set up the rendezvous, was now acting stiffly, and her mind was clearly elsewhere. The silence continued.

There was nothing at all here too inspire Wendy. How much she desired to retrieve that one moment in her past, that instant when she had savored to the full all of the passionate, warm love in the world. Her only thought at this moment was to place her lips once again on that broad, majestic forehead. It grieved her when she reflected on how that man, who had been in love with her, had thrown himself at her feet and would have gladly sacrificed everything for her, might now be consoling himself in the embraces of some other woman. Now she was really sorry. She had not needed to break up with him in the first place. She could have continued to spend her life secretly taking time for trysts at Beihai. She laughed at herself. Why was she causing herself so much grief? She had intended to do the right thing by both men, but had only succeeded in making them both hate her. Moreover, why—when she had wanted to be a good person—had she only two weeks later allowed her ears to listen to the blandishments of that handsome Wang Zongshe? And now? Now she had made yet another rendezvous, in the very same place, with this cheerless person!

She directed her gaze at Ou's aggrieved face. Once again she was extremely annoyed. She was even beginning to hate Ouwai Ou. Why couldn't he give her that fierce joy once again, that intoxication, that satisfaction of a kiss she was willing to die for! She had been very distracted on his account and had lain awake many nights. She had borne the pangs of her guilty conscience toward her husband. She had risked making herself the laughingstock of society and had rushed such a long way to offer herself to him. And he? What was he offering her? When she looked at his tightly clenched lips and his tiny eyes, staring so stupidly ahead, she began to rage inside. She wanted nothing more than to subject him to immediate humiliation. But she also hated not being able to thrust herself into his embrace and cling tightly to him, as she had with that other man. Now all of those things, the things she needed— those powerful, virile arms, those furious kisses, those insane, passionate, solemn words—assaulted her mind. Yet there was nothing she could do but remain standing there by the stone balustrade, biting her lip hard. Nor would it help to have a tantrum like a small child, insisting stubbornly and vainly, "I want it, I want it." In fact she really was on the verge of screaming like a child. She looked at his emotionless face and had to summon all of her strength to restrain her heart, which was about to burst into a frenzy.

Ouwai Ou's own thoughts seemed obstructed by something, and he dared not allow her to hurry on any further. He felt as if he were nailed to the spot by a pair of eyes, but he also did not dare look down into her eyes. He was only vacillating, wishing to be liberated from this torture as soon as possible. Such close scrutiny was unbearable for him. If he really did love her, then he would neither evade her eyes nor resent her silence. He would know how to deal with this fiery woman. But now? He regretted what he had done. If he had known earlier how this woman used silence and reproachful stares to intimidate people, he really would have preferred to let someone else be the victim. He would have stood her up this morning.

Just at the point when he was about to break under the tension, a voice, more gentle than any he had ever heard before, called softly to him, "Ou . . ."

There was no denying that this voice, against all his expectations, stirred his heart. It seemed to him that in his entire life he had never heard his name vibrate so musically on another person's lips and then lodge itself in his heart. As if in spontaneous echo to the voice, he looked down into her face and saw two curving eyebrows swept into a slight frown as she gazed out over the entire city. Her dainty lips were like piano keys still trembling from the final chord of a melody. In this moment he felt utter rapture, and everything that had preceded it was forgotten. And still, he could not do what she wanted. The most he could do now was look at her.

Wendy was clearly aware that she was doing nothing more than play-acting, but she still took herself completely seriously. She was feeling very sympathetic with herself in this situation. She heaved an imperceptible sigh and, using the new look she'd recently learned from the movies— her Garbo gaze—she stared out over the entire city below. Actually, she saw nothing at all. She just took on an inimitable air of pride, deep emotion, and sorrow. Also, as if impatient with her difficulties, she pulled off her little purple cap. Now her trimly cut hair was awry, falling loosely around her head, making her face both more attractive and more digni-fied.

Ouwai Ou also felt himself growing impatient. He did not know how to go about cheering this woman up even a little. All he could do was say to her softly, "Wendy, say something!"

Now her gaze was boring straight into him. Her eyes were fixed on him and she made no sound.

"Go ahead, say something!"

"What's there to say? I know now, Ou, that you're afraid of me!" She said this in an indescribable tone, as if her suffering could not be ade-quately defined even in a thousand sentences yet had all poured forth in this single one. Ouwai Ou listened, angry that he could not instantly present more than a hundred and fifty items of evidence as proof that he did not fear her. Yet he still did not risk making a move. He only repeated in a sincere manner, "I'm not, I'm not."

Wendy again pressured him with her eyes, without saying a word.

By and by, his words "I'm not, I'm not" only proved to be an incantation for bolstering his own courage. And as soon as her eyelids closed, his words, or what was left of them, died away altogether. Wendy heaved a deep sigh and said, "You are afraid of me! You are . . ."

Ouwai Ou stood there speechless. He could not summon up enough courage to begin explaining how he was not afraid. He really wasn't afraid. As far as women were concerned, he was very suave. He knew how to tame the kind of woman who got hysterical, like little Ajin. Wasn't he qualified? Wasn't he far more knowledgeable in such matters than Wendy? And yet she went on staring directly into his mind. How could he be expected to manage at such a time without telling lies? In fact, what was wrong with telling lies? Since Wendy herself was fully aware that she was play-acting, why was anybody obliged to fall for her wiles? As long as the performance of this drama was compelling, so that even the actors might forget themselves and break into tears or laughter, then wouldn't lying be the most truthful thing to do?

Wendy was also standing there mutely, not because she was equally enraptured by her own words, but because she suddenly detested herself. The drama which had hardly begun was already over. Their two hearts were now separated even further than before, as if they were two things which could not be linked. Once again they were both sunk deeply into their respective thoughts.

Ouwai Ou kicked lightly at the gravel on the pathway with the tips of his shoes. His feet were numb and it was still cold. Once more he caught sight of her two little feet encased in leather shoes. Her two well-rounded calves were hugged by sheer, flesh-tinted silk stockings which reached up to her knees. Once again he saw how charming they were, and felt like rubbing them.

"Are you cold?" he asked.

Wendy shook her head. When she noticed where his gaze was directed, her smile broadened. Her shameless behavior already distressed her, and she was worried about her husband at home. Nonetheless, she was unwilling to end things so easily. She asked him to take a look at his watch.

The long hand was between two and three. The short one pointed to ten.

"I can only stay another hour, Ou." Wendy did not think that she had made this declaration with any particular force. She was very innocently pleased with herself, and was actually thinking of her husband. He must have gotten up by now. She wondered whether or not he would be stunned by her absence, and whether or not the fire in the heater would still be burning brightly ... The impact of the statement, however, far surpassed the effect of her few earlier utterances, which had already given her cause for satisfaction. Ouwai Ou now began to look at her very tenderly.

This made everything perfectly clear to Wendy. She now resolved to sacrifice his self-respect, or rather, she was now determined to make a sacrifice of him. In this one hour, she was going to captivate his heart. She intended to grant him favors he had never enjoyed, and create in him some needs which would, in all of his future days, continue to be insatiable. Now she smiled adorably, even as her heart was reveling in a sensation of cruelty.

And so, not long afterward, Ouwai Ou, seemingly oblivious of everything else, began to swear solemn oaths to her—a maker of verses cannot help thinking that oaths are the most trustworthy things of all. Grasping her hands, he earnestly pleaded to hear her commands as to what he should do, and how he should deport himself in regard to her and her husband. He also announced his hope that she would belong to no one but him. But at this moment his words stopped, exactly as if he had suddenly lost all power of speech. The fact was, he was beginning to vacillate. He was beginning to recognize that he had gone too far in his declarations, for after all, if this woman really did attach herself to him, could he be so absolutely certain that he would dare to go on? The schoolteacher's disappointed face appeared before his eyes. Quickly he closed his eyes and bowed his head.

As for the woman, she too was thinking of her husband. Her husband was such a dear, sweet thing. Yet she could not turn a deaf ear to this confession, even if she scorned this man for mistaking momentary practical matters for love, just like all other men. Feeling the warmth of his hand, she clasped it tighter.

It was now time to return. The sun projected their shadows vertically onto the flight of steps. Wendy repeated, for the fourth time, "Please, let me go now. I must be getting back."

Ouwai Ou accompanied her back down the hill. At its base several people could be seen here and there. Wendy felt like going on alone, because she was concerned that someone might see them. But she was too embarrassed to mention it. The same thought occurred to Ouwai Ou.

"Wendy!" he said, "supposing we ran into Lao Zhang just now. What would you do?"

"Why would it matter? I'd say that I ran into you on the street and that we just came here to chat, that's all."

Ouwai Ou pressed closer to her and murmured, "I'd like it if he saw us together."

Wendy inwardly smiled at her success, but she kept her thoughts to herself and said nothing.

At the front gate of Beihai Park, he hired her a rickshaw. Watching her receding figure, he threw her a kiss. He was joyful, for in his opinion the woman was genuinely terrific, and he no longer dared compare her with little Ajin. But he was also overcome with shame at the thought that he still lacked the courage to take possession of her. The thought of the oaths he'd sworn made him even more ashamed. Nevertheless, he was still unable to decide whether he should refuse this woman or not. Some reflection advised him that the best thing would be to go and talk things over with Lao Zhao. Whereupon he too hopped smartly aboard a rickshaw.

As to whether Wendy had attained anything, even she herself did not know. She knew only that when she was seating herself in the vehicle and gazed at him one last time, she had been pleased by the thought of the words she had repeated over and over during the preceding nights: "He's afraid of me! Afraid of me!" But in fact, she did not cling stubbornly to that thought. She only hoped to return home quickly and fall into the arms of her husband, whom she would love eternally. In his embrace, she was sure she could attain everything she ever desired. She stamped her foot forcefully on the wooden floor of her rickshaw and called out in her well-practiced Beijing accent, "Faster, please! Faster!"

Translated by Ruth Keen and Hal Pollard

Yecao

"Yecao," written mid-year in 1929, was a turning point in Ding Ling's fiction because in it she changed the way she represented woman and man and the battle of the sexes. The story still contains earlier themes, for example, women's lust, women's weakness, women's independence, but they are connected here to a very new, important figure who would reappear many times subsequently in Ding Ling's fiction. This figure, the experienced author who has won control over her female feelings and failings, would emerge again in stories like "The County Magistrate's Daughter" (1939) and "When I Was in Xia Village" (1941). Yecao feels "like a woman" inside. She has flights of fantasy and regrets the indiscretions of her past. Yet what Nanxia sees in Yecao is what Sophia so longed for Ling Jishi to see in her: intelligence, strength, integrity.

This movement in Ding Ling's writing significantly changed how she depicted sexual difference in her subsequent work. She allows a common ground to emerge between male and female characters. Yecao and Nanxia share the human qualities of reason and feeling. As the narrator puts it, "human beings [are] intelligent things, but once they [become] caught up in emotions, they [grow] extraordinarily confused." Emotion is not the special essence of women any more than reason animates men.

A clue to why Ding Ling began to unravel the Victorian stereotypes she'd found so persuasive and valuable before, is the idea of work. Yecao may long for erotic abandon, but her vocation forces her to focus on things outside desire, just as her experience gives her the ability to foresee the likely consequences of indulgence. Hers is a qualified renunciation; she seems willing to leave open a time for love sometime in the future. But there is no question that work, the daily use of her will to struggle for clarity, is Yecao's road to self-respect. Perhaps the conviction forming a core part of Ding Ling's early literary imagination, that women are naturally weak, crippled by emotion, seemed less compelling once she had found this strong self in the work of writing.—TEB

Spring arrived; gentle breezes blew in through the window, bringing with them the fragrance of flowers and damp grass. Birds on boughs exchanged calls and the chalky wings of tiny butterflies brushed lightly against stalks of flowers swaying in the wind. Young men and women were changing into light-colored, new, unlined jackets. Tender cheeks enhanced by a rosy glow, black eyes sparkling; in little groups, here and there on outings, they were drinking in the beauty of the spring day with all the heartfelt happiness of young people. These were fleeting, precious days.

Yecao, a young woman of twenty-four, wearing a gray lined dress appropriate to a middle-aged woman, had shut herself up in a small room alone, worrying over the characters in her novel. She had forgotten spring. In the novel that she was imagining, however, there was a spring day, filled with ecstatic and impassioned love, raging like fire. In her stifling room, she couldn't help but recall the course of her own life. How unbearable, how terrible those already vanished days had been! The intoxications of the past, she seemed to believe, could be recaptured somehow. But as she gazed through the window at the white clouds, she came to understand that for her it was not necessary to have everything she'd previously enjoyed. Jaded by past experiences, even were she to have an impassioned romantic experience again, she would be totally untouched by it. Except when indulging herself with memories of a fantasy of two trembling hearts, she found comfort only in her writing. In her novels, she often alluded to her magnificent lonely heart.

Today she was terribly upset because she had endowed an extremely level-headed and rational woman in her novel with unduly passionate emotions. Also, she had let a slight touch of melancholy slip in. This definitely was not the character she had intended to create, but it was the flaw in women that she was able to understand best.[1] She didn't know what would be better, to tear up the manuscript and start over, or to go on writing, but not sympathize with the woman. She couldn't stop thinking about this perplexing problem, but gradually, she turned her thoughts to the social environment that caused women to overemphasize emotions, then to how pitiable women are. In a moment of self-examination, she began to detest herself. Could she stifle her own emotions? Even though it seemed that she needed nothing other than her writing, still there were times when, freed from external aggravation and lost in prior joys and happiness, she would think of the past—this was something so painful and so tinged with remorse that she could never bring herself to speak or think of it. She thought of the past with resentment and longing, and then, finally, with indifference.

Unavoidably, these thoughts made her a little sad. She felt that she was a useless person. She could not forget the man who had forsaken her for another woman. But neither could she forget their mutual love. Blessed with the ability to analyze herself, she knew very clearly that even if the man were to abandon the woman he now loved, forsake it all and come back to her, she still would not accept such kindness, nor would she find so-called happiness in it. She already looked upon love as a pitiable and laughable toy.

Her thoughts went back to her novel. As before, all she was able to grasp intellectually was the overall mood of the characters. At first a light, pleasant feeling was sustained; in the end only "uncertainty" remained.

At that point, she didn't know how to go about calming down enough to refocus her attention on the unfinished novel. Just then the door glided open; it was the amah with a letter.[2] Happily she took it, opened it, and read it through. She was reminded of something she'd forgotten.

This is what the letter said:

> I want to see you very much. But I feel too embarrassed. I don't know why you have such an implacable, neglectful attitude toward me. Right now my spirit is exhausted. I have no recourse but to plead with you: if it isn't putting you out, I will be waiting for you at nightfall on the lawn in French Park (I assume you know which lawn I mean). No need to sign my name, that isn't important. Written this very day.

Yecao read it with alarm. She had, of course, already put this out of her mind, yet she felt no need to reveal her position. Even if she had been in love with another man, was she expected to write this man to tell him that they could be ordinary friends? She believed that human beings were intelligent things, but once they became caught up in emotions, they grew extraordinarily confused. Nanxia was a typical example. In his everyday conversations, he could make things clear. But in his recent behavior toward her, as she saw it, he had unavoidably lost touch with his usual understanding.

She was reminded that she hadn't seen him for a couple of days and guessed that he had forgotten all about everything, so what a surprise to get a letter today. Presumably, these last few days had been rough on him, and his plight saddened her. She decided to go to the appointed meeting place this evening.

After dinner, carrying an old thin coat over her arm, she walked leisurely to the park in a soft breeze. In the tall buildings on both sides of the road, lamplight passing through gauze curtains looked soft and red. On a wall, new growth on sweet-smelling vines made the supple shoots hang down the outside. Raising her head, she sighed with longing. The street was both quiet and clean; only a few sparsely placed electric lights were shining, and shadows of trees were imprinted everywhere along the path. She walked under still leafless trees, and the shade deepened somewhat as she continued along in a lighthearted mood.

Most of the visitors to the park had gone, leaving only a few people clustered by the pond in a grove of trees. In twos and threes they sat knee to knee on the low iron benches, talking in hushed voices. Yecao made her way toward the lawn, following the path by the pond. But as time and again she thought of Nanxia waiting for her, this image merged with that of someone else. It made her feel a little ridiculous. Passing by some large trees, by a flower bed, she came to the outermost lawn. To the left a dark form was silently and rapidly walking toward her. At first she was startled, but then she recognized the hunched-over shoulders, the hands shoved into coat pockets, and the despondent and hesitant manner so characteristic of him.

"Oh, it's you, Nanxia," she said with relief. Nanxia did not answer as he shifted his weight forward.

She noticed immediately how the melancholy eyes shone in the dark as they gazed at her. She couldn't help feeling a little current of fear. She saw that his dirty jacket was open. His necktie too was untied, and an expanse of flesh on his chest was exposed by an unbuttoned shirt. His hair was all mussed; that made her feel all the more uneasy, while at the same time, a sense of loathing rose in her heart, as though she regretted coming. But there was nothing she could do now, so she said with a smile, "We've been having nice weather lately. Have you been going out?"

Nanxia did not answer her, but just walked her over to a place that had a few benches. She sat down, looking very tired.

"My but the park is nice at night," she said. "But I haven't been here for a long time—the last time was with you."

Why should Nanxia have to respond to this? A straightforward young man, full of passion, he found this meaningless talk irritating. He continued looking mutely at Yecao.

Yecao understood why he didn't answer, but she wasn't willing to let the silence last too long. This sort of uneasiness no longer held any fascination for her. She no longer required the sort of situations that at one time she had deemed best for goading people into the experience of immense confusion, excitement, and intoxication. Wanting to avoid all of this, she said, "Nanxia, you haven't said a word. Why? If I've done something to make you unhappy, I'll go. We can get together again when you feel better."

She was just getting up to go when Nanxia's eyes stopped her short. "I haven't said anything," he said in an imploring tone, "because so much of what has been said has oppressed me so cruelly that there's nothing I can say. Please, I beg of you, sit down for a moment and let me think." As Nanxia was speaking, he moved the bench a little closer and reached out to take her hand.

It was so obvious—she knew the role she was playing—that she thought she should leave. She felt that she ought to reject this man. But she also felt great pity for him, and as she grasped his bony hand, her heart was moved in spite of her feelings.

As she looked at him again, the lights along the path illuminated his face: ashen, his eyebrows knotted and his eyes filled with despair. Her gaze moved down to his mouth: lips raised in a grimace and, in the light of the lamps, the suggestion of a moustache. She couldn't help but be reminded of the past. Involuntarily, she squeezed his hand hard. Nanxia turned his head away and quietly sighed.

On a little path in the distance, a couple could be seen embracing, pressed together so tightly they appeared to be a single person.

Again, Yecao began to reflect back on events in the past. She recalled the spring day three years ago when she too was cradled against a man's chest. They would come to the park at nightfall for their outings and wouldn't go home until midnight. She remembered that when she had been in that man's arms, her heart felt as if it would break—such a youthful heart that could be filled with so very, very much happiness. Besides, she had to admit that she also knew how to tease a man to the point of blazing passion and so satisfy his needs. But now it was all over, all of it. She couldn't treat this friend with the same cruelty. She could only sympathize with him, a man who had misplaced his love, one who had chosen the wrong woman.

"I wish you could understand me better," she said to him sincerely. "The way you're acting saddens me."

"Yecao," he finally spoke. The bleakness of his voice made each word bear down heavily on her heart. "I am profoundly miserable, and this misery comes precisely from my understanding of you. I am no longer an adolescent who can innocently, romantically play my role in the script. But I am cursed in that I haven't the strength to suppress my impulses, either. Still, my desires are not excessive. If only you would say 'I love you' once, that would be enough. But, Yecao, I know you—your heart is harder than other women's, you are unmovable. You love only yourself and your work. Of course, there's nothing wrong with that. You never led me on. Your attitude toward me has been that you will laugh and joke with me, without ever making a point of the fact that you are a woman. But, Yecao, let me put it this way, and hope you don't think I'm too blunt. It's precisely because of your attitude that I honor you, respect you, and love you so much! For some time I have known that I'm wrong, but I can't disentangle myself! Sometimes I think I will simply go crazy, and even though the consequence would be that you'd have nothing more to do with me, I'd be willing. But I don't have the courage. Actually, I've often felt like a madman, only I've always managed to suppress it. Ah! What should I do?"

Forceful as the words were, Yecao reacted as a woman whose heart was indeed harder than other women's. For besides sympathizing with him, she also saw him as being slightly ridiculous. She wondered what good anything she said would do. If you feel so miserable and can't stand it, then you don't have to love me, especially since you know that my heart is immovable. Or, though misery is bitter, it can also be sweet; you can go on loving me. I do not have the right to interfere or forbid you to love me. So if you feel that you absolutely must go mad, take it out on me to satisfy yourself, then there is nothing more I can do about it. Since you insist on driving yourself so hard, go right ahead. Quite simply, of what use are words? Why ask me? Can I command you? Ai, you're no child! But she kept these thoughts to herself, showing him only the veneer of a smile as she took his hand once more and said earnestly, "I can't give you any comfort. I can only hope you will not lose sight of what is more important to you. As for me, I've put it all behind me. And it's not that I don't feel bad about that—there's an emptiness inside me—but I no longer have any desire for love."

Nanxia was silent again. Finally, he poured out his heart to her, disclosing his first impressions of her. He was so worked up that at times he appeared on the verge of tears.

The leaves of the white poplars rippled, the wind was cool; Yecao felt cold. She started to put on her coat, and Nanxia innocently helped her into it. Fearful that she might be cold, he suggested that they take a stroll. That sounded like a good idea to her, so she got up, and hand in hand they walked toward a darker place.

Tender new grass felt soft beneath their feet, and long willow branches were swaying in the dim lamplight. The night was quiet, not a sound anywhere. A half-moon had risen, shedding weak light. Yecao saw that her shadow and his slept with each other on the ground ahead of them as they walked along.

Appearing a little happier, he expressed his feelings for her again. He did not lie to her. Not at all. When they were together, they talked openly and honestly about everything, and he didn't seize upon her ambitions. But as soon as he left her, he was in agony; it seemed he'd rather die than fail to win her love. He began to feel sorry for himself. Again he asked her if she'd grown tired of him.

She shook her head and said softly, "No."

He smiled childishly at her, "Then I'll never leave you. I'll move next door to you."

"What if I've grown tired of you by then?"

"As long as you approve now, everything will be all right."

They walked up to a path. The dense trees in the darkness on both sides blocked the light from the lamps outside. Blown by the wind, the leaves of the willows and the palms rustled incessantly; they were so dense that even the stars were blacked from view. Because the path was narrow and dark, the two of them walked closely together, each feeling the warmth of the other's body. Nanxia put his arm around her waist. His heart pounding, he wanted nothing more than to take her into his arms and madly kiss her face and body, but he didn't dare. He could only test her out by saying, "Yecao! You know I love you. Aren't you afraid to walk with me alone here?"

The setting made her feel a little uncomfortable, but she wasn't the least bit afraid of him. On the contrary, she wished that he would let himself go so she would once again enjoy that intoxicated feeling.

"I'm not afraid," she said sadly (only she knew she was sad). "I'm not afraid, because I trust you."

Words formed in his mind: he wanted to ask if she would let him say "my love" to her. But before he could say anything, the path ended in a spot of bright illumination. They released each others' hands unaware they'd done so.

When they came to the pond, the clear flowing spring water gurgled lightly, and the moon on the surface of the water rose and fell like waves. Roses alongside the bridge gave off breaths of sweet-smelling fragrance. Yecao reflected on what had just happened, and felt that it was in terrible taste. She looked at Nanxia coldly.

A fish splashed in the pond, sending spray everywhere. There were already tiny white buds on the lotus pads.

As they sat beside the pond, she was preoccupied with various ways of describing a night scene. She was thinking how a certain scene would be perceived by one person and how it would be changed when perceived by another.

But Nanxia looked at her happily. He was wishing that every night could be like this one.

She wanted to go back. She wasn't at all reluctant about leaving. As for him, he still hadn't heeded the look in her eye that proved he'd made no headway. Feeling much happier than when he came, he just asked her if they could meet again the next night and if he could see her home tonight.

She turned him down. She still had work to do and was afraid that he would disturb her. On the way home she sang, apparently very happily, her newly composed, well-turned phrases.

Translated by Charlotte Calhoun

Shanghai, Spring 1930

Ding Ling wrote the two chapters that make up this novella in June and October of 1930. It was a time when she and "bourgeois" writers like her felt that the ground on which they stood, from which they spoke, had shifted suddenly and forcibly. Cultural figures increasingly saw it as their responsibility to resist Japanese encroachments and rightist reaction. It reflects the turmoil surrounding her that the two halves of this novella belong together only by force of a certain intellectual logic. But the disjointedness of the chapters is misleading, for each is the account of a heterosexual couple in domestic conflict. Side by side the parts recombine so that each gender contributes one progressive and one "bourgeois" protagonist in a neat four-cornered structure.

Ding Ling was also beginning to develop a more social cast to her fiction whereby relationships between people precede personality. Later this would develop into the cast-iron code that class relations determine personal identity. Her more socialist orientation accounts for the life she manages to breathe into what could have been a very ordinary plot. If, as the Communist writer Ding Ling would later insist, character emerges in daily practice, then personality is indeed malleable, not essential, and relations between women and men really are remediable. The literary practices to which resistance culture was exposed (from, for example, anti-imperialist Russia), as well as the new appreciation of European naturalism, licensed colonized writers to begin drawing on certain older, previously discredited conventions for representing human affairs in fiction. In Ding Ling's work, personality began appearing as the effect of prior social relationships, and also as a secondary focus, the new emphasis being plot mechanics.

Both Meilin (the Chinese name is significant) and Mary are women. Meilin seeks strength and social justice in a socialist community of comrades, while Mary, courage and intelligence notwithstanding, ruins herself with the work of being a woman: who to sleep with, what to wear, where to be seen. Sophia, we recall, really had nowhere to go but the grave. Meilin can step away from her enthrallment to bourgeois "love" and into service. The narrator's voice, though present in this story, seems less caustic and self-righteous than before. There is more dialogue and social detail to underscore the looser diction that is so very different from the imploded, tightly wound sentences of earlier works like "The Diary of Miss Sophia." More and more, it seems clear, Ding Ling felt herself empowered to represent reality.—TEB

Part One

I

When the elevator reached ground level, the sudden discordant clatter of leather soles sounded riotously through the long corridor. Half a dozen exhilarated young people strode toward the massive glass doors on their way out of the building. The way they looked at each other, their eager lips, they acted as if they had an inexhaustible supply of new ideas, yet they spoke little as they walked straight out to the street where they would have to part. They had just attended a big youth conference sponsored by a literary club.

One of them, a thin dark fellow named Ruoquan, strolled toward the north, images of what had just happened jumbled in his mind. The speeches, arguments, flushed faces, generous sincere laughter, bizarre suggestions, and stubborn prejudice . . . He could not help smiling. In fact, he felt that it had not been such a bad meeting at all. He relaxed his pace at the thought and soon had reached the crowded Great Avenue.

"Hello, where are you headed?"

Someone had caught up to him and grabbed his shoulder.

"Oh, it's you, Xiaoyun." He looked a little surprised.

"Are you busy now?"

"No."

The two of them turned and joined the flow of the crowd, exchanging a few words now and then about what had happened at the meeting. When Xiaoyun suggested that they go somewhere for tea, Ruoquan said no, that he wanted to go home. But then, abruptly, he said that he wanted to visit a friend and asked Xiaoyun if he would like to go along. When Xiaoyun found out that the friend was Zibin, he shook his head.

"No, no, I don't think so. I really don't feel comfortable seeing him these days. He just loves sneering at people. You'd better not go either. It's no fun there."

Ruoquan took leave of Xiaoyun anyway and boarded a streetcar for the Jing'an Temple. The streetcar swayed a lot, and he held onto a rattan ring with one hand and let his body rock back and forth. As he looked at the neat blocks of buildings through the windows, the tangle of activities at the meeting and Zibin's nonchalant manner soon faded from his mind.

2

Zibin had just come home from Great Avenue, too. At the Xianshi Store he had bought a piece of light green fabric for his lover to make a lined winter gown. For himself he had purchased several packages of paper and pens for the amazing work he planned to produce this spring. He was driven by an ambition to prove his ability to the pathetic readership, constantly misled by promoters' gimmicks, and to shame the second-rate, even third-rate, writers hanging around taking up space these days. What trash they wrote. The language alone was enough to get them sent right back to college for a few more years. It was only fad and profit-mad businessmen that allowed them to become "writers." This upset Zibin. More and more things upset him these days. Actually, he was getting to be a real grouch.

Zibin was still a rather celebrated writer who enjoyed the affection of a certain element of young readers. He showed considerable skill with language, for which one might say he was admired. But there were critics who took a different view and were quite uncomplimentary. They often dismissed his work for its emptiness and lack of social relevance. That was the reason he was often plagued with a vague depression, which he did not care to reveal to anyone, and even his lover knew nothing about this secret.

Zibin's lover was a lively young woman who had decided to live with him a year ago because she was a great fan of his works and was extremely sympathetic toward his personal history. Despite their differences in temperament, they never seemed to have major disagreements. Zibin was older and extremely fond of pampering her. She was energetic and unaffected. Her age and interests did not make her exactly the ideal companion for a despondent writer. Still, he loved her and he took good care of her, and she loved and worshiped him. Although people often gossiped about how badly mismatched they were, they had managed to live together in harmony for quite some time.

Blessed by society and the times, Zibin had gotten himself a pretty good position and, from among a small number of intellectual women, he'd been able to select a young woman who was above average in appearance, bearing, and culture. He was clearly quite fortunate in the area of finance, as well. They lived in a single apartment in a two-story house on a very clean and quiet alley off Jing'an Temple Road. There they had a bedroom, a living room, and a tiny study, and they employed a maid who cooked their meals, so they ate quite well indeed. Not to fear, however: there were still plenty of readers who, deceived by his works, felt sorry for him because of his poverty. In reality, he not only lived well, but often went to movies, ate chilled fruit cocktail, and bought gourmet candies. Sometimes he just squandered money on a whim.

The couple were looking at the fabric when Ruoquan walked in through the back door. They were a little surprised because two weeks had passed without one of his customary visits.

"Why haven't you been over to see us for so long?" Meilin asked, looking at him with her big eyes opened wide.

"Because something has . . ." Ruoquan began but interrupted himself when he noticed how thin Zibin had gotten. "Why have you lost so much weight?"

Zibin said he could ask Ruoquan the same question.

Holding up the fabric, Meilin asked for Ruoquan's honest opinion.

Ruoquan had supper with them. He felt that there should have been plenty to say to his old friend Zibin, but well acquainted with his temperament, he didn't know how to start. He smoked several cigarettes and felt that he had been sitting around too long wasting all that precious time. He was just about to leave when Zibin asked, "Have you got any manuscripts ready to be published?"

"No," Ruoquan replied. "I haven't touched a pen for a long time. I guess I've sort of forgotten about things like writing."

"How could you let that happen! Someone in Beijing is about to publish a literary supplement and wants the two of us to contribute. The rate is something like four dollars per thousand characters, maybe more for us. You can write up a few things, and I'll mail them out for you. I always feel somehow closer to northern readers."

Ruoquan looked at him and at Meilin.

"Sometimes I feel I could quit writing altogether and it would be no great loss," he said with a sigh. "We wrote some things and people read them, but after all that time, nothing at all has changed. Besides the money we got for it, can you see any other meaning to it? It's true that some readers were moved by a particular anecdote or passage, but look at the kind of readers they were! Nothing but petty bourgeois students in high school and beyond who have just reached adolescence and are prone to melancholy. They found that these works suited their taste perfectly because they described the kind of depression they felt but couldn't understand. Or else they found that those stories represented their ideals, and the characters were very adorable, so much like themselves. They also felt that the characters must embody qualities of the writers, and they fell in love with the authors and manufactured naive fan letters. So then we got the letters and naturally we were really excited, felt as though our art had had some effect. We wrote back, choosing our words with care . . . and then what? I now realize that we've actually done harm by dragging younger people into our old rut of sentimentalism, individualism, discontent, and pent-up anxiety! . . . What's their way out? They can only sink deeper and deeper into their own rage. They can't see the connection between their suffering and society. Sure, they can train themselves to write better, get involved in cranking out a few articles and poems, even get a few compliments from older writers; but tell me, what good does it do them? What good does it do society? That's why I for one am giving up on writing. And I wish the other writers we know would give some thought to this problem, too, change direction a little. Although it would be too much to hope for immediate success, it will be meaningful to the history of future literature."

Ruoquan hoped that Zibin would respond. It didn't matter if Zibin disliked his ideas, for Ruoquan wanted to continue this conversation, to argue, and finally to reach a conclusion even though it might irritate Zibin, really make him mad. They had often argued over trivia in the past and Zibin had gotten upset.

"Aha." Zibin only smiled. "Here we go again with your fashionable preaching!" he said calmly. "The push is on to promote proletarian literature these days. Batch after batch of proletarian writers are being produced. So where are all the great results? Aside from the critics, their own friends, who heap them with flattering praise, what impression have they made? Go ask their readers, China's proletarian masses . . . or are they their own readers? All right, all right, we won't discuss it any further. I don't think it matters who the era belongs to. You can't go wrong if you just keep on working hard."

"I don't agree . . ." Ruoquan began but was interrupted as Zibin gestured to Meilin.

"Get changed," he said. "We're going to a movie. You haven't been here for so long. No matter how progressive you've gotten, we can still have some fun. I still have a few dollars. You choose: Carleton or La

Lumière . . . either is fine." Zibin spread the newspaper out in front of Ruoquan. Ruoquan said he wasn't going.

Zibin grew impatient. He shot Ruoquan an angry glance, then quickly turned it to a smile. "Right," he said in a mocking tone. "You've even quit going to the movies!"

Standing by the door and looking at the two of them, Meilin did not know what to do. "Are we going or not?" she asked haltingly.

"Why not?" Zibin looked very angry.

"Ruoquan!" Meilin looked at him with her lovely, imploring eyes. "Come on, let's go!" Ruoquan regretted having made his friend so angry and wanted to nod yes.

"If you don't insist," Zibin said coldly, "he won't come!"

Ruoquan really felt a little angry too, but he acted as if nothing had happened and kept his eyes on the newspaper.

When Meilin came downstairs dressed to the hilt, the three of them walked to the street corner together. Leaning toward Ruoquan, Meilin whispered in his ear and asked him again to come along. But when Ruoquan noticed how annoyed his friend looked, it all seemed pointless. With a loud "goodbye" he walked off rapidly, heading east.

3

Zibin and Meilin did not enjoy the movie. They were too preoccupied to speak to one another. Meilin couldn't figure out what had made Zibin so angry. To her, what Ruoquan had said made a lot of sense. She loved Zibin. She appreciated everything he wrote, since she always found in his work exceedingly beautiful phrases and a certain elegance of style. She admired his talent. But she could find nothing in Ruoquan's remarks that was wrong or would justify such anger. She looked at Zibin. Even though his eyes were fixed on the screen, she could tell that he was agonizing over something. "Well," she thought, "this really is an odd situation. Why did he insist on coming to the movie?" She nudged him with her elbow.

"It's a good film, isn't it?" He took her hand and whispered, "Mei, I love you." Then the film seemed to absorb him again.

Yes, Zibin certainly was in a rage, but it was hard to tell just who had offended him. Ruoquan's remarks kept echoing in his ears as if every word had been aimed at him. It really made him feel uncomfortable. Was it true that his work produced only the kind of result Ruoquan described? He just couldn't believe it! The critics' words were nothing but an expression of jealousy. Ruoquan was completely unaware that he'd become the dupe of those critics. Zibin pictured Ruoquan's dark, thin face, and slowly he began to feel that it no longer looked like him. He recalled the Ruoquan of the period when they first met.

"Oh, we've grown so far apart, Ruoquan, my friend!" he sighed with regret.

They really had! Ruoquan had reached a point where Zibin could no longer understand him. No matter what Zibin thought of Ruoquan, that he was bad, or even evil, his friend Ruoquan occupied a very firm position. Confidently he strode toward a new age. He couldn't hesitate. He wouldn't wait.

Zibin looked at Meilin and saw on her tender face an aura of tranquility derived from never having had to worry. He found her adorable. Yet the very next instant he felt that, charm notwithstanding, something about her left him dissatisfied. He looked at her for quite a while, suddenly envious of her carefree attitude. He turned his head back and exhaled softly.

Yes, far apart! The woman had never understood him. They had always been far apart despite an intimate year of living together. But he had never gauged the distance between them, since it would prove only that a clever person like himself could make a mistake.

Though throughout Zibin's musing, one might have noticed only Meilin's simple charm and delicate beauty as she sat watching the movie, actually she was absorbed in what Ruoquan had said. There seemed to be a great contradiction between Ruoquan's words and those of the man she had always admired.

They went home late, exchanging few words. Neither one wanted the film mentioned because they were both afraid they wouldn't be able to answer any questions about it. The story line was a blur, really, nothing but a blur.

4

Time went by. Day by day two weeks passed. Ruoquan got very busy. He joined a number of new organizations and was assigned several jobs. He felt his ignorance and spent time and energy reading as much as he could. He lost weight. Deep, firm lines appeared on his face, but his spirit was unusually lively, as vigorous as the coming of spring. One day he was working in an office that looked like a residence. It was an exceedingly run-down, old-style alley house, huge and empty inside. A comrade and his wife (she had never been to school, but was quite intelligent) and two children lived downstairs. An organization took the upstairs as its temporary office. Ruoquan was leafing through several minor newspapers in search of the daily diatribes against inferior writers that one critic was writing under a number of different pen names.

The "inferior" writers being attacked were Ruoquan's new acquaintances who had common goals for which they worked hard. Ruoquan respected these people and was on good terms with them. The critic, however, called the ones who had established names for themselves opportunists and claimed that the others, having no means of achieving fame, had simply surrendered to a certain banner and were working like little soldiers, doing their utmost to flatter their bosses and attack whatever their bosses disliked. Once their opportunities came, their names started popping up in magazines, and so in the end they too became writers of that wing. Then there were some who were just villains and careerists from start to finish and who were training their lackeys and praising their patrons. They had knocked around literary circles for a long time as a way of lining their pockets. They often took aim at their patrons and collaborated with their enemies and so on, and so on. Ruoquan found this critic—who knew literary circles but whose viewpoint was totally wrong and whose behavior was extremely ugly—disgusting. He often thought of writing an essay that would thoroughly, systematically refute his misleading criticism, especially his mistaken and nonsensical literary theory. While Ruoquan did not have time to write, he could not ignore it either, and so every day he flipped furiously through the papers to see if a new article had appeared.

There was a racket on the stairs, and three people walked in one after another. The first was Xiaoyun, who came each day. The second was Chaosheng, staff member of the Worker's Association as well as a cousin of the woman who lived downstairs. The third was the woman herself. Her name was Xiuying.

Chaosheng shook hands warmly with Ruoquan because they had not seen each other for so long. Different demanding jobs prevented them from being together more often, but they had maintained a cordial friendship ever since meeting, and after brief greetings they started talking gleefully about the strike then under way in a textile factory. Ruoquan was very interested because he was hoping to take the plunge from the intellectual movement into the workers' movement. Chaosheng had promised to look for the right opportunity. That was why, whenever they met, they talked for the most part about what was happening to the workers. After a while, Chaosheng suddenly asked, "Are you still writing articles?"

"No," Ruoquan answered, slightly ashamed. But he gave his excuse proudly. "No time for it."

Chaosheng told him that their paper had a column called "The Club" that could use some literary things. He hoped that Ruoquan could take care of the thing or else invite a few of his comrades to do it. But, Chaosheng reminded Ruoquan, workers did not understand their style.

They had to make it a little simpler and shorter. He talked as well about the theory of popularizing literature and art from the perspective of the working class.

Before long Chaosheng left. He was very busy indeed. He said that he would come again to discuss the matter he had just proposed. He also asked Xiaoyun to give it some thought, for he really wanted to have a good, concrete plan. When only Ruoquan and Xiaoyun were left, Xiaoyun took a newspaper from under his arm, handed it to Ruoquan, and said, "I really wonder why Zibin had to do this."

Ruoquan was a little taken aback. Recently he'd almost seemed to have forgotten his friend, though their seven-year-old friendship made it impossible for him not to feel concern. Also he'd been hearing a lot of criticism of Zibin lately. He could no longer defend him as a close friend, but he had hoped that Zibin would abandon that stubborn attitude of his. He should bend a little, make a more sincere ideological change. Ruoquan sensed that something was wrong from the look on Xiaoyun's face.

"What about Zibin?" he asked and took the paper.

"Read it, you'll see."

It was a literary supplement titled in bold type: "Another Kind of Movement Activist on Our Literary Scene." It was signed "Xin."

"Did Zibin write this?"

"Who else? When he publishes short stories in *Shooting Star,* doesn't he sign himself 'Xinren?' Anyway, look at the article; it's obvious that nobody else could have written it. And look at the supplement—it's edited by Li Zhen, [the Party's] cat's paw.[1] Imagine sending in a manuscript to that kind of a paper and mocking people for no reason at all! It really puts those of us who are his friends into a difficult position. Maybe he considers the great gentlemen of the *Shooting Star* clique to be the good people, his dear friends, while we're beneath contempt. I feel sorry for him."

Ruoquan glanced at him and then started reading the article. The tone was teasing. It was just as beautifully composed as Zibin's other work, and Ruoquan read through it as naturally as water flows. The structure was good, subtle, and compact. But it still had all the old flaws. It was neither an essay nor criticism, just light and pretty, and totally vacuous from start to finish. You might classify it as satire. Yes, actually, the whole thing could be called a satire; only it was impossible to find the target. As for names, he listed a few he considered to be "another kind of movement activist on the literary scene," and some others too. But he didn't do more than list them. He didn't place them in an adversarial position or attack them head on. Neither did he express any objective judgment as a critic. You could see that the author had derived satisfaction from the article. He'd gotten to express some personal grievances. He may also have been able to convince a tiny number of readers (one or two at most) to feel as he did. But in the final analysis, the article had no strength. It wasn't worth paying attention to because the author had no position, no objective. The piece was useless, like a shot fired at the sky. All it did was let off steam.

Ruoquan was silent for a while as he thought about his friend. "I don't find anything wrong with it," he said slowly to Xiaoyun.

"In a word, it's his attitude." Xiaoyun looked unhappy and sighed. "His attitude stinks. A lot of people have been talking about it. I can't defend him at all."

"Then let the others talk. If he isn't concerned, why should you worry?"

"You don't really understand. I'm convinced at this point that he does have regrets. He's no brave fighter. I know him really well. That's why I hate him and feel sorry for him at the same time. Otherwise I'd have joined those who are attacking him."

"Don't I know him," Ruoquan nodded. "He's so smart but he belongs to a different age. We can't drag him over to our side. I often feel sorry for him. I am sure that he has really been frustrated recently. Why don't we go to see him tonight?"

"It's useless. All you can talk about is food, drink, or entertainment. If you raise the real issue, he'll avoid arguing by giving you the cold shoulder or else he'll get really sarcastic. I don't want to see him."

"Why should that bother you? Let's drop by for a casual chat. I just want to see him cheer up a little. Being happy can actually give you courage to live. Let's go see him tonight. Are you free?"

Reluctantly, Xiaoyun agreed.

5

Although it was already eight o'clock in the evening when Ruoquan and Xiaoyun got to Zibin's house, the living room presented a lively scene. Three young men in Western suits were there with Zibin and Meilin. Zibin was a little surprised at their arrival, but he introduced them around with ready pleasure. Two of the three young men were students in a Shanghai art school and the least handsome one had just come down from Beijing. They were all unknown young poets willing to dedicate their lives to literature and art. So when they heard Ruoquan and Xiaoyun's names, they were delighted. Cautiously they extended their hands as they made admiring sounds.

Not a trace of displeasure showed on Zibin's face. Although he was thin, he didn't seem as pale as before, and there was a rosy glow of excitement on his face as though he were in such a good mood that he could go on talking forever. He talked a lot about life in Beijing, and about American architecture, and he took out a dozen or so photographs that a friend had sent from the United States. Later he also spoke of Japanese painting and told them a friend of his was doing very well in Japan selling paintings.

The maid brought in a mound of candy and fruit. Zibin ate the most. He picked up a famous chocolate, praised it highly, and urged his guests to help themselves. "Meilin just loves this. Right, Meilin?" he looked at her.

"Sure she likes it," Xiaoyun thought to himself. "But you were the one who instilled this taste in her because it shows class. If she only liked *dabing* and *yutiao,* you probably wouldn't be so happy to put her on display." [2]

Actually, what Meilin retorted was, "No, I don't like it any more. I'm tired of it. Yours is the taste that never changes."

Zibin frowned a little, and quickly changed the topic.

Ruoquan felt that Meilin was less talkative than she had been before, and mostly just sat there silently observing people. He walked over to strike up a conversation.

"Seen any movies lately?"

"Sure, a lot." She seemed very upset. "But I don't like to go because I don't get any happiness from them."

Zibin looked right at her but acted as though nothing was wrong.

"Why?" Ruoquan's eyes fixed on her. "Why don't you feel happy?"

"I don't know why," she glanced over at her husband. "Life is just so tiresome . . ."

"Find a job," Xiaoyun said, looking at Meilin in amazement. He'd never heard her say that she was unhappy before. "You'll feel better if you have some work to do."

"What can I do? Sometimes I still think about going back to school."

"Mei, darling," Zibin, interrupting them pointedly, tried to change the subject. "Are you talking about going back to school again? Weren't you tired of student life? I try to get you to read English every day here at home, but you won't, and I'd love to see you write but you're too lazy. So what's all this talk about going out to work?"

Meilin stared at him resentfully from the corner of her eye. "You're the one who likes that sort of thing, I don't . . ." she mumbled.

At nine o'clock, one of the students had to leave. He lived in Zhabei near the Tiantong convent, and if he waited much longer it would be hard to get home. The other two students then thought that they had better leave, too. One of them kept asking for Ruoquan's address, saying how much he'd love to visit in the future and solicit some advice. Then Zibin saw the three of them off.

The other two guests were still unwilling to leave. Zibin turned around, looked at their eyes tiredly, and sank weakly into his chair. He touched his cheeks. He could tell he had a fever. Listlessly, he picked up a tangerine and ate it.

"You have so many guests!" Xiaoyun had waited a long time to blurt this out.

"Yes! What can I do about it!" Zibin replied. "I can't refuse them. They often keep me from work and they wear me out. They sit here as though they're never going to leave. I just don't have the time to entertain them."

"It's all because 'guests flock to the good host.'" Xiaoyun almost made the conventional response but swallowed his words. He was afraid Zibin might imagine he was being mocked. Lately, Xiaoyun had begun feeling he had to be more careful with this friend than with anyone else.

"Why can't you refuse them? You can, you know. I guess there must be lots of these meaningless functions." Ruoquan was absolutely sincere.

Zibin didn't want to admit that and said nothing.

Meilin also believed such functions were completely unnecessary, but she didn't want to say anything. "If nobody came," she finally said, obliquely criticizing Ruoquan and Xiaoyun, "that would be terrible too."

Everybody looked at her but only Ruoquan responded.

"Quite right, it would be lonesome. But we could figure out something else to do. We could get together more and discuss real, concrete issues or form a reading group, since reading alone is not very inspiring. You don't learn as much and it's pretty superficial a lot of the time. It's not that we don't want to get together, we just want to cut back on the wasteful functions. We still want plenty of contact with people."

Meilin's big eyes sparkled. She seemed lost in thought. She was just about to say something when Zibin seized control of the conversation.

"It's not a good idea for her to do the things you're talking about," he said. He didn't want any more discussion along this line and changed the topic again.

By ten o'clock, the conversation had really taken a turn for the worse. There was no focus and each felt walled off from the others. No one was willing to express an opinion or to give others the opportunity to express one. It was too obvious. As soon as anybody said anything, the split opened up. Then everyone began yawning. They felt tired, but it seemed that nobody wanted to stop the conversation. They kept on talking, but all of them had the same deepening sense that their fragile friendship was deteriorating. They were drifting farther apart with no possibility of compromise.

Finally it was Ruoquan who stood up and made a resolute gesture to Xiaoyun, who nodded in agreement. The two said goodbye and walked out without the slightest regret. Zibin saw them off graciously as he always did, but he had no wish to prolong their visit.

When they had been escorted out through the back door, Ruoquan turned and spoke loudly as he would to children: "Get back in now, both of you. All right?"

"Come again in a few days, OK?" Meilin suddenly said in a sharp voice. Her voice was quivering and everyone noticed.

"Yes," said Ruoquan, "we'll come again for sure." And Xiaoyun repeated it.

6

"You're crazy! Screaming so loud!" Zibin was furious and scolded her.

He had never shouted at her before in anger. This was the first time he had shown his violent side. He did not know why his disgust with Meilin had surfaced at this moment, and he didn't know what it was that he hated about her. All he knew was that nothing felt right, that words could not describe his unhappy feeling, and that Meilin only intensified it as though she meant to cause an explosion. She not only didn't give him the consolation and the courage to live that a lover should (she never understood how hard life was), she made things worse and added to his agony. That was why he had yelled at her, and she may have had it coming. But since he had pampered her for so long, he now felt regretful. Though he actually felt worse than ever, he just said gently, "It's very late. Let's go up to bed."

Meilin said nothing as she went obediently upstairs.

Zibin tried to make up by talking to her sweetly and giving her two big apples. But she was thinking, "You always treat me like a child."

Before long Meilin went to bed like a good little girl. Zibin kissed her good night, but did not go to bed. He was very excited and still wanted to work. He went up to the attic, to his little study.

But sleep would not come for her, and she lay in bed thinking about life. She didn't deny that she was fortunate to have his love. But she didn't know why she suddenly felt dissatisfied. This surprised her, for she had lived her life in a muddle for so long. In the past she had read his fiction and had worshiped him. Then he had fallen in love with her, so she had fallen in love with him. He had proposed that they live together, and naturally she had agreed with him. However, she should have known that as soon as she moved in with him, her separate social status would disappear. Only now as she thought about it did she realize that except for him she had nothing. In the past, having read a lot of classical and romantic fiction, her ideal had been to throw over everything for love. Once she fell in love with him, she really had left everything behind and plunged into his embrace. She had gone along quite happily the whole time thinking muddle-headedly that she was fortunate. But now things were different. She needed something else! She wanted her own place in society. She wanted to have contact with many, many people. Even though they loved each other, she could no longer be locked up in the house as one man's after-work amusement. Yes, she still loved Zibin and, no, she would never leave him, of that she was certain. But she felt that he was somehow stifling her. Worse than any old-fashioned family, he did not allow her any freedom. He pampered her, petted and amused her, and satisfied all her material wants. But he only wanted her to love his ideas and what he loved. She wondered why he was like this. He was so tender, yet so autocratic.

Meilin could not sleep as her mind was flooded with thoughts of the person closeted in the attic. She had only just now discovered that he was unhappy. She had no idea anymore whether or not he had been happy in the past. She certainly had not been aware of any problem. His laughter, his praise of her, his constant assurances of how content he was, and his appreciation of her generosity had all made her think he must be happy. From time to time, he got angry over some little thing and would dash off some articles to let off steam. She had felt uneasy and at a loss then, but it had never lasted very long and he'd soon be feeling better again. He could admit later that he had forgotten what they'd fought about and that he had an irritating temper. Then the unpleasant episode would pass without a trace like white clouds blown away by the east wind. Now, however, she sensed that he was often annoyed, even though he pretended that nothing was wrong. He locked himself in the attic a lot to avoid seeing her. What was he doing there? He often came to bed very late and then said that he had been writing. But she had taken a look at everything he had done lately and discovered that his recent output was pitifully slight. He was eating very little, although he denied it and often said, straight to her face, that he was overeating. What did it all mean? Didn't he trust her anymore? He had never talked with her about any of these matters, and he never talked about his problems to his friends, despite the fact that his articles were full of discontent. He often wrote long letters filled with gloom and doom to people living far away, but they always contained the same old complaints. Things had been at this standstill for the past few years! But none of this completely explained the basis of his unhappiness. What was really causing it?

Meilin's thoughts eventually turned to Ruoquan. She and Ruoquan had known each other even before she met Zibin, but it was his friendship with Zibin that drew him so close that he began treating her like a member of the family. She didn't think about him as being right or wrong, but got along with him very well. After quite a few arguments between him and Zibin, however, she concluded, from her limited perspective, that the cause of the problem between them was Zibin's stubbornness. Ruoquan was very sincere and modest, and what he said was not unreasonable. Zibin, on the other hand, was quite unreasonable. He mocked Ruoquan, treated him coldly, and avoided him. Why did he behave like this? They had been such close friends before. Meilin could tell that Zibin meant to abandon his friend because he no longer so much as mentioned Ruoquan to her. This was quite a different situation than before. Not once did Zibin suggest visiting Ruoquan even when he had not come over for a long time. This was also quite different from before. In fact, it was more than just Ruoquan. Zibin was intentionally keeping a distance from a lot of his former friends. Why was that?

The more Meilin pondered, the more puzzled she became. Quite a few times she was about to go up to the attic hoping to get to the bottom of things, but then reconsidered since she knew he'd never reveal anything to her, and would just caress her and sweet talk her into going back to sleep. He'd never let her know what was bothering him. Finally she realized that he would always treat her like a child.

The clock struck two o'clock. He still had not come down. She sank deeper into her thoughts and the anxiety of waiting. What was he doing?

Zibin was suffering from a headache. He had fever and a cough. He sat at his desk as usual. He had grown used to looking into a small round mirror when he sat down and he was saddened to see how much more weight he had lost. In the past this sight might have made him shatter the glass by throwing it into a corner of the room, but since a woman now shared his place, he just tossed the mirror into his desk drawer. That way he wouldn't be stuck for an answer to her interrogation. It was the same that night too. But after he tossed the mirror aside, he also made a resolution: "I'm not going to look in the mirror ever again."

Once seated, as was his custom, Zibin lit up a Beauty brand cigarette. White silky smoke floated slowly up and then dispersed. His mind was like the silky smoke—directionless, empty, tangled, and drifting—yet he could feel a heavy pressure. Zibin was depressed. He struggled against his physical discomfort and tried not to give in to bed. As though he were angry, he wanted to persist and to write a gripping masterpiece that

night. He made a quick calculation and realized that if he went two more weeks without writing for *Creation Monthly,* it would be fully two months since he had communicated with his readers. As for *Shooting Star,* he seemed to remember that there was nothing left to send it either. Readers could easily forget a writer, and critics were merciless. It saddened him that these people couldn't accommodate a talented writer more kindly. Meanwhile, however, he could only keep plugging away, because he was afraid people might think, mistakenly, that he had burned out creatively. He was a capable and prolific writer whose work was superior to others—that, at least, was his own conviction. The day was sure to arrive when his masterpiece would shake contemporary literary circles. Yet at the moment, life was extremely irritating, for he lacked prolonged periods of time to think and could hardly finish even the shortest piece.

Zibin read through several old unfinished manuscripts one more time. He felt that each one of them was too good to be discarded. But now, no matter what, he was not in the frame of mind he needed to finish them. He pushed the pile of manuscripts aside for a time when he would be more free and could finish them off. He took out a clean sheet of paper to write on, but for some reason his mind was a blank, and he grew anxious. His hopes were one thing. Reality was a different story altogether. Yet he refused to believe that what really prevented him from producing anything was a lack of talent. Time was passing and exhaustion began to overtake him. His mind, however, was clearer than ever. He cast the manuscript aside and angrily lay down on his chair. He was beginning to hate his friend.

Once upon a time Zibin's mind had been calm, the very thing that creative writing needed. He was quite intelligent to begin with and had a probing intellect, but he couldn't stand challenges. Whenever Ruoquan came around, he left Zibin with a terribly uncomfortable feeling. Ruoquan's news had to do with social concerns that lay beyond Zibin's understanding. This puzzled Zibin, but it also made him resentful of the blow to his pride. Further, Ruoquan's self-assurance and confident attitude toward life made Zibin feel unsettled and jealous in a way that was hard to explain exactly. Zibin felt contempt for Ruoquan (he never had respected his writing) and called him shallow, a blind follower. He had deliberately talked himself out of respecting his friend, yet he could not forget him. He hated Ruoquan for no particular reason, and then, as Ruoquan displayed more sincerity and worked more steadily, the more disgust Zibin felt over his efforts, and the harder it got to forget him. Zibin felt equally resentful toward people who were like Ruoquan and toward those who were even more diligent and resolved than he, though

to Zibin they all seemed very far away and insubstantial. He could rattle off the names of those who deserved to be mocked, but they weren't engraved in his mind, as Ruoquan was, as constant pain. Zibin found it possible to respect anonymous people who really were working hard, but Ruoquan's bunch he just could not believe. They were nothing but shallow, confused opportunists.

At two o'clock he heard Meilin coughing. His own cough was even more severe. He was thinking it was really time to go to bed when he recalled Meilin's recent unspoken stubbornness and her closeness to Ruoquan that evening: it made him feel that even Meilin had drifted away from him. He was standing all alone in this frustrating position that demanded so much struggle. Out of pure spite, he refused to go to bed. He wrote two long letters to two far-away readers whom he didn't even really know. At this moment, there was no one else he could feel close to. The letters were pretty much the same. As he wrote them his mind relaxed, and by four o'clock he had blanked out from exhaustion and fallen asleep at his desk.

7

"I wonder why my life shows no sign of improving," Meilin said to herself. It was true. They had endured a life without pleasure or hope into mid spring, Shanghai's most exciting season. Pot-bellied businessmen and blood-sucking devils wizened and shriveled from overwork on their abacuses were going at full tilt in the careening money market, investing and manipulating to increase their exploitation of the laboring masses and to swell their astronomical wealth. Dozens of newspapers being hawked in the street carried banner stories about antagonists on various battlefronts, but the news was contradictory and unreliable. Beautiful young aristocratic ladies, faces rouged and eyes radiant, strolled through the streets wearing their new spring outfits. They crowded the amusement parks and took outings to scenic suburban spots to gratify their pampered bodies and untroubled moods. Amusements like these were bound to keep them young, beautiful, content, and confirmed in their ways. As for the workers, although they had endured winter's rigor, their lives got harder with spring's arrival because rent and the price of grain were up, and working hours lengthened. They worked harder and got weaker. The old and feeble who didn't have their wages cut were fired and replaced by children who never had enough to eat and whose age and build were obviously below the legal limit. The workers suffered so much that they simply had to resist. And so struggle began. Every day brought news of strikes and the beating and killing of workers. Subsequently, revolutionary young people, students, and members of the

[Communist] Party found themselves extremely busy. They sympathized with the workers, supported them, and under the leadership of various people rushed around all sweaty and excited . . . It was mid spring. The wind was soft and the weather intoxicating! But every evil, pain, agony, and struggle unfolded under the soft clear sky.

Meilin wore a new outfit every day, green ones, red ones. She went out regularly with Zibin, but got no sense of fun or pleasure from it. She imagined that each person she saw on the crowded streets had a more meaningful life than she. Meilin did not want to die. Quite the contrary, she wanted to really live and she wanted to be happy. It was just that she could not find direction and needed guidance. She wished that Zibin could understand, that he would feel the same way, so they'd be able to talk things over and set out on the same road of life together. Yet looking at Zibin made her miserable because the man she'd once worshiped had become so inscrutable. He seemed to be her exact opposite. He wasted life seemingly without intending to. He was deeply thoughtful yet never revealed what he was thinking about. When people disgusted him, he prided himself on staying civil. (He had never felt so pained in front of company before.) When he did speak out against someone, he'd immediately retreat into self-hatred. Sometimes he showered Meilin with affection; other times he was indifferent. His behavior was contradictory and his misery self-inflicted. Sometimes Meilin tried to talk to him about life, but then things became really hopeless because he never answered her, just smiled silently. And the smile hurt her too, because she could sense its bitterness and she knew how agonized he must be.

This situation lasted until one evening around eight o'clock when the house was empty of guests. Tired from running around all day, Zibin lay on the bed reading a book of poetry. Meilin sat on a chair by the bed reading the latest issue of a magazine. On the table by the bed sat a lamp with a red silk shade and a pot of tea. In bygone days it would have been a sweet night. Now, however, Zibin felt listless as he flipped through the pages, glancing at Meilin from time to time. Meilin also looked over at him now and then, but neither seemed to want eye contact. In fact, each hoped for comfort from the other and both looked pathetic, he sad and she anxious. Finally Meilin reached her breaking point. She threw down the magazine.

"Don't you feel we're awfully quiet? Come on, Zibin, let's talk," she said.

"All right," he replied, pushing his book to the corner of the bed.

But the silence continued. Neither knew what to say.

Five minutes later Meilin spoke in a trembling voice, "I think you've been very miserable lately," her eyes fixed on him. "Why? It makes me sad to see you like this!"

"You're imagining things . . ." As usual Zibin gave his phoney smile, then turned away and heaved a long sigh.

Meilin was deeply moved. She walked over and took his hand. "Tell me," she begged in an anxious, tender voice. "Tell me everything you've been thinking about! Tell me about all your worries!"

Zibin remained silent for a long time. Lots of unpleasant thoughts were tangled in his mind. If only he could tumble into Meilin's arms and cry out loud as he had with his mother when he was little. Then all problems would vanish and he'd be able to start over, living vivaciously for her sake, making discriminating plans for their future, slowly straightening his own life out. But he understood—he gritted his teeth as he thought about this—that it actually would be useless to cry because this woman was more weak than he and could not bear the turmoil. If he cried he would frighten her. Anyway, even if he did cry till his tears dried up, what good would it do? All the conflicts and agonies of reality would remain to be faced. Unless he died and left behind the world he knew so well, he would never be able to free himself of all that. The result of this was that he said nothing, and just endured his growing pain. He held her hand tightly. His face twisted grotesquely.

His fearful face made Zibin look like a tortured, wild animal. "Why are you making such a face? Have I whipped you?" she screamed at him, baffled. "Tell me! Damn it, I can't stand any more of this! If you don't talk I'll . . ."

She shook her head as she looked at him. He turned his face toward her. Tears flowed across his cheeks. He held her neck, drew his face close to hers and said brokenly, "Mei, don't be frightened. Darling, you love me, so let me tell you slowly. Oh my Mei! So long as you don't abandon me, I'll be all right."

He held her tight. "Well, there's really nothing," he continued. "Yes, I have suffered a lot recently. I can't describe it. I know that my health isn't good. Everything has gone wrong because of that. I need to recuperate is all."

After a while he went on, "I resent everybody, every conflict in the world. All I need is love and you. I think of us leaving here and everything familiar. We could go to an isolated island or an empty village. Publications, fame, it's nothing but shit. Only you, only our life of love really exists!" And on and on he went at great length.

Meilin wavered. She abandoned her desire to be more ambitious and involved in life. For his love and what he had just said she pitied him. She wanted to help him because, after all, he was a man of talent. She was in love with him. Finally, she cried too. She comforted him for a long time because she wanted him to believe that she would always be his.

For his health's sake and peace of mind, she hoped that they could leave Shanghai for a while. They could take a trip to somewhere where mountains were green, waters clear, birds chirped, and flowers danced, to spend a delightful spring. If they were a little frugal and sold just one more book to the Shooting Star Bookstore, they would have enough. What did it matter if they were slightly short? They figured that if he collected his smaller, unpublished drafts, he would have about seventy to eighty thousand words. That would just about do it. The trip would not be hard to arrange. Imagining herself and Zibin strolling around all day at some beautiful scenic spot cheered Meilin up. Zibin also felt good about leaving the city for a while, since he just couldn't put up with all the new pressures anymore. For his health's sake, he needed a trip or a long-term rest in the country. Therefore they resolved that night to go to West Lake, since it was fairly close and Meilin had never been there.

Both felt much happier, which made for a wonderful night such as they hadn't enjoyed recently; and that was because they both saw a ray of hope for their future—however dim it might be.

8

The next day they got part of the money for the manuscript. So they did a lot of shopping but waited for the rest of it to start their trip. But the day after that the weather turned and the rain started, now pouring, now drizzling, and their mood clouded over too. Meilin spent the entire day in bed complaining nonstop. Zibin, unhappy also, made another futile trip to the bookstore. He would have to wait a few more days to receive the rest of his money. The rain continued day after day with no sign of letting up. Both of them stayed at home; neither was in a mood to do anything. The days lengthened, became excruciatingly dull. At first Zibin had kept telling Meilin about West Lake scenery over and over, but now it bored them both. They grew tense waiting for the money, yet when they finally did get the full sum six days after deciding to go, it didn't make Zibin happy. "What should we do?" he said indifferently to Meilin. "It's still raining. We might as well wait a couple more days."

It was hardly a reason at all. The rain was not heavy and West Lake not far away. If he had really meant to go, they could have left right then.

Meilin was neither angry nor surprised. It seemed perfectly natural to remain at home and suffer, since they had no urgent need to go to West Lake. The delay cooled their excitement, and both sank at once into the same private thoughts that had tortured them before. Zibin often heard news that depressed him. Quite a number of friends and acquaintances were involved in activity outside the world of bookstores. None asked about him. He was forgotten. It was most unbearable news. He despised them, hated them, but felt he should not run away. He wanted to stay in Shanghai, keep an eye on them, and wait. Also he would apply himself and really show them. What would he get out of going to West Lake? Temporary peace and temporary separation from the world, but he wasn't sure that he could forget it all and go on living in peace. Also he was sure that it would not be hard for the world to do very well without him. When they heard about his trip, his friends would almost certainly mock him for being frightened into hiding out of fear of the new era. Then everyone really would forget him and even his name would become unfamiliar. Worst of all, the young students who worshiped him and the learned celebrities who praised him would be cut off from all intelligence of him, and slowly the good impression he had made would become weak and blurred. This he feared above all else! He could not act like ancient hermits who fled everything. He had lots of desires. He did not want to lose what he had gained. He decided that going to West Lake was foolish. But he was very afraid that Meilin would insist they go. If she did, he thought, he would have to go against her wishes, or he would go with her for two or three days and then come immediately home. Staying for a long time would never work out. Seeing that Meilin was not as anxious to go as before, he relaxed, and yet finally there came a time when they had to discuss the matter. He just told her his idea, and said that the reason for not going was that he had to write an essay and did not have time right then. It would be better, he felt, for them to take the trip next month. He spoke eloquently, for he was afraid that Meilin would disagree or would at least pout and get angry. He was amply prepared with the tender expressions necessary for coping with a lovely, delicate woman. When he finished what he had to say, he leaned his head toward the back of her chair so that his lips grazed her white neck, and his breath brushed her lightly.

"What do you think?" he asked softly. "I'll do as you wish. It's up to you."

Meilin agreed in a few words. The matter was resolved without any untoward display of emotion. All Zibin had to do after that was get to work on what he hoped to accomplish. He was a literary man possessed of ample self-confidence and was not made for other kinds of struggle. He had decided to stay in Shanghai to satisfy his ambitions; yet the danger was that if he went on locking himself up in that little room, getting angry and writing discontented letters as time passed and other people went forward, then he would always be a malcontent and would end his life in meaningless misery without ever having had any success worth mentioning. Even if he had exceptional intelligence, it would be useless.

So far as Meilin was concerned, a life of leisure was no longer accept-
able. Action had become an instinctual need. She wanted to be with the
masses, to try to understand society, and to work for it. She was no
longer a woman who could live happily in seclusion. Already she had
lived far too long as the wife of a gloomy man eight years older than she.
She felt that living with him had made her more subdued and taught her
to worry and to be depressed, and yet she still hadn't reached a level
where she could understand her husband. It just wasn't the life for her.
Ever since the beginning of spring, she had been feeling uneasy with her
husband's new agonies. The role of wife, the role of lover, did not satisfy
her. She gave a great deal of thought to doing something about it but
lacked opportunity and someone to guide her. She did not know what to
do and it depressed her. She knew perfectly well that her depression
would never win sympathy from Zibin, and that compounded her unhappiness. She couldn't figure out why just a few days earlier she had
suddenly wanted to go to West Lake. Of course it would have been an
improvement, but as they had delayed the trip, she came to feel that
spending somebody else's money and going on a holiday with him and
wasting time while so many other people were working hard not only
wasn't right, it was actually disgraceful. It was fine with her that Zibin
now didn't want to take the trip. Yet his reason—that he didn't have
time and had to write—made her feel that whether she went or not was
unimportant, because it looked as though she really was a person who
had nothing at all to do. The thought made her ashamed. She wanted to
find something to do, and she believed that sooner or later she would.
But she figured it would be best not to talk it over with Zibin. For the
time being, she kept it secret.

9

Ruoquan received, unexpectedly, a letter that had been forwarded to him
through a chain of friends. Meilin's name was written on the envelope in
large characters, and concern for Zibin's health filled him as he opened
it with surprise. He was nearly certain his friend was sick again. It made
him sad. Whenever he thought of his friend it was like this. The letter,
however, scrawled at a horizontal slant like a telegram, read:

> I assume that you're free Sunday morning. Do come to Zhaofeng Park,
> please. I have something important to discuss. I'll wait for you. Meilin.

It didn't sound like Zibin was sick. Then what was it? Had they quarreled? He'd never seen the two of them arguing. Ruoquan still suspected
it had something to do with Zibin, because he did not think that Meilin

had any other reason to come to him. He had known her for two years now, but they weren't really close. He wasn't all that familiar with her background and had never paid any particular attention to her. She impressed him as a young woman who was naive, pampered, and definitely not bad looking. Thinking of Zibin, he decided he would make the long trip to the far west end of Shanghai the next morning.

At seven o'clock in the morning, Ruoquan was preparing to leave. He picked up a handful of coppers and two silver coins, brushed the dust off the old Western-style suit he was wearing, and rushed out of the house. He figured that he would arrive at Zhaofeng Park around seven-forty. Meilin and Zibin were people who got up very late, so she might not even be there by then. But, he thought, there would be no harm in waiting for her. He had not visited the park for over half a year, and the opportunity to walk around and breathe fresh air would do him good. Lately his lungs had felt bad.

After transferring trolleys three times, Ruoquan arrived at the entrance to the park. He paid admission and stepped through the gate. The soft breeze bore a pleasant spring fragrance. Ruoquan stood up straight, unbuttoned his suit jacket, inhaled deeply, and felt refreshed right away. The tension and exhaustion he usually felt left him without a trace. Anyone arriving at this verdant carpet of grass, leaving behind the noise of the world, feeling the spring breeze, warmed by the morning sun, would forget everything and unshoulder all cares. Visitors to the park would relax their bodies and allow the quiet environment to give them such pleasure that they would forget where they were.

There were not many people in the park. A few Westerners and some children's carriages were visible here and there. The green of old and new leaves surrounded him. Dazzling sunlit white cotton clouds moved and shifted shape slowly in the vast blue sky overhead. Ruoquan walked lazily across the undulating grass for quite a way, almost forgetting why he had come. He felt very comfortable and the air was just perfect. Just then he heard a swishing sound on the grass not far behind him, and when he turned to look, he saw Meilin standing there wearing a *qipao* of white with grey stripes and a dark red woolen sleeveless jacket.[3]

"Oh, I didn't know you were here," he said without thinking. "You're early!"

Meilin was very calm, but a touch of happiness and a slight flush showed on her face. "I've waited for you for a long time!" she said sweetly. "I hope it won't bore you," she continued in a more serious vein. "But I want to talk with you. That is why I invited you here. Shall we go find a place to sit?"

As he walked along eastward with her, Ruoquan watched her high-heeled, brown leather shoes as she minced along. She had on flesh-toned stockings. Were her feet really that tiny, or did the elegantly crafted shoes make them look so pathetic and feminine?

"How's Zibin?" He tried to strike up a conversation. "Is he in good health?"

"Yes. He's started writing again," she answered without much enthusiasm.

"How about you? Are you writing too?" he went on.

"No."

He noticed that her face twitched and an unhappy expression appeared.

They sat down on a red painted bench next to some trees. On the left a group of huge hydrangeas were blooming luxuriantly, the massive flowers exuding a delicate fragrance and pink glow. Ruoquan didn't know what to say. He was still in the dark about the point of this talk, about how Zibin was doing and how the two of them were getting along.

She looked at his puzzled expression and said with a smile, "Did you think it was strange to get a letter from me?"

"No. I didn't."

"So then you know why I wanted you to come here?"

"Well, not really," he answered hesitantly.

She smiled again and said, "I didn't think you'd know. But I must tell you that the reason is I've been feeling awfully depressed for a long time . . ."

She paused and glanced at him. He lowered his head, gazing silently at the lawn. Then she continued on at great length. She stopped frequently and, because she appeared somewhat nervous, did not seem able to get it all poured out freely. But from start to finish Ruoquan uttered not one word, and did not even look at her because he wanted her to finish what she had to say. She told him all the fragmentary recent notions and hopes she'd had until she finally felt that she desired his comment.

"What do you think?" she concluded. "You don't find this foolish, do you? I guess I'm quite naive."

Ruoquan remained silent for quite some time looking at her tender, dignified, and honest face. He hadn't expected the woman to be so frank in expressing her discontent with life and her bold determination to get involved in society. He felt extremely happy because her unexpected attitude encouraged him. After a long silence, he extended his hand, grasped hers warmly, and said, "You are just wonderful, Meilin! I think I finally understand you now!"

Meilin was so happy she blushed.

Afterward they were much more open in talking about their feelings and newly acquired knowledge. They were both in good spirits, particularly Meilin, because she could speak freely and Ruoquan not only listened to her and understood her, he was willing to help. She saw a light ahead. She was anxious to know how to start working immediately. He hesitated, but he did promise to see her again in a few days. Possibly he could introduce her to some people who would find her work.

IO

Meilin kept smiling after she got home. She could not hide her joy, and at times the words nearly slipped out. She felt that she should inform Zibin, but restrained herself because she was afraid that he would interfere and sabotage her plan. Zibin noticed nothing. He was considering a novel and the mischievous, taunting language he would use to describe his main protagonist, a Chinese Don Quixote. It would be vivid writing, sharp satire. He figured that if there were no unexpected interruptions or upsetting events, he had two undisturbed weeks of writing time. He could shock the world with a novel of one hundred thousand words by the summer of 1930. Then, as the author of such a work, everyone would know his name. Temporarily he brushed aside all potentially troubling matters. He wanted to clear his mind, once so keen. He had been at home in seclusion for several days now, avoiding all contact with other people.

It was a different story with Meilin. Two days after her meeting with Ruoquan, she attended an afternoon meeting of [the Communist] study group on literature and art. Over half of the fifty people attending were workers, and the other half included a few young writers and a good number of lively students. Meilin had never experienced this sort of life and it made her feel excited. She looked around amicably, wishing she could shake all of their hands warmly and converse frankly with each one. Aside from Ruoquan, she did not know anyone there, but she did not feel awkward. On the contrary, she felt quite comfortable because she and they were all "comrades." Aside from being slightly apologetic about her beautiful outfit, simple but well-tailored, she was completely enthusiastic. It was a general meeting, so the number attending was large. Except for a few workers with unavoidable time conflicts, almost everyone in the organization was there. When the meeting began, the chairman asked a young man wearing a Western-style suit made of Hong Kong fabric to deliver a political report. Everyone was solemn and silent. Meilin fixed her eyes on him, raptly intent on the simple ideas she was hearing for the first time. The speech was simple, but it presented the world's political and economic situation very clearly and analyzed it accurately. The speaker was young, no older than twenty-five. Later Ruoquan told her that he was a worker in a print factory who had had two years at university. Meilin felt inexpressible shame. Everyone there, she felt, had a better grasp of politics than she did and was more capable than she. Following a number of work reports, the discussion turned to organizational work. Meilin did not know how to participate since she was not familiar with the whole situation, but the chairman kept looking at her to solicit comments anyway. It made her feel uneasy, but she was quite sure that before too long she could be retooled and her ignorance remedied. The last matter they took up was what action to take on [May Day].[4] At this point somebody else stood up to make a report. He was a representative from an organization directing [the Party]. Then the decision was made. On [May Day] they would all mobilize and go to [the designated] avenue and occupy it. The meeting ended on this high note with everyone tense and excited.

"Day after tomorrow," people kept reminding each other on the way out. "Don't forget, nine o'clock, just go to [the] avenue!"

Meilin stayed a little longer to chat with Chaosheng, who had just chaired the meeting and worked for the labor confederation and a few others. They all treated her with great cordiality and respect. A woman working in a textile factory was particularly friendly.

"We want to make a revolution," she said to Meilin. "But we also want to learn about literature and art we can understand. You writers need a revolution too, so we've united. I am afraid we're too busy to do a good job. In a few days I'd like to show you some things I've done. Chaosheng said that you're a woman writer. I've just begun to learn how to write, and it's all because Chaosheng has encouraged me. I have a lot of ideas, but I can't express them. Next Monday I'll be able to find some free time. I would like to write a newsletter for the factory because Ruoquan says they need one."

Meilin said she couldn't write literature either. She also said that she would love to work in a factory.

Then the woman described various hardships at the factory, including a couple of tragic incidents. She said that she would try to help if Meilin really wanted to go to the factory, but she worried that Meilin would get sick right away because of fatigue and dirty air. Chaosheng also said that it was not difficult to get in and expressed the wish that some of the intellectuals in this group would go to work at factories to get a real understanding of the [proletariat], and get [proletarianized]. It was the only way to create an authentic [proletarian] literature.[5] However, Chaosheng had reservations about Meilin's health. She, on the other hand, insisted that she could train and get stronger.

Since Meilin had more free time than the others, she was assigned to work for two hours each day at their organization office. They gave her the address and told her that she would probably get more hours in the future because as [May] approached, more needed to be done. Far more workers wanted to join and they had to be trained, as well. As a beginner, she had shouldered a heavy load, and she knew she had to work extremely hard.

I I

The [first of May] arrived.

From the time, at eight o'clock, when Zibin discovered Meilin's absence, he felt uneasy. He asked the maid, but she didn't know anything about it. He couldn't imagine where she could be. It dawned on him that recently she had often gone out without telling him where. Also he recalled that she had not spoken much to him recently. He kept waiting and waiting, but she didn't show up. In a fit of anger he stamped into his study, swearing that he would waste no more time thinking about the woman. He'd finished part of his writing already and wanted to get on with it. He sat down at the desk, but his mind was elsewhere. He opened the drawer, and there he discovered the letter Meilin had left him. He read hurriedly, as though to swallow it whole. The letter was clearly written, as follows:

> Zibin, I simply can't hide the truth from you anymore. When you read this letter, I will probably already be on [the avenue] as assigned by the organization to carry out [a Communist] movement. I imagine that you will be unhappy to hear this news, but I feel I have to let you know and explain it, because honestly I love you very deeply. Even now I still hope that you do not misunderstand me. That's why I'm reporting to you now. I hope you will give it some thought, so that when I come back we can have a rational discussion. We should both criticize each other very sincerely and thoroughly. I have a lot of things to tell you, some about myself and some about you. I'll talk to you more later on.
>
> Meilin

For a long time Zibin was stupefied. He could barely breathe. He had never wanted this. It was too unexpected. He thought back to all the unpleasant news and all the familiar faces, and then he thought about Meilin . . . Oh, such a woman, so gentle and soft. Now she too had abandoned him to follow the masses. He had great ambition and talent, but it was in vain because he could not go that direction. He was left all alone. He was despondent and wanted to cry, but couldn't. In his imagination he pictured what [that avenue] must look like at that moment, full of terror and danger. Despite a deep anxiety, he did not look forward to Meilin's return. He did not want to see her again, because she would bring him so much pain, pain that would worsen over time. He could not bear to have her in the same room with him anymore. He ripped the letter to pieces angrily. Then he saw his notebook, yawning open like a mouth, and the paltry few pages he'd written. He grieved over it silently before slamming the cover shut and throwing it in the drawer. Then he heaved a long sigh.

Part Two

I

At dawn on an early spring day, a moist breeze swept in softly through the broken window, brushed everything gently, and left quietly. The pale light of the sky reached into every corner and coated the room with a mysterious color. The bustling noises of the city had not yet begun. It was a good time for peaceful sleep, but Wang Wei, who had stayed up very late, awoke with a start. He opened eyes that were heavy with sleep, looked dumbly at the sky for a while, and then, as if he hadn't thought of anything, closed his eyes, turned over, and dozed off again. He was a likable, bronze-complexioned young man. Just as his eyelids closed, a beautiful vision sprang into his mind. He turned over, as though startled for a second time, and sat up. Seeming to doubt himself, he took out a terse telegram from under the pillow, which he reread:

Taking steamer Dairen to Shanghai tonight. Arriving morning day after tomorrow. Meet me. Mary

The bronze face shone with joy. He rubbed the stubble on his chin and beamed. Even more happily, and with an occasional "whew," he put on his old black woolen trousers and thought over and over to himself, "This is really a strange one. When I was longing for her letters, not a word. Now, when I'm up to my ears in work, she comes. Oh, Mary, you strange creature."

A pleased, happy expression adorned his face as he spoke that adorable name. After splashing some cold water on his face, he dashed out into the light fog and headed toward the Bund.

The streets were quiet. Only a few horse-drawn garbage carts and several listless street cleaners were out. Now and then, an apprentice, half asleep, stepped out of a small shop to take down the shutters over the doors. The fog made the streets damp. Everything seemed to be enshrouded by a thin white cloud. It was cool, but pleasant. Wang Wei walked to a streetcar stop and after a short wait boarded a streetcar headed for the Bund. The din of the iron wheels shattered the surrounding stillness as the car swayed violently down the tracks. Wang Wei wasn't thinking about any of this. He ignored everything and thought only of the place he was headed in the thick fog, in which he kept seeing a flowerlike, petite, and charming face. He had met her at an informal banquet last summer. On that occasion, she hadn't even noticed him. She had talked a lot, been very lively, and her drinking had attracted considerable attention. But she had hardly glanced in his direction. Yet, somehow, he had found her nonchalant arrogance captivating. Noticing an occasional inadvertent frown, he felt that she must be very lonesome in a way that was incomprehensible to ordinary people. Because of this he felt very close to her, and when he heard her laughter, his heart unexpectedly raced. The next day he plucked up enough courage to visit her. He was warmly welcomed, but a few days later she left for Beijing to study. Not daring to believe that there was a firm friendship between them, he felt somewhat pessimistic and disappointed. Later, however, a few letters were exchanged between them, and thoughts of what might happen led to wishful thinking. Suffering from the uncertainty, he felt he simply had to go to Beiping.[6] There they lived together as happy as could be for a while before returning south together. Since this had happened during winter break, she insisted on going home, agreeing to return to Shanghai after the Lunar New Year; but she did not keep her word. Only after a long time did he receive a short letter from her from Beiping. She gave no explanation, asking only that he forgive her.

His anxieties would have overwhelmed him if a new hope had not brought him encouragement. By then he had become very interested in contemporary politics and economics, was reading diligently and insatiably, and was also gradually becoming involved in practical struggles. As a result, even though he often wrote to her, missed her, and felt sorry about losing her, after a short time his letters became shorter and he didn't miss her so much. Sometimes he even forgot her for a few days. Yet despite everything, her pretty face was deeply engraved on his heart, comforting him after his hard work. Only he knew how much he loved her. When yesterday he received this telegram out of the blue, it revived many hopes and dreams and brought back the sweet past. He wished he could see her at once and tell her many things, about his recent work above all. In no time at all the streetcar arrived at the Bund.

On the Huangpu River several large ships, their iron chains rattling, were ready to weigh anchor. The air reverberated with sharp, loud whistles. Small sampans carrying workers across the river were well out toward the center of the river. The sun had already risen, casting its pale yellow, warm rays from the other shore, and giving people on the road long thin shadows. Wang Wei took a deep breath of the morning air, and as his flushed face was touched by the pleasantly cool breeze, he felt very comfortable. His whole body seemed filled to the bursting point. He was carefree, yet anxious to find the Riqing Company quay.

When Wang Wei found the quay, it was surprisingly quiet. There was no boat, only a rippling stretch of river. At a loss, he fixed his eyes on the water, not knowing whether he was late or early. He feared that the telegram was a trick Mary was playing on him, because with her taste and temperament, she was quite capable of such cruelty. Often all she considered was the satisfaction of her own impulses. He did not know what to do, but finally decided to go to the company office and inquire. The company's answer was that the boat would not reach the quay until two-thirty in the afternoon. This gave him new hope, although he still felt listless on his way back home.

After breakfast Wang Wei went to his workplace, where he sat for two hours translating newspapers from English into Chinese and from Chinese into English. He had been working hard recently, sometimes delivering documents to other organizations. He also attended frequent meetings where such topics as the business of the organization, various theoretical problems, and the correctness of recent political policies were discussed. Because of this, he was often so busy that he didn't return home until midnight. Yet there were also times when he could not rest in the morning because he had to draft planning outlines, organizational outlines, manifestoes, and correspondence. He had not had enough sleep for quite a few nights, so when he went to work this day he looked exhausted.

A unit of the [underground society] temporarily occupied this office-like room. The [society] had been established under the direction of the [Party] and was an organization that promoted the proletarian literary activity of a number of intellectuals. Since the organization's activities were illegal under the present government, an embroidery goods company sign was hung above the door. Several staff members came regularly, but young Wang Wei was the most respected among them as one who was never late or absent from work. When he arrived this morning, aside from the cleaning man, only the short secretary, Feng Fei, was there. Feng often came late since he lived far away, but today he was sitting there alone smoking leisurely. When Wang Wei entered, he was surprised to see him there.

"Hey, Feng, why so early?"

"It's not really early."

Noticing that Feng's slightly flat face was beaming, Wang Wei asked, "What is it? You look so happy."

"Oh, nothing . . ."

Yet Feng could not get a certain fortuitous encounter out of his mind. A month ago, he had noticed a woman ticket-seller on a bus, but they had never had an opportunity to talk. He would see her at the same time every day, and each time he saw her his respect for her increased. She was so unaffected, a capable woman whose face had that healthy color that came, not from makeup, but from working with a will and high spirits. From her appearance and her speech (she often argued with passengers and forcefully expressed her opinions), he concluded that she was an educated woman who had a kind of simple, clear understanding of politics that resulted from having class consciousness. He nearly spoke to her many times, for he was already feeling very close to her; but because of his habitual timidity, he always missed his chance. This day, however, he had left home earlier than usual to handle some extra business; and while at the bus stop, head down, as he thumbed through the pages of a local paper, he had suddenly heard a familiar voice. Turning around, he saw her standing behind him calmly looking at him and smiling, making him ill at ease.

"Hi there. You're early today," she said.

"Yes . . . right . . ." he sputtered.

"I'll be busy today," she continued. "I have to take another girl's place, so I won't have a break all day. She's sick, but can't ask for any time off. Tonight I'll have to buy some medicine to make an herbal brew for her. And you, sir, where do you work?"

"I'm on the staff of a company," he replied.

Looking him over, she shook her head and remarked, "No, you don't look like it. You look like you're still a student. I'm good at figuring people out."

After they had exchanged a few more words, the streetcar came. She had hopped aboard gracefully and, after saying hello to another ticket-seller, had taken over the wooden ticket board and canvas coin bag. When Feng was about to get off, he had casually remarked, "See you again," as though he were addressing an old acquaintance.

Now he was thinking again about what had just happened. He had never had much contact with women, and disliked the usual young misses who were students. The ticket-seller was the first woman he had ever paid any attention to. He made a lot of guesses about her background and created a glorious, gripping history for her. He did not notice that freshly shaven Wang Wei, despite being exhausted, was showing an even greater joy on his face.

On this day Wang Wei left early and also missed a meeting. At the dock, he finally fetched his dazzling beauty and several pieces of luggage, and took them home.

2

A sedan drove from the Huangpu River onto wide, smooth Victoria Avenue. Wang Wei took a small tender hand in his. Not knowing what to say at first, they just smiled silently at each other. They were both very happy. After a long time she broke the silence, "How are things going? You look like you've lost quite a bit of weight."

Touching his freshly shaved chin, he answered with a laugh, "I thought I looked better today."

He thought of how his beard was growing so rapidly lately and smiled again. He was going to tell her about it, but changed his mind. He would wait for her to discover it by herself. Holding her hand tightly, he said, "Mary, you look more beautiful than ever!"

He drew her soft hand up to his lips. She moved a little closer to him. He sighed and, with a sad look on his face, said, "Ah Mary, don't leave me again!"

She tenderly turned her face toward him, and the two pairs of lips that were longing to join pressed tightly together. Intoxicated and dizzy, they embraced each other gently and forgot everything else.

At a sharp turn, the car shifted suddenly, jolting them back to reality. They pulled apart. He hastily steadied the little suitcase that was swaying violently, and then, looking at the small round mirror up front, he noticed the driver's smile. This made him feel a little annoyed and embarrassed, but all he could do was smile back at that sly, grinning face.

After arriving at Wang Wei's apartment, they got out of the car in high spirits. Four times he ran from the small back door to the third floor. Her luggage was lined up on one side of the stairs. As he searched his pocket for the key, he looked at Mary and said, "The room might be too small for two people, but we can move somewhere else later, all right?"

The room was certainly not big and had only a few simple things in it: a bed, a desk, two chairs, a bookshelf, and a wardrobe. Because there weren't a lot of things, it really didn't appear to be all that small. It was just that the ceiling was low, which created a closed-in effect. Since Wang Wei was seldom at home, usually just to sleep, he hadn't noticed this. But Mary, who had just spent two days on the vast ocean, felt it immediately. She did not want to say anything, though, and on the contrary, praised the room for being clean and the occupant for his neatness.

"The credit goes to the woman who rented the room to me," Wang Wei explained. "She does all the cleaning. The furniture is hers too. She even provides me with tea. All of this convenience is the reason why I live here. Why don't I ask her to bring us some boiled water."

Mary stopped him. Looking at her wristwatch, which said about five o'clock, she asked, "What do you do about meals?"

"That depends. I don't have a fixed time and place to eat. Are you hungry?"

"I'm starving. I only had a bowl of thin rice porridge in the morning, and at noon I was in such a hurry that I didn't eat. Let's take care of filling our stomachs before we do anything else."

"All right." He picked up his hat and started to go.

"Where shall we go? Where do you usually go?" she asked.

Small, filthy, crowded restaurants flashed through his mind. Then he glanced at her outfit—the imported velvet coat with a fur collar, the neat gloves, and the shiny satin shoes—and burst out laughing, "We can't go to any of those places. Mary, lately I've been living in the style of the common people. Today let's go to a nice place as a treat to welcome you. We'll work out a long-term plan tomorrow. Tell me where you'd prefer to go."

Mary looked at him and smiled sweetly. "You'd like to treat me? How much money do you have?"

He figured out what was left in his pocket; perhaps four yuan or so. If they weren't extravagant it should be enough. Mary liked Cantonese cooking, so they hired a rickshaw to go to a restaurant that was quite far away.

They had an excellent and leisurely meal. Mary was in an agreeable mood and generous with her beauty, often taking a captivating pose for no particular small reason. She had taken off the hundred-and-twenty-yuan coat and was wearing only a thin, light green, tight-fitting, soft silk *qipao* that delicately revealed the intriguing parts of her body. She talked a lot about funny occasions when she had missed him and how she would never leave him again. She told him why she hadn't kept her promise and how, although she had known he was able to forgive her, she had suffered twice as much. Ah, how painful her recent life in Beiping had been. She hadn't wanted anyone else to know about this pain and had not understood these feelings herself. She said she only wanted him to know about this pain, and that if he gave her a little more love it would be all right. She spoke very movingly, even excessively, and he felt her pain himself. A kind of physical instinct pressed upon him, making him wish that at that moment he could press her down and enjoy again the wild intoxication of her beautiful flesh without having to use words to express his love. Several times he said, "Let's eat up quickly!"

It was different for Mary, though. The atmosphere of the restaurant stimulated her. The red lights shone over them and made Wang Wei look more handsome than usual and so earnest. As for herself, she had a slight fever and was sure this made her more attractive. As she sipped wine or black tea, her excitement increased. She enjoyed sitting with her lover on the soft seat, whispering hypnotic words, and forgetting everything else. She enjoyed the exciting sensations that made their hearts burn with barely controllable desire. Wanting very much to prolong this feeling, she was unwilling to leave. She was afraid that going back would break the mood. That place was cold and cheerless, and there were trivial things waiting for her to do. Wasn't her luggage still piled up in the middle of the room? She sipped her wine ever so slowly.

Wang Wei, on the other hand, gradually fell silent. Just a while ago he had been suffering from an unfulfilled beautiful desire. Controlling himself, he felt his entire body burning hot. Red capillaries filled his eyes and seemed ready to ignite. He remained silent, trying not to listen to her, to be vulnerable to her seduction. This was because he was really feeling more pain than pleasure. He even tried to think about some trivial things in order to relieve this unbearable emotion. He stayed silent, and pretended to be listening to her, but actually, his thoughts were slowly drifting away to many small matters. He should be forgiven for this because Mary was simply unaware of the suffering a young man commonly endures in the presence of a pretty lover.

The big clock in the restaurant struck seven. Wang Wei was shocked, for he suddenly recalled that he absolutely had to attend a meeting at seven-thirty that evening. Over twenty people would be waiting for him, the chairman. He looked hesitantly at his beautiful partner, not knowing what to do. He really had to go, and even if he set out right away, he would probably still be late. But how could he do that? How could he just leave Mary alone in the restaurant? He became very nervous and angrily snapped at the waiter, "Hurry up and bring the rice!"

Mary gave him a wondering look, but said in a charming voice, "All right, let's eat."

They finished eating in a great hurry, after which Wang Wei stood up and walked out. Mary had not even put on her coat, so she was a little irritated. She did not, however, let her feelings show, and silently followed him as he walked quickly out onto the street. They hopped into separate rickshaws and were soon flying toward home. She felt an indescribable annoyance, but she forgave and followed him.

Once they arrived, Wang Wei felt sorry for Mary. He took her into his arms, kissed her, and stretching her full length on the bed, begged, "A thousand apologies, my love! I've got to leave you for a while, but I'll be back soon. I'll explain it all when I come back. Anyway, you must try to understand me. I love you very much, but I have too much work to do. Later on, maybe I'll find a way to do less, but for now there's no way. Well, sleep tight. I'll help you unpack your things after I get back. Okay, close your eyes. Don't hate me! I have to go."

Mary was baffled. Disheartened, she lay in the bed and looked at him. Wang Wei turned and rushed out the door. All she heard was the sound of his feet running quickly down the stairs.

As soon as Wang Wei left Mary, he forgot about her. Running like crazy down the street, he thought of the people who were waiting for him. They were certainly even more anxious than he was.

3

The beautiful, lively young woman who had been left behind lay on the large bed alone. She really had a gentle, beautiful heart. She had many intense interests that she had brought with her from afar. She would generously give this man much affection and tenderness if he would adore her. In fact, it was only her need for this kind of considerate care and some measure of excitement that had sustained her through all the trouble of coming here. Now what? What was she getting? She was treated coldly. He left her here all alone and went somewhere else. What could be more important than the reunion of two lovers after a long separation? She lay on the bed in frustration for quite some time. The dim yellowish light of the sixteen-watt bulb reflected off the ceiling. She thought about Wang Wei. She didn't understand, but she couldn't help feeling angry, for what he had done had hurt her pride. She thought of moving all her things to a hotel in a fit of pique, but she really loved him too much. In fact, she had become less bold than before and was willing to put herself at risk to forgive him. Perhaps he really did have something more important to handle. Perhaps he would be back any minute. She cheered herself up, got out of bed, and started to straighten up her things. Her face felt a little uncomfortable and she wanted to wash it. Also, most important, she wanted to change her clothes, because her coat was too good to be rubbing up against the things in this room. She opened up a fine leather suitcase that contained quite a few colorful playthings. She took them out and set them one by one on his desk, which she discovered was completely bare. Next she took out several nicely wrapped packages that contained fine gifts she had brought him—a beautiful tie, two colorful silk handkerchiefs, and some other things, such as buttons. As she held these things, her heart softened. She imagined how happy he'd be and how lovely he'd think she was when he saw these gifts. Lovingly, she pushed these things to a corner of the desk. Last, she took out a thin, quilted *qipao*. It wasn't quite new and was made of black satin.

She took off her coat in front of the wardrobe mirror and in the dim light looked at her pretty figure. Her slightly flushed face was framed by thick black hair and was held high by the high collar of her light green dress. She looked quite dignified and exciting. Slowly she unbuttoned her dress to reveal the lace of her pink slip. She looked at her half-nude body with affectionate, playful eyes. Only after enjoying the sight of her white neck and shoulders for a long while did she reluctantly cover them with the quilted *qipao*. This dress was so long that the hem covered her ankles, making her look taller. She was truly beautiful and a pleasure to behold. It seemed that whatever style and color she wore only added to her beauty. She opened the wardrobe and found it practically empty. There wasn't a single item of clothing, just a few pairs of socks in a corner and several empty hangers. She was puzzled, and suspected that there must be a suitcase somewhere where Wang Wei had placed his clothing. She hung her beautiful dresses in the pitiful wardrobe and then started to look for his suitcase. She found two of them lying under the bed. As the bookcase was full of books, perhaps he hadn't taken his clothing out and still had it packed in his suitcases. She thought of how Wang Wei wasn't one for dressing up, how he often ruined good clothes and wore old, worn-out things. She continued to unpack her own things, but even though many items that she wanted to use were placed in a convenient place, the room was still a mess. Several gaping suitcases lay open on the floor, and used wrapping paper was scattered all over. She was very tired and really felt unable to straighten everything up at once. Actually, there wasn't that much to do, but she couldn't handle it. She became angry and, not wanting to see the pile of trash anymore, lay down on the bed again and tried to sleep.

It was already eleven o'clock. When she had been occupied with her lovely treasures and passing the time admiring herself, she hadn't realized that it was so late. However, tired though she was, she still couldn't fall asleep. She was feeling lonely and couldn't get Wang Wei off her mind. She felt more anxious and distressed than when she had been on the ship. She simply couldn't understand him. Why wasn't he back yet? Why had he left her alone in such a desolate room for such a long time? Something was up, for in their past there had been only tenderness and affection between them.

Mary was young and pretty. For years she had easily attracted the interest of men. She was clever enough to realize this and accepted it with pleasure. Yet she loved no one but herself. She knew she was basking in the radiance of her own youth. She wanted to hold onto this throne forever instead of letting someone seize it. Having read many works of fiction and seen many movies, she knew that marriage was the end of a woman's life. First one became a tender, docile housewife, then a good mother who loved her husband and children. What might be called the tender love of family would then take away many other possible joys, and in the blink of an eye, a woman's hair would be white, her emotions exhausted, and she would be allowing her husband love affairs on the outside. All she could do then was set her loving old woman's heart in order and calmly wait to become a grandmother. What was so wonderful about that? She didn't need that. She was quite happy with what she had. She was leading a life of freedom, and the money she received from home, though not enough for her to be extravagant, was certainly sufficient for her needs. She also had many friends who adapted to her every change of mood like obedient servants. She had lived happily like this for a long time. Strangers might think that she had considerable experience and had known frustration, but actually, her heart had never been touched by anyone. All that had happened was that her face had become more beautiful than ever and she had cultivated a distinctive style that made her even more attractive.

It might have been possible to live according to her ideal because her appeal to the opposite sex would not have diminished that quickly. However, she had been conquered by Wang Wei's affection, and her entire view had changed. Although she had once despised men's love, Wang Wei's every move expressed a masculine love that did not deserve humiliation. She was moved by his behavior, and could not control herself; so she had fled to Beiping because she did not want to yield. In Beiping there were a number of men who loved her even more than Wang Wei. Once she had been happy to live there, but now, even though she joked with people as she always had, there was a firm, reserved figure that she could not forget. She was deeply impressed by his special qualities and wanted to be with him again. It seemed that what he had given her was not love, but a boundless new hope for life and an energy that she had never experienced before. Then just as she was longing for him, he had rushed heroically to Beiping like a legendary passionate warrior. This action suited her perfectly, and she responded to his bravado with generous affection. For some time they lived together romantically and tenderly. During that period, she was genuinely happy and enjoyed life as never before. However, being accustomed to freedom, she slowly began to feel that the sacrifice was too great. She was afraid—afraid of living an ordinary life, afraid of becoming a mother, and afraid of losing her friends. To lose all of her admirers for one man would not be worth it. She loved Wang Wei and wanted to hold on to that feeling, but for the time being she wanted to be apart from him. They could be a pair of free lovers and lifelong friends, but she didn't want to be husband and wife, cuddling up against each other like two tame doves. So she made up her mind to flee. She went back home, but after staying for a short time, she felt even more disgusted with family life, and became more determined than ever to leave Wang Wei. That is why she didn't keep her promise and went to cold Beiping. She wanted to stay in that tranquil ancient kingdom for two years, until she graduated from college. At first everything went fine. But soon she began to think of Wang Wei. As his letters dwindled off, her mind grew more and more confused. She was afraid that this warm-hearted person would drift away. In the end she decided to sacrifice everything and go to Shanghai. She simply could not leave this man. She cursed her stupidity and thought of her earlier life. "Ah, that was life! But what is this?" She went anyway, taking her passionate heart and casting it into the bosom of her lover, whom she had loved and respected. He was the man of her dreams.

Now what? This time he had really offended her. How could he treat her like this? She was both angry and sad. She waited until twelve o'clock, then one. Finally she heard the sound of light footsteps running up the stairs. She knew they were his. Suddenly a feeling of sadness overwhelmed her, and before she knew it, a teardrop had fallen silently onto the sleeve of her long black *qipao*.

4

Wang Wei tiptoed in. At this moment all problems and activities disappeared from his mind. He was prepared to suffer in patience the torture of her love and to give her extra tender affection. He knew that it would be hard for her to understand and forgive him for his behavior tonight because she didn't know about the recent change in his outlook on life. But afterward he could let her know, and she would not only be sympathetic, but would encourage and join him. He walked softly to the bed and bent down to look at her. She didn't make a sound, as though she were asleep. He sat down next to her, but dared not disturb her. He looked at the messy room. It was like the tangle in his mind, where there was so much to think about and so much confusion that he couldn't straighten it out. For instance, he thought of his work and what it would mean to live with Mary. He didn't think he had the time or energy to do all that was expected of him. The best thing, he thought, would be to tell Mary everything right away. She would be happy and they could work together. Besides being in love, they could discuss many important questions, such as the world economy, politics, and how to liberate the laboring masses. Their opinions might differ and then they would argue. Perhaps Mary would be correct. In the end they would agree and still be lovers. He lowered his head again and looked at her. She had such beauty, such noble beauty. Every inch of her body testified to the fact that she was fit only for a happy life, nutritious food, and pure fresh air. Her every movement was fit only for high society. Yet, he thought, if Mary gave up her extravagant clothing for a coat of homespun cloth, it would highlight her distinctive qualities even more. If she could learn to be a little less delicate, she could have a different style of beauty. It was possible. As he looked at her again, she seemed to change form and become his ideal. She was strong, fit, and slightly masculine, but she still retained her original, seductive beauty. He wanted to kiss her, but he stopped for fear of waking her. He continued to think about many things, all of them dreams of being together with Mary. Ah, they were such happy dreams, but they were not something that Mary could understand.

A long time passed. Wang Wei lay down next to Mary in utter exhaustion, but his mind was very clear. He saw the fulfillment and glory of his future life. He held his happiness in his own hands, just as a helmsman holds the rudder. He could not fall asleep because he was overtired, his head ached, and his mind was still working. Now and then he smelled the fragrance of Mary's body. This excited him, and he began to have wild desires.

Wang Wei was too close to Mary. She could hear his heart beat, and his rapid breathing brushed softly against her, making her skin tingle. She hadn't been asleep, just a little angry and unwilling to talk to him. When she couldn't stand it any longer, she turned quietly away, thinking of moving a little farther from him.

"Are you awake, Mary? I've been waiting a long time."

He reached toward her. She pushed his arm away and said in a soft, cold voice, "I haven't slept a minute."

Her tone of voice said it all. He moved closer, hugged her apologetically, and pleaded.

"Will you let me explain, Mary? You should know that you've misunderstood me. Have pity on me! You've already given me too much. Even if you only stayed for one hour, I couldn't express in an entire lifetime my gratitude for your coming from Beiping. If you want to be cruel, I deserve any pain you inflict upon me. But don't misjudge me, Mary. I can bear being wrongly judged, but when I see you angry because of your misunderstanding, I feel hurt. I know that you're angry with me, and perhaps you are suspicious of me too, but can you let me explain? In fact, it's really because . . ."

"No, don't say anything. I don't like to hear explanations. Explanations are nothing but high-sounding excuses. I'm certainly not angry with you. You have your freedom. You can arrange your time however you want. I only hate myself for being too weak and valuing love too highly."

"Mary, I don't want us to spoil our life together. I don't want to quarrel with you on this first happy night. I'm in the wrong, but you will forgive me eventually. You really don't know how much I love you."

Wang Wei reached out again to hold her. Her anger was not appeased, but she did not want to talk about it anymore. She let him hold her.

Wang Wei used loving phrases and slowly mollified her. He wasn't afraid to utter moving expressions, and at the right moment he was mischievous and cute. It was not that he liked to be hypocritical like this, but he knew that some of these techniques were indispensable if he was to make her love him a little more. Also, they were sincere. As a matter of fact, Mary soon forgot the recent unpleasantness and, cradling her head in his arms, said, "I was worried because you came back so late. Do you often come back this late?"

He answered that he often did. He usually had work to do, and even when he came back early, he still was unable to sleep. He said that he felt lonely in the room all by himself. His head was bowed, and from time to time he stroked Mary's face and hair. Mary felt that he was much thinner than before. She held his cheeks and said, "You've lost weight, Wang Wei!"

"Now I can start getting healthier because you're here."

But Mary was thinking that perhaps he'd be even busier and have less time to rest.

They forgot how tired they were and went on chatting. Sometimes they talked like little children, and said funny things that only people in love could understand. Only when dawn was breaking did they try to fall asleep in each other's embrace and lie there quietly with their eyes closed.

Because they were madly in love, he was still very passionate and she became more tender. So they lived together happily and peacefully for a short while.

5

Wang Wei usually got up every day at about eight o'clock, a little earlier than she did. He would straighten up the room, then read the newspaper, soaking up all the news he could. He wanted to learn everything he could about the world economy, developments on revolution in China, and evidence of the daily weakening of the ruling class, so he could prove the correctness of the political line that had been decided upon. He also searched for opposing arguments in reactionary papers and looked for indications of rumor and deceit. He was most interested in *Western Newsworld,* for it was more accurate than all the major Chinese newspapers and published exciting news that couldn't be found in China's [Communist] newspapers. This paper carried shocking stories under banner headlines and openly discussed the Chinese revolution from its capitalist, imperialist standpoint. It called for the Chinese warlords to wake up to the development and the strength of the power opposed to them, to recognize that this power was definitely not just bandits or a mob, as they thought it to be. Wang Wei, naturally, wasn't happy with this view and looked only for actual news stories that would encourage him. He also had to read some other papers in which he looked for speeches and reports on both domestic and international policies, decisions on construction and revolution, and news about factories. Sometimes he had to write things, like outlines of a plan or tasks ahead. At such times his brain seemed to expand as many thoughts and proposals welled up within it, but he had to find a place for them. Since he wasn't all that accustomed to this kind of work, he had to think carefully about it, put it in order item by item, and then lay it out on paper. Three months before he had still been a melancholy student who could easily and very quickly have produced moving, clever, and touching lines in a poem of equal length. When Wang Wei was about to finish this daily task, the beautiful one would awaken. She looked so enchanting, with her hair spread over the pillow; and when she noticed that her man wasn't beside her, she would hum softly, and Wang Wei would know that it was time to finish up. He would put everything aside and walk over to the bed. Two long arms as snowy white as lotus root would stretch out above the green quilt, and sometimes he would catch a glimpse of her breast under the white or pink embroidered collar of her sleeveless undergarment. Her skin, with its rosy hue after a good night's sleep, highlighted her eyebrows, eyes, nose, and lips, and made shadowy areas more distinct. Wang Wei would be even more bewildered by this beautiful form. Sometimes he would kiss her violently, and sometimes, not daring to kiss her, he would just gaze at her quietly with sincere admiration. When that happened, she would be both charming and reproachful, saying to him with the air of a spoiled child, "You've sneaked out of bed and left me alone again."

Then he would explain, sometimes with words but more often with actions. He was still completely enraptured with her and passionately in love with her. Even though she was sometimes unhappy with him for not spending as much time with her as before, she could only forgive him. She would have to lie in bed for a while before getting up, and he would lie there beside her. This was such tender enjoyment! They would forget everything as they kissed and made dreamy conversation. For him, her innocence was absolutely lovable!

If she had a slight headache from sleeping too much, she would stretch lazily before kicking the soft quilts with her snowy white bare feet and climbing out of bed. Then Wang Wei would hustle back and forth looking for little things like garters, dainty silk underwear, and a variety of feminine paraphernalia whose names he didn't know. She would then comb her hair and get dressed while he took meticulous care of her. She was very pleased with him, this tender slave who was also such a fortunate slave!

Later they would walk hand in hand to a small nearby restaurant to eat. Sometimes they went to a Cantonese restaurant because she liked Cantonese food. Occasionally they went to a small Western-style restaurant because she liked its quiet setting. At times like these, he would become nervous because he could see the clock on the restaurant wall moving very quickly, and he didn't have a lot of time to keep her company. Saying goodbye was always the most difficult part of the day for him.

After eating they would go back home. He couldn't help rushing, and she would realize that it would soon be time to part again. Hating to see him in such a hurry, she'd be silent for a long while, and then he would pause for a moment before going. But such moments were not pleasant, and eventually he had to kiss her cold cheek apologetically and rush off.

Now it was always he who was a late arrival at that place where he had to go. He appeared more rushed in doing his translations, and when several others would discuss something at another table, even if he wanted to listen, he didn't have the time. All he could do was glance at them once in a while. Once the short fellow, Feng Fei, who always had a happy expression, said to him, "What's happening? You seem to be preoccupied with other things lately! You look more tired every day."

Wang Wei simply answered with an "umm." He really hadn't had enough time lately to observe Feng's increasingly radiant face. Feng Fei and the woman ticket-seller had already become close friends.

Wang Wei would quickly finish what he had to do, then hurry off to somewhere else. It was not the same place every day. Sometimes he had to go a long way to attend a meeting, and this took time as well as physical and mental energy. Many controversial issues would be waiting for him, and there would always be disagreement. They would continue arguing for a long time and not end the meeting until it was time to eat. Then, because of the distance, he couldn't return home quickly, so most of the time he wasn't able to eat supper with Mary. In addition, he usually was busy at night, and although he tried to reduce his workload, he couldn't. As a result, the earliest he could get home was eleven o'clock. And even that did not mean that he had solved all the day's problems.

Only occasionally was Wang Wei free to return home by dinner time. This was the happiest time for Mary, since she could have him alone the whole evening. In the enjoyment of love, Mary was forever insatiable. She'd drag him out onto the street to look for little restaurants that they had never been to before, or sometimes they would go to larger ones. After dinner they would walk along the brilliantly illuminated, bustling streets because it was still too early for the late movie. She often paused before windows that had the most delicate items on display and would say in a tone of surprise, "Oh, that's really nice!"

Wang Wei didn't have the slightest interest in such things, but he had to smile and go along with her. Sometimes she was not satisfied with his response and would turn to look at him and ask, "Do you mean it's not good? But it's gorgeous, really gorgeous!"

Wang Wei then had to answer, "Yes, it's very nice. The rich really know how to enjoy life. There'll come a day when we confiscate it all."

He meant to make her happy with such banter, but she would get angry and answer him seriously, "You're the only one who thinks so. I'd never want to possess such luxuries."

She would start to pout and walk away from the window as if she didn't care. At these times she looked as beautiful as an imperious queen. Wang Wei would say a few words of praise, and slowly she would forget her pique and start smiling again like an innocent child.

When there was still lots of time, Mary would insist on going to large stores to buy fruit. The fruit, naturally, was good, but it was expensive. Mary, however, was not one to think about small numbers, so she would ask Wang Wei to pay without a second thought. Wang Wei had become so poor, however, that he often walked long distances instead of taking a third-class streetcar, so on these occasions, they usually used Mary's money. He felt that they were spending too much, but reluctant to say anything, he simply obeyed her.

After this they would go to a deluxe movie theater, buy tickets, climb the elegantly carved stairway, pass through the doors where handsome ushers were standing, and take their seats. At such times she was happy. It didn't matter when the movie started or if she liked it or not. She had spent a lot of money, and spending money was the best way to satisfy her vanity. At these moments she would be sitting in Shanghai's first and foremost place of entertainment. Not far from her sat well-dressed foreign wives, and from time to time one could smell the fragrance of their superior perfume. She was prettier than they were, and her makeup probably cost as much as theirs. Some people would look at her, then size up Wang Wei, who was good looking in a masculine way. He displayed a very male determination and an incontestable dignity. Mary loved him for this. However, Wang Wei did not have a natty appearance. He often wore shabby clothes, and no matter how many times she mentioned it, it was still the same. Over the past few years, he had not had even one new outfit made. Now, because he was so short of money, there was even less chance that he'd buy something. She had once wanted to get him a nice lined overcoat as a gift, but he had refused it. In fact, he did not think he needed an overcoat or had the time to go to a tailor.

When the movie started, Mary was happy, no matter what it was. She did not come for an exciting plot, because the ones she imagined were always better. Even less did she need to look for ideas and art from the Americans. She was very familiar with what appeared on the screen. If she wanted to find ideas and art, she could read books. Coming to the theater was strictly for enjoyment. Of the one yuan that she spent to attend the movie, eighty cents was for the soft, cushioned chair, the shiny brass banisters, the velvet curtains, and the pleasing music. Only a country bumpkin would come solely for the movie.

As for Wang Wei, in the past he had been fascinated by these pictures. He had often come when he had nothing else to do to see the romantic plots, the stirring tragi-comedies, and the half-nude bodies. Now that he was so busy, he no longer had an interest in such meaningless works, no matter how many millions of dollars had been invested in them. Now he considered these movies senseless, or even hateful, because they so easily numbed people's minds and influenced society for the worse. He and people like him could not approve of these things that were merely entertainment for ignorant capitalist matrons and young ladies. However, for the sake of Mary, the person who loved him, he put up with it. He thought of how he often left her home alone and how this was a way to make her happy. It was a sacrifice for him but a compensation for her.

They would amuse themselves until late at night before heading home. It was never enough for Mary, but when she saw that Wang Wei was exhausted, she controlled her excitement. Wang Wei would be so tired that his eyes would be red, his face puffy, his joints stiff. As soon as they reached home he always fell fast asleep, something that Mary also regretted.

6

Leading a life like this could be considered enjoyable, but when it lasted too long, problems arose. Wang Wei was worn out from the constant lack of sleep, while Mary had too much time on her hands. Loneliness annoyed her, and she often said to him, "I feel that our past was so wonderful. How can I make you come back to me and belong to me forever? Now I feel that this is probably just a woman's illusion. Ah, Wang Wei, whenever I think of my weak points, a woman's weak points, I start to hate men." [7]

Wang Wei knew that they were an incompatible pair. If Mary were a peasant girl, a factory worker, or a high school student, then they would get along very well because there would be only one idea, one outlook. He would lead her and she would obey. But Mary was from a relatively well-to-do family and had never experienced hardship. Her intelligence made her proud and her learning confirmed her attitude toward society. She was engrossed in the pursuit of pleasure. She believed in herself and would yield to no one. Sometimes she could become very firm and determined. Wang Wei saw this crisis, like the world economic crisis, spreading out before his eyes. He loved Mary. First, she possessed flawless beauty. She was intelligent, had skill in dealing with others, and was courageous. Her shortcoming was her upper-class upbringing, which taught her to indulge herself in a world of fantasy. She had no desire to deal with the real world because it was too troublesome and too tiresome, especially those things that she saw as ugly and commonplace. She was already twenty years old, and the most important thing for her was to keep looking young. She did not want to let anything snatch away her youth. Wang Wei understood this well. He often searched for a way to change her, but his methods were slightly clumsy, and Mary would realize what he was up to. Then she would mock him.

"In a word, Wang Wei, you've wasted your efforts again. If I wanted to join the revolution, I would have done so long ago. You'd better believe that I haven't lacked the opportunity. It's not that I don't believe in revolution: I'm just tired of it. You really don't need to use your propaganda on me. And as for yourself, let me tell you right here and now, just wait and see, one day you will lose your life for it. Ah, it isn't worth it. You're much more useful alive than dead."

She spoke from the heart, for she really was growing tired of all this. She had never discussed his work with him and had never read the books and newspapers he brought home. Her interest focused entirely on herself. She had read some of the minor newspapers, but they only reported news about campus queens, sports celebrities, film stars, and pimps and prostitutes. Wang Wei disapproved and sometimes, unable to control himself, would say to her, "Mary! I don't think that this is very worthwhile entertainment. You didn't have this inclination before."

Mary would respond, "If you stayed at home, I wouldn't have to read these. I'm just too lonely. I need something to while away the time, but your books don't amuse me."

"Then come along with me, how about that? You can treat it as a lark."

Mary would give him a sour smile.

After he urged her several times to come to work with him, Mary began to waver. Her lonesomeness was getting unbearable. So one day she decided to go with him to a routine meeting.

After lunch she began to make herself up very carefully. She expected that the people at the meeting would all be quite ragged, even more pitiful than Wang Wei. She had heard that these people were all very poor. She did not mean to be arrogant or show off, but she wanted to shock them with her beauty. She wanted to disturb the minds of those revolutionaries. She was very happy about this romantic notion and its imagined success.

Mary gazed into the mirror until she could not find a single flaw; only then was she satisfied. She sat down and waited anxiously until three o'clock, when Wang Wei ran back pantingly to pick her up. She wanted to look in the mirror one more time to seek his approval, but there wasn't time. Seeing that she was ready, Wang Wei said happily, "Wonderful, I was worried you might not be ready. Let's go. I'm late again." Paying no attention to her clothes or appearance, he walked hurriedly ahead of her.

As predicted, they were late. A discussion on a general plan and concrete steps to carry out a program was already underway, so no one greeted the latecomers. They only glanced their way and then returned to their discussion. As Wang Wei sat down with Mary at one corner of the table, someone whispered to him, "Wang Wei, good heavens! You're always late for meetings. If this happens again, you'll be disciplined."

Nobody paid any attention to Mary, except for one or two who scanned her face for a second. It did not please them.

Mary looked at the seven or eight people. Two were wearing long scholars' robes and the rest were in Western suits. They were quite young, and two of them looked like little street urchins. They all shared a common quality, namely, that they looked dynamic, vigorous, and full of vitality. Mary had already sensed this. She alone did not have this quality.

Mary was often high-spirited too, but what stimulated her? It was definitely not to make progress in life. Her excitement lay in erotic pleasures, in the pursuit and enjoyment of physical desire. Of course, at certain times and places, this was enchanting and bewitching, but in this place it was obviously colorless and ugly. She became faintly conscious of this and started to feel an inexpressible unhappiness.

At this time Wang Wei seemed to have forgotten her completely. He appeared more cool-headed and methodical than ever. He had the most ideas and he was the one most to the point. He not only didn't pay any attention to Mary, he didn't even look at her. Several times she nudged his elbow to express her discomfort, but instead of taking the hint, he moved his arm away. Slowly she became angry with him.

The longer Mary sat there, the more bored she felt. She stopped listening, for what they were doing had nothing to do with her. She did not know why, but she even started to hate these people. All she could think of was leaving, but there wasn't any opportunity to say something to Wang Wei. Five o'clock. Six o'clock. Night fell. She saw that there was no sign of a break. She had sat so long that she was feeling fidgety all over. She was contemplating showing some anger. Finally she stood up with a determined look on her face. Only then did Wang Wei ask, "What do you want?"

"I have to leave to do something," she answered defiantly.

"All right, I'll be finished in a little while."

Wang Wei rose slightly and handed her the big red leather handbag she had forgotten. By now everyone was looking at her. Their eyes followed her out of the room with a look of disapproval. She stalked out of the room with the haughty stride that only an aristocratic woman possesses.

The meeting went on without interruption until seven-thirty. As Wang Wei took his hat and was about to leave, the chairman of the meeting, Shuyin, asked him, "Are you busy tonight?"

Wang Wei thought for a while and said no.

"Let's go and have supper then." As he spoke, Shuyin looked at the one-yuan bill he had just taken out of his pocket. Wang Wei was reminded of Mary and said he had to go back home.

"There's not enough time. From here to your house takes at least an hour. Are you worried that she's waiting impatiently for you?"

He began to waver.

"Is the young lady who came today the one you're about to recommend for membership?" Shuyin asked.

"Yes. I think she's very capable, and I hope she'll like being one of us."

Frowning a little, Shuyin unconsciously lowered his voice, "In my opinion, Wang Wei, you won't succeed! She's a woman set in her ways."

Wang Wei nodded gloomily and answered, "I've been worried about that painful stage because Mary could never put up with it. I realize now that she has endured too much already."

In the end Wang Wei decided to go home to eat. He waited there for Mary for quite a long time, but she did not come back. It was sheer agony! He recalled how Mary had often waited for him like this and felt more sorry for her. He prepared to wait for her and show her warmth after she returned.

7

At midnight, when Wang Wei was so tired he nearly fell asleep, he heard the click of her high-heeled shoes coming up the stairs. Wang Wei awkwardly got up to greet her. In the dim light, he did not see the trace of unhappiness on her face as she said in a cheery, sharp voice, "Why aren't you in bed? Sorry to have kept you waiting so long."

Standing in front of the mirror, she examined her warm face. Wang Wei asked in a relaxed manner, "Where have you been, Mary?"

"You don't have to know. It has nothing to do with you. Tell me, when did I ever question you?"

"But . . ." Wang Wei walked over to her with a pitiful expression on his face. "Ah, Mary, are you angry with me?"

"No." She laughed and kissed him on the cheek.

"But, Mary, you have to tell me."

Mary laughed happily. Seeing the wrinkles of worry deeply etched in his face, she savored the joy of victory. She actually began to have a cruel desire for revenge, wanting to torture him for his neglect, which was intolerable for a women who craves affection.

She would never forget that moment at the meeting when she had stopped existing as a person, especially in Wang Wei's mind. She had been sitting so close to him. Why for so many hours hadn't he thought of her or looked over at her and realized that she was not used to such activity. Moreover, when she left, he hadn't seen her off or talked with her. Such behavior was nothing less than mistreatment for a proud woman. When she walked out of the meeting, she had almost burst into tears. She had hated Wang Wei, those people, and that so-called meeting! After sitting there for several hours listening to all that talk, she found not even one word earned her admiration. Sitting like that and talking all day long came as a disappointment. She was not, definitely not, opposed to a revolution and was certainly willing to work hard. But she didn't see how all this talk was going to create a revolution.

Naturally, this idea sprung from her vanity, but from this point on she lost some respect for Wang Wei. Because she looked down on his work, she felt an unreasonable hatred and scorn toward him. His leaving her alone at home became unbearable. In the past, she had accepted the situation because she loved him and, rather than interfere, respected his wishes. But now she understood everything. She would have to drag him back. He should not have a life separate from her. If he resisted, she planned to make him suffer, to avenge the love she had granted him that he had not returned sufficiently. Once her mind was made up, she had begun by going out alone for a walk. She prepared first to give him something bitter to taste and make him wait anxiously at home for her. She had gone to a restaurant for dinner. It was crowded with young couples and groups of young people, and she was the only one there all alone. Many people looked at her in surprise, making her feel uncomfortable. She kept thinking about Wang Wei, but soon she heard a surprised and happy voice from a table opposite hers: "Well, Mary, hello. Is it really you?"

She raised her head and saw a woman of medium height, wearing a Western-style outfit, rushing toward her. She was so happy her heart jumped.

"Oh, Molan!" she called out.

They grasped each other's hands and looked at one another for a long while before Molan asked Mary in a puzzled voice, "Are you by yourself?"

Mary felt a little embarrassed and told her that she had come with a girlfriend who had had to leave earlier, and that was why she was alone.

"Ah, then, you are lonesome. Come join us."

Mary wanted to say no, but Molan had already called to the white-clad waiter. She had no choice but to follow Molan to the other table. Two men and a woman were sitting there. As Molan introduced them, Mary looked them over. They were all good-looking, fashionable people, but none of them looked as good to her as Wang Wei. Wang Wei didn't have that common air. Mary braced herself because their eyes were following her every move. Partly out of flattery and partly out of admiration, Molan complimented Mary, "Well, it's been almost a year since we've seen each other, and you're more beautiful than ever, Mary. How do you do it?"

Everyone trained their eyes on her outfit and on her. This was the result of the several hours she had spent in front of the mirror preparing to elicit compliments.

Mary and Molan had been very good friends in the past. Now they had met again at a time when she was lonely. How could she not be happy? So even though at times she still thought of Wang Wei, she ate her dinner in a good mood.

Molan wanted to go to see where she lived, but she preferred not to return right away and invited Molan to see a movie. Molan liked a good time, so naturally she agreed. Mary intentionally chose a place relatively far from home, so it would take longer to get back and Wang Wei would have to wait even longer.

The result was exactly what Mary had hoped for, with Wang Wei waiting for her anxiously. Even without looking carefully, she could tell that this was a time to be satisfied. Although she finally yielded to his repeated questioning and told him where she'd been, she did not tell him about

Molan. He felt sorry for her and said that after this he wanted to keep her company, because he realized how lonely it was to be alone, particularly in Mary's situation. Mary, however, did not say much, as if she did not really care one way or the other. She yawned a few times, took off her long *qipao,* lay down on the bed, and fell fast asleep.

The next day saw their usual morning routine. Wang Wei got up before getting enough sleep, and Mary lay down on the bed and fell asleep. The day after that was once again the same, and Wang Wei got up before getting enough sleep. But then Mary awoke with a start and jumped out of bed. She didn't help him at all as he did the tedious job of cleaning up, paying attention only to making up in front of the mirror.

"Mary, why are you getting up so early?" he asked her.

"I can't sleep," she answered indifferently.

She was ready at half past ten. "How about going to eat a little early?" she suggested.

"Why not, let's go." He was a little unhappy because she was making him postpone his morning assignment.

They went out to eat, but spoke very little as if there were nothing to talk about. On their way back home, however, Mary said with a smile, "I don't think that either one of us needs to go back. You can go to work, since you probably have a lot to do. As for me, I want to visit a friend whom I haven't seen for a long time."

She bade him goodbye with her eyes and walked off quickly in the opposite direction. Wang Wei ran to catch her, asked where she was going, but she gave him a determined look and asked angrily, "Why are you trying to control me?"

Wang Wei had more questions, but she jumped into a rickshaw. He could only stand there at a loss, watching as she went away. He then walked home listlessly.

His place was a total mess. Clothes and stockings that Mary had worn were everywhere and the washbasin was full of dirty water with grease from cosmetics floating on the surface. He had thought of using this extra time to do some work, but he was preoccupied with thoughts of Mary. He wasn't angry with her; he felt sorry for her. He decided that she had left him today because she was still angry with him, and that although she had acted indifferently, she actually was feeling depressed. He lay down on the bed, that bed that still retained the fragrance of her body, and sank deep into thoughts of Mary and her future. She was so intelligent. He didn't want to imagine that one day they might part. He wanted to walk with her hand in hand down the same road. He hoped that Mary would keep up with the changes of the era and stop drifting. He really needed to be with her.

8

From then on, Mary was seldom at home because of her visits to Molan and other old friends. She didn't feel lonesome when she was away from Wang Wei, but since she was still in love with him, she often felt a slight ache. Wang Wei was also suffering. He saw things more clearly than Mary did and thought that if one day she should leave him, although it would be awkward for him, it would be hardest for her. The reason was that he was busy and could become absorbed in his work. His faith would still exist and would not change at the loss of a woman. Although at the time he would feel sad, he could use another kind of power and his reason to fill in the void left by that love. But as for Mary, she was only a woman who liked fantasy and pleasure. If her surroundings turned bad, she would not have the strength to pick herself up, and she might be beaten down by her sorrow. He considered every aspect of her situation and wanted, for her sake, to pull her back. However, because Mary came back too late every night, sometimes when he was already fast asleep, he didn't have a chance to do it. In addition, in the morning Mary often got up earlier than he did. She had become indifferent, and when he wanted to say something affectionate, she employed various means to stop him. Although he had good intentions, he didn't have much time, so how could he devote his whole mind to this affair? They continued on like this until one night when Mary came in just as Wang Wei was turning back the covers. She seemed to have had more wine than usual, and her face was rosy. Without thinking, he said to her, "Mary, go look in the mirror. You're so beautiful!"

Had this been in the past, hearing the compliment would have thrilled her and she would have given him a charming smile in return. Now, however, she only said coldly, "None of that nonsense!"

Seeming to be completely wrapped up in herself, Mary kept her mouth tightly shut and went to bed. Although Wang Wei was lying in bed next to her, he didn't receive the slightest trace of warmth. He thought of their past affection and love, and sighed without meaning to.

"Why are you sighing like that?" Mary asked. "You're keeping me awake."

"I was thinking of our past . . ."

"The past is history! What's there to think about?"

"Those were sweet times! But now . . . I hate to tell you, Mary, but you've made me suffer quite enough!"

At this Mary became very angry. Using the direct, frightening manner that was one of her special qualities, she yelled at Wang Wei, "I made you suffer? Nonsense! It's you who has made me suffer! What pain do

you have? During the day, you go out to 'work.' You have a lot of comrades! You have hope! You have goals! At night you come home and rest.
You have a woman whom you can kiss anytime you want! As for me, I
have nothing. All day I roam around. I have boredom, loneliness, and
the deep regret that comes from losing my love! Yet I still put up with it.
I keep you company and serve as your amusement after your tiring day.
I've never uttered a word of complaint, while you sigh and complain
about me . . ."

Anger choked off her last words and her entire body was convulsed.

These irrational words almost made Wang Wei lose his temper too,
but when he saw Mary in such a state of hysteria he controlled himself
and just said, "Don't be like that! Don't be like that!"

Mary was silent for a long time with her head buried under the covers.
Then Wang Wei heard the muffled sound of sobbing. Unable to bear it,
he touched her even though he was still afraid of rejection. But Mary,
although she ignored him, didn't react. She had been defeated by her own
tears. He took her softly into his arms and said tenderly, "It's all my fault.
I understand. Forgive me, please, Mary! I beg you not to cry! You'll ruin
the eyes I love so much."

She ignored him and continued to sob.

At a loss, Wang Wei waited patiently, constantly repenting his mis-
takes, scolding himself, and making some rather silly pledges. But still
Mary went on crying. This saddened Wang Wei because they had been
on such good terms from the time they met each other. Now at the start
of their break-up, Mary was in such pain. He thought of the causes and
felt that there was no way to save the situation. Maybe they couldn't be
reconciled, and Mary would be leaving him. This thought made him so
sad that, even though he had not cried for years, he burst into tears.

When Wang Wei's tears fell on her face, Mary was deeply touched. Her
heart softened and she lifted her hand to feel his face. The wet face and
gaunt cheeks made her feel sadder, and she began to cry out loud.

Wang Wei held her tight as he moved his wet face over to rest against
her still wetter face.

"Mary, I love you!"

Mary embraced him and let him kiss her. Then she said, "I will always
love you, Wang Wei!"

The obstacles that had separated them disappeared. The resentment
that had been in Mary's heart rushed away, and she fell into his arms.
She told him in detail about her suffering, and he talked about his hopes.
Mary felt once again that he loved her very much, and that she was
fortunate. Wang Wei was happy too. He had a chance to express his
thoughts, and this woman believed him and believed in him. It seemed

that what he had imagined was not that far from reality. He felt that women were always like this; it was better to move them by love than to convince them by reasoning. This phenomenon was the opposite of what he'd hoped to find in women. However, since Mary was like this, he was glad to handle it this way, and to prove as well that he really loved her.

The two of them were filled with tenderness, the kind of tenderness that follows heartbreak. Holding each other tightly, they talked all night long, then slept through the following morning.

9

In the afternoon, Wang Wei managed to return home early. Mary, who was still very tired, hadn't gotten out of bed. Her eyelids were slightly swollen and the pure white light coming from her face made her look a little weak, but in his eyes she just became more pathetic and lovable. He took her hand. It was completely limp.

"How come you came back so soon?" she asked.

"Slowing down, of course!" he answered with a smile.

She was very happy, but then said, "Don't do this again. I don't want you to do this."

For many days Wang Wei came back relatively early, and he did not go out at night either. He told everyone he was sick, which was believable since he looked so wan and sallow compared to two months earlier. Besides, his exhausting work schedule in the past was evidence that he was no shirker. Wang Wei, in fact, really did need some rest. However, from the very beginning he felt uneasy, because all he was doing was sitting at home keeping a woman company.

Mary did not go out and run around anymore. She waited for Wang Wei, and while he was out even cleaned the room for him. She wanted to move to a better place and see about getting one or two pieces of finer furniture. Wang Wei agreed. He certainly didn't want Mary to lead as hard a life as he did. The weather was becoming warmer, and Mary wanted to make some fashionable light dresses. Only if she wore something nice would going out be enjoyable. Not going out in spring to have a good time would really make her sad. She also wanted to read several Soviet novels that Wang Wei had bought especially for her. Wang Wei's idea was that these works would have some influence on her, and he hoped that slowly she would change her ideology and her interests. She knew Wang Wei's intentions, but read them only as something to pass the time, although she did say that they had fresh plots. If Wang Wei wanted to extend the discussion, she would talk about the beauty of the language. He could not do anything but embrace his original position: "Slowly it will come."

They lived peacefully like this until April, when, through his involvement with the National Trade Union, Wang Wei's work became more urgent and he had less time than ever. Most days he was only at home to sleep at night. In the beginning Mary put up with it, but after a few days she began to feel resentful. When she asked him to go out for some relaxation, he refused. When she asked him to stay at home a little longer, he expressed impatience. When she asked about moving, he shook his head. Mary threatened him several times: "Wang Wei, if you keep on like this, never being at home, there'll be a day when you'll come home and not find me here. Do you think I'm some docile wife? Do you mean to tell me that being in love with a woman doesn't rate any time? Wang Wei! What do you say? I insist that you stay home now. Otherwise . . ."

Wang Wei, who did not know what to do, shook his head and said, "Why look at it that way? Mary, I hope that you're a rational person. Think this over carefully. Right now I really can't wait any longer. I've got to go right away. You should be more understanding and forgiving, and you shouldn't be living like this anymore. If you like, just say the word, I can find some suitable work for you right away. We really need workers now."

Mary angrily threw herself onto the bed and when Wang Wei took the opportunity to run out, this upset her even more. There was no doubt about it: Wang Wei's work was more important to him than she was, and he considered love worthless. How could she go on living with a man who didn't love her! She thought about what he had said: "If you like, just say the word, I can find some suitable work for you right away." Ha! What would suitable work for her be? She recalled the boring meeting she had attended. She knew herself well enough to know that she could never join such an organization, because there was no appeal to vanity and no praise, only dullness that could never stimulate her interest. Yes, it was true. She was not rational. She relied upon her emotions completely. She did not deny it. She was born that way. So now, since Wang Wei was no longer excited by emotion, she did not have to force herself to conform to his hopes. Furthermore, she concluded that no matter what she did, even if she left him, it wouldn't affect him very much. In fact, he did not need her anymore.

The unhappy times were wearing her down. She felt that she had aged a lot. She really could not go on like this, especially after she discovered that he did not seem to be troubled at all. She no longer said much to him, since she knew it was useless! He did not talk much to her, either, because he didn't have enough time and knew that she wasn't interested in his work. Now the room became dreary, and because Wang Wei was hardly ever at home, this dreariness surrounded only Mary. The more excited Wang Wei became about his work, the more it upset Mary. She realized how incompatible they were but didn't know what to do about it. If she couldn't blot out her identity and become a person with a mind like his, then she had to try hard to drag him back to her again. But could she succeed? She was not sure and was as a result even more depressed. Originally, he had not been this kind of person, and she hadn't been away from him for all that long a time. Yet he had changed completely. What was it that had such power? It was beyond her comprehension and very frightening. But she could never follow him. Their backgrounds and personalities were too different.

10

Time sped by without a trace, but the pain grew greater and greater. When Mary could no longer stand it, she had no choice but to take the ultimate measure. So it was that one night when Wang Wei returned home, he sensed that the room was somehow different. He still didn't think about Mary possibly leaving, until he went to bed and discovered that only his dingy cotton quilt was left on the bare bed, and Mary's soft, thin satin quilt was gone. He was astonished. He opened the wardrobe and discovered that all of the dazzling Chinese dresses had disappeared. All that remained were a few tangled hangers and his old coat. Mary's suitcases were missing, and her dainty makeup things had been removed from the drawers. Only then did he realize that the day he had dreaded had finally arrived. He gazed blankly around the empty room. He didn't know what to do. Shanghai was so big. Where could he go to find her? Besides, he knew that even if he found her and brought her back, he wouldn't know how to deal with her. Could he be with her all the time?

"Ah, it all happened so fast."

He reflected on their first encounter, their sweet life together, their separation, and her coming to Shanghai . . . He felt sad for himself, but he felt even more sorry for her. It was he who had ruined her! If he had not fallen in love with her and had not pursued her, she would still be leading the happy, carefree life of an innocent maiden. But now, he had been unable to change her and had only given her many painful memories. She would never be happy again unless she could find someone who would offer her an even purer and warmer love. Only love, the most lofty love, not Wang Wei's kind, could rescue her. He knew that he had treated her poorly, for which he felt extremely remorseful. But he was unable, and would always be unable, to comfort her. He lay disconsolately on the bed and silently repeated that lovely name, "Mary, Mary . . ."

Wang Wei awoke the next morning exhausted. He was lying in bed with his clothes on and his eyes were wide open, but he could not get up. When he heard the old landlady's knock on the door, he shouted, "Come in!"

A gray-haired old woman entered the room. Her reddish face wore the same smile it always had, which gave her a friendly expression.

"Forgive me, sir," she said. "I forgot. When the young lady left yesterday, she asked me to give you a letter as soon as you returned. I waited up for a long time, but you came back too late!" As she spoke, she drew a letter from her bosom. Wang Wei snatched it from her.

"The young lady said she had received a telegram from home informing her that someone there was sick. She said that all you had to do was read the letter to understand everything. Is someone in her family really sick? She gave me two dollars. I'm very grateful to her. She is so kind."

Wang Wei opened the letter, but noticing that the old woman was still standing by the bed, he said, "Yes, something has happened back home. You can go now."

Finally the old woman walked out slowly. The letter was quite simple:

Wang Wei, I am leaving. I know this will not surprise you, but I must tell you. I am going to stay at a friend's house and wait for your letter. If you still love me, I hope that your reply will be satisfactory. Otherwise, we will not have another chance to see each other. You should understand the reasons that caused me to leave. They are your unfaithful love and your work. If you can't give a full explanation and find a way to solve this problem, then you need not respond, because no answer means no solution. You should know my temperament and the reasons for my leaving. In a word, to make it even clearer, all I want to tell you is, if Wang Wei doesn't belong to Mary, Mary prefers to suffer alone.

Mary

P.S. The address is GPO, Box 1782.

Wang Wei read the letter and didn't say a word. He could not deny that he was still very attracted to this woman. He thought of how carefree he felt when he was in her arms.

That afternoon Wang Wei took some time off and went to the post office, but the post office maintained absolute secrecy and he failed to find out anything. In the evening he decided to write her a letter, even if it wouldn't be able to satisfy her. If she came back he would be grateful, and if she didn't he would naturally feel sad. However, he was not going to shoulder the responsibility for their separation. It wasn't his fault. He rubbed his drowsy eyes as he read the letter again, and then he started writing on a white sheet of paper.

Oh, Mary, you can imagine how cruelly time weighs on my hands. The room where you left me with a lot of memories is now as desolate as a graveyard. I am forcing myself, despite a piercing headache and sore eyes, to carry out this heartbreaking job according to your order. I don't need to defend myself. There is bound to be a day when you will understand whether or not your Wang Wei has loyally fulfilled his responsibility to love, and you surely know that your lover didn't do anything whatsoever to deceive you. I am sure that this is not overstated and that you will understand. Yet the fact is clear that you felt compelled to leave. You were dissatisfied with my behavior, which is to say that I could no longer please you. This situation was not what you had hoped for and it hurt you a lot. But this was not what I had hoped for either, so I should not be the only one to blame. I've suffered a lot, and maybe I started to suffer before you did. I also tried to ward off this terrible moment. You are intelligent and should have understood my painstaking effort. But it was only my fantasy. Your old outlook on life couldn't be changed in the least. You are proud by nature. I don't want to go on talking about this, now that the crack has become a crevice and you have left with your mind made up. I do not have the heart to blame you for your cruel treatment of me, because I know that you have fallen into hopeless misery because I could not offer you a satis- factory reply. Yes, I could say that I will give up everything and join you in a carefree life if you will come back, but I don't want to deceive you (I have never lied, you know that); and even if I tried to get rid of my present work, my ideas could not change. Wang Wei probably will never be a lovable man in Mary's eyes.
    That's all I have to say. It's all up to you now. How can I behave like an innocent child crying for his Mary? I await your final judgment.
                                                                    The Offender,
                                                                    Wang Wei

Quite a few days passed after Wang Wei mailed his letter. He waited uneasily and anxiously hoped, but there was no reply. He inquired all around, but learned nothing. His reply had obviously made Mary decide to suffer rather than return to him. From this point on, they were sepa- rated, and no one could devise an alternative ending for this sad story.

                                      11

Wang Wei's life reverted to what it had been before Mary's arrival. He was busy, and getting even busier, but no matter how busy he was and no matter to what degree the image of Mary faded in his mind, even to the point of disappearing at times, when he lay down on his bed alone, he could not help missing her. He worried about her. He couldn't stop worrying about her. He couldn't imagine her life and how bitter she must be. He had asked around in the hope of getting some news to console himself, but he had failed. Mary had left, taking all traces with her. Yet he had a turbulent heart and was still enthralled by that will-o'-the-wisp.

One day near the end of the month, around the start of the third week since Mary had left, Wang Wei was sent to a busy part of the city to deliver a speech. When he arrived he saw that crowds of his organization's people were spread out along the street, at the entrances to shops, and at the trolley stops, and that demonstrators, all of whom were students, were coming and going. A tall Sikh policeman was pacing vigilantly but calmly in this tense atmosphere. Because it was still early, Wang Wei slowed his pace on the sidewalk to examine the situation.

He felt an excitement that he couldn't control, as if he were seeing a surge of roaring waves toppling the mountains and churning up the seas. He also seemed to see an erupting volcano engulfing the city in its raging flames. It was possible that this might happen immediately, since so many people were ready for it! And he, he would accelerate the great storm and ignite the flame! Some acquaintances were also there, and a fire had begun to burn in their hearts too. Their outer calm could not mask their inner turmoil. The joy of anticipation had brought a slight flush to their faces. At that moment, two people approached him. He raised his eyes and saw Feng Fei, secretary of the organization, whose round face shone with a proud smile, and the ticket-seller, a healthy woman whose hand was clasped tightly in Feng's. As soon as Feng saw Wang Wei, he went over to him, smiling as if he had a lot to say. Wang Wei winked at him, nodded slightly, and walked past. However, there was something extraordinary about Feng Fei's happy expression that made a deep impression on Wang Wei. The image of Mary swiftly sprang to mind. Ah, his former dream had now been realized by Feng Fei! That woman was a true revolutionary. But he had no time to think about this because the hour was drawing nigh. As he reached the public office building, even greater crowds were gathering, and many of his acquaintances had grouped together to await the first order. The minutes passed. At exactly nine o'clock the deafening roar of firecrackers was suddenly heard across the street, and immediately after came the thunderous yelling of slogans. Astonishingly loud shouting filled Wang Wei's ears: "Charge in! We'll occupy the assembly hall first! Charge!"

As Wang Wei pushed himself into the public office building, a great crush of people squeezed against him. They forced their way in, and in no time the assembly hall was filled with people. A hubbub of voices filled the space. While Wang Wei and two others were trying to get to the platform, someone shouted, "Quiet please! We'll start the meeting now. Presiding officers!"

The crowd became quiet immediately. By now Wang Wei had already pushed his way up to the base of the already crowded platform. Someone called to him, "Comrade Wang Wei, you first."

Wang Wei leaped onto the platform and stood in the chairman's place. He was hailed with prolonged cheers and applause, but he was able to slowly calm the crowd with shouts and gestures. Then he spoke calmly and seriously in a loud voice: "Today we have come here to hold our meeting. First, we have to understand the meaning and mission of the meeting! That is to say . . ."

Two gun shots were heard outside, and a phalanx of policemen rushed in. The ranks of the masses began to waver and disintegrate. Shouts of "charge" were heard, and the sound of excited, trembling voices filled the air. Some people tried to escape quickly from the iron batons and bullets as the meeting place was turned into chaos. At the sight of this dramatic change, Wang Wei tried hard, but unsuccessfully, to calm the people, for as more policemen rushed in the masses panicked. Someone beside him whispered to him, "Things are looking bad. Let's go down and blend into the crowd."

Wang Wei jumped down but was promptly seized by a big hand that reached out from the crowd. It held his arm tightly, and then a giant of a man squeezed out in front of him. All Wang Wei heard was the man cursing him: "You bastard, I've been trailing you long enough. Let's see you try to run off now. Hah, if you want to make trouble, do it in the police station."

Wang Wei's hand was twisted painfully, but when he looked at the detective's face he felt that there was no use saying anything. He continued to shout loudly toward the masses: "We must prepare quickly for the [Communist] general demonstration! We will destroy imperialism."

A big fist hit him on the face and stopped him from shouting. Then he was dragged out onto the street. Many of the masses were still scattering. Wang Wei noticed their angry faces, their encouraging and consoling eyes. He also heard fragments of slogans and saw that in a few places the masses were fighting the police. He was pushed over to a large, black iron truck, already filled with fighters who had been arrested, and thrown on top. As he looked out through the wire mesh, he spotted a charming lady by the entrance to a big department store. Ah, it was Mary! She was still so attractive and graceful, like a queen from a distant land. She looked happy, yet serious. Obviously, she had been out shopping, since she was carrying parcels. Moreover—yes, yes, it was true—there was a handsome young man accompanying her. Wang Wei looked in amazement at the sight and thought to himself, "Good, she's happy again. That's the kind of person she is, and I don't have to worry about her anymore. Goodbye, Mary!"

At this moment there was an uproar inside the truck because two more people were thrown in almost on top of him, and he heard several voices cursing: "Damn it! Damn! If we're going, let's go! What are we waiting for?"

The truck started abruptly, and all the arrested people fell down. Quickly, however, they pulled themselves up and began shouting slogans together: "Down with . . ."

Translated by Shu-ying Ts'ao and Donald Holoch

Net of Law

"Net of Law," which was written in 1932, lifted the four-cornered relationship of *Shanghai, Spring 1930* out of the middle-class, French settlement in Shanghai and put it back down into a subproletarian slum in the central Chinese factory town of Hankou. Ding Ling moves the complicated plot forward in a new way. She abandons the omniscient narrator who speaks over the action to explain how and why the story will progress, revealing motives and feelings hidden even to the characters themselves. Events in "Net of Law" occur as the consequence of people acting inside relations of dominance and submission. Characters, in combination, represent larger patterns at work in history. As Gu Meiquan puts it, "Just as you weren't the person who caused me to lose my job, I was not the person who killed your wife."

The continued influence of Chinese Marxist theory in this work is seen in the way Ding Ling recasts gender oppression in the context of plot development. This is a story about the personal travail of a brutally oppressed, subproletarian woman. But Acui's tragedy, while it instigates action, does not remain central to the story. Indeed, it ends up being rather peripheral. A matter-of-factness suffuses the story. Of course women suffer more than men. Of course women die so that men can unite in proletarian brotherhood and a war of national salvation. Of course poverty inflicts injustice. Of course a miscarriage of justice and a miscarriage of a fetus are synonymous.

Ding Ling's New Realist stories show sexual oppression within class oppression, and she goes to great lengths to show that men are not the agents of women's oppression but merely the immediate instruments of the oppressors. The Party of the Proletariat has, of course, the responsibility to remedy society's ills. What seems remarkable in this story, none-theless, is Acui's exaggerated passivity. In "Net of Law," Ding Ling goes out of her way to deny historical agency to the female subproletariat.— TEB

I

It was nearly dark and the shift had ended. A great mass of people surged out through the iron gate like a tide of water. Near the place where the dike had broken, Gu Meiquan pushed those in front and was pushed by those behind as he squeezed his way out. Only when he reached the center of the street could he exhale a deep breath. After making sure of his direction, he turned out of the crowd and headed toward the entrance to a nearby alley on his left. The cobblestone street was wet throughout the year, and soft mud often stuck to the tops of the stones. The alley entrance was somewhat dark and low. Just as he reached it, someone came up to him from the side. He turned his head and saw on the face of his wife, Acui, a little smile that expressed her happiness.

"Have you finished dinner?" he asked.

"Yes, it's ready. We have a gold carp."

The houses along the alley were lined up in tight rows like pigeon cages, one after the other. They had walked past several rows when someone coming toward them shouted, "Lao Gu, are you on your way home?"

Meiquan smiled and nodded, lightly tossing the hair that always hung down over his forehead. Then the man who had asked the question saw his wife walking alongside him. He made a face and walked off.

They walked to the seventh row of houses and turned in. Acui brought her smiling face up close to him and whispered, "Someone has moved in upstairs next door."

He looked at her for a moment and took a cigarette out of his pants pocket. After lighting it, he entered the house.

Meiquan's wife served him attentively. She took off his dirty work clothes and washed his hands and feet in a wooden basin. After drinking some water, he stretched out in the chair, holding what was left of his cigarette in his mouth. His limbs, numbed by a full day's work, began to feel tired. He started humming a tune from his hometown and began to rock gently back and forth.

A three-year-old child from upstairs to the rear heard his voice and groped his way down the steep, narrow stairway that tottered as if about to collapse. Acui stood by the stairway and said in an attempted Hunan dialect, "Gou Yazai, have you eaten? Uncle's home. He's bought some candy. Hurry over."

"I haven't eaten. We're waiting for Daddy. He's not home yet," Gou Yazai answered brightly as he groped his way into their room.

By now the room was dark. Gou Yazai felt his way over to Meiquan. Meiquan put him on his lap and sang a children's song, "A red bird, a green tail . . ."

When the food was brought over, they lit a small oil lamp. Gou Yazai sat off to the side and watched them eat. In his hand he held a piece of turnip.

They were cooking upstairs too. The spicy, peppery odors made Acui sneeze. But Gou Yazai wasn't bothered. He could already eat lightly spiced food.

"People from Hunan are disgusting, with all their hot peppers," Acui said as she wiped her eyes and nose with her sleeve, looking straight at the child.

"People from Hunan are disgusting," Gou Yazai imitated her.

Acui laughed, then turned and said, "The people who have moved in next door are from our part of the country."

Just then Gou Yazai's father returned through the rear door; he stuck his head into the room and glanced at the people inside. His face was flushed from drinking. Acui said hastily, "Brother Zhang, have you eaten? Come in and have a seat. Meiquan's just relaxing."

Zhang Zongrong strode into the room, his hat set jauntily on the back of his head, bringing with him the foul smell of liquor. Noticing his father's condition, Gou Yazai quietly slid off of the bench and headed upstairs.

"The little bastard, the son of a bitch can't work, but he sure knows how to eat! That bastard Little Li out front asked me again for candy money."

Zhang Zongrong had been unemployed for more than two weeks and was completely dependent upon his wife, who worked in a cigarette factory. He had recently taken to drinking and often stole clothing to swap for liquor. Then when he returned home, he'd rant and rave. Compared to Gu Meiquan, who had a regular income and had just married a young wife, Zongrong's temperament was understandably bad. However, because Meiquan and Acui were so kind, they often comforted this family that shared their living quarters. As soon as Gou Yazai's mother went to the factory, he spent most of the time with Acui, who loved small children.

Gu Meiquan knew that Zhang Zongrong was about to start ranting and raving again, so he pulled out a cigarette, stuck it into his mouth, and said, "Bite! Don't let it get you down. Let's sing some mountain songs."

"I'm not up to it." Zhang Zongrong inhaled deeply on his cigarette and took off his hat.

Gu Meiquan, however, pushed his rice bowl aside and tried to get him started by singing, "The young girl's skin was white, so white. The young lad's skin was black, so black."

Without being aware of it, Zhang Zongrong leaned over. His drunken eyes looked at his happy friend and he started singing, too: "Black ink writes on white paper. Have a look, don't the colors match?"

Acui smiled as she gathered up the dishes. Gu Meiquan pushed Zhang Zongrong up the stairs. The alley was filled with coal and wood smoke. Small children were yelling and crying. Women were cursing loudly and spanking them. This was especially true of the local women. Even in everyday conversation, they seemed to be angry. This was the voice of Hankou women.

Gu Meiquan lit another cigarette, leaned back in his chair, and watched Acui as she went about the room doing various little chores.

"The new neighbor seems to be newly married," Acui said. "She's very young, and has a ring on her finger."

He listened and looked at her, but didn't respond. She continued, "I'm really very happy. It's so nice to have someone from our home for a neighbor. I'll understand her language and temperament. We'll be able to talk about things back home and have a lot of fun. These people from Hunan and Hubei are so smooth and superficial, and they have such tempers. They can be nice, but they just aren't the same."

She discovered that he hadn't really been listening to her and, with apparent irritation, said, "What's wrong? Why aren't you paying attention to me?"

"I'm listening. Go on!" He took another long drag on his cigarette.

Upstairs in back, Gou Yazai started to cry. His mother, who was scolding him, was crying too. Acui went on, "They're so pitiful. His wife told me that when they were young, they were farmers in Hunan and did quite well, but later, they became poorer and poorer. One year it would be drought, the next year flood. When they couldn't survive any longer, they fled to Hankou. He worked for a long time as a dockhand, but because it was such difficult work, he later took a job in a soap factory. She found a job in a cigarette factory. They worked very hard, wanting to earn enough money between them to return home. Who would have known that they wouldn't make it, that instead they'd become worn out. Brother Zhang has stopped working and now relies on her. She works in the factory and can't take care of the house. Sometimes I can't bear to see what's happening, so I do her washing and look after Gou Yazai. She's always thinking of me. Can't her husband find some kind of work?"

"Finding work isn't easy. Hasn't Wang Laoqi, who lives in front, been out of work for three months? His wife goes out every day to beg. Now there are too many beggars, and the people aren't giving money the way they used to. The floods rose too high this year, and more people than ever are fleeing the devastation. I can't imagine what it'll be like this winter."

Acui's thoughts turned to her family. There hadn't been any letters from them for a long time. She wondered what the floods were like back home. She had left home to marry Gu Meiquan and come with him to Hankou. If they were careful, they had enough clothing and food to get by, so there was no need to worry. But what about her family? They had said that they'd be going to Shanghai, but she didn't know what had come of it.

As for Gu Meiquan, although he talked about the floods and the difficulty of finding work, he was thinking about the relatively good life that he had now. During his life he had struggled hard. As an apprentice he had been beaten day and night and then he had worked a long time as an unpaid assistant. Now he had this twenty-five-dollar-a-month job as an ironsmith, had married a woman with a pleasant personality and good looks, and . . . she seemed to be pregnant.

2

Swish, swish, swish, swish . . . the sound of splashing water. Acui and Grandma Wang from next door were washing clothes by the back door. Palm fiber brushes rubbed hard across dirty cloth. Amid the soap suds, gray, blue, and black clothing was becoming a bit cleaner. At this time the only people in the alley were a few small children with runny noses who were squatting on the ground. Most of the adults had gone to the factories, and it seemed to be much quieter. Acui noticed Grandma Wang's trembling hands and saw how she frequently splashed water out and wet the ground. Time and time again, her oldest granddaughter brought water from the street well in a tin can. Along the way, she spilled some, too. Acui couldn't keep from saying, "You're too old for this. How can you wash clothes with your hands so shaky and weak? I think you should stop. Your hands have turned white from soaking in water all day long. It's not worth it for so little money. Shouldn't your two sons be taking care of you? Three copper coins for one piece. What kind of price is that? I hear that in my town of Wuxi, it's several cents per piece."

"Young sister, how can you understand? In a few days the weather will turn cold and there will be fewer clothes. My eyesight is so bad I can't take in mending or stitch shoe soles. Of what use are my sons? They can barely feed themselves. If my daughter-in-law hadn't died, it would be better. I have several granddaughters. When my eyes close and my feet are stretched out in death, then I won't have to take care of things. But as long as these old bones are working, I won't give them my trouble. Although I'm washing clothes cheaply, my customers aren't particular about how clean they are, so I can do a so-so job. Sometimes the soldiers are quite nice. If I can get ten or twenty pieces a day, isn't that enough for my food?"

Acui felt that what she said made a lot of sense. In her mind she figured it out. If she washed thirty pieces a day . . . three times three is nine . . . nine hundred copper coins. In five days she would have a dollar. In a month she'd have six dollars. She was still young. If she took advantage of the present and saved some money for when the child was born, then she would be able to buy a few more things. And so she asked, "Grandma Wang, how about helping me to get some once in a while? I'd like to have a few clothes to wash too."

"Sure. So you're going to take up this hard work too, eh? I think you'd be better off finding needlework to do. I'll keep you in mind, but it's also been hard to find needlework recently. Some families don't send their needlework out any longer, and the number of needy sewing women in the street has increased. They've all fled the countryside to escape the floods. They're willing to sew and mend for half a day for half a bowl of putrid rice porridge. They've taken away our regular business."

When she heard the world "flood," Acui thought once more about her family and said, "I thought that floods only happened where we lived. It was really scary. How could I know that it's the same everywhere. My husband told me yesterday that tens of thousands have come from south of the river and that quite a few have been killed. He said that they were lawbreakers and troublemakers. Grandma Wang, your Hubei Province is so different from where I come from. Over there no one ever heard of killing people without a good reason. Here in Hankou, they're chopping off heads all day long. Young students are being arrested, and beheaded too. It's really frightening!"

"The world is changing more every day. It's even worse than during the time of the Taipings. It's certainly going to get even worse. It'll have to before things can get better. These poor people are nearly starving to death. How can they not rise up? If I were younger—if you don't mind a little joke—I also would be rebellious."

"Mama! Candy!" Gou Yazai came over from the entrance to the alley. His hands were completely covered with black mud. He was holding up a piece of black and red ginger candy.

"So, you little scamp, when did you go out with Xiao Li, that bastard! When your daddy comes home, he'll give you the beating you've been asking for. Grandma Wang, his dad's a worthless bastard too. He can't find any work, he complains about his wife and son, and he drinks from morning to night. If I had a man like that, I'd hang myself."

"He's not to blame. In that kind of situation there's nothing anyone can say. His empty stomach makes him that way. He can't steal, and he's so full of anger that he takes it out on his wife. We women are so pitiful. Who among us hasn't lived their entire life in sorrow? I'm a good example. When I was young, I was beaten by my husband. That guy was really an animal. Eventually, he died right in front of me. These two bastard sons of mine aren't any better. No matter whether I've done something or not, they get angry and curse me like a dog. They deserve to be struck by lightning, but, ah, they're still my sons. When I think of how they've never enjoyed happiness or received any benefits from their parents, I feel that I should just let them be that way and forget it. How can poor people talk about filial piety and etiquette?"

Hearing this made Acui feel miserable. Her mother regularly had tears running down her face too. Now she was wandering about destitute someplace and Acui didn't know where.

Just then the young woman who had recently moved in came down from upstairs. "Ma'am, which lane has water for sale?" she asked in a Shanghai dialect. "We don't even have any cold water, and I can't get anything done!"

Grandma Wang didn't understand her dialect, so she just smiled and shook her head. Acui looked at her plaid shirt, her black pants made of foreign cotton with the oversize pant legs, her gray shoes, and her smooth, combed hair. She felt a sense of great satisfaction and said with a smile, "Sister, Grandma Wang doesn't understand your dialect. When I first came it was the same. It was very hard. You're from Wuxi, aren't you? I'm from Dongxiang District."

Unexpectedly, Xiao Yuzi had found a young person from her hometown. A big smile appeared on her face, which was covered with cheap cold cream. She was so happy she practically seemed to be shouting as she said, "You're from Dongxiang? I'm from outside Nanmen. How long have you been here? Do you live next door? Oh! I'm so happy. You must come over every day!"

"All right. And you must also come over here. We live on the first floor. I saw you yesterday. If you want water, there's still some in my water vat. The water shop has boiled water for sale. If you want to buy river water, stand by the alley entrance and wait. Someone will pass by carrying some. I'll go with you. Sister, have you just come from Wuxi?"

"I've come from Shanghai. My mother accompanied me here. She's going back tomorrow. I'm so depressed. I've never been to Hankou before. Oh, it's so good to have someone from my hometown here. Is your husband from Hankou?"

"No, he's from Dongxiang too. He's an ironsmith— So you've come from Shanghai. I wonder how conditions are there. I heard that my mother wants to go to Shanghai. It's easy to find work there, I guess. She'll die going there for the first time. My younger sister is going with her."

"Shanghai . . . " Many memories of hardship appeared before Xiao Yuzi's eyes. She had been an embroidery worker along with her mother. The two of them had lived well enough, working hard, but getting by. She often sewed some new clothes and also went to the Great World Amusement Park and Cheng Huang Temple. Because there were only two of them, they even saved a little money. For this reason, when she was betrothed to Yu Axiao in the spring, they didn't even ask a dowry from him. They figured that he had a job. But then the floods came. Even though Shanghai wasn't flooded, the embroidery shop where they worked went bankrupt. Other embroidery shops were unwilling to add new workers. Rice became more expensive. Oil became more expensive. Everything became more expensive. The two of them, mother and daughter, couldn't find work anywhere. They anxiously watched their savings disappear. They wrote several letters to Axiao, and finally he sent a reply asking her to come. But he only wanted her. He was not willing to support his mother-in-law. This was why she was returning to Shanghai. One of her younger brothers worked in Shanghai pulling a rickshaw for a wealthy family, and maybe her mother could find work as a maidservant.

Acui felt a great sadness as she listened to Xiao Yuzi tell of her troubles. Ah, finding work in Shanghai was so hard. How could her own mother and sister find a job there? They couldn't keep living at home, for their house and fields were gone. Elder Brother had left to become a soldier. Father had become a long-term laborer who could only support himself . . . Oh, Mama, Little Sister.

Xiao Yuzi also told her how many refugees in Shanghai lived in county guild hotels that were filthy beyond belief. They had nothing to eat. Some were starving and others were dying of disease— Ah, those people. Maybe Acui's mother was among them, and her sister . . .

Acui's conversations with Grandma Wang were made up of this kind of worrisome talk, and now she wasn't talking about happy things with this neatly dressed new arrival. However, since all of them were suffering hardships, she still felt some comfort.

After Acui finished washing her clothes, she went with Xiao Yuzi to buy boiled water and plain water. Then she went to Yuzi's home and sat with them for a while. Yuzi's mother was a very warmhearted person. Gou Yazai tagged along with her to play. Acui asked Yuzi's mother to ask around in Shanghai for news of her mother and sister.

When Gu Meiquan came home from work, Acui told him what she had learned about their neighbor. She happily went into every little detail. Gu Meiquan wasn't the least bit surprised, and said, "I know. I found out when I went to work. I was wondering who it might be, and it turned out to be Axiao. He works in the coppersmithing shop. This past spring he asked for time off to go to Shanghai. There are no more than seven or eight people in the factory from Wuxi, so of course I know him. Heh! Several days ago this guy was still trying to make time with some of the women. Now that his wife has arrived, he'll probably behave himself. Of course I know him."

Acui thought of telling him that she wanted to take in some laundry or find some needlework to do, but she changed her mind. She wanted to save up some money to send home to her mother and sister. She didn't need to tell him. She was afraid he would object.

3

Xiao Yuzi's mother left. Because Hankou was a strange city to Yuzi, she became close friends with Acui. They were often together. After their husbands went to work, they went to one another's home, with Gou Yazai always tagging along. They did their laundry and shopping together, and sang songs like "Wuxi Scenes" and "Meng Jiangnu Cries at the Great Wall." Grandma Wang's granddaughter liked to have them teach her songs. Some people in the alley called them sisters. Although Yu Axiao was younger than Gu Meiquan, Xiao Yuzi was a year older than Acui.

The two husbands often spent time together after work. They smoked cigarettes and talked about the factory, about which foremen were good men and which ones were bad. They talked about workers who had gotten their faces slapped for flirting, and others who went to hotels with their female coworkers. They talked a little about the past and even did some bragging over their hardship-filled histories. During Gu Meiquan's apprentice days, for instance, he had been beaten and whipped daily. Even if he had wanted to cry out, he wouldn't have dared to. Now, however, he said, "Hmph! That son of a bitch sure knew how to give a beating, but I wasn't afraid. I knew things about him, and if he had beaten me, I would have told everyone in the neighborhood. His wife was a real slut. Her husband couldn't satisfy her, so she had affairs with his workers. Sometimes she came over and touched me, but I pretended not to understand and ignored her. She hated me for that. You don't see many women like that."

Because Yu Axiao was younger than Gu Meiquan, he was less experienced and less knowledgeable about everything. He also lacked Meiquan's ability to boast. He listened more than he talked and often invited Meiquan to go to a teahouse. Although Gu Meiquan was quite experienced and had seen a great deal, he treated Axiao well. But then, he was nice to everyone.

Acui asked Grandma Wang several times to find some work for her. Even washing clothes would have been fine. She was worried about her mother and wanted to earn a little money to send to her. However, Grandma Wang always told her there wasn't any work.

One day when Acui was returning home from shopping for food, she saw some soldiers in a rice shop. After hesitating for a while, she finally gathered her courage and went over and said, "I'm a washerwoman. Do you gentlemen have anything that needs to be washed? I'll wash them clean for a low price."

One of the soldiers looked at her pretty young face and called out with a laugh, "Old Zhang, come on over! There's a woman here who wants to find clothes to wash. Bring your dirty clothes. Heh, she's a sweet young thing."

"Okay. You can take them. You're going to wash my dirty clothes. How about this dirty body? It needs washing too. How much for a piece of clothing? How much to wash this body?"

Acui timidly replied, "Four copper coins a piece . . . "

"Not bad. Okay, tomorrow come a little earlier. We've got a lot of clothing."

And so Acui carried a load of dirty clothes home in her arms. After that she always had at least ten pieces a day. At first, because she wanted to save soap and had to scrub extra hard, she felt the strain, particularly since the clothes were so dirty. Sometimes, Xiao Yuzi helped her ladle water. After a while she got used to the work.

One day when she was returning the clothes, the soldiers stationed at the oil and salt store across the street from the rice shop shouted to her, "Why don't you wash our clothes too? Aren't we good enough for you?

A pretty girl like you passing by here every day and mixing with those guys across the street, that's not right! How much do you charge for one piece? We want you to wash our clothes too."

This little bit of extra work was already causing Acui a lot of trouble. The soldiers all had foul mouths and she was constantly having to ward off those filthy hands. They dilly-dallied when they paid her and gave her a hard time. But then she thought of her mother and sister and endured it. She was frightened when they stopped her, but she was happy too. "It's the same for everyone," she said, "four copper coins."

"Hey, other people only charge three. How come you charge four? Why are you different?"

"If I say four, it's four, and you have to come and sit around every day."

Thus it was that on this day Acui carried home two loads of dirty clothes. After washing all day, she was completely exhausted. Just as she lay down to rest, Xiao Yuzi rushed in and whispered, "Grandma Wang is mad at you. At first I didn't understand, but then I knew what it was. She's saying that you stole her business. She told Mapi, the pockmarked woman who lives in back."

The suddenness of these words left Acui feeling very confused. Then she realized what had happened. "Oh, I forgot. I forgot that she's supposed to take care of those clothes from across the street. I'll go tell her. I'll return them to her."

The two of them walked out. When they reached the rear door, they could hear Grandma Wang's voice.

"The world isn't the same now. All the women fight shamelessly for money. Oh, how they want money. They have no pride. Wouldn't it be better if they just went out and sold what they had between their legs?" Acui had been holding in her anger for a long time, and when she heard Grandma Wang curse her this way, she snapped back without even thinking about it.

"If you want to wash clothes, say so. How can you insult someone this way?" Tears suddenly began to well up in her eyes.

Grandma Wang came running out of Mapi's house. Two old eyes stared angrily from her completely wrinkled face. Her toothless mouth hung open. Her withered lips trembled: "Curse you, so what? You slut, you daughter of a whore. You pussy-selling dog. You stole an old woman's food. Let's see what happens to you!"

"You're the real slut, the real whore. I didn't go looking for those clothes. They insisted that I wash them."

"Why wouldn't they insist that you wash them? You and your sexy ways. Your stink is enough to kill, you whore."

Mapi also came running out. She tugged at Grandma Wang and said, "Don't get angry. If you die from anger, your sons won't be able to afford a coffin. I've always said that none of those people from downriver were any good. They're all cheap goods. Look at the prostitutes in the International Settlement. They're all from downriver. Don't bother with them. After this we'll be hearing a lot of jokes. They're stinking up the whole street."

Acui couldn't control her grief any longer. Tears flowed in a torrent, and she was fit to be tied. In her anger all she could think of was lighting into those women. She was shaking all over. She held onto Xiao Yuzi, unable to speak. Xiao Yuzi was angry too, and joined the fray. "Where do you get off bullying outsiders? You're the real filth!"

"You're all no-good, cheap stuff. You witch, with all that smelly face cream!"

Grandma Wang's granddaughter made faces at them. Gou Yazai was so frightened that he started crying. As a large number of people from the alley gathered round, Acui and Xiao Yuzi went inside to get away. Grandma Wang hatefully told her story to the people who had gathered there, and some of them helped her curse them. Acui wanted desperately to cry, but she wouldn't let herself. Her face was pale. Xiao Yuzi was as angry as she was, and stayed with her. Together they cursed the others in low voices. Acui didn't cook supper that night. She just lay under the covers and cried.

4

The next morning, as Yu Axiao was setting off for work at the factory, Gu Meiquan caught up with him at the alley entrance. His usually happy face was solemn as he said, "Something's wrong with my wife. She cried all last night and has tremendous pain in her abdomen. She's two months pregnant, and she might lose this one. She looks like she's about to die . . . Axiao, I want to stay with her today. Please go to the cashier's office and notify them for me . . . "

Axiao thought of saying some comforting words, but Meiquan turned and ran back home.

Acui's hands were pressing down on her abdomen. Her breast was still filled with anger from the previous day. She didn't dare tell Meiquan. She felt that she was going to miscarry, that she would lose this child. This made her even sadder. She was worried that Meiquan would be angry with her, for although he never said so, Meiquan had liked the idea of having a child. Acui tried to put on a calm appearance, but she couldn't do it. Her tears continued to flow. Meiquan hadn't gone to work, and the expression on his face was very unpleasant to see. When Xiao Yuzi came over, she grabbed her hand and burst out crying.

It was afternoon before several clots of blood appeared. They all knew what was happening, but no one wanted to say anything. Gu Meiquan was very anxious and upset, but when he saw the sadness on his wife's face he maintained his silence. Acui hid under the covers and wept quietly. She was hot all over. Xiao Yuzi didn't know how to comfort her, so as evening approached she went home.

Mapi ran to Grandma Wang's back door and the two of them talked in loud voices. They said that this was retribution. Acui shouldn't have stolen an old woman's business because heaven has eyes. This conversation carried to Acui's bed. Grandma Wang's granddaughter came to the doorway to take a look too, and there wasn't any sympathy in her eyes.

The news of Acui's miscarriage was passed along the entire alley. It was taken as very ordinary news, and not a single person sent an expression of sympathy. Gu Meiquan held in his anger against fate and his resentment toward Acui. He thought that it was all her fault, that she had brought on the miscarriage by all that unreasonable crying. He cooked his own rice and made rice porridge for Acui. She refused to eat. All she wanted was some boiled water. Her fever showed no sign of receding. He couldn't express his anger, and could only try to cheer her up.

The evening passed as was followed by a long, sad night. Once again the sky turned light. Gu Meiquan had no choice but to go to work. He felt his wife's forehead. It was still very warm. He hesitated for a long time, but in the end he had to go. All he could do was say, "Don't worry. Relax and lie here. This evening I'll ask a doctor to come and see you. After you take some medicine you'll feel better. Axiao's wife will be coming over soon. Have her sit with you. Later on, I'll buy something to return the favor. Okay, I'm going."

Gu Meiquan had taken a day off work, but he felt even more tired than usual. He had no energy at all. Spiritlessly, he walked slowly out of the alley. The street was full of people coming and going, people with uncombed hair and sleepy eyes on their way to work. Some women workers had bound feet or off-center buns in their hair. Doddering old women and young girls of twelve or thirteen squeezed their way forward through the crowd.

Gu Meiquan walked to the cigarette factory where he had worked for two years. The iron gate was still wide open. The female workers, who were in the great majority, were busily rushing in. He bent forward and slipped in through the gate. Just then someone shouted, "Gu Meiquan, go over to the pay office."

He looked and saw the gate guard staring at him.

"What for?"

"I don't know. You'll find out when you get there."

Although he hadn't done anything wrong, something didn't seem right. He felt very uneasy as he walked to the pay office. The cashier rolled his eyes a few times and looked at him from behind his glasses. Then he handed him a small packet.

"Twelve dollars and fifty cents. Wages for half a month. You're two days short of half a month, but no deduction has been made. Count it yourself. You don't have to come back again!"

These words were like an unexpected thunderclap. Gu Meiquan was left standing dumbfounded in front of the counter. Finally, after a long time, he was able to speak: "This can't be. Why am I being fired? I didn't break any rules. There's no reason . . . "

"What do you mean by 'reason?' Do you think this factory is yours? When you feel good you come to work, and when you don't feel good you stay home and sleep. If everyone were like you, the factory would have to close its doors. Hmph! And you want to talk of 'reason.' "

"This isn't fair. Yesterday my wife had a miscarriage and a high fever. I had to stay with her all day. I asked Yu Axiao to come and ask for a day of vacation. Aren't I permitted to ask for time off? I've never heard of that before."

"Bullshit! Not fair to you. Maybe Yu Axiao's ghost came by. Go look for it! You wanted to be with your wife. Ha!"

When Gu Meiquan heard that Axiao hadn't come, he was so mad that he nearly jumped into the air. However, he controlled himself and said with a smile, "My wife is really very ill. Axiao's not coming isn't my fault. I asked him to. Please show mercy one time. How can I stop working? We have no money and my wife is sick in bed. It's hard to find work these days . . . "

"I don't want to talk about it. It's not me who doesn't want you. It's the foreign boss. You're wasting your breath with me. Who told you not to come yesterday?"

"I asked Axiao, that bastard, and the bastard didn't come over and take care of things. Missing one day shouldn't be enough to fire me."

"Your mother's pussy! What are you squabbling about? You've got your money, so get out! There's nothing more to say!"

"This shouldn't happen."

"If you don't get out, I'll have you arrested."

"You damned dog, get out of here fast! You're just asking for a beating!" Someone else in the pay office joined in cursing him.

"Get out? Where can I get out to? I've worked here two years and never done anything wrong. Why do you want to drive me away? I insist on staying here!" As Gu Meiquan became desperate, he also became aggressive.

"Call security!" The cashier looked at him again from behind his glasses and matter-of-factly turned his head away.

Gu Meiquan dashed out like a crazy man. All he could think about was hitting someone. Some late-arriving workers were in the compound. They gathered around him and he appealed to them in a loud voice for justice. His only thought was to find the boss and beat him up. He rushed over to the copper shop to find Axiao, but two guards came up and grabbed hold of him.

"Get out! If we see you in here causing trouble again, we'll throw you in jail, dog fucker!"

Grabbing and pushing, they rushed Gu Meiquan out the main gate and gave him a kick in the rear. He stood there in the middle of the street feeling a little dizzy. A great darkness pressed down. Where could he go? He couldn't leave the factory. His life and the life of his wife depended on this place. For the past two years, he had been able to eke out a living. After this . . . look for work . . . what hope was there . . . twelve and a half dollars.

"That cashier is no good," he thought. "And Axiao, the bastard, how could he not go to ask for time off for me? Hmph! We're from the same area too. He won't be able to face me!"

Thousands of unconnected thoughts passed through his mind. There was no solution. He became angrier. The unjust firing by the factory, Axiao's rottenness, and the fear of unemployment all compressed together to form a tremendous pain that swallowed him up. If only he had an iron fist to smash this catastrophe. Time had become something cruel and heartless. He stood there staring at the factory for a long time. All of the passersby looked at him. A homeless dog ran up and sniffed his dirty pants. A policeman walked over and cursed him. Only after he saw the policeman's raised billy club did he fearfully and aimlessly walk away.

"Hey, brother! Have you come from the factory?" Zhang Zongrong stumbled up in front of him. He laid a hand on Meiquan's shoulder, smiled, and then laughed as he looked at him.

Gu Meiquan suddenly felt very sad and nearly started to cry. He held on to Zongrong and forced out the words, "Brother Zhang."

Zhang Zongrong's smile widened as he pushed him along. "I thought you were a man! What's so unusual about a woman having a miscarriage? She'll sleep a few days and be fine. It's better for a child to die this way. Some poor devils never get a chance to grow up and have to be sold along the way. That's worse than dying like this before they're fully formed. Are you thinking about having descendants to take care of all that property you own? You're worrying too much."

"Brother Zhang . . . "

Zhang Zongrong didn't pay any attention to him. He dragged him into a teahouse and talked all kinds of nonsense to him.

There were quite a few people in the teahouse, including local hooligans and unemployed people with no place to go, who paid two copper coins to come in and sit for long spells. They were all talking and interrupting each other, and Gu Meiquan angrily poured out his tale of woe.

"Hmph! That Axiao is worthless. He doesn't deserve to live. It's all his fault. How could he forget to go to the cashier's office for you? You're from the same hometown and your wives get along like sisters. People from downriver just don't place any importance on loyalty. He doesn't deserve to live. If you want some help, you can count on me. We'll see what that guy can do."

Zhang Zongrong seemed to be angrier than Gu Meiquan. His face was red and he spat as he talked. His words moved Gu Meiquan to action. Pounding the table, he said, "Okay, I'll give the bastard a beating and knock the devil out of him. If it weren't for him, I wouldn't have lost my job. We'll wait for him till his shift ends."

After deciding on a plan, Gu Meiquan felt somewhat relaxed. Instead of going home, he wandered around outside all day.

5

The kerosene lamp had just been lit. In the dim light the room took on a sorrowful appearance. Acui was still in bed, but she was already feeling much better, and Xiao Yuzi was still there with her. Suddenly a great clamor came from down the alley. This was followed by a large number of people, who crowded up to their house. People were talking loudly among themselves, but what they were saying couldn't be heard clearly. Then Gu Meiquan came in with several other people. His head was bleeding. As soon as he saw Xiao Yuzi he rushed up to her and cursed angrily, "Whore! You're not welcome here! Get out of my house, you fucking . . . "

Xiao Yuzi drew back in fright.

"This has nothing to do with his wife," someone said.

"Aren't you going home? Your husband is hurt, too," someone shouted.

Xiao Yuzi flew out of the room.

"Ai . . . " Acui screamed in fright.

The room was jammed with people. Gu Meiquan had completely lost his sense of reason and his usual calmness. He cursed like a madman. "That bastard has no conscience. I'll kill him! How could he have forgotten? Hah! We'll see if he holds on to this job. If I let him go, I'm not a man."

"It's so hard to find work now. Axiao is inhuman," someone added.

"He didn't do it on purpose. He's sorry, but it's too late. Forgive him and be done with it. We should all be friends. Everything is up to fate," someone said to calm him.

"Why blame Axiao? Why not blame the boss? Axiao didn't fire you."

"Ah, his wife just miscarried. What's he going to do? There are so many people looking for work."

Acui was lying in bed. She didn't say anything, but she understood most of what was happening. Her tears began to flow quietly once again. She looked at her husband's angry appearance. She'd never seen him like that before. She was very frightened. She didn't know how to comfort him.

"The bleeding hasn't stopped. Put some ashes on it," a woman called out. Someone burned a little rice straw and brought the ashes over.

Gu Meiquan washed the blood off with cold water, removed his clothes, and started cursing again like some kind of hero. The people who had just squeezed into the room looked at him with curiosity as others went to the bottom of the stairs next door to watch. Women were yelling for men to come home for supper. Gradually everyone left, until all that remained were a few children who kept running in to take a peek.

The alley began to fill with coal smoke, wood smoke, and the smell of cheap cooking oil. A steady din filled the air. The dim lamplight in the house was a dull gray color. Acui huddled weakly in the dirty bed, while Gu Meiquan sat by himself, growing hungry.

Acui became feverish again and cried without stopping. Gu Meiquan started to feel disgust toward this woman, but he still patiently comforted her. "Don't worry. Maybe I'll find a job. How can heaven allow people to starve to death? If Hankou doesn't work out, we'll go to Shanghai, where my fellow apprentices are." The next day he bravely set out.

Xiao Yuzi didn't come to visit her again.

Grandma Wang was back washing clothes all day long by the back door. They were the clothes that Acui had once washed. The sounds of the palm-fiber brush rubbing the dirty cloth and the water splashing around became unbearable. No one came to see her. Gou Yazai didn't have anyone to take care of him, and he was like a homeless puppy. She didn't know where he was playing. He hardly ever came to her room, and when he did, he just looked at her and walked away. She couldn't get him to stay.

Gu Meiquan didn't find a job. He went back to the factory once and asked for work, but they refused. He also wanted the remaining half month's wages, because he was paid by the month, but he was beaten and thrown out.

With no work to do, the days were too long. He couldn't bear staying at home, so he started hanging around with Zhang Zongrong and some other unemployed workers. He also took to drinking. When he returned home at night he would look at his wife, who had no vitality whatsoever, and get angry. If she hadn't miscarried, he thought, he wouldn't have lost his job. Now he even had to take care of her. She lay in bed all day, as if she were dying, but she didn't die. At first he cursed her; then he beat her. Once he got used to beating her, there were times when he beat her savagely.

Acui could not defend herself, and could only cry. Since crying only made him angrier, however, she had to hold it in. She was feverish and racked with pain, but had to get up and do some work. Her husband had become a tyrant, and she didn't know what had become of her family. Daily necessities such as food became a problem. She had never looked for work before. Every thought became a lash on her body, which had already grown so thin.

The twelve and a half dollars were used up quickly. The eight dollars they had saved were also spent. Then she gave him the two dollars and thirty cents that she had earned from washing clothes. He didn't ask where the money had come from, just took it and went out. The weather turned colder. He still couldn't find work. She also inquired at several places, but female workers were not in demand. She even went to a number of employment agencies, but there were already too many people sitting there. After their money was used up, they had no choice but to sell their clothing, which was all single-layer and old. It wasn't worth much, and then it was gone too.

Gu Meiquan and Yu Axiao had another fight. Meiquan wanted to borrow travel money to return to his hometown, but Axiao wouldn't agree. After being beaten, Acui spent the day in bed.

It was Xiao Yuzi who took advantage of a time when both men were out to come over. The two women hadn't talked for a long time, and when they saw each other they felt only sadness. Most of the mutual resentment that had built up in their hearts disappeared, but Acui still said in a trembling voice, "Axiao doesn't have a conscience. He hurt us so much. You shouldn't have stopped coming to see me . . . "

"Don't blame him. He just made a mistake. Your old Gu is like a mad dog. He shouldn't be let out. My husband's leg still hasn't completely recovered. Yesterday he slept the whole day."

"Ah! His temper really has become terrible these days. I . . . Gou Yazai's mother is better off than I am. There are times when I think it would be better to die." Tears flowed down Acui's face. Xiao Yuzi felt very bad.

"Does he really beat you a lot? That's what Grandma Wang says. She also said that she feels sorry for you. She doesn't hate you anymore."

"Oh . . . " Acui started to cry. "How can he help but beat me? We've no way out. Our food is gone. We've pawned everything. We've begged. We've waited for temporary work. It's no use. Starvation is all that's ahead of us. I don't dare eat enough to fill myself . . . Naturally, he's impatient. He has to take out his anger on me. I'm afraid of him. I hate him, but I understand him. He was never like this before. I want to hit someone too, but since I can't find a place to vent my anger, all I can do is cry alone."

Xiao Yuzi looked at her leaning forward over the table, sobbing steadily, her head in her hands. Her arms were much thinner than before. She looked so frail, like the withered leaves of autumn. Xiao Yuzi felt very bad, too. Life was miserable. For a long time she didn't know what to say. Then her hand touched something in her pocket. She pulled out two coins, laid them on the table, and said, "Your days are hard. I know what it's like. When I was in Shanghai and lost my job, it was scary. Maybe after a while you'll find a job. Don't worry. Are you really thinking of going to Shanghai? In my view, your chances of finding work are slim. There are so many people there looking for jobs. Old Gu wanted Axiao to lend him ten or twenty dollars, but Axiao really doesn't have any money. With my coming here and my mother's leaving, he's already taken on a lot of debts. His hands are really empty. It's not that he wasn't willing to give him a loan, but Meiquan didn't believe him and started a fight. He's so wild it's scary. But you and I were like sisters before, and now you have nothing to eat and are suffering greatly. I don't have any money, but I feel so sorry for you. That's why . . . these are two silver dollars my mother gave me when she left. Since they were new, I couldn't bring myself to spend them. I've kept them all this time without telling Axiao. Now I want you to have them. We've been like sisters. You take them."

Acui looked out from under her hands. She looked at the silver dollars and started crying again. "I don't want them. I don't want them. You keep them."

Xiao Yuzi comforted her once more and then left. She left not only the silver dollars, but also a great deal of warmth in the heart of this pitiful woman.

The two silver dollars were exchanged for food, and when Gu Meiquan saw food on the table, he didn't make a sound. He still went out regularly with Zhang Zongrong to drink tea and wine. Gou Yazai began spending time with Acui again. His mother was very kind to her. After returning from work, she always went to her room first to see how she was doing. Occasionally, Acui also went to visit Xiao Yuzi. Grandma Wang was talking to her again too. Then just when she was getting along a little better, something unexpected happened.

6

Gu Meiquan went to the factory gate again, wanting to see if they had any temporary work. It didn't matter what it was, packing or transporting would have been fine. Although he hadn't said anything, he already knew that only a little bit of the rice was left at home. He stood there with some other men for half a day. Then just as he was preparing to leave with nothing more than his usual feeling of hopelessness, a short fellow with a harelip nudged him and said with a glint in his eye, "I know all about what happened to you. Ah! You were betrayed. Do you know that you've been replaced? The person who filled your vacancy is Axiao's cousin."

"Really?" Meiquan grabbed him.

The harelip spit out a string of indistinct words. "It's true. It's been a week already. I saw them walking together."

"I'll kill you if you're lying to me!" Gu Meiquan was shocked by the news that he had been betrayed. His face turned crimson from anger and he ran off. He asked around. Some people shook their heads and said that they didn't know. Others said it was true, that he'd been at the factory for a while. There were also people who said that this had nothing to do with Axiao, that the other man had found the job himself and was earning five dollars a month less than Gu Meiquan had made. That night Meiquan looked up the drunkard Zhang Zongrong. The two of them cursed Axiao long into the night before returning home.

The cheap sorghum liquor worked its mischief in Meiquan's stomach. He was falling-down drunk. He was so dizzy that Acui had to help him lie down. Then he began to curse Yu Axiao again. He complained that he had been stabbed in the back by that damned Axiao and that if he didn't get revenge he would have wasted his life. Yelling that he wanted to kill him, he ran into the kitchen to look for the cleaver. Acui was scared to death. She hung on to him for dear life. Only after he fell down was she finally able to drag him back to bed, where he fell asleep.

Acui didn't dare sleep. She kept watch over him until it grew light outside and the alley began to stir. The honey bucket cart was coming, so she went out to pour out the commode.

Gu Meiquan awoke with a terrible hangover. His mind was filled with confused thoughts: Yu Axiao's betrayal of him, hunger, his emaciated wife, tears, death, revenge. But could he really kill him, kill a person and forfeit his own life? He vacillated momentarily, but hatred continued to eat at him. Could he forgive him? No, everyone would laugh at him for being a coward and say that he deserved to starve to death. However, then he thought that scaring him would be good enough. If he forced Axiao to come up with ten or twenty dollars, that would take him a long way. He could go to Shanghai. That's the way to do it, he thought, and smiled a satisfied smile.

It was then that Acui entered the room. When she saw his pale face and that cruel hideous smile, her heart trembled. She knew he was thinking evil, frightening thoughts again. "Something very bad is going to happen . . . " She walked aimlessly out of the room, controlled by one emotion—fear. She stood for a moment by the rear door and her mind cleared a bit. She rushed next door, ran up the stairs, and pushed open the door to Yu Axiao's room.

Xiao Yuzi was curled up in bed, her eyes still not fully open; Axiao had just gotten out of bed and was putting on a short cotton jacket.

Acui blurted out, "Axiao, leave quickly! Hide! That wild man is going to pick a fight with you." She turned and rushed back home.

"A fight? Am I afraid of him? If he comes today, I'll take care of him. This bastard is too violent for his own good!"

But Xiao Yuzi begged him to leave, and he walked out without even washing his face. Acui stood in the doorway and watched him leave. She breathed a sigh of relief.

Having sent her husband away like this, Xiao Yuzi felt uneasy. If things were going to keep going like this, she thought, it would be best to move. Slowly, and with a bit of apprehension, she sat up in bed, and just as she was reaching out for her clothes, a head poked in through the doorway and frightened her.

It was Gu Meiquan, a cleaver under his arm, who had sneaked over without even his wife seeing him. All he wanted to do was punish Yu Axiao by scaring some money out of him. In one rush he dashed to the foot of their bed. Yu Axiao, however, was not there.

Meiquan hadn't cut his hair for a long time, and it hung down in wild disarray. His face was frighteningly pale with pulsing blue veins bulging out on its surface. His red, sunken eyes were opened wide and from them emanated a fierce, evil glow. The cleaver was in his hand.

Xiao Yuzi saw the approaching doom and abruptly came to her senses. She drew back in fright and started to call out. But before she had uttered a sound, the cleaver cut into her throat. She couldn't cry out, but she continued to watch him, her body shaking in convulsions. Then the next blow struck her forehead and she had to close her eyes. Then the third thrust, the fourth . . . sliced across her body.

Gu Meiquan was a crazed man. He hacked away confusedly for a long time, like a man caught up in a dream, then suddenly awoke from his frenzy. Instinct called to him, "Escape!" He threw down the cleaver, wiped off his hands, and ran.

Xiao Yuzi was unconscious for quite some time, but gradually her pain awoke her. She had little strength left. Blood flowed from her wounds. She struggled to her feet and dragged herself over to the window. She stuck her head out and pounded on the windowframe.

The first person to spot her was a small child, who screamed in terror. A blood-covered head with scraggly hair was hanging out of the window. Then others saw her and rushed like the tide to her room. They were shocked by what they saw. In a moment the entire alley knew about it. Someone found Yu Axiao and told him to return home at once. Someone else informed the police. The alley seethed with excitement as though heaven itself had overturned.

When Yu Axiao saw the condition of his wife, he had a pretty good idea of what had happened. He embraced her blood-stained body. Xiao Yuzi was already gasping her last. She rolled her eyes and looked at him, whispering with great difficulty, "Gu . . . Mei . . . quan . . . "

The police arrived. Many people crowded into the house next door and brought Acui over. Her head was bowed. There was nothing that she could say. A steady stream of tears flowed from her eyes.

The corpse was placed in the middle of the room to await the arrival of the coroner. It was covered with blood.

The people's hearts were as one, but they didn't know what to do. Some competed to give their report of events. Others didn't say a single word. This tragedy was branded onto their hearts.

Yu Axiao wept in grief. He gnashed his teeth, stamped his feet, and pledged that he would gain revenge. He wanted Gu Meiquan to pay with his life. He filed a charge against him and said that he wanted to post a reward. He wanted to put everything that he had, everything that a life of toil could earn, into a reward. He wanted to catch Gu Meiquan.

Although some workers went to work, the people of the alley didn't want to leave this house. Some passersby from the street and a number of peddlers also crowded in. The coroner conducted the postmortem, made some entries in a notebook, and left.

Yu Axiao didn't go to work, but most of the people at the factory knew what had happened. In the afternoon he bought a thin white wooden casket, carried it to the public cemetery, and buried it.

Acui was taken to jail. Two days later the *yamen* interrogated Yu Axiao, Grandma Wang, and Zhang Zongrong, and disinterred the casket for another examination.[1] The murderer, however, was not there, and nothing was decided. Yu Axiao and the others were allowed to go home. Acui remained in jail.

7

Gu Meiquan struggled with terror, with hunger, and with the agony of his criminal act. After passing through many places, he escaped to Shanghai and found his former senior apprentice, who was working as a clerk for an ironsmith in Zhabei District. When he saw Gu Meiquan dressed in rags and looking worse than a beggar, he couldn't help but let him stay. It was possible now to say that Gu Meiquan had a place to live, but he still could not find a job. Sometimes he went with his former fellow and helped out for a day. He certainly wasn't going to receive any pay, but he hoped to get some food. Yet even this didn't make the boss happy. He worried about his crime and his wife, and wondered how things had turned out. He felt regret and often hated himself. He didn't sleep well and sighed constantly. Day by day his appearance became less human. If he didn't have visions of Acui, his teary-eyed wife, all day, then he saw Xiao Yuzi's terrified look. If not them, then it was Yu Axiao that he saw. He didn't understand how he could have hacked away at that woman like that. He had never hated her. He thought, a demon must have taken possession of him at that moment. Ah! Why had she been so afraid? Why had she tried to yell out? Sometimes he blamed himself; sometimes he blamed others. At times he was afraid that someone would come and arrest him; at other times he feared that Xiao Yuzi's spirit would come and haunt him. He was terribly restless.

At first Meiquan's old workmate didn't have any suspicions, but later he felt that something was wrong. He asked Meiquan several times but got no reply. One day, however, when Meiquan could not keep it to himself any longer, he told him the whole story. He felt that if he confessed, his mind would be at ease. His friend didn't throw him out because of this. Instead, he agreed to ask someone who was going to Hankou to inquire into the affair. Not long afterward a letter arrived. From it Meiquan learned that Yu Axiao had filed charges against him, that the documents had arrived in Shanghai, and that Acui had been locked up in jail. Grandma Wang had been to visit her once and said that she was very sick and on the verge of death. Grandma Wang and the others said that she could be released only if her husband were apprehended. Otherwise, her life could not be saved.

When Meiquan heard this, he felt as if he had been stabbed in the heart. His wife had committed no crime, but because of him she was suffering. All he could think of was saving Acui from jail. She was so pitiful, so innocent. But he was not brave enough to give himself up. He thought of several things to do. None would work. Finally, he decided to write a letter to Axiao. The letter went like this:

Axiao!
I'm sorry. In the past I was too confused. I didn't mean to do what I did. I only wanted to frighten you. I don't know how it happened that I actually did what I did. I regret it, but what is done cannot be changed. You hate me, and you should. If you have me arrested and want me to forfeit my life, there will be nothing for me to say. It's just that what, after all, does this have to do with my wife? I hear that she's in jail and very ill. I can't go to visit her. She has no relatives in Hankou. We knew each other well once. She was on such good terms with your wife. I beg you to show mercy and say the word so that she can be released. She still has a father in Wuxi. Maybe she could live there. If you save her, she'll be grateful for your mercy. I'll be grateful for your mercy too. I'll always remember your goodness. I want to repay you.

Gu Meiquan

The letter was sent and a long time passed by. There was no news at all.

Still Gu Meiquan could not find work. He was often hungry. The weather turned colder and his clothes were thin. Because of the things on his mind, he felt uneasy day and night. It was then that he became acquainted with several unemployed Shanghai ironsmiths and finally learned that it was much harder to find a job in Shanghai than in Hankou. Not only did employers arbitrarily fire seasoned workers in order to hire cheap new workers, but there were large-scale firings, dismissals, and closings at many factories, leaving thousands of workers milling around the streets. Everything was high priced, but the factories still made deductions from wages, had workers on extra shifts, and extended the working hours. Shanghai had tens of thousands of unemployed workers.

Gu Meiquan often went with other unemployed workers from place to place. Although he was still hungry, he seemed to understand more things. Formerly he had been terrified because he had become a murderer. Even when he had felt regret, it was only because he had harmed himself in a moment's anger. Now, however, he didn't even feel any hatred for Axiao. What did any of this have to do with Axiao? Where could he have found the power to fire him or frame him? This was all the doing of those wealthy, powerful oppressors! Originally he and Axiao had been brothers. They had stood together. They should be fighting the enemy together. He hadn't understood this before and had made Axiao his enemy. After he realized this, he felt even worse. Once again he wrote to Axiao:

> Axiao!
> You probably still hate me and would like to boil my flesh. I, however, don't feel any hatred for you anymore. I don't know how you've been getting along recently. I feel very sorry for you. Your wife was hacked to death, and you must feel very sad. I am very regretful, but I am also clear about things now. This is why I don't hate you anymore. You shouldn't hate me either, because just as you weren't the person who caused me to lose my job, I was not the person who killed your wife. Although it can be said that you forgot to ask for time off for me, the ones who fired me were the oppressors. Although it can be said that the person who killed your wife was Gu Meiquan, Gu Meiquan did it only because he had lost his job, couldn't find food to eat, and lost his head. Only because I mistakenly blamed you could I do such a confused thing. I feel even more hatred for that power that makes us so miserable. You still don't understand this. You still hate me. I hope that you don't steadfastly maintain that I'm your enemy. We used to be brothers. We were both brothers in poverty! How is my wife? Has she died? She is really being treated unfairly. If you're able to save her, then please do it. Now it's winter. What good does it do you to keep her locked in jail?
>
> Gu Meiquan

The letter was sent, but still there was no reply. Although Meiquan was still very unsettled, he gradually put these things out of his mind. Then war broke out in Shanghai. The place where he lived became a battlefield, and on the first evening it was destroyed by artillery. After this there was burning and slaughter as the Japanese soldiers came. Gu Meiquan and his friend fled together and, with no place to go, joined a voluntary military unit in Zhabei. All day long they rescued wounded soldiers at the front line. Airplanes flew overhead. Machine guns, assault guns, small cannon, and rifles fired ceaselessly around them like the firecrackers on New Year's Eve. Bombs and large shells exploded nearby. Bullets whizzed past their ears.

Gu Meiquan was frightened at first. However, the brave soldiers were disobeying orders and fearlessly blocking the approaching tanks and Japanese imperialists who were burning, killing, and raping everywhere. Why did his soldiers persevere: They did it for the toiling, hopeless masses. They gave him courage. In addition, he also saw refugees in the combat areas being seized, bayoneted, and disemboweled, then left to die. Children were lifted out of their mothers' arms and stabbed to death. Then their mothers were raped by Japanese soldiers until they died. Gu Meiquan had never witnessed events like this before. He had never imagined them. Now he was aroused by them. He was drawn into the magnificent anti-imperialist feeling. His companions, the volunteers in the unit, the commanders, the relief groups that rushed out from the International Settlement, the common people of all ages, enthusiastically supported both the soldiers who were resisting Japan and the strikes by tens of thousands of workers. He and his old workmate were busy all day. Meiquan was utterly exhausted and unbearably filthy. He got less rest than when he had worked in the factory, but gradually he became happy and whole again. Eventually he forgot about having killed someone and being a criminal.

8

And what of Yu Axiao? Because of what had happened to his wife, he didn't show up at the factory several times without asking for time off and was fired. He spent every day looking for Gu Meiquan, but he didn't find him. Clothing and food soon became a problem, and then he had no choice but to look for work. He went to all the places where there were people from his hometown. It wasn't that they didn't want to help, but that they couldn't find work either. All they could do was lend him a few cents and send him on his way. He also went to the Wuxi guild house, but the gate guard chased him away. Sometimes he spent the whole day looking without finding any work. At other times, in order to get just a few copper coins, he ran errands for shopowners who knew him. He thought of pulling a rickshaw, but he wasn't familiar with the streets of Hankou and the rickshaw company wanted a deposit. He inquired at several small coppersmithing shops, but none of them were hiring new workers. He couldn't afford to rent a place to live any longer, so he slept at Grandma Wang's under the stairs. Seeing how miserable he was, Grandma Wang let him stay without paying. Detectives from the *yamen* often came to pressure him, and he felt it necessary to treat them to some tea. Sometimes this pressure made him feel fed up with this "official matter." Eventually he began to think about Gu Meiquan less and less. Formerly he had thought only of catching him and boiling his flesh. Now he looked at the matter with less intensity. If he killed Gu Meiquan, what good would that do him? Yet he never completely forgot his desire for revenge. His unemployment, his lack of a home, and the tragic death of his wife were all the work of Gu Meiquan!

Several letters from Acui asking about her husband's whereabouts were taken from jail. Because of her own suffering she often hated him, but she didn't wish for his capture, since he would have to pay with his life. She thought of her own life. She would become old and die in this dark, sunless, flea-infested jail. Her food was a coarse rice that was worse than husks. She slept on an ice-cold dirt floor. She was beaten by the guards and had to endure their loathsome advances. She was only nineteen years old. Ten years. Twenty years. Who knew how many days she would spend there. The thought terrified her. She thought longingly of her family and all the people she knew. She yearned for a ray of sunlight and a breath of fresh air. At times she thought that if Gu Meiquan were captured, maybe she could be released from jail, but . . . that would mean the end of his life! If he died, what would happen to her? And so she grew thinner and fell ill.

Grandma Wang came to see her once. Gou Yazai's mother brought him over once too. Just seeing them increased her sadness. All they could give her were women's tears. The weather turned cold. Although there was no wind or snow in the jail, she could not get away from the cold air. And so her illness worsened.

When the first letter came, many people in the alley ran over to have a look. This was news! Gu Meiquan had written a letter home. When Yu Axiao received it, he grew even angrier. It stirred up a great deal of hatred within him. However, Grandma Wang told him, "This is the truth! What does this have to do with his wife? If she isn't released, she'll certainly die in jail."

Axiao also thought of that morning when Acui had run over and told him to hide. Acui had been their friend.

Someone else told Axiao, "Gu Meiquan is speaking honestly. He had no reason to want to kill your wife. Naturally he knows he was wrong, but now he can't show his face. The *yamen* has a legal case, so as soon as he shows his face he'll die. Now you're only harming his wife, and she hasn't committed a crime. In my view, Axiao, you should go and plead for leniency. Have that woman released." Many others added their agreement. They all said he shouldn't have the woman locked up in prison until she died.

In light of their opinions, Axiao went to see someone at the *yamen*, who promptly cursed him for being stupid. He asked Axiao if criminals should be able to come and go as they pleased. This woman could be released only after the murderer was caught and tried and it was verified that she really was innocent. As for her illness, there were sick people all around, and some criminals even feigned illness.

Everyone felt that Acui was innocent and was being harshly treated, but no one had any power. All they could do was hate this unreasonable law. Grandma Wang then took an old padded jacket and went to see her again. She told her that a letter had come from Gu Meiquan and that Yu Axiao had tried to have her released. Acui cried again.

Gu Meiquan had still not been captured, and Axiao was having more difficulty getting by. He too fell in with a large group of unemployed workers. The drunkard Zhang Zongrong was also there, but he drank very little now. There were all unable to find work and their stomachs were making things hard on them, but as a group they managed to come up with some solutions. Gathering together and demanding solidarity, they went to social welfare offices and municipal party offices to demand a place to stay and a food allowance. The first time a few policemen were used to scare them off, but the next time they came with more people and the police were of no use. The only thing to do was deceive them and give them a little something. But deception could not last long, and then they were back again. As this went on, Yu Axiao came to understand more. He no longer cared about where Gu Meiquan was.

Then Gu Meiquan's second letter came. This letter made things clear, and Yu Axiao understood Gu's meaning. He completely forgave his friend. He also talked with many others, who encouraged him to drop the legal case and be done with it. Why should he want Gu Meiquan's wife confined until she died and Meiquan unable to show his face for the rest of his life? What they said made sense to Yu Axiao. Even though Gu Meiquan had wronged him, he would forgive him. So he asked someone to submit a petition to the *yamen* saying that he wished to rescind the charge. The *yamen*, however, replied that this would not be permitted. This was a murder case, and such a serious charge could not just be dropped. Acui still could not be released. All Yu Axiao could do was regret that he had charged Gu Meiquan.

Since facts had proven that they didn't have the slightest bit of power, Yu Axiao found it best to put this matter out of his mind. Maybe Gu Meiquan wouldn't be caught. Perhaps Acui would gradually get better. Instead of thinking more about this problem, he enthusiastically joined the group of unemployed workers in planning ways for everyone to make a living.

9

Although Axiao and Meiquan had forgotten the matter and didn't want to think about it, there were people who didn't want to forget. After the Shanghai Detective Bureau received notification, they kept the case in the active file. Also, because they had received orders to forestall anti-Japanese activity, they disbanded some volunteer units. And since they feared that even though these volunteer units were disbanded, they might still be secretly active, they tightened up undercover surveillance of the units. It was through this investigation of disbanded volunteer units that they found out about Gu Meiquan. One night, intimidated by the guns of more than ten men, he was tied up and taken away. It was like the capture of a great bandit. Then, because this was a major case, it was decided that the trial would be held in Shanghai. Yu Axiao, Acui, Grandma Wang, and others were to be brought there at once.

The news saddened Acui. She thought of the prospect of seeing her husband again, but when she remembered that he might lose his life, she grew anxious, and her illness worsened. Grandma Wang didn't want to go to Shanghai, so she went into hiding. Yu Axiao wanted to hide too, but he was caught and escorted to Shanghai. On the day that the trial started, he saw his enemy, Gu Meiquan. The two of them had grown much thinner and much dirtier. They looked at each other. There were many things they wanted to say, but they were not allowed to speak. Xiao Yuzi's mother came too. As soon as she saw Axiao, she started to cry. She hated the murderer.

Gu Meiquan presented everything according to the facts. Some of those who were listening couldn't keep from shaking their heads. They couldn't decide whether he was right or wrong. The judge also questioned Yu Axiao. He too spoke according to the facts. Then at the end, he added this statement: "I wish to take back my written complaint. I don't want Gu Meiquan to forfeit his life. I want to forgive him and be done with this. He committed a crime, but he cannot assume all of the responsibility. I regret very much that I have filed this 'official matter.' It hasn't been good for me at all."

The judge listened to him with a completely expressionless face. All he said was that everything would be decided according to the law.

The next day the verdict was announced. Gu Meiquan was taken to Caohejing and shot. Acui died in the Hankou jail at about the same time. Yu Axiao found himself charged by the detective bureau for not paying any of the reward that he had agreed to provide. The detectives had not volunteered to capture someone for him. So he was arrested and locked up in jail. No one knows when he will finally gain his release.

Translated by Gary J. Bjorge

Mother

Ding Ling wrote the novel *Mother* over the months between May 1932 and April 1933. She was at the time reeling under horrible personal tragedies and a worsening political situation. She wrote it for money and never had a chance to revise it. It was long as a consequence and considerably more disjointed than this excerpt suggests. The original novel is twice the size of this selection and is divided into four chapters of equal length and weight.

Chapter 1 does not appear here since it is the chapter least connected to the novel's central plot line, the education of the "New Woman" Yu Manzhen. In the initial chapter, Ding Ling introduces the rural Jiang family and their old slave Yao Ma, and she seems to toy with the idea of making Manzhen a perfect Confucian widow. Manzhen is sick for most of the narrative and revives only to greet the old family servant who has come from Wuling to take her home to the Yu family. It thus seems most logical to excise this part.

Other cuts have deleted repetition and obvious padding. Some cuts have been made out of consideration to Western readers. Drinking parties, extra characters and discussion of their kin relations, a visit to Manzhen's Jiang in-laws at Wuling, a lavish party at Du Shuzhen's mansion all delight the reader accustomed to old-fashioned Chinese domestic novels. Chinese readers are trained to luxuriate in these huge casts of characters and to appreciate the ways in which kinship ties connect them all. They also have the cultural background to connect the elaborate descriptions of hair, costumes, and furniture to actual garments and objects. These interesting but, from the point of view of the English reader, dispensable extras have therefore been sacrificed.

A great deal happens in this novel despite the cuts. In chapter 2, Manzhen leaves the country for the city, a movement that represents the movement of her social class in general. Chapter 3 finds her entering a women's academy, where her political consciousness expands, her patriotism deepens, and her relations with other women become modern and exciting. In chapter 4, Manzhen swears a revolutionary oath of political sisterhood with her friends in her father's garden. The novel describes in loving detail the new world that liberated Manzhen and her sisters create. They unbind their feet and push their fragile bodies, scale down their elaborate gentry hairdos and silver bangles. At each step they redefine their social relationships and make decisions on the basis of how their personal behavior can benefit the nation.

One of the many peculiarities of this novel is the way Ding Ling portrays her mother in it. The portrait of Manzhen doesn't resemble anything else she'd written to that point, and it certainly flew in the face of her own published opinion that political writers (like herself) ought to stop writing from autobiographic experience and start writing about proletarian or peasant subjects. It remains one of the few fictional representations of the gentry women's liberation movement.—TEB

Spring

Chapter 2

Manzhen's family was like so many other families. Most of their land was rented out to tenant farmers. However, for convenience' sake, to keep their servants fully occupied, and to project an image appropriate to the gentleman farmer, they always set aside the land right outside the gate closest to the house for themselves. They'd farmed more land in previous years when there'd been a lot of servants. This year, as only Changgeng was left, they prepared just one *shi* and divided the rest up between the tenant farmers. Despite the fact that he was the only one left to do the work, Changgeng was happy as ever. He'd wake up every morning at dawn, as the clear, cold dawn wind blew through his little room, whistle a tune, then throw on his short, light padded clothing, and go to the kitchen where roaches were still scrabbling over the stove. He opened the side door and walked out onto the stone embankment. Constantly in flux, countless blue, purple, yellow, red, and gold clouds banked the silver sky as the sun broke over the mountain. The cocks in the back garden began to crow joyously. As Changgeng headed away from the house, one of the dogs fell quietly in behind him while the other followed far behind. The scent blown on the wind breathed spring. The wind carried the smell of the moist, bedewed mud. It was deeply satisfying! The spring dawns were cold, but Changgeng was oblivious to it. The mud under his feet was moist, but he was oblivious to that as well. *Mu* by *mu* he circled the field. The soil was awakening. The surface soil had already turned color and purple weeds were in bloom on the field. The sun shone down on him. Bees flew about. And Changgeng? Changgeng, as he'd learned to do from his father before him, sat up on the bank of the field, looked around at the purple sea stretching out everywhere, opened the buttons of his shirt, lit the pipe he'd just learned to use, and gazed lovingly about as he thought to himself: get to work!

Changgeng really couldn't afford to rest there for long. Each day was busier than the last and each day the work was harder. But it was the kind of work that resulted in something. When he stood in the field and pulled open the ears of grain, when the golden grains were unleashed into the wooden barrel, and when he carried it bushel by bushel from the field to the house, his heart overflowed with joy! Her head wrapped in a cloth, as was her custom, Yao Ma would greet him at the side of the road with a bowl of cold tea. Although the grain belonged not to him but to his employer—the person he called "master"—who could really claim that the land and the grain weren't rightfully his? He loved it as though it were his own child. He was never far from it. He tilled it. He stood in the middle of it and soaked his feet in its moist, mild, muddy water; even in his dreams he was never free from the thought of what it needed to thrive. After the harvest, he'd carry the grain to the master's granary, but the master never loved it. When the grain had been husked and was boiling in the caldron, giving off its indescribable fragrance, only Changgeng could smile to himself. Or when the grain had been carted away, sold by the master to pay his debts, only Changgeng grieved and mourned! Changgeng was the son of a tenant farmer and had become a hired hand. He'd grown up on the land and had known neither dire poverty nor great wealth. His employer was magnanimous. He was contented to remain the young fellow he was, with only his labor to sell.

Yao Ma seemed restored to youth. She made her rounds ceaselessly, allocated each his or her work, and not the slightest detail escaped her notice. Her second son left home, but her young grandchild still came over, for he had learned to ride herd on the cow. And he was good for other tasks as well.

Every night when everyone else was asleep, Yao Ma came to Manzhen. "Nainai," she would say, "Let's hatch some more chicks this year, and not do a slap-dash job of it like last year. When we get them to market, I think we can get two hundred *qian* apiece for them, or more, and probably five apiece for the eggs."

Manzhen would look at her and smile. She wouldn't answer. Manzhen had never given thought to the fact that perhaps it was her turn to become a chicken peddler. She knew Yao Ma's intentions were good. But from her point of view, chicken peddling was simply out of the question. Still Yao Ma continued.

"We'd best not limit ourselves to an increase of one or two hundred chickens. We probably should raise some more piglets as well. It's a disgrace to waste the leftovers, and we've got our own husks for pig-feed right here on the farm. Laotou hasn't anything else to keep him occupied now, and when autumn comes they'll bring us a good income. Don't look down your nose at it, Nainai. You can't compare the present with what's past and you are going to have to calculate carefully now to get by. There just isn't anything left of the old family prestige, so the best thing to do is put all that behind us. If you would cut back on your social obligations, we'd have fewer expenditures. The days of lavishness and high society entertainment are behind us now. You can't be longing for those days back again, not until your little son makes a success of himself, now can you?"

Sometimes Manzhen could be swayed to take some interest in Yao Ma's plans. "I just don't know anything about farming," she'd say. "And what if my husband's brothers say something about it?"

"What are you afraid of? They'd do the same as you if they found themselves in your shoes. How can they say anything if we sell off our surplus to meet everyday expenses? If they want to mind our business for us, they should mind it all. Are they going to bring up your orphans for you? It's not like what happened in the past. Your son's great-grandfather had a different situation. His uncles treated him as if he were their own son, and he worked hard to repay them for it. He earned his high place in society through his own struggle and effort, and he lived up to their expectations of him. The way I see it, we have to make our own calculations. Qiuchan has free time. For quite a while I've been thinking of exchanging last year's raw cotton for some processed cotton. Then everyday we could spin a little cotton thread. When I'm free or when a wet nurse has some time, we can spin too. One wet nurse has to go. Even with a large pot of rice, it's worthwhile since it's one less mouth we have to feed. You're familiar with this kind of thing, naturally, Nainai, so don't you bother about it. You just let me handle it. But I need your approval, Nainai. There's a master in every house, and I'm really only just a slave."

"Whatever you say," said Manzhen. "Do whatever you want. Just don't let anyone know that we're selling things."

Manzhen didn't have a better plan. She had only thought the problem through to the point of how she was going to get new clothing for the children, and no further. All she really possessed was a determination to endure hardship, and for her children's futures she was prepared to sacrifice a great deal. Destiny had decreed that she undergo a great hardship, and she was planning to set about it without fear. But in truth, she had no idea what hardship was, no inkling of what hardship really entailed.

Yao Ma did let one wet nurse go. When the woman left, Manzhen gave her two old dresses and packed a basket with three *sheng* of rice and some yams and taro. Qiuchan spent her time spinning at the squeaking loom in the back room. At first she thought it was a lot of fun, but later on she began to get listless and lazy. Yao Ma came in to chew her out.

"You think you're spinning just for me, do you? You think later on when you get married you aren't going to need clothes yourself? How much money is Nainai supposed to spend to buy you ready-made clothes in town?"

So Qiuchan spun on. Only Manzhen sat with nothing to keep her busy. When she'd first been married, Manzhen had tried spinning just for the fun of it, so now she came over to watch Qiuchan at work. Qiuchan understood that her mistress wanted to try it.

"Can you spin, Nainai?" she asked. "Would you like to try?" and up she jumped from the spinning wheel.

The wet nurse humored Manzhen as well. "It's as easy as pie, but I'll bet Nainai never did it before, right?"

"I have done it before. Why shouldn't I be able to. I can probably spin better than you can . . ."

And so Manzhen sat down with them. She was lighthanded and did spin a very fine, uniform thread. But after a few minutes her hands became too heavy to lift and she gave it up. Anyway, watching the others spin was just as interesting for her.

. . . .

Several times during the fair weather, Yao Ma came to urge her mistress: "Nainai, the peach blossoms are out. Walk around the gate. The rain was excellent this year and last year the heavy snows came at just the right time. Go take a look. There's a bit of a wind, but nothing to worry about. Walking is a good way to relieve anxiety, and you can lean on Qiuchan."

After a glance out the window, Manzhen consented happily. So the whole group of them set off—Qiuchan and Shuner leading Xiao Han by the hand, and Yao Ma. As they reached the gate, three dogs joined their ranks.

"Oh, it's really and truly spring! Its been so long since I ventured past these gates that the scenery has changed quite a bit. Isn't that row of red flowers over there by the pond peach blossom? Have the magnolias the Chens sent us from their garden dropped their flowers already?"

"No," Qiuchan answered. "Those aren't peach flowers, they're lilacs. Aren't those the peach over by the path leading to the vegetable garden? Oh, the flower garden at the old mansion must be lovely now. They have so many flowers there that there can't be a single one they don't have. Isn't that right, Yao Ma?"

"My, my, my," said Manzhen. "It's been so long since I've been outside I feel as though my eyes have gone bad. Oh, over there in the distance. Aren't those rape flowers. The rape are in bloom!"

Without her noticing, happiness flooded Manzhen. She gazed all around with warm, tender eyes. The wind carried a scent with it. Had the swallows come? Were their nests still intact? Xiao Han walked along in front of her mother, skipping and babbling her own little song.

They walked slowly along the paved stone road. The cedars on both sides were bedecked with fresh green growth. Suddenly Manzhen walked in among the trees, took a hairpin from her head, and slashed at a large spider web. "These really deserve constant attention, you know!" she said to Yao Ma.

"We just don't have enough hands to go around anymore," the old woman replied. "There are so many things that need to be done. When you recover your health, Nainai, then we can set to work on these things one at a time. You take the lead and it will be simple. In a couple of days, we can get some laborers in to fix things up and a gardener to straighten out the garden and take a look at those trees. Then everything will be fine again, I guarantee it."

Yao Ma brimmed with enthusiasm. She hoped that Manzhen would get started, would talk things over with her and pay attention to all the arrangements she was making. All Yao Ma could think of was how to improve things for the family.

When they reached the end of the road, Manzhen sat down on a rock. Off in the middle of the far field was Changgeng, his jacket slung over his shoulders, as he urged the ox forward from behind the plow. And the purple sea, the tiny purple flowers that he so adored, waved and rolled as he passed through them, turning them under the sod. When he saw the women, he stopped immediately.

"Old Mother Yao! Nainai came out with you as well? Nainai, I hope you're feeling well. The weather is magnificent today, isn't it?" he shouted in greeting.

Manzhen simply nodded at him, so the robust young man put his effort into getting the ox moving again.

"He's a useful fellow. A dutiful fellow. As long as you don't get in his way, he'll work for you as though he were working for himself. He's got a head on his shoulders." This Yao Ma murmured to Manzhen in the way of explanation. Then she shouted to Changgeng, "Don't forget to go to the market place for the piglets."

"I haven't forgotten. I'll go tomorrow," came the cheerful reply, floating back to them because he did not turn his head.

There were others, as well, off in the distance, turning the dirt in their fields. That land also belonged to Manzhen's family. If you proceeded beyond that, the land belonged to the Seventh Master. Seventh Master's house was visible from where they stood, although you could really only make out the white wall and black tiles. A number of households lay outside of Lingling Hollow, but they were just tenant farming households. On the other three sides of the hollow were low-lying hills tipped with trees that provided firewood. Beyond those hills the land belonged to other families. The foot of the hills were surrounded with houses. Lingling Brook flowed out of those back hills and made a steep bend. It was a very long stream that meandered in circles around the thickets of the hilltops, down around the hollow, out to Chaizhu Wall, and then . . . to places unknown. Because it was such a small stream and did not follow a large road, no one paid it much heed, and there was no specific name attached to it. This was truly a peaceful place, and no noise, beyond that of the birds and butterflies or the bees and insects, disturbed their peace. Manzhen and the others lingered for a while, until at Yao Ma's urging they continued on to the pond. It was so still that they could see the reflected clouds in the blue sky floating on its surface. The tan ducks and red-beaked goose bobbing leisurely on the pond swam off at the sight of the women. Tiny purple flowers dotted the wild grass at the road side; white flowers and soft branches reached up onto the sides of the road. Manzhen needed to lean on Qiuchan to make the going a little easier, for although she had changed into flat shoes, she was getting tired. But Yao Ma wanted to take her to the vegetable garden. Yao Ma's pretext was that Manzhen should view the peach blossoms. Actually, she wanted her to see the garden itself. Laotou and Laifa (for that was their grandson's name) came out of the garden to welcome them.

"Go on in and take a look, Nainai," Yao Ma said. "I've settled everything with Laotou. We don't need much produce this year since the family is smaller now. So we've planted a large portion of the garden in peanuts and set up a trellis for pumpkins. Since it's just not appropriate for you to be selling things, Nainai, you can send these as gifts, instead, and avoid having to spend any cash. We'll certainly have enough to eat after planting this. Little Laifa here is a good boy, and he'll keep ahead of the insects and do the weeding. Look, it's not just the peach trees that have burst into bloom, the willow are turning yellow as well . . ."

Manzhen knew very well that Yao Ma was giving her the soft sell on the garden. Yao Ma still wanted to drag her over to see the chickens, pigs, and new bamboo, but it just wasn't possible. Manzhen's feet and her soft, weak body forced her to demur, and leaning heavily on her maid, she returned to the house. Yao Ma and Xiao Han stayed outside.

Day by day the weather got warmer. Manzhen ventured outdoors a few more times, and even brought the infant. Occasionally she spent several days outside in a row. Qiuchan fixed her a willow chair, and she would bring the children out to bask in the sun on the flat embankment. In past years she had had little chance to spend time outdoors, because usually the house was filled with guests. It wouldn't have been appropriate to sneak off by herself with all the servants around, and she'd never quite figured out how to manage it. So even when she'd thought about it, too many things had worked to prevent it. Now there was nothing to fill her days, and since it was spring and there was no one at home, the maids and women servants encouraged her to spend her time outside the house. Yao Ma filled her in on all the things that she would need to know now that she was a gentleman farmer. So frequently she would spend the day sitting and talking with the wet nurses.

"Are things pretty much the same where you come from?" she might chatter. "No matter how high the mountains are where you come from, I'm sure they couldn't be anywhere near as high as the ones in Guizhou. When I was little, I went there with an uncle. It's a terrifying place. When you look down at the foot of the mountain all you can see are clouds, as if there were a huge river below you. For scenery, of course, Yunnan is the best, really exquisite. The weather is fantastic, neither hot nor cold. But it's too far away. It takes two months to cross that mountain road. I hear that now you can go through a foreign country and cross the ocean and get there faster than if you go overland, but I don't know precisely how they do it . . ."

Guizhou, Yunnan, the scenery, and so on, made absolutely no sense to the wet nurses, who simply listened politely. But one of the women couldn't restrain her curiosity over Manzhen's last statement. "Foreign Country?" she asked. "What do you mean 'Foreign Country'?"

"Foreign countries are foreign countries, and there are a lot of them! Years ago, right after Miss Han was born, my husband, the Third Laoye, and his uncle went to Japan to study, but it was just too hard on them. They only stayed a year and then back they came. They had cut off their queues in Japan, so when they came back they were afraid to let anyone see them. They put false queues on their hats, and let me tell you, it wasn't easy getting those false queues to stick. The country I called Japan is not much different from our own country, although they don't wear the same kind of clothing we do. Much further away there are places called England, France, and so on . . . People from those countries don't look like us at all. They have green eyes and red hair. In 1900, the year of the Boxer Rebellion, they attacked Beijing. The Emperor and Empress Dowager had to flee to Shaanxi. I don't know how many people they killed, but they had foreign guns so all they had to do was aim at a person and he was dead. There's a church in Wuling now that they preach in. They don't believe in worshiping the ancestors or the Boddhisatva.[1] They believe in some kind of god, and a Jesus. I've heard that a lot of Chinese believe in him too. The church is rich. I suppose there's merit in turning convert, though I can't see it myself."

"Nainai," said the wet nurse. "Is it true that foreigners kidnap children and cut their eyes out to make medicine?"

"Actually, I'm really not sure whether that's true or not. From what I've read in books, I do know that their doctors use knives. They even lance little boils with them."

"I've heard," said the other woman, "that foreign women don't wear trousers. Do you know if that's true?"

"Has anyone ever seen one of them? You'll only find out if you get to see one yourself. All I know is that foreign women are different from Chinese women. They don't bind their feet; they bind their waists. Have you ever seen that clock stand of ours? The foreign women on that clock stand have such tiny little waists. They can go to school, though, and are free to do all kinds of things like going into politics or becoming an official. They have a much better life than we Chinese women have. It's the rules of etiquette that are the cause of our suffering, and with us Chinese the richer your family is, the harder it is to be a woman."

"Poor women have to suffer in their own way," the wet nurse countered.

"Yes, you're right . . ."

Then Manzhen raised her eyes and looked all round. Everywhere she looked, her gaze was returned with joyous colors. It made her feel that she should stop talking about suffering. This was such a joyous place, and she had lived here for so many years and had never known it until now. She had read many ancient poems that had just this kind of setting. This was the pastoral life she had thought of so affectionately, the leisurely, disengaged country life she had wanted. Though she was now a poor woman, still she would not have to surrender this house and the surrounding hills and fields. She could avoid most of her social obligations and wouldn't have people coming to visit with her much. She could go along with Yao Ma and the servants and toil away earnestly at the work to be done. They wouldn't lack for anything and would be happy. As soon as she had the time, she would begin to teach Xiao Han some characters, and as the baby grew, she'd be able to teach him as well, and wouldn't have to hire a tutor.[2] Life was not completely without hope. All that was needed was for her to make the decision. Let the past be buried. Her old life was not something to waste time pining for. The new must start afresh and everything and everyone was waiting for her. She must strip off the gown of the mistress and put on the garb of the farmer's wife and capable mother. Manzhen straightened her back, looked proudly out into the distance, then back at the house, as though to say, "All right, I'll show you all!"

So many things depended on Yao Ma for their impetus. Frequently the old lady was too busy even to comb her white hair into place, and it hung loose on her forehead. Often she'd seek out a flat rock on which to sit and rest and knead her tiny little feet between her palms.[3] Qiuchan and Shuner both helped her around the house. But they also liked to work outside, for the weather was beautiful, and anyway, there were considerably fewer restrictions on their activity now. Manzhen's spirits rose with the passage of each day, and her health improved correspondingly. Just then, however, the family in Wuling sent a messenger and a sedan chair out to the farm.

"I really must go see them. Oh, dear, how time has flown. It's been six or seven months, hasn't it." Her mother had been dead that long.

So she turned over most of her affairs to her husband's Fourth Uncle, some to one of Xiao Han's paternal uncles, and placed authority for the family, the little farming family she had just joined, into Yao Ma's hands. One day at dawn, she left with her children, the wet nurse, and Qiuchan.

Left behind, Yao Ma sat on the flat stone at the mouth of the road, gazing in the direction of the departing sedan chair. The sad loneliness of an old person welled up inside her. For some time she dwelt on thoughts of her mistress. Oh, how lonely her lot was! Manzhen was so totally alone, and there were so many barriers she would have to overcome. She had the two children dependent on her, and she herself was so fragile, so ignorant in the face of hardship. Yao Ma saw the sedan chair off into the distance. The further they went, the tinier they were to the naked eye, and the more Yao Ma was filled with a floating feeling. She thought she'd feel better if only she could say something to someone, but when she turned her head, she found that the servants who'd been standing behind her had all left. All that remained was a flock of newly hatched chicks, pecking at the ground a short distance from where she stood.

"Tsk, tsk, tsk," she called to them. The chicks fought each other in their rush to get to her. "Hold on, hold on," she said lovingly. "I'll go fetch you some grain. I'll feed you and then later you'll feed me. Grow big and plump for me, my little darlings. She'll come back this summer, so let's get everything done for her."

Yao Ma got to her feet, turned, and slowly walked home, the chicks peeping along at her heels.

Manzhen was feeling sad too, as if life was the wind and she a leaf, blown in its wake. She huddled down in her sedan chair in dead silence, totally dependent upon the bearers to take her where she was going. She stared stolidly at the distant horizon and then shifted her gaze to the scenery passing by the sides of the sedan chair. The loneliness at the bottom of her heart grew even more profound. But a strong patient strength started to grow inside her as well. If she was to lead her children forward from this lonely destination, she could not afford to be intimidated by anything. She must not be afraid of the things that hurt her the most, the things that could most easily destroy her courage: no mate, no help, no sympathy!

Throughout the journey, Manzhen used every bit of strength she had to comfort and control herself, to somehow get herself through the day.

It was evening before the sedan chair entered the little west gate into Wuling. By that time there were very few pedestrians out. The shops were shut down for the night, shutters in place, doors locked. Only through the cracks in the wooden doors did a little light spill out into the street. Only a little inn around the corner emitted the sounds of laughter and conversation. The sound of a flute playing the haunting love song "Long for You Every Season of the Year" came wafting out of someone's courtyard. Before long the sedan chair stopped in front of an imposing stone gate from which hung huge lanterns with the words "Prefect Yu's Residence" written on them. The bearers sounded the brass ring on the iron gate and announced simply "Fifth Daughter is home." It brought a rush of sounds from within and then the outer and inner gates swung open. Precisely as the sedan chair reached the central hall, a frightening chorus of female wailing began in the third hall. At the same time, out from under the lanterns and candles strode a beautiful and intense young man. In one rapid motion he moved to the front of the sedan chair, supporting the half-fainting Manzhen with his hand.

"Fifth Elder Sister! Manzhen!"

"Oh, Yundi, Little Brother!" Her strength had already given way. Most of the year, during the most recent past, she'd borne her hardships. But now as her very closest relative, her strong, capable younger brother sprang up before her eyes, a new weakness overcame her, a weakness she had never before experienced. She broke into bitter tears when she perceived anew her own isolation and her need for the pity of others. She wept until she felt empty. She had longed to weep without restraint on her mother's bosom. Now nothing inhibited her tears, but she would weep not on mother's bosom but at her dead mother's altar.

Women servants and maids supported her, and surrounding her, the group moved toward the back room. A beautiful young woman, her sister-in-law, Third Mistress Yu, greeted Manzhen, looking as though she had already cried herself to exhaustion. Manzhen ran to the altar, knelt down before it, and then prostrated herself on the ground, sobbing. Everyone present wept in response. Terrified, the children began to wail. Xiao Han crawled on the floor too, grasping at her mother's clothes, crying piercingly. Only very slowly did Manzhen calm down. By then only her sister-in-law and brother remained to console her.

"Fifth Sister, Manzhen, your health is important. Stop, stop. I beg you both, don't cry anymore," Yunqing said.

Then only Manzhen continued to cry. Finally, influenced by their warm feelings, a mixture of heated towels and hot tea, and their soothing talk, Manzhen slowly stopped her spasmodic weeping.

She had no rest that evening. She and her brother and sister-in-law and an elderly wife of one of her cousins who lived with them talked until late in the night. She questioned them at length, listened at length, and at last, she told them her story. What passed between them was almost unendurable, and even harder to bear were the memories, and so they divided their time between talking and weeping. It was not until the third watch sounded that they went to bed. Ensconced in her quilt, Manzhen could not avoid solitary, silent tears. She was so unlike her brother. He had such potential. Since childhood he had been a boy whose brilliance and capacity won praise. But Manzhen, Manzhen was merely a weak, incompetent girl. He was possessed of a fertile estate, and she had to sell her land to pay her debts. She was only a year older than he, and as children they had always played together. She had been as strong as he in everything back then. But later on he had studied, while she had been sealed up in her room learning to embroider flowers on cloth shoes. He had entered the academy, and she had coveted his glory "from behind the screen." Now the discrepancy was too great to overcome. He had

education, ideas, and a profession. The brilliance of his future was un-
limited. And she? All she could do was take Yao Ma's advice, hatch her
hundred chicks, raise little piglets, and grow peanuts and pumpkins!
Yunqing's children would become like him, like their grandfather. But
her children would have nothing to depend on but her little chicks. She
couldn't help resenting, and was particularly unwilling to submit to the
fact, that she had been born a woman. She wasn't afraid of hardship.
She longed to create a world for herself out of hardship itself. But in this
society she was not even allowed to meet alone with her own eldest
brother-in-law. What use was served by a tiny, willowy woman with
bound feet entertaining such high ambitions! Restrictions were fixed by
all the books and all the rules of common etiquette. What single individual could break through these restrictions?

Her eldest and third oldest sisters came home to see her, and several
female cousins from her father's side of the family came as well, as did
female cousins from her mother's side of the family, and the wives of
cousins from her father's side. So the household was full of life despite
the daily sound of weeping.

. . . .

But as time wore on, even more emptiness slipped into Manzhen's life.
She wanted to detain her eldest sister—whose husband had already left
for Honan and who had no children—for another two days.

"No," her sister said, in a quandary. "I really should go home. I'll be
back in a few days to see you again, all right? I'm not going far."

"No," said Manzhen. "You must stay. I still have a number of things I
want to discuss with you. You stayed with me for eight or nine days once
a long time ago."

"You don't know, Fifth Sister. Things will be far better if I come back
in a few days."

"What do you mean?" Manzhen asked.

Unable to come up with a plausible excuse, Eldest Sister had no option
but to stay. Still, during dinner she announced to them all, "Manzhen is
acting like a child. She insists on keeping me here even though I must go
home. There are things needing to be done there."

"If it's nothing important," Third Mistress Yu said clearly, "you can
certainly stay a few more days and keep Manzhen company. You're in
your own home, so there's no need to be so formal." Manzhen's sister bit
her lip and changed the subject.

During all this, Manzhen had come to feel that something was missing
in the family. Had this scene unfolded in years past, her sisters wanting
to leave and all, their gentle elderly mother would have chided them
sweetly, "What's so urgent. You're forbidden to go, dear. What is it here
that's making you so uncomfortable? It's true, isn't it, what they say

about daughters, that they're fated to marry and favor their husbands over their own families!"

And so it was the next day: her eldest sister left, and Manzhen made only a half-hearted attempt to get her to stay. Now Manzhen understood that this house was not her home. Eldest Sister apologetically tried to make her feel better: "Tomorrow or the next day, I'll send someone to fetch you so you can stay with me for a while. Stay the latter part of the year, all right?"

Manzhen felt no grudge toward her sister-in-law. Third Mistress Yu was being far more hospitable and considerate than in past years. She was even paying attention to Xiao Han's needs. In the past she'd never been as attentive as she was now. She was such an outstanding, clever, competent person, that everyone envied her as soon as they met her. There were four sisters in her family, all of them famous for their beauty. She took excellent care of her appearance, paying equal attention to her makeup and clothing. She usually wore clothing of simple elegance, and her cosmetics were delicately applied. She had dainty eyebrows, lively moist eyes, and a row of bangs that hung over her forehead evenly smoothed off to one side. During mourning she wore only a small pearl flower in her bun. She had an exceptionally tiny waist, and when she walked she swayed provocatively. Her voice was clear and crisp, so when she talked she seemed so lively and bright. Her husband was someone she could boast about in the presence of others. She was rich, and she knew how to flaunt her status. Although she was only twenty-six, she already had four children, the oldest daughter seven years old. Now, after her mother-in-law's death, she was free to run the family. She was skilled at needlepoint, and the flowers she produced won universal praise. She knew a good number of ideographs as well, and she kept her accounts in meticulous order. Busy from morning to night, she always managed to find time to teach her children to read. Zhuer already knew nearly a hundred ideographs; little five-year-old Yuer knew several dozen. As soon as it was afternoon, she set the older children down on stools to read ideographs printed on little squares of paper. The method of recognizing the picture and learning the ideographs from flashcards was new. On each card an ideograph was printed on one side and a picture on the other. A bookstore in Shanghai had printed them, and they had been very popular. Manzhen, who happened to be walking by during their study time one day, saw the flash cards; she too thought they were wonderful.

"Why, aren't these nice. Where did you buy them?" she asked.

"Their daddy brought them from Shanghai, but I've heard you can buy them in town now, because a kindergarten is going to open."

"I suppose that a kindergarten is a school?"

"Schools themselves are not that rare, but they're going to have a women's school. Apparently there are two women's schools in the provincial capital. Wang Zongren used to come over to our house every day, and my husband was happy as a lark. They were very busy for over a month, though I don't know what they were doing. They'll open the new school in September. One class will be an accelerated teacher's training course and the other a kindergarten. They've already found a place for it. It's on Shitou lane, in the house where the Cai family used to live. Do you remember them? Wang Zongren will be the principal. When September comes around, I'm going to send these little folks to kindergarten."

When Manzhen heard this bit of news, she didn't dare believe it. "Are you sure about this? Who is Wang Zongren? What's a teacher's training course?" she asked.

"Wang Zongren is Wang Guoqing's son. Wang Guoqing was father's disciple. They disregard the master-student relationship now, and just call each other by their first names when they meet. They went to Japan together. He was also close to your husband. As for teacher training, I don't understand what it's all about either. Apparently it's a course devoted to teaching people to be teachers. There will be women teachers—a strange turn of events."

"Daddy said that when I get big he's going to send me abroad, Auntie Manzhen." Zhuer's speech was just as sharp as her mother's.

As they were talking Yunqing came into the room. "Hurry and find me a suit of clothing," he said, so pressed for time he couldn't greet them properly. "I've got an appointment with the county magistrate, and I've got to change my hat too.[4] I'm so busy, Manzhen, I just can't find the time to sit down and have a chat with you."

"It's good to be as busy as you are," she replied. "There's nothing for people like us who have to look for things to do. Do you know how boring it is to sit around with time on your hands?" When Manzhen saw how spirited her brother was, she couldn't help but envy him, and she sensed that time was passing her by.

After she had brought him his clothing, Third Mistress Yu handed him a hat with a queue hanging down from it like a black snake. Then Yunqing revealed his barbered head, and his unusual appearance struck Manzhen as rather unattractive.

"Haven't you grown one out yet?" she asked him. "Or have you cut it off again? Are you going to spend your whole life like that? You really can't take your hat off when you're at someone's house."

"No, I haven't grown one; none of us are going to. One day we'll all have to cut out queues, and just think how splendid it will be when that time comes."⁵ Yunqing gave a meaningful smile. There seemed to be so much he left unsaid.

"I won't be home for dinner tonight," he said as he walked to the anteroom to change, holding his clothing. "When Wang Zongren comes, I want to rush on over to Wu Dingguang's and wait for my response."

"All right."

The two women gazed at each other and both knew why he had to go out—especially Manzhen, who seemed at a loss for words to describe her own mood. The world was changing. Yunqing was changing. Although they hadn't said much to each other, she could see that his behavior was really different. He was teaching now in a boy's school that had just opened, but what he taught had little in common with what his father had taught before him. He did not spend his time teaching people how to write essays. Instead, he taught his students how to go about putting the country in order. He talked about civil rights, the Republic, and other strange novelties. Now he wanted to run a women's school. But what use was it for women to be educated? Could women possibly become government officials? For Manzhen the idea of an education that was really useful was terribly exciting.

. . . .

However, after that day's conversation, Manzhen felt as though something had stuck in her heart. There were many questions she had no answers for but was too embarrassed to discuss openly. Her interest had been greatly piqued. She had envied her brother since childhood. She was not willing to spend her life hiding in the house. She'd read a few foreign novels in translation and couldn't say how much she envied the women in them. You see, the second daughter-in-law in the Cheng family had left Wuling and gone to school, and now she too was a teacher. Of course, she understood much more than Manzhen did, and she could be independent, asking nothing of anyone. And she was only a few years younger than Manzhen . . . But really, after all, Manzhen was only thirty. And other people had husbands who understood the new learning to advise them. How could she compare? What kind of a family was the Jiang family? The quality of scholars in the area was uneven, and the young Jiang masters were restricted to studying in the family hall.⁶ What chance was there for her, a daughter-in-law, to go off to school, book bag slung over her shoulder? Even if it were allowed, could she master the subjects? All of this she kept hidden away, turning it over and over in her mind every day when she was alone. After a few days, an invitation suddenly came from the Cheng family. On the envelope only the words "Cheng to Yu" appeared, so they all guessed that the second sister-in-law had returned from her mother's home, and that their eldest sister was throwing her a welcome-home party and was inviting them. Indeed, the servant delivering the message said that not many people were invited, just a few married women who visited most often, but particularly the Yu sisters. When the day came, Third Mistress Yu had a great deal to cope with at home, and Da Zhishao Nainai had gone to visit an uncle up the street, so neither of them went. Manzhen, however, was extremely pleased at the little dinner party, because she was very anxious to see this person who had become a teacher. She took four boxes of *dianxin* and wore a soft blue tunic with a black border showing a hint of silver and matching sleeves. The skirt was of pleated black silk, decorated only with a silver border. Her shoes were flat-soled white with dark blue. On her head she wore white mourning thread and a few silver enameled pins and one cloisonné ornamental flower in the shape of a lovebird pecking a peach. The effect was neat and tidy.

Although the Chengs had only invited ten or so guests, everybody had arrived early in a great commotion. They were all very fashionably decked out in finery such as "four-seasons flowered brocade" and "ten-colored brocade"; bedecked with flowers, with gold borders edging their gowns, they looked very colorful indeed. The jewels and flowers in their hair and on their hands, the tiny embroidered shoes peeking out from beneath their skirts, made it impossible to tell who was virtuous and who was not, who was beautiful, who ugly. Only Manzhen, being a chaste widow, was dressed simply yet elegantly.[7] Of course, no one could have guessed how peculiar the second Cheng sister-in-law actually looked. Her face was absolutely clean, without a speck of powder or rouge. Her coiffure was plain too, employing a single gold hairpin to secure her hair in a bun. She wore no earrings or rings. Her gray silk tunic had only a narrow border. The sleeves were cut much smaller and the body of the tunic shorter than the norm. A black skirt with large pleats was hitched up high, completely exposing her feet. These, indeed, had been unbound and were quite large; she had thrust them into plain black silk shoes that even had the white soles showing.[8] Everybody made polite small talk, flattered her, asked her all sorts of questions, even as they were harboring a single thought: "She looks terrible."

Then a woman named Mrs. Li asked, "Second Sister-in-law, you've come from the big city and have seen a great deal of the world. Tell us something about it so we can broaden our horizons. All we've heard is that Shanghai is a glittering world, a foreign world, where people from all over the world gather, and there are big merchants and lots of money. Anyway, is it that exciting? I hear the married women and young ladies dress rather oddly yet are still really quite exquisite. At your female academy, for instance, it must have been a lot of fun with everyone there. I suppose everyone dresses the way you do, though, right?"

Although they did not really esteem her, she continued answering them always very honestly. Then someone else said in a shrill voice, "What do you mean, 'Second Sister-in-law'? We mustn't talk that way. Even on the invitation it was written, 'Teacher Jin, Jin Xiansheng née Qiong.' From now on we shall call her Teacher Jin, Jin Xiansheng."

"That's right! Let's call her Jin Xiansheng!"

(In fact, she was called Jin Xiansheng from that moment on.)

"It's always good to travel," Manzhen then said. "If nothing else, it broadens your horizons. We're no better than fish in a well. What do we know? Did you read a lot of books in school? They say there's a female academy in this province, but the students are probably all really young. I'm afraid it would be preposterous for someone our age to go."

"No, not at all," Jin Xiansheng hastened to say. "It's still not too late if you want to go to school, Fifth Elder Sister. There are others there who are forty. The school offers a variety of subjects, including national language for cultivating one's moral character, geography, history—more than ten altogether.[9] But it's not hard. You'd catch on as soon as you began your studies."

"Oh, no! That's terrifying!" someone interjected. "Ten subjects right in the beginning. Men studying in the past had a much easier time of things. I'd never be able to cope with this academy of yours even if I spent my whole life at it."

"We can just forget about it," said another of the wives. "Yesterday I heard my younger brother say they had to do drills and run. That's really tough. Never mind the embarrassment, it would just kill these little bound feet."

"It's not that hard. If you're willing to unbind them, just loosen and shorten the binding cloths and they'll get bigger naturally. It would be best for someone like Fifth Elder Sister Manzhen, who's free of housework, living a boring life at home, to enroll. School would give you something to do, and moreover, you'd also have company." Jin Xiansheng was very encouraging.

"Fifth Elder Sister wants to enter school. Manzhen! Go ahead and do it. Study for two years and then you can be a teacher, a *xiansheng,* too."

"I wouldn't dream of becoming a teacher. I'd just like to study a little more and learn a skill."

It grew late as they talked and laughed. After the banquet the guests thanked their hostess and dispersed. As Manzhen was about to leave, her eldest sister stopped her.

"What's the hurry?" she asked. "Stay a little longer! I'll send an extra man to follow your sedan chair."

After the other guests had all left, Jin Xiansheng invited Manzhen and a young woman who had just turned fifteen and put her hair up to come to her room for some tea. Manzhen's eldest sister, Dagu Taitai, was there to keep them company.

"Fifth Elder Sister," Jin Xiansheng said, "I don't want to sound pushy, but you've obviously been thinking about this a bit anyway. This is one of the Wu family's younger sisters, and she'll also be attending school sometime in the next half year. Her elder brother, Mr. Wu Dingguang, Wu Dingguang Xiansheng, is very liberal minded and says that she will attend with her sister-in-law. Since her sister-in-law is at the very most only two or three years younger than you, what should you be scared of?"

"I don't mean to be evasive. I've been longing to go for a long, long time, but as I was afraid it wouldn't work out, I didn't dare mention it. Also I've never understood exactly what's involved. You must tell me."

So the three of them talked for quite some time, getting more and more enthusiastic.

Dagu Taitai did not approve of her younger sister. However, she found it hard to oppose her to her face. "It would be better," she just said coldly, "not to think about things you can't do. I can't imagine the Jiang family letting a young widow run about outside the compound, can you? Manzhen, you really should keep an eye on your reputation."

Manzhen heard this and it felt like a knife twisting inside her. There wasn't anything she could say. She didn't blame her elder sister because, in fact, there really wasn't much hope she would ever go to school.

. . . .

Yao Ma's dispatch of someone to fetch her back forced Manzhen to make a final decision. That evening she sat down to talk things over with this younger brother who had such new ideas.

"Well, what do you think?" Manzhen asked after relating all her difficulties and her hopes. "I made my decision only after mulling it over to the point of distraction. There really is no other road to take." That was how she solicited Yunqing's advice.

Yunqing sat opposite her, his white fists resting on the desk. For a long time he didn't utter a sound. Third Mistress Yu sat near the shelves, even more mute, if that was possible. The only audible sound was when she dragged the high desk lamp over in front of her and picked at the wicks in it.

"I'm assuming that you will agree, of course," Manzhen said, seeing that her brother had remained silent for so long. "You're helping Wang

Zongren run the academy, and asking girls from other families to study, so you can't really say no to your own sister. I know what the difficulties are. It's because Xiao Han's father is dead and I still wear a white mourning cord in my hair, because on both sides of this family we're scholar-officials, so it's not proper for me to show my face in public. I don't think any of this should matter. I can monitor my own behavior. I won't take a single false step. I'll even think twice about going to places that young women are allowed to go to. If people gossip, I won't pay any attention. In the end everything will be clear. Really, the Jiang family already has so many arches and tablets to virtuous widows. How could I do anything so scandalous that my son would loose face? As for the Jiangs, I'll cope with them myself. Since the masters neither pay my debts nor support my orphans, they can't really restrict me that much. So long as I'm well-mannered and don't violate etiquette, I needn't fear them.[10] I also understand your feelings and would never make things hard for you or put you in a position where you had to make excuses for me. If they talk, you are, after all, my younger brother, not my elder. Still, if I'm going to study, I do have to move to town. I plan to sell all my property and buy a house here. There are lots of things I'll need to ask you to do for me. Only if you agree to go to the trouble can I dare start anything. I am, after all, a woman, and you are my only relative."

Yunqing paused a while. He knew Manzhen's character. It would be useless to try to stop her. Not only that, but the world was changing day by day; so as long as no one from the Jiang family came forward to raise a stink, what difference did it make? At any rate, there was neither a Gonggong or Popo involved, her eldest brother-in-law was dead; the second one had left the family to become a monk. On top of that, what Manzhen had to say was completely reasonable: If the Jiang family wanted to manage her affairs, they should manage them all. Yunqing thought a bit further before answering.

"Yes, I think it would be good for you to do it. You're not afraid of hardship. With your will, even a stranger would help out, to say nothing of our own sisters.[11] Don't worry. Let the whole issue of buying and selling property wait a while. It's not easy. If no one from the Jiang family comes forward, nobody will dare take it. Stay at our house. We can certainly afford to feed you. But school starts as soon as the summer vacation is over, and before then you have to register and take an exam. Will you have time to go home? You still need to tell the Jiang Yeyes."

"I don't think so. If I tell them, they are sure to forbid it, and that would make things awkward. It would be better to start school first and then tell them. I'll wait till fall when the work in the fields is over before I go home. I asked them some time ago to sell my land, and the lineage temple agreed then. They know a lot more about my little piece of property than I do. They won't make a fuss if I move to Wuling. It's not as though the Jiangs have no sons, you know. So long as you don't stop me and you're willing to help me out with business, I'll have the courage."

There was nothing more Yunqing could say, so they just chatted about family matters and things happening in the schools outside the family compound. Manzhen was satisfied. She didn't return to her room until she heard the second watch sounded. They saw her to her door, where Lamei emerged, a small candle in her hand, to light her way.

"When I said I wanted to study, you forbade it," Third Mistress Yu shouted angrily as soon as they got to their own room. "The minute she even mentions it, you help her out."

He drew her down, his hand tugging at her sleeve. "How can you compare yourself to her?" he said, smiling. "If you went to school, would you expect me to take care of the house and children?"

"Huh," she turned away, grumbling. "I tell you, it doesn't really make much difference if mother and children eat here all year round, but when she goes to school, she'd better take the children with her. Who's going to look after them at home? I have enough to do; I can't manage any more. You really do know how to make people think you're so wonderful . . ."

"Oh? Don't be like that. Of course her children will go to school, but right now they're too young. If you help her out a little, you'll give me a lot of face. She's eager to do well and not end up being dependent. She's doing this because she has no other options. Who'd have thought she'd have such a fate? Initially, when her marriage was first arranged, her father-in-law was prefect of Guizhou. When Ma was dying, she made us swear in front of our brothers and sisters, repeatedly, that no matter what happened in the days to come, Xiao Han would be married into our family as a daughter-in-law.[12] She's a good child, and it was the old lady's wish, so I can't imagine Fifth Elder Sister refusing. I think we can make the betrothal as soon as Xiao Han's father's tablet is put up and they are out of mourning. Don't be like that. She's not necessarily unconscious of things, you know. Everybody says you are virtuous and intelligent. So," he said, stretching out his arms to her, "I'll be the first to thank you . . ."

"All right. Forget it. Just listen to that sweet talk! Meaning that I shouldn't go to school but should be your slave, watching your house all my life. And even then I'm not virtuous . . ."

But she couldn't continue, for something had stopped her lips.

Chapter 3

"What style of characters have you learned? I like the Wei Tablet best; it's so dignified.[13] But my younger brother wants me to learn the Zhao style. He says they're more appropriate, but you know Zhao-style characters have to be written well to look good. If there's the slightest deviation, they don't look right. What do you think?"

This particular day Manzhen was wearing a single layered gown of silvery gold from which the old flower border had been removed and the cuffs and waist cut down smaller. She'd just slipped shoes made from a new pattern onto her feet. There in her father's study, she was energetically entertaining people she'd only recently gotten to know.

"Zhao characters," said an intense, nearsighted young woman. "Nothing is as beautiful as Zhao-style characters. Ordinarily I like them the best. But studying calligraphy isn't easy. It's a field of study in itself if you want to be a connoisseur. Even if you specialize in one school, you still need to get a more varied view so that when you write your hands will do what your heart wants. In any case, at least you can write fine-looking characters. My experience with calligraphy at home is very restricted. Not like Fifth Elder Sister, who comes from a family of generations of scholars. My elder brother often says that calligraphy master Yu's seal-style and running-style characters were outstanding. Even Yu Yunqing is said to be close to specialist class. If it's convenient some time in the future, I'd like to borrow some of your stone rubbings and take a look." [14] The nearsighted young woman's name was Yu Minzhi. Her older brother was also a well-known figure in Wuling; having just returned from an officers' military academy in Japan, he was about to go to the provincial capital to become an official. Since the family she was engaged into was not that great, she wasn't too eager to marry and she was still delaying at the age of twenty-two. She read and practiced her writing a lot at home, and could, in fact, write a handsome Zhao-style character. She had also absorbed quite a lot of the Four Books and Five Classics. [15] Ordinarily, she did not have much contact with people, was rather scornful of others. She was, however, extremely intelligent. Unfortunately, she'd been born with a pair of nearsighted eyes and a dusky complexion. She also had no idea how to style her hair, and it just hung there in a single long, thick braid. Her shoulders were bowed, her feet not bound straight; she had no sense of makeup, and the color of her tunics and skirts always clashed and looked hideous. Consequently few people liked her. She had just come in from the country and was staying at her elder brother's place before entering school. Her elder brother was very good friends with Yunqing. Because Manzhen and her friends were all worried about having no intimate friends when they went to school, they included her in the invitation to come and meet them.

"Yes, I have long respected Miss Minzhi's calligraphy," Manzhen said modestly. "In the future I'll have to depend on your guidance, so please don't be too polite to teach me. When I was little, all I wanted was to write the sort of inscriptions that you find on drawings, but eventually I abandoned it because people said it was useless for a woman to practice calligraphy. I only started in on it again a few days ago—too little, too late, I might add—and, hands shaking, found a copybook and a proper lamb-hair brush. Well, that aside, I shall just trail along behind you, and I shan't mind exposing my clumsiness. One day I'll write out a couple pages and show them to you, and hope you won't laugh at me!"

"Fifth Elder Sister is being terribly polite," Wu Dingguang's wife said in a coy tone. "She knows all of us are going to depend on her lead." Though already in her late twenties, Wu Dingguang's wife was still quite the tease. She was tall and had piled her hair up high on her head to reveal the long neck that rose very neatly from her shoulders. She was one of those women who loved to read novels, particularly *Flowers from a Brush* and *Lady Mengli*.[16] Today she'd come over to visit Manzhen with her husband's younger sister, Wu Wenying. Because she had no children and because Wu Dingguang was giving her encouragement, she planned to go to school for the fun of it.

"Look at you, ladies, talking of nothing but scholarship, throwing about learned words without taking a sip of tea. And now it's all cold." Third Mistress Yu entered from the hallway where she had been standing with Jin Xiansheng for some time. "Fifth Sister-in-law! Manzhen! Do ask the ladies to eat some of these plain cakes. Miss Wu is really very polite. I'm so stupid," she continued in this polite vein. "Not knowing enough to sit down when there's a chair right there. Oh, Jin Xiansheng is probably right. Unbinding feet probably will be best after all. Lamei, go bring Dagu Taitai's pipe before the smoke bugs come crawling out." [17]

Manzhen's eldest sister, Dagu Taitai, and third eldest sister, Sangu Taitai, were sitting at another tea table. Third Sister never finished her endless complaining about her irritating family affairs, how the second wife was discourteous, how disobedient the maids were . . . She'd originally been quite adept at the social arts of mingling, poem writing, taking wine, but she was now entirely consumed by life's minor worries. She had no interest at all in what was making her younger sister so busy and happy and turned a cold shoulder to the new young guests.

"Wu Yaomei [Miss Wu] is certainly quiet," said Jin Xiansheng following Third Mistress Yu into the room. "Just yesterday her old grandmother was telling us how worried she was that Yaomei was too withdrawn. I told her that if Wu Yaomei learned to be naughty at our school, I was afraid the old lady would end up in quite a tizzy herself. Yaomei! Don't be so formal! Come on out and have some fun too. Have a look at the garden. It must be a bit larger than yours. You can see people walking on the city wall quite distinctly."

"The garden is not that big, but is designed fairly well, entirely according to my father's plans," Manzhen said, inviting them out for a look. "In the past it was quite complete. Since the old gentleman passed away, what with my elder brother not at home and my younger brother too busy, it's deteriorated more each year. When I was at home, I'd come here every day to walk with my father and play chess. Now I seldom come back here myself. Third Aunt Yu! Have the girls pick lots of flowers in a little bit, so the ladies can take them home and put them in vases."

Then everyone walked up to the verandah. It was not very wide and had low eaves. Two delicate, horse-shaped iron wind chimes hung there, and when the wind blew they made a tinkling sound. Before their eyes stretched the blue sky, and beneath it a long line of beautiful gray walls drawn on the horizon, their topmost green tiles reflecting the sky. Pieces of white cloth were laid on the green tiles to dry, while in the blue sky white clouds transformed themselves without pause. This was not a particularly breath-taking scene, but to city dwellers it was very pleasant. The garden lay below. Seen from above, it really wasn't very large. Yet the artificial rocks and water, the trellises, and the flower stands were all placed so as to make the whole look natural. Even the buds and each blade of grass appeared situated in just the right place. Everywhere, however, bits of broken tile, moss, spider webs, and bird droppings were apparent, so that although the red blossoms and green leaves were luxuriant, they couldn't cover all the signs of disuse. The studies, too, appeared a little dilapidated.

Two green porcelain drums and several little Hunan bamboo chairs had been set out on the verandah. A light breeze blew gently, wafting in the fragrance of grass and flowers but bringing a certain heaviness as well. Small bees buzzed over and circled them. Wu Wenying was afraid of bees and shrieked. Everybody laughed, then went on talking and joking happily. Lamei and Qiuchan ran into the garden to pick flowers and a quantity of fragrant orchids, which Third Mistress Yu rushed to put into their guests' hair. Only Manzhen wore none. Then Third Mistress Yu placed a single flower in her own hair, and arrayed against her pretty, dimpled, smiling face, it made her look even more beautiful. After that, at her suggestion, everyone wandered out into the garden, except for Eldest Sister and Third Sister.

.   .   .   .

Manzhen and Third Mistress Yu served dinner before calling for sedan chairs and sending the guests home. After a few days, Wu Dingguang's family invited them to dine. Jin Xiansheng also invited Manzhen over in her eagerness to befriend her. Even Yu Minzhi borrowed her elder brother's place and entertained people. Manzhen got to know several more new friends who were also preparing to enter the school since they were all to be future classmates. What a new term "classmate" was!

Wuling summers were uncomfortable, but this year they didn't feel the heat because there were so many new things to keep them busy. The visitors never failed to praise Third Mistress Yu's maternal virtue and great capacities, and not one of them could touch her for beauty, so she appeared even more beautiful and acted even more virtuous than ever.[18]

Manzhen couldn't avoid socializing with lots of people, but she never forgot the bitter determination hidden in her heart either. Early every morning she would rise when the house was still absolutely silent. The breath of wind blowing in through the window from outside still carried a little of the chill of the night dew. A red glow filled the sky, forecasting the imminent rise of the fiery red sun. The sky was boundless, and its great emptiness made one feel either too big and clumsy or too short and tiny. Under the eaves a new spider web was stretched each morning. The little creature certainly was industrious. Every day Sanxi would sweep away the web with a bamboo net, and every evening the spider returned to weave a new one. There would always be a good many little insects snared in it, and flies resting on the draw cord of the blinds as well. Menzhen never wakened the maids. After standing a while by the window she'd sit down abruptly at the table. A large mirrored vanity box sat in the middle of the table, yet she never bothered with her hair. Rather, pushing aside the box, she's reach into the drawer and take out a big copybook. The ink slab was filled with ink ground the evening before, so she'd start concentrating on copying. She had made rapid progress and really did write much better already.

By then the old maidservants were most likely up, and the sounds of doors opening and gentle sweeping began. The wet nurse usually slept on in her side bed, cradling the baby. Xiao Han would already be crying for Qiuchan from the back room. The child was never willing to sleep late and started calling to get up in the early morning. Manzhen never paid attention to any of these noises, proceeding until she had three drafts of the Nine Palace characters, throwing down her brush only when her wrist started to ache. Usually about this time, Qiuchan brought Xiao Han into the room to greet her mother.

One morning when Xiao Han came in, her hands were filled with almond bean cakes, she was wearing nothing but an old shirt, and the pieces of white mourning cloth on her shoes were really dirty. It made Manzhen think about her household goods: in the country they could probably have found some cloth to make Xiao Han new clothes, but in Wuling city they would have to buy cloth for that purpose. She made a few calculations. She needed a few new clothes herself, and new shoes.

Besides tuition, she was going to have to put aside a little for buying things. Qiuchan came in carrying the wash water for her face. Qiuchan hadn't brought any fall clothing for Wuling either. "See if you can do something about Xiao Han when you have a moment," Manzhen directed the girl. "Look how dirty her shoes have become, and you still haven't changed the cloths . . ." With that she walked behind the bed and brought out a pair of gold mesh phoenix hair ornaments, part of her dowry, which she'd only used three or four times. They were of little use now, she thought. She gave the two ornaments to Yunqing. That evening, Yunqing brought back a string of fifty small coins good at Li Yuanheng's cloth store. The money made her both happy and sad.

Writing ideographs was not so difficult. To prepare for the exam, she practiced writing essays at home. In her father's library, she found volumes of the Four Books, the Historical Records, and other basic books and read them studiously all day long.[19] Yunqing found a few volumes of poetry and essays for her. When she came across parts she didn't understand, she'd leaf through the Kang Xi Dictionary or ask Yunqing. "Don't turn into a book worm," Third Mistress Yu would say to her with a laugh. What caused her much greater pain were her feet. Right after she cut the binding cloth short, it hurt terribly just to put them on the ground because without the extra bindings her arch and ankles had nothing to support them. It hurt to bind loosely for the same reason. But she longed for her feet to grow bigger, faster, so she endured it. At night she slept with only a pair of socks on her bare feet. During the day, she used only five or six feet of cloth bindings and bound very loosely. Sometimes, just like the days when her feet had first been bound, they hurt so much she could hardly bear to touch them on the ground. But out of fear that she'd have to walk at school, she always stood a little longer, then walked round and round the house. Third Mistress Yu did not entirely approve of this.

"Feet like Jin Xiansheng's and Yu Minzhi's are just plain ugly," she would say to her. "Look at how Yu Minzhi walks, always turning up the edge of her skirt. Now big feet may be fashionable in places like Shanghai, but here they're not popular at all, at least not yet. It seems to me that it's easy to make feet bigger. What if small feet become fashionable again, though? That would make things very difficult. You don't see Wu Dingguang's wife unbinding her feet. And she's pretty enough, though she's a little too tall and her complexion is bad. What do you think?"

"Big feet are better no matter what the fashion is. I saw country women who could go up mountains and through water, almost the same as men. How I envied them. As to whether they're nice looking or not, I don't care. I'll be satisfied so long as I can walk on them a little and get some use out of them."

"You aren't going to be asked to climb mountains or ford rivers. You'll only be reading books at the academy, and everyone there will be very refined. If your feet unbind well, you'll be all right. But what if they end up half-way in between, neither fish nor fowl? That would be no improvement at all. I'm worried about what to do with Zhuer's feet. Her father says they mustn't be bound so she can go abroad for study, but if I don't bind at all they'll be as ugly as a man's. I think in a few years I'll probably have to bind them just a little bit." Third Mistress Yu had a good pair of feet, and she was not willing to unbind them under any circumstances. She'd suffered a lot for those feet, and their fame had cost her dearly. If all of a sudden no one wanted tiny feet, she would feel unspeakable remorse.

Manzhen could see that their points of disagreement were not limited to feet. On every subject, no matter what, they always held two, diametrically opposed, points of view. For example, Manzhen felt great sympathy for Yu Minzhi's desire to study more and not marry, while Third Mistress Yu sneered at her appearance. If Minzhi's brother had not been an army officer, she would not have respected her at all. Third Mistress Yu also loved bad-mouthing Wu Dingguang's wife, saying that she came from a merchant family. She also went around saying that Jin Xiansheng was not well educated, and together with Third Sister, she'd light into the secondary wives.[20] Now that her mother-in-law, Popo, was dead, moreover, she often hit her maids, who many times would sneak off to Manzhen's room to complain. Once or twice Manzhen had put in a good word for the underlings, but she knew the limited power of her words, and though in her heart she knew what was going on, she couldn't say so out loud. Often when she got to the verge of a clash with Third Mistress, Manzhen changed the subject.

The examinations for school were completed. Very few people took them because most were afraid. Everyone who did passed, and all were enrolled as normal school students. Now they had only to wait till July fifteenth when the school opened. Classes started on the twentieth. Wang Zongren had long ago prepared to hold a gala celebration on that day.

. . . .

The next day everyone was up bright and early to dress. Breakfast was early too. Then they streamed out in four sedan chairs, a child inserted in each one. Elder Sister and Manzhen were in front, Third Sister and Third Mistress Yu in the rear. The three maids Qiuchan, Lamei, and Yingchun followed the chairs along with Sanxi, the footman, as they went directly out the main gate of the Yu family mansion and headed east, turned two nearby corners, and were there. From a distance they could see a flowered wall. The sedan chairs had only just been carried in the front gate when several soldiers shouted from the second gate for them to halt. In the outer court, they got out in an area where off to one side there were already several empty sedan chairs. Five or six soldiers were clearly visible standing by the second gate, wearing short tunics with the ideograph "bravery" sewn onto the chest and back, signifying that they were irregular troops. In addition to them, six or seven other people who didn't appear to be either footmen or strong-arm men were standing around in tight-fitting outfits.

"Please enter," the soldier said mildly as the group of women stepped out of their chairs.

From inside the second gate, two large-footed servants who'd come from the Mayang region appeared. "Nainais, please, come in all of you!" they said.

The children stuck close beside the grown-ups, and the maidservants followed close behind too, as they all went inside. Being a male servant, Sanxi was not allowed in and swerved next door to a small courtyard where the men teachers lived.

A very lively scene met them as they turned around the large screen. The room was already full of women, most dressed as though they were from big wealthy households, some pretty, some not. They were sitting together in twos and threes talking.

Jin Xiansheng emerged from a house in a small side courtyard. "Oh. How come you've only just arrived!" she cried, rushing over to meet them. "Let's go right in my room and sit down!" She led them to a small room beside the main hall. The hall, they could see, was already hung with red satin banners across which the words "Eight Immortals Crossing the Sea" had been written. Four large palace lanterns hung far above.[21] In the center of the hall sat a big square table with a red table cover and an embroidered cloth. Fragrant sandal wood smoke was already wafting up out of a big incense burner. A pair of enormous candles and a packet of longevity incense remained sealed in red paper. Squarely at the front of the hall hung a portrait of Confucius with a piece of red paper pasted up right next to it that read "Spirit tablet of Master Confucius, foremost among teachers." Also at the front of the hall hung gold words on a black background, written by the retired magistrate of Wuling county, that read "Women's Normal College." On the walls on both sides hung couplets presented by all the well-known figures in Wuling. Next to the table was an unknown object with several chairs lined up beside it. A good many women were walking back and forth gazing at the thing. Behind the great hall were numerous rooms filled with people amusing themselves.

"That's the classroom," Jin Xiansheng said, pointing things out. "Tomorrow Fifth Elder Sister will have classes there. Over there there's a big drill ground and a dining hall. After a bit, I'll take you to see them. A banquet has been prepared. Mr. Wang Zongren says that you ladies must stay for it."

"We aren't women students. We've just come along to watch. So we get banqueted too?" asked Third Mistress Yu with a laugh.

"Why not? All students' families and relatives are to stay for the banquet."

"About how many students are there?" Manzhen asked.

"Thirty or forty, thereabouts. I've heard that several more counties will be sending people, and if that's true then it'll be more. There are even more children. Forty to fifty have already been registered."

As they were talking more people arrived. When the big clock in the hall struck ten, one of the Mayang maids began vigorously ringing a big brass bell.

"Fifth Elder Sister," Jin Xiansheng said hurriedly. "The ceremony is about to begin. You come with me. The rest of you please stand here and watch. Are the children coming?"

Several more large-footed female teachers also emerged, and scurried around busily. The people scattered about the school had no idea what was happening and pushed toward the big hall.

"The entire student body please come and stand in line. Visitors please stand outside." The students didn't know what was meant by 'stand in line,' so they all stood around haphazardly in the middle of the hall gazing at each other and giggling. The spectators pushed to the front again.

"Jin Xiansheng, please pull them back and tell them to stand in a single line. I'm afraid they don't understand me." A young eighteen- or nineteen-year-old athletics instructor was getting anxious as she looked at this group of students with the tiny feet. The students all stared back at her strange appearance. Her feet were nearly the size of a man's. Her clothing was tight, and she'd combed her hair up onto her head in a way that didn't resemble either the style of a monk or the old-fashioned women's coiffure. She spoke a quick shrill provincial dialect, and it was quite true that hardly anybody could understand her.

Jin Xiansheng stood watching for a while, then consulted with her a moment before asking two other female teachers to help pull the students one by one until they were lined up in four rows facing the front of the hall.

Manzhen found Yu Minzhi and her friends from where they'd gone to play in the back earlier. They stood together. There were about a dozen or more children lined up in two lines in front of the normal school students. Spectators outnumbered students two or three to one. They were squeezed along the sides of the hall, and Jin Xiansheng and the other teachers had to ask them repeatedly not to laugh or talk.

Then a female teacher in her forties entered. She wore her hair combed into a high bun and walked over in front of the students with quite a strict air. The students all stared at her not daring to make a sound.

"Please don't talk and don't laugh," was all she said. "In a minute the retired magistrate and officials will be coming along with a number of male guests. Just do as I do." She invited several onlookers to sit in the area set aside for honored female guests, but most of them smiled and refused. She was the school administrator, surnamed Chu, and she'd been a teacher already for a year in the provincial capital. A servant raised the brass bell and swung it back and forth again. Everybody thought that this was very funny. Then there was the sound of footsteps outside, and a number of people appeared at the door. Some of the married women looked down in embarrassment.[22]

The retired county magistrate, a man in his fifties, strode in wearing sacrificial robes and a hat with a crystal button on top. Headmaster Wang Zongren came second. He was only about thirty, with a round face wreathed in smiles. Today he had on a long pale gauze gown, a black vest, knit satin shoes, and his hat was crowned with a tiny coral button. Following him were several middle-aged gentrymen, some of Yunqing's youthful friends, two old teachers, and a few staff members. The group of them were not exactly walking in step, but they strode along respectfully into the ritual hall.

Some of the female guests standing further off were commenting privately on the retired magistrate and headmaster. Then two masters of ceremony emerged from among the male guests. As at a wedding there was music. It was created by the athletics instructor, who walked over to the unknown object, sat down at it, and pressed on it to produce a rather baffling sort of noise. After that the retired magistrate, the headmaster, and the school administrator led the group of women with bound feet as they bobbed up and down kowtowing on the concrete floor in reverence to the sage Confucius. When they finally finished kowtowing, which was a considerable hardship in itself, they had to stand straight and stiff and bow to the retired magistrate, the headmaster, the administrator, the teachers, and even to the guests. Then the retired magistrate made a speech in which he went on and on and on, even though no one had any idea of what he was saying because he was from Baoqing and they couldn't understand his accent. Then the headmaster made a speech. Then the guests made speeches. By this time, several of the female students could hardly endure the pain in their feet and were on the verge of tears. Most were getting impatient, and although they could think of nothing else but retiring to the side to sit down, they were afraid to move. A few of the children did go off looking for their mothers. Finally the ceremony drew to an end. The male guests left to the music. Then, like released prisoners, the students dashed about gleefully. Even perfect strangers walked right up to each other and asked, "Aren't you just dying of agony? Wasn't that awful?"

Manzhen and her friends hurried to Jin Xiansheng's quarters. Third Mistress Yu and the other wives quickly made room for them. "Come and sit down!" she said. "I was so anxious for you. Why didn't they at least give you benches?"

"I'm sick and tired of standing. In all my days, in my whole life, I've never had to endure such hardship . . ." Yu Minzhi pulled up her skirts and flopped down on the bed.

"Never mind. Tomorrow when we have classes, it will be the students' turn to sit while the teachers stand. Fifth Elder Sister, come over here. I'm not that tired." Wu Wenying approached a chair, then offered it to Manzhen. Some people they didn't know squeezed into the room to see them.

"Fifth Guma!" Third Mistress Yu said. "Manzhen, did you know there was even somebody here from your own Jiang family?"

"There couldn't be. I don't believe it."

"It's true," Third Sister added in verification. "An old amah was around here just a minute ago saying she recognized you. She said she'd seen you once in your Third Master's house. She said her Nainai wanted to greet you but was afraid you might not recognize her. I forget which branch of the family she mentioned. You still don't believe it? She'll probably come around looking for you."

"Maybe so. Only there's so many people in the Jiang family, a great many of whom I don't know, and I can't be sure of the family branches. She's not likely to be a very close relative. The closest ones all live in the country and wouldn't be coming to Wuling. They'd most certainly drop over to our house for a visit if they did, don't you think?"

"It's always that way. People with the same surname can always find some family connection," Third Mistress Yu continued. "For instance, doesn't Miss Minzhi have the same name that we do? We're not really related, but if you were to follow it out to our ancestors, we'd all be descendants of the same family in the end." Third Mistress Yu's wise-acting made them laugh.

As they were chatting, in walked Jin Xiansheng, dabbing away at the sweat on her forehead with a handkerchief and saying as she came through the door, "I'm so sorry I couldn't attend to you and keep you amused. Please hold on a little longer; the banquet will begin immediately. Elder Sister, please help keep the Third Aunties here.[23] Fifth Elder Sister, you all are hosts here, so don't stand on ceremony. Could I ask you students to go to Chu Xiansheng's room to visit a little? She's a guest in Wuling and hasn't any relatives to visit with. Chu Xiansheng comes from a respectable family. Shall we go and meet her?"

"Certainly, of course. I'm not sure we know how to talk to teachers, though."

"You needn't worry about us, we're quite all right. We're going to amuse ourselves a bit longer and take a look at your academy. I don't think we'll attend the banquet, though. With a crowd of maids and children, it wouldn't feel right. We're not exactly famine refugees, are we, Eldest Sister-in-law," said Third Mistress Yu to Manzhen's oldest sister. "Let's go and see the grounds in back. Who knows where those little rascals have run off to play or whether there's anyone watching them." Third Mistress Yu hurried out ahead of the rest. Manzhen and her friends followed Jin Xiansheng into a room across the hall.

The crowd went to the back to unwind. By this time, the people attending had scattered and many had gone home. There were still some ensconced in the big sitting room nibbling melon seeds and chewing betel nut. They appeared to be the female members of some household. Children, maid servants, and amahs were everywhere. People had picked branches of pomegranate blossoms from the back garden, and the fiery red flowers were quite exquisite. The group of women passed by the classrooms and felt very strange when they looked inside and saw blackboards hung at the front and the maps along the sides. Then they passed a study and peered into the three dormitories further back. Each had five or six beds in it and tables and benches too, though these were rough-hewn. Outside were washstands. In the tiny courtyard, several small banana trees had been planted. The windows were covered with white paper, and in one room mosquito nets already hung over three of the beds. On the tables were some combs and brushes.

"If I were young, I'd come here for fun of it too," Elder Sister said. "It's always best to have lots of company. If I did, though, I'd certainly change the paper on this window. I'd hang the row of glass below with pink screening, because outside is a moon gate and green plantains. Everybody will be sleeping in the same room, working together. It'll be so interesting. The later you're born the better. When it gets to Xiao Han's time, who knows what things will be like. Ma never dreamed Manzhen would ever get to go to school or to have an audience with the sage: Confucius is taking female students now."

"Well," insisted her younger sister, "Ma's generation had its own kind of vitality. If they had started a women's academy, it probably wouldn't have been like this. Today there was no ostentatious ceremony at all, not even the degree we'd have at our house for a small birthday party. In the old days if someone entered an academy, there'd be a huge stir at the temple, and even people in the streets and markets would celebrate like crazy. What ridiculous music they played for this one, letting a wretched little girl press on that what-do-you-call-it, that foreign thing. They didn't even have any firecrackers. And did you notice those soldiers standing at the door, totally feeble? What sort of thing is that? As for these bedrooms, they're frightfully crude. How can they expect young ladies to sleep in them? Lamei and the servants have better than that, don't they? . . ."

"Third Sister-in-law," Third Mistress Yu interrupted. "You're really— this school has been founded as a place where there is equality, independence, where you take care of yourself, where you study. It's not for officials or even like the *Flowers in the Mirror*.[24] You always want ostentatious rituals, and that just won't do here. Let's go over there and take a look at those huge trees."

After turning through yet another gate in the wall, a big courtyard appeared in front of them in the middle of which stood two enormous mulberry trees, so big that it took several people holding hands to encompass them. Mulberries lay scattered all over the ground. The north-facing great hall with five adjoining rooms had been dismantled to make an all-weather drill ground. Around the yard were some dumbbells, balls, and bats. Nobody knew what these things were, and they all went over to touch them. Zhuer, Xiao Han, and the rest of the children, including a few from other families, were picking up mulberries in the middle of the yard.

"Lamei! Do you want to die?" Third Mistress started scolding immediately. "See if I don't beat you to death when the missies get sick from eating that stuff! Those berries are rotten. How can you eat them? Why don't you hurry up and take them somewhere else to play."

"We don't eat them, we're just playing." Zhuer came over with her little brothers.

Xiao Han saw that her mother wasn't there and tugged at Qiuchan to go find her.

Turning out of the courtyard, they came to the dining hall. It was a very large room that could hold more than a dozen tables, though right now it had only eight. On one wall there were two big openings. The rice and vegetables were handed out from here. Next door was a big kitchen. They passed the place where the male teachers lived. Two of the servants from Mayang were preparing lunch.

"Won't you ladies wait for the banquet before you go home?" they said smiling. "It'll be ready immediately, so you can sit here and wait."

Third Mistress Yu didn't answer. "You all planned for us to eat here?" she finally said with a smile. "I think we might as well go home. We've got some cured meat steamed in bean sauce and fried hot-spiced root at home that's actually tastier than some sort of banquet. What do you say? Shall we go? Tell Lamei to go to the gate and tell Sanxi to see to the sedan chairs."

"Let's go home. In a minute there'll be students and teachers here, and we'll be in the way," Third Elder Sister agreed. "We should go now."

So they all left without even telling Jin Xiansheng. The children went with them, all except Xiao Han and Qiuchan because the little girl was just then with her mother, playing happily with the female athletics instructor.

"Now that you say so," Chu Xiansheng was saying eagerly to the other women, "You're pretty liberal-minded here in Wuling. The headmaster was telling me yesterday that although any number of people opposed the opening of a female academy, you actually ended up with a lot of students. A few years ago when the headmaster of the Zhaonan Female Academy in the province had just returned from Japan and wanted to start the school, there was some support for it, but no students. For lack of a better plan, they decided to get the school started anyway. So they brought in young ladies from their own relatives' families in sedan chairs every day. No music or drill. Just an old gentleman to expound the texts with a blind hung between him and the students. Teacher and students could hear voices, but they couldn't see anybody. Gradually some of the big families began to send students. Finally they took down the blind and added other courses. The government saw that the headmaster had done a good job and asked him to start a woman's normal school. Now each school has more than two hundred people and several dozen graduates. There still are those who revile him, but he's getting more praise each day. Wang Xiansheng is a graduate of Zhaonan. She knows the real situation there and all sorts of funny stories."

Wang Xiansheng was the athletics instructor. Though she had big feet and was very liberal-minded, she was, after all, very young and easily embarrassed, and she didn't know how to socialize with strangers very well. Usually she didn't talk much, just smiled.

There were two other young female teachers, one named Zhang who taught drawing, the other, Chu Xiansheng's daughter, who taught handicrafts. She was adept at making flowers and appliqué. In her room hung two horizontal screens made using appliqué techniques and a plum blossom in a glass box. The flower was so beautifully crafted it looked real, and everybody loved and admired it and were amazed that such a little girl could have such clever hands. Manzhen loved the flower the most and thought that she'd like to make one too, to put in her room.

Although all of them were total strangers, they hit it off very well together. Particularly Manzhen, who felt both envy and respect for them all.

After opening day, the school became very lively. People often came to observe. After a few days, classes started and most of the students arrived in sedan chairs. Altogether the school employed six female Mayang servants. Most of the kindergarten class had maidservants or amahs following them around to take care of them, so often there would be ten or twenty maidservants sitting in a room together gossiping. Before class there wouldn't be a single man around. The school was large, so it was a lot of fun. Wang Zongren strolled over occasionally. When he saw that there were more students every day, his pudgy face took on a glow of satisfaction. The teachers from outside Wuling got to know people and felt more at home. Every day crowds of students sat around in their rooms. Day by day they started to change, until they'd become different from what they'd been at home. Now their clothes imitated the styles of the teachers from the provincial capital. The younger ones, like Wu Wenying, found it very easy to unbind their feet at once and let them grow bigger. They all wore white cloth socks and black satin shoes. Some changed their dangling earrings to small hoops, and many stopped wearing them altogether. The jewelry on their hands gradually disappeared as well. They all liked to stay longer in the school. Boarders gradually increased. The boarders were even more hard-working, all being competitive young girls. Yu Minzhi was boarding in now too. Her elder brother had already left for the provincial capital. As soon as classes were over, she would drag Manzhen and Wu Wenying to her room to sit. Wu Wenying's sister-in-law only attended ten days of class, then refused to come to school, saying it was too hard. By this time, the neighboring county had sent some students over. Of course, there were lots of people who left school midway, like Wu Wenying's sister-in-law. But Manzhen kept on so stubbornly that she was never even late for class.

As soon as it was light Manzhen would rise, following her old habit, and write two pages of characters. While she was washing Xiao Han would arrive, as well as Zhuer and Yuer, who also liked to gather in their Guma's room. They were all very loving to her. She needed to give some care to the baby, who was a year old and was learning to say "Mama." He was very weak and not willing to get down on the floor and walk. Strangers frightened him, and he'd bawl when anyone came in. So he usually hid in his room all day, playing with his wet nurse and Qiuchan. When his mother came to see him, he'd reach out his arms for her to pick him up. Usually Manzhen wanted to hold him a little while, but by that time Zhuer would be calling, "Guma! It's time for breakfast," from the doorway, and Xiao Han would start in: "Eat breakfast, go to school, Mama! Eat breakfast, go to school." So she'd have to leave him, have breakfast with the children, and then take the large sedan chair to school.

Because she was mild and friendly, a great many people were very cordial to her. But she was always too busy to socialize with them. First she'd drop the children off at the kindergarten where Jin Xiansheng was already standing in the middle of a crowd of children. Jin Xiansheng always greeted her quickly: "Fifth Elder Sister! Good morning!" They would exchange pleasantries briefly and watch the children off to play before continuing on to their own classrooms, where, as soon as she entered, someone was bound to call out, "Sister Manzhen's here!"

Manzhen's new classmates quite loved her, partly out of sympathy, partly from respect. This was particularly true of those from counties beyond Wuling. Among these was a woman with a lot of endurance named Jiang Yu, who came from a not very well-to-do family and whose brother, a well-known reform movement figure, had packed her off to study. Unfortunately, that had infuriated her future sister-in-law, who'd spoken out strongly against it. Jiang Yu paid no attention, just pinned her hopes on becoming independent through hard study. Jiang Yu's bed was near Yu Minzhi's, so of course they became close friends.

Manzhen's greatest friend was another young girl of sixteen named Xia Zhenren, who came from Pu County, at least five or six hundred *li* away.[25] Zhenren had read newspapers that she got from a cousin of hers in Shanghai and had developed a prodigious ambition—to save China. She knew that a young lady at home was not much use, so as soon as she heard that there was a women's academy in Wuling, she'd argued with her father repeatedly, and the upshot was that she arrived at the school with her young sister-in-law. Xia Zhenren believed that saving China required learning and a group of friends bound by a common purpose. Not long after she arrived at the school, she became close to Manzhen because she thought Manzhen was better than the younger ladies. Although Zhenren was very young, her accomplishments had made her precocious, and her discernment outstripped all the rest. After a few talks, Manzhen's admiration for Zhenren grew, and seeing her diligence, simplicity, and dedication to work led Manzhen unconsciously to change some of her own habits.

At first Manzhen hadn't wanted to take part in physical education class, since quite a few of the other students with bound feet didn't. She knew her feet were not right yet, and she feared other people would mock her.

"Manzhen, Big Sister! Don't be afraid," Xia Zhenren encouraged her zealously. "Let them laugh. At most they'll laugh for three days. Your feet won't get any bigger if you are not willing to go out for physical exercise. Small feet just won't do. You must come with us."

Manzhen took her words to heart. Naturally there were people who scoffed to themselves and those who whispered, "Look at Yu Manzhen, trying to do physical exercise with such tiny feet . . ."

Especially when they practiced running, she was never able to keep up and always fell behind all by herself. Then Wang Xiansheng would say, "All right, you can stand to one side for a while." "Elder Sister Manzhen," called the women who, having no class then, sat around on the benches amusing themselves watching, "Come sit over here for a while."

People tried to persuade her to give up. But she felt that Xia Zhenren was right. She wouldn't stop, soaking her feet in cold water each day. The consequence of her nearly unendurable effort was that the size of her shoes began to increase noticeably, and after half a month she could wear a larger pair. Soon she had completely removed the binding cloth and only needed to wrap her feet with a square piece of cloth like a man.

"Her feet really came unbound quickly," her classmates started saying then. "Maybe the bones weren't fractured by the binding process. In any case, she's quite something. Look how much stronger she looks now."

Even more than the unbinding of her feet, Manzhen's determination came through in her school work. She could not be counted best in her class. Yu Minzhi and Xia Zhenren were both better students; but unlike Manzhen, they had nothing else to concern them, whereas she was snarled in petty worries. But she threw herself heart and soul into ensuring her progress. For instance, right after class she went directly to the kindergarten to see the children, who'd finished for the day. The naughty little brats would already have gotten ink and mud all over themselves. She'd have to wash them up even though Yingchun —herself a child and not equipped to manage them—was supposed to be taking care of them. Sometimes the girls had gotten into a fight and were crying. Then she'd have to provide comfort. They'd listen and then start home with her. Often the sedan chairs weren't there yet, and she'd have to lead the band of children home on foot since it was so close and on a familiar road. Sometimes Zhuer and her brothers would already have been picked up, leaving Xiao Han to sit by herself on the sandy ground or beneath the trees, her little cloth pomegranate-flower bookbag beside her for company. Then Manzhen felt such a wave of sympathy for this daughter of hers that she couldn't help rushing over to give her a hug.

"Mama, Mama! Bugs, look at the bugs," Xiao Han yelled one day as she galloped toward her mother.

"Are you all by yourself?" Manzhen asked as she brushed the dust off her daughter.

Xiao Han thought a moment. "Mama's here!" she answered.

"Yes, Xiao Han has her Mama!" Manzhen said, picking up the child's bookbag. "Xiao Han's not afraid. Come. We'll go home. Your little brother's waiting for us."

Several times she came late to find the kindergarten empty and deserted. Not finding Xiao Han anywhere, Manzhen assumed she'd gone home with Zhuer. Then not finding her at home either, she'd have to race back to the school. There she would finally find Xiao Han either sleeping comfortably in Jin Xiansheng's room or else at the normal school students' dorm being fed cakes by everyone and singing "The Little Rooster."

As soon as they got home, the wet nurse would bring the baby, who now had a name—Da—over to Manzhen.[26] Da had been sick a number of times recently. His mother always looked for a red flush on his face, but he just sat weakly in her arms and caressed his mother's face with a tiny finger. He was a sweet child, though he almost never smiled. "Da," Manzhen often asked him, "Da, what are you thinking about?" He didn't answer, just looked at her so intently that she decided he must be thinking of something. "Strange child," she thought to herself. It made her love him specially, more so even than Xiao Han, though all their visitors and everyone else had praise only for her daughter.

Manzhen could not spare a moment's delay, however, and soon she'd turn to her books. Then the interruptions would start: "In the future," Qiuchan might come in, sad-faced and muttering, "it would be better if Nainai kept the wet nurse from visiting the back quarters. City people take advantage of her lack of sophistication. We must rely on your prestige . . ." Another time it was, "Lamei got such a beating today, her head was all bloody. She went on cursing and cursing because she was afraid I wouldn't get it. Huh, fortunate for Nainai, that Nainai didn't have to hear it all. It's so maddening . . ."

So when Manzhen saw Qiuchan coming with that look, she knew what to expect and cut her off early: "I know. I forbid you to talk so much. I think it would be best if you just stayed in your rooms when I'm not home. You're always getting into trouble!"

Seeing Manzhen had stopped listening, Qiuchan pushed the wet nurse forward as her advocate, but the nurse was rebuffed too. Secretly they blamed Manzhen for being useless.

Manzhen paid them no mind and always turned back to her lessons. The fear that she'd fall behind her classmates kept her up late every night. Her progress was so remarkable that she found herself able to compete with those clever girls, and that made her very happy. However, there were really problems blocking her way. A letter from her husband's fourth brother urging her to come home arrived, along with another from one of the Jiang uncles pressing her to get home quickly so she could attend to her land sale. Yao Ma, in particular, kept sending letters with various people asking how Manzhen was doing—in other words, when she'd be home. As a consequence Manzhen consulted with Yunqing once more before deciding that she would go home mid-October and return in time to take a make-up exam before school started again. She left Xiao Han in town, taking with her only Da. She left Qiuchan too, to keep Xiao Han company.

. . . .

Chapter 4

The school added and lost students. Quite a number of young ladies still felt that it was too grueling or that they couldn't keep up and just quietly stopped coming. That was the case with Manzhen's distantly related sister-in-law Du Shuzhen, who withdrew two weeks into the second semester. She kept inviting people over though. Manzhen was among those invited, but she did not want to go and tried to keep Du Shuzhen at arm's length. One day after school, however, as Manzhen was getting ready to go home, Du Shuzhen came over.

"Fifth Elder Sister!" she said, grasping her hand. "Don't reject me. After all, we're from the same family and I've got no one at home. I wanted to study but I can't spare the time from my domestic duties. Really, I just want to make a few friends, but you all look down on me. Now I'm inviting you over with no motive other than my hope that in the future you'll treat me as a friend and drop in often for a little fun."

"Thanks so much, but I'm afraid I really couldn't. With two small children, there's always something to be done," Manzhen replied with hypocritical politeness.

"Really! What are you afraid of? You're never home as it is. Your wet nurse looks after the little one. Let the big one tag along." Just then Yu Minzhi came along, interrupting them. "Perfect! Big Sister Minzhi is much franker. Fine. I'm depending on you, Minzhi. If Fifth Elder Sister doesn't come tomorrow, I'll be asking you why not." Having delivered this, off Du Shuzhen went to look for the others.

"She's such an amiable person. Why do you dislike her so much?" Yu Minzhi asked Manzhen.

"It's nothing, really. Did you know that she's the proprietor of the Jiang's Taichang Store? They're among the first families in Wuling. That her store is big is nothing, but they have extensive land holdings too. Even at a low estimate, they must yield seven or eight thousand *dan* in taxes a year. Naturally, some in the Jiang family are better off than she is, but a great many are far worse off. We, of course, couldn't be compared to them. We were always distant, and our branch of the family didn't have much to do with them. We also depended on our land for a living, but we're scholars and have a family practice of mercy and courtesy. They're really pretty awful if you start poking into their habits. I don't know how they've been behaving since they moved to Wuling, but there were lots of terrible stories about the families where we lived in Ping County. They were really wicked. Sometimes when we've more time, I'll tell you some of them."

. . . .

Du Shuzhen was the daughter of a rich merchant. She had lost her mother as a child, and since none of her stepmothers had known how to manage a house, she had often helped her father out. In the process she'd become extremely capable and used the abacus expertly. On the Jiang side there was a shortage of capable hands. Her own husband was a sickly young man, and although there were plenty of nephews, they all had their eyes on the store here in town and did everything possible to shirk other responsibilities. The Jiangs brought her in specifically as a daughter-in-law. In her five years here, she'd managed the house for two, during which time the family had added more than a hundred *dan* of land. Now that her husband's health was a bit better, he had placed everything into her hands to manage and had gone off to the provincial capital to study at a middle school. Except for an old second wife, no one else lived in the Wuling house. The old Second Wife, who recognized how capable she was, liked her a lot and pretty much gave in to her. The nephews were all afraid of her and said that she was fierce. The result was that she was independent and had no one controlling her. She had no plans to return to Ping County because her mother's place was here in Wuling. Also because her mother's family were merchants and the people on her husband's side weren't serious about their studies, she put great stock in education. That her husband was at the provincial capital studying this time was, of course, the consequence of her prodding. So although she wasn't able to study herself, she was eager to have friends who did, and that was why she entertained them so enthusiastically.

Everybody drank tea for a while and ate some of the cakes prepared in Du Shuzhen's own kitchen, chatting casually until they broke up. Du Shuzhen had the maids bring out some Western toys. Her younger sister was still very childlike and loved playing with them. Some people went into the garden. Du Shuzhen called a photographer. At first nobody wanted to have her picture taken, but after some pushing and giving ground, finally everyone posed and each had one photograph taken.

"I'm going to say another stupid thing, so don't laugh at me," Du Shuzhen singled out Manzhen and Xia Zhenren particularly. "I think it would be quite a good idea to ask a few people to take an oath of sisterhood. We should all share similar aspirations, be single-hearted. That will make it easier to help each other in the future. Though I can't attend school now, I haven't given up on the idea and I'd still like to work with you. I'm not much use, but I can help a little in other ways. Well, what do you think? Come around to my house another time and we'll talk it over, all right?"

They both smiled and agreed, but immediately changed the conversation to other topics. That day everyone stayed for dinner. After they had dined, sedan chairs sent them home.

People actually did go to her house frequently after this. She'd often send her servant women to the school to get them. Manzhen and her friends, however, stayed their distance. In addition to their reservations, they were the most hardworking of all and really did feel pinched for time.

At this time Yungqing's Langjiang Society was already producing an eight-page newspaper called the *Light of Langjiang,* with Jian Xiansheng's husband, Cheng Renshan, as editor. They not only brought out the paper, but they also often served as distributors for papers and magazines from Shanghai. A good number of Wuling's youth made the newspaper office their headquarters. These papers and magazines had a wide circulation in the school. The topics of discussion in the school now began to change. One student would ask about the contents of the Xinchou treaty. Another spoke in praise of Lin Zexu.[27] "It would be wonderful if everyone were like Commissioner Lin. It's the Emperor who chickened out! . . ."

Manzhen understood most clearly what the disastrous effects of opium were, so she often told them about her family. Almost everyone smoked, and there were always several lamps burning.[28] They couldn't keep the young people off it because their fathers and elders smoked, so by the time they were teenagers, the children were already addicts. Xiao Han's father had started at the age of fifteen and by the last years of his life was consuming six ounces of cake opium nearly every day. If his portion was reduced, he became quite irritable. This bad temper was especially true of the friends who came over. Lest they get out of hand, they too were offered this substance. The men spent all their time lying in a stupor, and the women learned it from them. As a consequence, this generation was far less capable than the one that had preceded them. Even if one discounted the cost in honor and economy, their bodies were so desiccated they were almost inhuman. Opium culture had been imported into the family by Jiangs who'd been officials elsewhere in the country.

After they'd exhausted the matter of the Opium War, their conversation turned to the Christian missions. Jiang Yu's family had lost a law suit against a convert, so she hated foreigners the most.

"They're a bunch of riffraff," Yu Minzhi said disparagingly. "A decent person would never willingly break up their ancestral tablets to become a Christian. There are already two churches in town. The officials fear them yet can do nothing about them. They've already bought land outside East Gate."

"Look at our map—how much has been lost in the last dozen years! The time for dividing up China is upon us, and we'll soon be slaves in a conquered country. If we don't wake up and unite to chase off the Manchus and set up a country ourselves, it will be terrible!" Xia Zhenren often used words from the *Minbao* newspaper and was obviously the most ardent of the friends.

"I think my brother and Cheng Renshan may have something to do with the revolutionary party," Manzhen said. "They've all been to Japan, where they specialized in law and politics. But although they are running a paper and spreading propaganda in the schools, still they don't seem very willing to talk to us. If they did we might know more about the outside world . . ."

Xia Zhenren didn't wait for Manzhen to finish. "Looking down on women, eh?" she interrupted. "There are women like Qiu Jin. If we only read more, and not that gassy old-style writing, we'd be more competent and not afraid of the men. Personally, I've always felt Qiu Jin was a bit too foolish . . ."[29]

"There's Madam Roland from overseas . . ." Wu Wenying showed her naiveté.

"For something like revolution, you need people first and money second," said Yu Minzhi. "Haven't you noticed how they run around like chickens without heads soliciting from overseas Chinese? We can only sit and watch. Not even Cheng Renshan and his bunch can pull it off. I've heard that the money for the newspaper comes right out of their own pockets. Wasn't Jin Xiansheng just mentioning that they want to sell some land? I think that it's really my elder brother who would be of some use. At least he has soldiers and foreign guns. But he also keeps his affairs very secret. Elder Sister-in-law knows. Elder Sister-in-law entered the Zhounan Girl's School. We need a sum of money. What do you all think?" After finishing, Yu Minzhi gazed at everyone from behind lenses as thick as drinking glasses.

"Yes, I've heard Elder Sister say that Renshan wanted to sell land, but his parents wouldn't allow it. As a matter of fact, they haven't got much land. As for you, you're all green girls. You put up an enormous fight just to get yourselves to this school. That in itself is a considerable achievement. As for me, though I can be more independent, I'm only a penniless scholar. We want to do something for our country. There's no real chance of getting money. But I do have an idea. First we get people together, invite as big a crowd as possible. Then I'll go and tell my younger brother openly that if they really are revolutionaries, we'll work with them and do whatever they tell us to. If they aren't revolutionaries, the sole reason, I think, is that they lack connections to the outside. If they approve of us, then we can join with them to make such connections. Do you approve?" Manzhen's recent happiness showed in her face.

"Great! I agree! I'm not afraid to die if it's necessary!" Xia Zhenren gripped Manzhen's hand tightly.

However, Jiang Yu said, "Of course there's nothing wrong with it, but if a rebellion led by scholars with examination degrees hasn't succeeded in three years, then how can ours? We haven't the strength to hurt a mouse nor the ability of Guan Zhong.[30] Observe, beginning with the Zhongxing Society, how many times they've started rebellions, and not one has ever succeeded, except that some people get their heads chopped off.[31] I say it's better to study and wait."

"Jiang Yu's right. Even Jin Xiansheng doesn't meddle in outside affairs," Wu Wenying agreed. She loved hearing stories about assassins. She felt that the assassins were all adorable, especially young Shi Jianru, who had blown up De Shou. When she thought about the cruel tortures they suffered, however, she began to feel rather frightened. She hadn't the daring to approve of Xia Zhenren and Manzhen's enthusiasm, and said so quickly. She was afraid of having to take real action.

Nothing came of their conversation, but everyone was glad to talk a second and a third time, after getting new stimulus from the papers. However, even though they talked, they still let things go on as they had before. Among them only Xia Zhenren was genuinely committed. She saw that every one of them was still a young lady. Though they had learned something about national affairs from geography lessons and from newspapers, and though they seemed to discuss these matters very enthusiastically, they took an equal interest in handicraft class or drawing class and were still interested in clothes. Zhenren really wanted to leave this place and move somewhere else, but she didn't even have traveling money. Being confined here, she couldn't help feeling unhappy. The thought of the shamelessness of traitors to the country pained her greatly. One day after class, she followed Manzhen to the kindergarten all by herself. Manzhen often couldn't find Xiao Han in the kindergarten, but she always went there first. Today Xiao Han happened to be there, sitting in a swing holding her bookbag. As soon as she saw Manzhen, she stood up and called, "Mama!"

The swing started to sway. Manzhen quickly grabbed the rope. "How come you're here by yourself?" she asked Xiao Han.

"Big Brother Yu wouldn't let me go with him. He kicked me, and I told Teacher." Xiao Han cocked her head and peered at Xia Zhenren trailing behind her.

"Don't quarrel with them and don't tell Teacher. Come down and go home with Mama."

"Mama, Auntie is laughing over there." Xiao Han pointed at Xia Zhenren and began to laugh. Manzhen turned her head. "Who were you trying to scare?" she said with a laugh, catching sight of Xia Zhenren.

"No one. I just wanted to talk to you. Ah, you love children so much! Xiao Han is so easy to love. Elder Sister Manzhen, we must educate her well. You mustn't favor your son over your daughter." She lifted Xiao Han out of the swing. "Xiao Han, do you like to study? Shall Auntie buy candies for you?"

"I like to study. I don't want candies. I want a foreign boat." Xiao Han still remembered an ingenious big steamboat she had seen at Du Shuzhen's house.

"All right, I'll be sure to get one for you." Xia Zhenren too thought of Du Shuzhen. She led Xiao Han to a long low bench and sat down, asking Manzhen, "What do you think of Du Shuzhen?"

Manzhen sat down too and said, "Her? Maybe she's really nice, but the rich never have good people around them because they only like being flattered."

"Well, then, what do you say about Yu Minzhi and the rest of them?"

"I'm saying, is that plan of yours going to be carried out or not? Maybe you're better off than I am because you always have housework. I don't now why, but lately whenever I think of national affairs, I feel as though I'm being pricked in the back by pins and needles. I feel uneasy all the time. I came to Wuling because I felt too isolated by myself and wanted to find some teachers and friends. Now of the people here, I think I can only discuss matters with you. I noticed your strength long ago. If others were in your position, they would have fallen long ago. Who would have struggled on like this? And you're the only warmhearted person. If you didn't have the children burdening you, perhaps it would be even better. Don't you think so?"

As Manzhen listened to her, she began to feel sad. Ordinarily she was not willing to complain to others about the bitter days of the past or about her present lonely struggle, but not it all swirled before her eyes. She had never heard anyone speak to her like this before, and had not known that the young Xia Zhenren could understand her. She thought of the children. Wasn't Xiao Han listening to them with a look of understanding in her sparkling eyes? She gazed at Xiao Han's two little loose braids.

"No," she answered. "In the past, I was so fortunate because my father and mother loved me so much. And now I am still fortunate because my children are so good. You say I would be better off without the children.

I don't understand. I really have the courage to live only because of the children. At that time—ah, at that time I didn't have even a friend like you. Now, over this past half year, I've gotten so much help from you, all of you, that I finally understand some things. Before I didn't understand anything. For instance, I'd heard of the Gengzi Incident, but I'd never paid any attention to it before.[32] So long as the soldiers didn't come along and fight right in front of my face, it had nothing to do with me. It's only now that I know a little about the world outside that I think about such affairs and get angry. However, if I really went to assassinate the emperor now, I still think that it would be for my children, that they may grow up in a good, bright world and not become slaves in a vanquished country!"

Xia Zhenren picked up Xiao Han and put her on her knees. Because Xiao Han didn't understand what her mother was saying, yet seemed to feel that it had something to do with herself, she reached out and held her mother's hand uneasily. So Xia Zhenren hurriedly cuddled her. "Xiao Han!" she said. "Mama likes you and Auntie likes you. Don't fuss." She touched her with her face then went on, "Elder Sister Manzhen! What you say is right. I believe you. But can you really leave the children or not?"

"Those events are, of course, still very far off. When we're facing them, we can talk it over again. Maybe it will be this way, maybe that. For now let's just talk about the present. You're really still young and full of dreams."

This made Xia Zhenren laugh. "Then let's talk about the present," she said. "According to your plan, we must first gather some people. How do you propose we get them together?"

"How to get them together?" Manzhen looked at her and smiled. "If you act as though you're rushing to the front or to assassinate someone, you'll never gather people in an entire lifetime. Even young gentlemen would be scared away, not to mention these young ladies. I think we should first count our numbers to see how many there are and then invite them to a get-together. We could make up a name and say we are going to study, help each other, and support each other in the future when we are working in society. If we do it this way, I'll guarantee that they'll all come. Gradually we'll understand more, and you'll propagandize all the time. We'll ask the headmaster to give a few talks too. He's a reformer, so that will make it easier. Later I'll talk to my younger brother. Some people need not be told anything, and we'll not tell them. What do you think? Will it work?"

"Yes! Yes! Let's do it. Xiao Han, you'll be in it too!" Xia Zhenren jumped up like a child and began counting people. "You, me, Yu Minzhi,

Wu Wenying, Jiang Yu, my sister-in-law would be all right too. Tang Yun is pretty good. What do you say; that's still only six or seven. Oh! Should Du Shuzhen be invited? You won't agree to that."

"Yang Yi is very good. Though she doesn't talk much, I think she's very solid. Don't you think so?" Manzhen asked, without responding to her question.

"Good, that's right, she's very good. But how about Du Shuzhen? I feel it might be good to have her. Didn't she even tell us that she'd like to become sisters with us?"

"I know. Having her would be an advantage, but this advantage is not dependable. I came out of that kind of family. However, if you insist, then I guess it'll be all right. But we mustn't have the feeling that she might contribute eight hundred or a thousand for the public good. It wouldn't be realistic. I think let's do this. Tomorrow, or even today, you go to her house and say that in keeping with her idea we will become sworn sisters. Tomorrow I'll talk to Yu Minzhi and the rest. Now I'd better go home. The child at home will be looking for me, I'm afraid. Recently he's begun getting fussy around this time. Xiao Han, where's your bookbag?"

"All right. I'll go to Du Shuzhen's today. Let me see you to the gate." Xia Zhenren picked up Xiao Han's bookbag from the swing, and the three of them left the kindergarten.

As expected, all those invited agreed cheerfully. Everybody made suggestions for a great celebration on the day. Du Shuzhen wanted to invite them to her courtyard, but Yu Manzhen insisted on being the host. She said that she was older. Finally it was decided to have the event at Manzhen's place. Before her marriage, Manzhen had felt that the sisters among her relatives didn't visit each other often enough, and had sworn sisterhood with some in this back garden. They had several parties a month and were very lively. Her father and mother spoiled her and, seeing that the sisters only talked about needlework and novels at their gatherings, or played chess and drank wine, did not interfere. Then everybody married. Some left Wuling, and those who didn't leave were tied up with housework and could not move about freely. It was no easy matter to find an opportunity to meet and talk for an afternoon. To get everyone together was impossible. Before Xiao Han's father's death, when Manzhen returned to Wuling, she often felt lonely and missed those childhood friends. Her mother would often get some guests together, but they had changed, and hypocrisy showed through their warmheartedness. Then after Xiao Han's father's death, she was unwilling to think of anything. If someone came to see her, in her heart she would be grateful. If no one paid any attention to her, she felt no blame. She had had enough of the world's cold and warmth. She had never thought to receive her new sisters in this back garden or realized that these new sisters would no longer be satisfied with gathering together merely for conversation and laughter, but would want to unite as one forever and strive together in society in a common cause. In the past she had been afraid of loneliness. She had struggled forward on her own, not daring to hope for friends. Yet now she had so many friends. At least they all understood her, sympathized with her, and were willing to help her, while at the same time they needed her help. She was unspeakably happy. She said to Xiao Han, "Do you know, in a little while a lot of aunties are coming, your real aunties?" She said to Da, "Don't be scared of them, as though they were strangers, understand? The aunties all like you." Xiao Han saw that Mama was happy and jumped about laughing. Da began to laugh too. She told Third Mistress Yu and invited her. On this day she was the only guest. Third Mistress Yu accepted with a smile. Recently she had become much more friendly toward Manzhen. The reason was that Manzhen was now living separately and taking care of everything herself, while looking after her two children in school at the same time. The maidservants and amahs from the two sides also made much less trouble now that they were further apart.

Just then Yunqing was preparing for a journey. He had fussed for a long time about going to Shanghai, and now he was really going. Manzhen asked Lamei to come and help. The whole family knew that Manzhen was giving a banquet to swear sisterhood.

After breakfast they started arriving one after the other. Du Shuzhen had prepared a special gift and went with Manzhen to see Third Mistress Yu. Then they went to fetch Auntie. After sitting with her for a while in front, they went out back. Ever since Manzhen had come here to live, the back garden had been kept very neat. Now it was late spring, and although some flowers had already fallen, others, such as the magnolias over the shed and the peonies on the flower terrace, were in full bloom. The hydrangea was still forming large white balls, and the small roses in the pots were still producing a deep fragrance. Purple iris and white plantain lilies next to the path under the trees were blooming brightly amid the soft green grass. It was very lovely.

The large windows near the garden were hanging open. It was another very clear day. Numerous butterflies and bees were flying into the room, and small sparrows were flying to the steps outside the window, where they chirped away. The women sat inside the room and competed to put forth their ideas about the ceremony. The bright red, gold-speckled certificates of sisterhood lay on the table waiting for Yu Minzhi, who was going to do all of the writing, to fill them in. Third Mistress Yu had sent a pair of large candles, some firecrackers, and some pastries as a way of congratulating them. Both Qiuchan and Lamei had tied up their braids with thick red string. Finally, in accordance with the idea put forth by Manzhen and Xia Zhenren, they did away with all ceremony and just exchanged the certificates. On the certificates they added current popular statements like "We will work together and help each other, and if anyone breaks their vows they will be cast aside by humanity and the gods." The candle on the table was lit, as was the sandalwood. Yu Minzhi leaned over the table in a most respectful manner and wrote very carefully for two hours. Everyone signed their names, and it was finished. Because there was no reason to keep the firecrackers, they were set off in the courtyard. The children picked up a few too, and they went off to the flower garden to set them off for fun.

. . . .

After this there were numerous other times when they drank wine. Some schoolmates wanted to be friendly toward them while others disliked them, even though they didn't say anything. These friends didn't pay any attention to such things. They really were working harder because the school director had told them that although their graduation examination would be held at the end of the term, they would still have to continue on. At that time they would shift to the regular courses. Now they were doing the preparatory courses. Worried that they would not be listed among the top students when they graduated, they studied harder. Those who didn't care for them saw that their grades were good and dared even less to go against them. Those who wanted to be their friends came around even more.

At the end of April, Yu Yunqing really did go to Shanghai. Before he left, as a result of Manzhen's recommendation, the school director invited him to the girl's school to lecture. His topic was "How to Save China," and his impassioned attitude and words evoked great admiration in the hearts of many people. This was especially true of Xia Zhenren, who said to Manzhen, "Your younger brother is truly a revolutionary!"

Manzhen was very happy too. On the evening before Yunqing was to leave, she asked him, "Do you have a purpose in going to Shanghai?"

"No, no. It's just that it's so boring at home and I want to go somewhere else. If I have the opportunity, I'll do something."

"It's good that you can go," Manzhen replied worriedly. "But you must be very careful. You're almost thirty years old and have four young children. Our family is small and your wife is young. If you don't have something to do there, you should come back soon. You can do the same things around here. As I see it, it would be good if you taught and published a newspaper. That wouldn't be ordinary work. What do you think?"

"You worry too much!" Yunqing said with a laugh. "Relax, relax. I'll be gone at most a year, and I might be back in six months. Actually, I'm taking advantage of your being here and the children still being too young to travel. If I can find some work there, I'll do it. I certainly don't need to worry about there not being enough to eat at home. If I can stand on my own out there, it would be good for me. The world is changing every day. If we can't catch up, it will be terrible. When Yuer and the others grow up, they'll all probably have to study science. Even if China is not sliced up like a melon, we still must expel the Manchu dynasty. This has to be done. I want to quickly learn some useful things. This is why I want to travel and see the world."

When Manzhen heard these words, she relaxed. Then she asked another question: "Cheng Renshan is probably a member of the revolutionary party. Have you joined with them? There are several in our school who are thinking of joining."

"I don't know. He may have some relationship with them, but this wouldn't be unusual. I know several members of the party, but I'm not one of them. What is the Wuling revolutionary party? It's just a few poor bastards who have accumulated a few hundred ounces of silver and think that they're doing wonderful things. Everything always depends on money, so if things can't be done here, one has to go elsewhere."

Finally, Manzhen made a request. "If you find an opportunity somewhere, there are several very enthusiastic people here. Please keep your eyes open for the others."

After Yunqing left, the door of the house was closed more tightly and the people in the household could only go out if they had some business to take care of. As soon as supper was over, the wooden bar would be fitted on the main gate.

. . . .

Taking care of the children kept Manzhen busy. She left early and came back late, and it never seemed to her that the summer days were long. Soon it was time for summer vacation again.

On the day that Manzhen completed her final examination, she realized that because of being busy with the exam she hadn't had a leisurely chat with her friends for a long time. So she made special arrangements to have Xiao Han taken home early, and then she went to the dormitory in back. The bedrooms were all quiet. She couldn't hear a sound. There were only the densely growing banana plants gently waving their giant leaves. She went straight back calling, "Minzhi! Minzhi!"

"Ah! Sister Manzhen, can you sit down? I'm washing my hair." Xia Zhenren came out from the small courtyard in back holding her long hair, which had been flipped to the front.

"Oh, a rare visitor! You haven't been here for a long time, Sister Man-zhen. Sister Minzhi has gone to the reception room. Her father has come." These words were spoken by another student named Zhang, who was there washing handkerchiefs.

"Vacation hasn't started. How come everyone's gone? As I was coming over here, I didn't hear a sound. Miss Zhang, aren't you going home during vacation? I'd like to wash my hands, please." Having said this, Manzhen walked toward the washstand.

"I'm not going back, but she is," Miss Zhang replied, looking at Xia Zhenren and her lips puffing out.

"Really?" Manzhen asked.

"Wait a minute and I'll explain. I'm done washing." Xia Zhenren had already wrung out her hair and let it fall down the back of her head. Now she was combing it with a large comb.

At this moment Xia Zhenren's chubby sister-in-law, Xia Youmei, came walking out of the dormitory. She had just woken up, and her eyes were still red. With a touch of embarrassment she said, "I didn't sleep well last night. I kept thinking about the physics exam I had to take in the morning. As soon as I handed in my exam, I ran back here and went to sleep. I didn't even go through the book to see if I had made any mis-takes. Sister Manzhen, I didn't even know that you had come. Ah, it's so hot. I'd like to wash my hair too."

"When you sleep during the day, of course you feel hot. It's really pretty nice today. The hot days are yet to come. Is anyone else around? Where is everyone?"

"We'll go look for them together. Just wait a moment." Xia Zhenren parted her hair and formed two loose braids. She was young and short. Her sleeves were rolled up high, and she wore loose-fitting pants. Because of the heat her face and her thin, unbound feet were slightly red. Al-though she wasn't very pretty, she looked very lively.

"Zhenren," Manzhen said with a laugh. "You really look good this way. Usually you look too old-fashioned. You're still young. You look so much better today."

"Hey, you're making fun of me! I say it's all right to be a little ugly. I don't care," Xia Zhenren replied very matter-of-factly, without paying the slightest bit of attention to Miss Zhang, who was trying to keep from laughing.

"Where's Xiao Han?"

"I sent her home."

As they walked out of the dormitory together, Xia Zhenren picked up a banana-leaf fan and started to fan her wet braids.

"Why do you want to go home? It's so far away. Can you return in time for the next term?"

"Let's go over there. That's where they must be. It's a place we recently discovered. It's nice and cool and hard to find. If I hurry I can make it home and back. Going by water is the fastest way, so that's how I'll go. Sitting on a boat for more than a month is really tough, but it will be good to go back for a while. My third eldest brother will be home, and I want to take advantage of his being there to have him talk to my father for me. Otherwise my father won't approve of my going to school. Just being stubborn with my parents won't convince them. There's also the problem of my fourth sister-in-law. After she left with me, there was a lot of idle talk at home. Several of the sisters-in-law gathered around my father and complained. Actually, Fourth Sister-in-law doesn't use any family money. You know how frugal I am. That's because I didn't want Fourth Sister-in-law to use the family's money and was giving her some. Now my father has written me a very angry letter. I really think that it's best for me to go home and straighten this matter out and then come back. But Manzhen, what if I went to the provincial capital to study? Would you approve? Everyone says that the school there is run better."

By now the two of them had walked over to the mulberry trees. There were a few small silkworms dropping from the trees, and in the trees above large mulberries were forming. They leaned against the stone terrace that circled the trees.

"Going to the provincial capital? Of course that's good!" Manzhen became more excited. "You ought to go. This place, of course, can't compare. If your family approves, you should go. However, you'll have to write me often."

"Don't spread this around. After I go home I'll tell you more. Really, the land route from my home to the provincial capital is shorter than it is to here. If the provincial capital works out, I'll write you a letter. You could go too."

"I don't have any hope of doing that. Look, I have two small children, and I don't know where my money for going to school next term is coming from. My house still hasn't been sold. Well, let's not talk about this now. Let's go find them."

. . . .

Manzhen's thoughts went back to Lingling Brook, that beautiful, tranquil home. She saw the low hills at dusk, the narrow road with flashing fireflies, the grove of trees sighing in the wind, and the little birds in the trees stretching their wings after being awakened by the starlight. She also saw the water of Lingling Brook playing with the moon and then rushing off downstream. She really missed that place. That was a quiet world filled everywhere with the ripples of a tender, beautiful life. It belonged to her and her children. The spring breezes there blew away her cares and gave her the strength to live. She loved that place and Xiao

Han would never forget it. Yet as she thought of it, her heart was invaded by an indescribable feeling of distress. That home and everything there, including the sky and the ground, the flowing water and the air, would soon belong to a stranger. She and her children would never possess that place again. Moreover, as far as a home was concerned, she couldn't think of a place that could be called hers. She was a person without a home. Wherever her children were, that was now her home.[33]

. . . .

As soon as vacation started, the school took on a deserted air. Many students had gone home, until only Yang Yi and six or seven others remained. Headmistress Chu was gone, and Jin Xiansheng had moved back home too. Wu Wenying and the others seldom came out, and so it took Manzhen five or six days to arrange for several people to get together at the school for some more fun. But the students whose homes were far away were carefree and happy. The school grounds were large and cool, and there weren't any restrictions. After they tired of reading books, they tried their hands at crafts or went to the exercise field to run. Sometimes they sent the Mayang servants who had stayed at the school out to buy some cold noodles and things like jellied fruit. While eating they would play chess or take turns telling stories. It was all very enjoyable.

The back garden where Manzen lived was also nice and cool. Sometimes in the evening, Third Mistress Yu would be so bored in the front part of the house that she would bring Zhuer to the back and sit for a while. Sometimes Yuer and Zhonger would come along too. Then all the children would coax their aunt into telling a story. She wouldn't have any choice but to tell them something from *Waterfall Cave, The Windy Volcano,* or the like. They all listened with great interest.

On days when no guests came, Manzhen would have Qiuchan and Lao Ma work at putting thin cloth or a layer of palm fiber on the doors or making socks and shoes for the children. Her own shoes were too small now, so she had to have new ones and some extra ones made. She calculated her money again and found that she really still had to be more frugal. She thought of Da's soon being two years old and how, after that, she wouldn't need a wet nurse and Qiuchan could take care of him. Xiao Han was already well-behaved, and there was no need for someone to look after her. Besides, she was in school all day long. Moreover, there was a little grain in the countryside and Yao Ma would definitely be sending her some money. Manzhen had already written a letter asking her to do so. She made preparations for quite a few things and then passed the time with her heart at ease. She thought that if something went wrong, she would just have to get through it because time kept moving. She also wrote letters to several friends who had gone home.

She was waiting for this summer vacation to pass by. Then it would be time to start school again, and she would once more be busily attending classes.

It was, however, still only July. The streets were frequently full of rumors. The person who brought the rumors back was always the gatekeeper, Lao Yu. Lao Yu would tell the rumor to the cook in the rear courtyard. Lao Ma would hear it and then tell the wet nurse and Lamei. Third Mistress Yu would see them talking and ask what was going on. They would tell her that Taiping soldiers were coming or about a rebellion somewhere. Third Mistress Yu would scold them and tell them not to say any more, but Lao Yu continued to tell the latest news and he still told it to Manzhen.

One day when Lao Yu was playing out front with Yuer and his brothers, he started to teach Yuer how to box. Just then Third Mistress Yu came out to get him. When Yuer saw his mother, he quickly called, "Ma! Ma! Watch me. I can box. Lao Yu taught me how. Lao Yu says the 'Long Hairs' are coming back!" [34]

"Hmm. Good, you're doing well," his mother replied. Then she looked at Lao Yu, who was standing motionless, and asked, "Say, just where have you heard these stories? You've got everyone seeing spirits and ghosts all over the place. You know that when the master's not at home you shouldn't listen to so many rumors. If there's something reliable tell me, and I'll have one of the male cousins come over."

"It sounds pretty serious. The magistrates have all gone to the provincial capital to ask for soldiers. I can't tell what's really going on. Some say that there are scoundrels in the city. Some say that the provincial capital is even more unsettled. All of the fortunetellers say that according to the stars there will be armed conflict this year. I don't know if the master has mentioned this in his letters. Really, are things still peaceful over there?"

Third Mistress Yu didn't know whether to believe Lao Yu or not. She could only say, "The master's letters have never mentioned this. If there really were some trouble, he would certainly return home, but he's never said that he was coming back. I think that all of this is simply rumor. Remember the year they said that there would soon be a war, and afterward, we never heard another thing about it? See what you can find out, but don't tell wild stories in the house and scare people."

Several days later, Da Zhishao Nainai brought some new information from the home of one of the nephews. As she talked to her aunt, she was almost breathless with fury.

"They know a lot. Second Elder Cousin goes to the Langjiang Society every day and gets the news. I asked him about these rumors so I could refute them and keep everyone at home from becoming alarmed. Who could have guessed that both he and his wife would scold me and say that I'm excitable and like to listen to what the women servants are saying. That's preposterous! I wouldn't have thought much about being scolded, but last night they were talking about when to move and what things they were going to take. Their maidservant Fuer heard a lot of what they were saying, and early this morning she came back to tell us. When I went over there, my brother's wife actually was packing up things in chests. Auntie, would that make you angry or not? If something really is going on, they ought to tell me. I have a son living in the city, and they know full well that Uncle isn't home, so there's no one here with you. They ought to come over and talk about taking care of you. When they conceal something like this, what are their intentions?"

"Is this really true?" Third Mistress Yu asked, her heart starting to feel uneasy.

Then Da Zhishao Nainai recounted some news that was almost the same as what she herself had heard. After hearing this, Third Mistress Yu sent someone to the back to get Manzhen so they could talk it over.

"I don't think that any fighting will spread to Wuling. If there really is fighting, this city isn't something to be fought over. I think it's nothing more than people getting excited about what they're imagining." When Third Mistress Yu heard Manzhen express this opinion, she felt much more at ease.

"Maybe there will be fighting, but we can't be sure. If they're going to throw out the Manchu Qing dynasty, they'll have to fight toward the capital. That's so far from here that we really have nothing to fear. Right?"

After this conversation, the household proceeded calmly through the next several days. However, one evening in the back courtyard Lao Yu started waving his arms and shouting, "Look! Do you see it? Far off, over there. There's a long strip of light."

"Oh, I see it. Really!"

In the western sky there was an unusual grouping of stars clustered tightly together to form a triangle. The appearance of these stars unsettled the minds of everyone in the city. They had been seen for three days and were growing larger every day.

"Go tell the mistress. They'll definitely still be here tomorrow, and they'll certainly be closer too. Go! Tell the mistress!"

The children also saw it. It was a strange star with a tail. It was very scary. The adults didn't say a thing, but their hearts were filled with wonder.

As the days went by, the star came out later and later in the evening. Everyone in the household would stand in the eastern corner of the courtyard and gaze fearfully at this star that was coming nearer. By now it could be seen clearly. In the front there was a large star and close behind it there were countless small stars that couldn't be distinguished. It looked like a river of white light in the shape of a broom hanging horizontally across the sky. It was already more than two feet long. Every day it appeared for a while and then disappeared. The star brought a sense of mystery to everyone's mind, and as it appeared at a time when rumors were rampant, the rumors grew even more numerous.

Manzhen joined everyone else in looking at the star, but after looking at it she would talk to her children and tell them the little bit she knew about astronomy. The children listened and slowly lost their fear. Even more interesting, they often asked questions that no one could answer.

This large, unusual star appeared in the sky for eight straight days, and then suddenly it wasn't there. The children waited in the courtyard for a long time and began to feel disappointed. Just as they were pestering their aunt for an explanation, there was the sound of someone forcefully striking the copper ring by the front gate. The knocking could be heard even inside the house. Terror gripped all of those sitting in the courtyard.

"Isn't Lao Yu outside?" Third Mistress Yu asked anxiously. Then they heard the confused sound of many feet running toward them. The children all hid near the adults, who stood up. "Mother Zhang!" Manzhen ordered quickly. "Go see what's happening!"

With a creaking sound, the middle gate was pushed open and a crowd of people came through. In the dim lamplight coming from the house, it seemed that it was a group of women. Third Mistress Yu was flustered by this and asked sternly, "What's going on? How dare you burst in like this?"

The group of people suddenly drew closer together and stopped. From the middle a trembling voice asked, "Third Aunt, is Manzhenjie at home?"

"Ah! So it's you. What's wrong? Hurry in and have a seat!"

The hearts that had been beating so rapidly finally calmed down. The new arrivals were taken into the central room of the house and seated. The lamps, including the white safety kerosene lamp that hung in the middle of the room, were lit, and then Yang Yi and the others slowly told them about what had frightened them.

Just before it was time for supper, one of the Mayang servants had run in to report that a lot of scoundrels wanted to start a rebellion and that first they were going to take over the women's academy and then make their move during the night. Then just as the meal was being served, the cook said the same thing to the servant through the food window and added that it was absolutely true. After this they sent a servant next door to ask, but the school director wasn't there. They also sent someone to his home, but he wasn't there either. They didn't dare stay in the back of the school, so they had all gathered in the front and listened to see if there was anything going on. They didn't want to believe the rumors, but at eight o'clock an old teacher from the school rushed in and said that probably what they feared really was going to happen. He wanted them to leave the school right away and hide somewhere. It was after this that they had hurried over to Manzhen's house without even picking up a change of clothing.

"I saw several hooligans outside the gate looking around," someone interjected.

"During the day today, several women came to the school. When I asked who they wanted to see, they said that they were just looking around. They were probably spies out to check the place over," someone else quickly added in a voice still showing some fear.

Everyone was very jittery that night. Manzhen stayed in the room that was temporarily prepared for them and talked until nearly daybreak.

Early the next day, they sent someone to find out what had happened. It seemed as though nothing whatsoever had occurred at the school. The Mayang servant who watched the gate was out using a bamboo broom to sweep the leaves that had fallen in the courtyard. When she saw the person sent out from the Yu household she said, "My, last night those young ladies were scared to death. I wonder who the devil started that rumor."

After they heard that nothing had happened, everyone felt a bit embarrassed but also a bit disappointed. They laughed and joked as they ate their breakfast and then returned to their school. Still, however, there were rumors every day and night, and none of them could sleep well. Then the school director, Wang Zongren, turned around and announced that the beginning of school, which had been drawing close, would be delayed a month. After this, the students living in the school didn't want to stay there any longer. Each of them hurried about making arrangements to return home.

Manzhen went to Jin Xiansheng's home once to find out what was going on. However, Cheng Renshan wasn't home.

"I'm afraid that the revolutionary party is going to start its revolution," was all Jin Xiansheng could say. "Some say it will happen in Nanjing, some say Guangdong, and others say it will be in Hankou. But we here probably don't have anything to fear. Even if there is an incident, it can't be too big. There aren't even two hundred soldiers in town. I don't know if they have foreign guns or not. The place where you live shouldn't be bothered. It's on a back street. I don't think it's something to worry about. These rumors are so aggravating."

Eldest Sister also said that there wasn't anything to worry about. She came back with Manzhen and stayed with her for several days.

On the streets, however, there were people who were moving out. On the river the price of boat tickets was rising. A letter came from Yu Yunqing. He said that he would be returning home, but he wrote nothing about the reasons why.

Manzhen bought several newspapers and brought them home to read, but she couldn't find any clue about what was going on. Believing that any happenings were still far off, she put the papers aside. However, Third Mistress Yu came and told her, "Today our neighbors left for the country. They don't know when they'll return. They have so many children."

Lao Zhishao Nainai had already long since gone to the countryside. She had two sons, one living in the city and one living in the country. She had left by boat with her son and grandson and hadn't even come to tell these aunts. She hadn't talked about taking them along because Yu Yunqing didn't have a house in the countryside.

Eldest Sister did rush back to their house and asked them if they wanted to go with her, because her mother-in-law and father-in-law wanted to go to the countryside to stay. They were preparing to live in a village, and the house there was quite large.

Third Mistress Yu didn't want to go. She wanted to wait until after Yunqing came back to talk it over with him. Also, they didn't have a house in the country to live in, just a house in a village. There were two village houses, which were said to be large. However, they would certainly be very dirty. She didn't want to go, so the next day all of Eldest Sister's family left.

With each passing day the streets became more empty, and as soon as darkness fell the city gates were closed. An invisible fear increased. Manzhen and Third Mistress Yu talked the situation over and agreed to send someone to Lingling Brook. If they heard worse news, they would make preparations, and when they really had to go they would head for Lingling Brook. This was the plan they agreed to. Then they waited for the news, which worsened day by day, and for Yunqing, who should have returned home but still hadn't arrived.

Another niece's husband hired a boat and took his entire family to the countryside. He came by once and said that he would take them all with him, but when he heard that they were preparing to go to Lingling Brook, he didn't insist on his idea and went on his way.

It was said that there was a revolutionary party in the city and that many hooligans were also mixed up in things. There were also people who had seen with their own eyes foreign ships loaded with foreign guns and ammunition, and it was said that as soon as a rebellion broke out they would respond. It wasn't just one place that was like this. The provincial capital was also said to be in great turmoil. Manzhen began to believe all of this hearsay, and so once again she talked things over with Third Mistress Yu. Both of them wanted very much to ask Cheng Renshan about what was happening, but they also realized that they wouldn't receive any straight answers. The fact that Yu Yunqing hadn't returned also created suspicions. Finally, on the day when the rumors reached a peak, they decided that Manzhen would take Zhuer, Xiao Han, and the other children, two maidservants, a wet nurse, one of the old women servants, and Lao Yu, and start off for Lingling Brook first. Third Mistress Yu was going to wait for several days and see what conditions were like. Perhaps Yunqing would arrive at home during that period.

However, by this time they couldn't find anyone in the sedan-chair business in the city, and they couldn't hire anyone to work for them. The price of sedan-chair transport had already tripled and the number of bearers had doubled, though there still weren't enough of them. There was nothing to do but wait. Fortunately, Yu Yunqing's major tenants, two brothers named Liu, came into the city to see them that day. Using the boat that they had hired on the morning of the very last day, that is, on the day before the rebellion broke out in Wuhan, they took Manzhen and the group of children to Liujiaping, a small village in the country.[35] It was located fifty *li* outside the city.

That very night there was trouble over by Kaopeng. With the occasional sound of foreign guns coming from afar, Third Mistress sat in the main room of the house holding Yuer tightly and watching the slowly reddening sky where fires were starting to burn. After a while she could no longer hear any more sounds, but she didn't sleep all night. The maidservants and the old women servants didn't dare sleep either. There were probably only three families on the street who hadn't left.

The next day the street was quiet, but no one dared open their gate. During the previous night, the county magistrate had fled. Several soldiers had been killed, some had run away, and those left had surrendered. Some of the hooligans had been killed too, and the rest had dispersed. Several old members of the gentry who hadn't gone to the countryside preserved order in the town. Some younger members of the gentry who had cut off their queues were there too. They were probably members of the revolutionary party.

After the noon meal, someone came and knocked on the gate of the Yu family residence. Very cautiously they opened the gate and let him in.

It turned out that he had been sent by Eldest Sister. He had made a special trip to pass on some terrible news. The night before, their brother-in-law Cheng Renshan had been struck by a bullet on the left side of his chest. They had carried him home, but within an hour he had died.

Translated by Catherine Lo, Tani E. Barlow, and Gary J. Bjorge

Affair in East Village

Under the terms of the Second United Front against Japan, Communist writers adopted a new line on literature in the late 1930s. No more class struggle of the kind Ding Ling had described in "Net of Law," in *Unexpected Collection* (1936), and in this final elegant New Realist story. She wrote "Affair in East Village," right before she crossed into Yan'an fleeing house arrest, and it shows her deep sympathy to the world—miserable, war-torn, and famine-ravaged—of North China's peasant villages.

Almost automatically, one senses, she wrapped her plot around the story of a benighted peasant woman and her misbegotten lover. Within a plot that shows the rural poor avenging themselves on the body of the tyrant who has oppressed them, Ding Ling succeeds in showing why the peasant family itself formed an obstacle to social transformation. The Chen family purchased Qiqi when she was an infant, a rather common practice called *tongyangxi;* under pressure, they just reconvert her back into capital. The Chens are not bad people, only poor and oppressed. In the view of this story, the prerevolutionary rural family has no other option, because to remain a family requires that fathers be valued over wives. Feudal morality retains its power in these patriarchal exchanges. "Affair in East Village" recalls previous stories to the degree that Ding Ling connects a female character's personal tragedy to an ensuing string of acts and events. The tragedy of Qiqi has major importance in the story-telling sense but, subtly, little force in itself as a source of suffering.

This story is important also because so many plot elements from it reappear in Ding Ling's major work *The Sun Shines over the Sanggan*

River (1948). In that novel, however, intimately knowledgeable about village attitudes and enjoined by threat of punishment to produce politically correct plots, Ding Ling relates a tale of thwarted love and class conflict but does not connect them in any relation that might conceivably be interpreted as causal.—TEB

———————————

Greenish smoke, aromatic with pine, fled the tongues of flame, licked at the sooty lips of the hole in the top of the stove, and flew swiftly upward. Handful by handful, Guijie tossed coarse chaff into the maw of the stove. She sat between heaps of straw and husks. Her complexion was the color of the straw, but the flames reflected in her eyes made them glitter brilliantly. Opposite her, on the other side of the smoke, the indistinct figure of "Ma" Chen stood in the vapor rising from the wok. She was stirring food.

"You have to look at what time it is! Stuff in more grass . . . the chickens have to go into their coop . . . and you're not worried . . . after a bit you'll have to wash the bowls . . . it's really too much . . ." Ma Chen had become more and more impatient of late. A look of anxiety and restlessness seldom left her face.

All of the dried-up pine needles were stuffed into the maw of the stove. With a crackling and sputtering noise, the flames leaped as high as Ma Chen's expressionless, blank, even somewhat forbidding face. Yet before the daughter's eyes appeared another face. She was thinking about Laoma, her little brother, who gathered kindling. She couldn't help saying, "Ma, tomorrow I must boil up some congee for Laoma and leave out the broad beans. He can't even move. Third Aunt said broad beans can't be digested. I felt his belly yesterday, and it was really hard."

Hearing no reply, she sank deeper into her imaginings. Laoma, her eight-year-old brother, now asleep in the next room, had recently been bitten by a dog, and she was very worried about his injured foot. What if it started to fester . . .

The heavy silence was abruptly, startlingly, shattered by Ma Chen as she straightened up and shouted angrily, "The food's ready. If you want to eat, then hurry up! This minute!" After this outburst Ma Chen muttered, "The beasts and the birds know what time it is, but the people in this family—all useless good-for-nothings . . ."

Chewing on the stem of his bamboo pipe, "Pa" Chen ambled in silently and went to sit down at the table placed against the wall. He looked into the wok and licked the end of his pipe.

"It's like you're dead! . . . Don't you know enough to bring a bowl and chopsticks? You had better realize your father is now a dignitary, so you'd better serve him properly . . . Next year he'll be appointed to office. Hummph! Now would you look at him. He looks like he's waiting for someone to feed him . . ." The wok paddle stirred around furiously. Scalding hot bits of this and that splattered all over. Ma Chen certainly was not looking directly at anyone.

"Whore! You crazy bitch!" These unspoken words merely rattled around inside Pa Chen's mouth. He stared at his old lady's back and at her head of disheveled hair. Taking his pipe out of his mouth, he spat in her direction as hard as he could.

"Go look for your Second Brother. I'm afraid that good-for-nothing has fallen prey to an evil spell these days. If he were here, he'd be frowning or scowling. Dammit, if it weren't for this retribution from a former life, things would be a lot more peaceful."

The daughter, accustomed to taking orders and constantly being scolded, set a bowl before her father as though nothing had happened. With gentle eyes she glanced meaningfully at that emaciated face with its sparse yellow whiskers. Her father rewarded her with a sympathetic look.

Her brother never did come home. Ma Chen alternately cursed and lamented. Angrily she set aside half a bowlful of leftover broad beans. Standing in the doorway, she looked at the distant hills as they gradually sank into darkness. A light evening breeze floated across the harvested paddy field as the crickets nearby in the thin grass began to scrape their legs and wings in their final song.

Choking back her incoherent resentment, Ma Chen walked outside. All she could hear was the staccato beat of bamboo poles made by Third Aunt out on the level ground. Third Aunt's sharp, staccato chatter rent the night air: "The Peasant Association, he must have gone to the Peasant Association. Wang Jin came yesterday. He stood under the willow tree most of the day. Li Xiangsheng, Second Brother, and lots of others chattered away until they saw me and then they wouldn't say anything . . . Why wouldn't they let me listen? I left them alone. Did they think I don't know what's happening? Lots of rumors have been flying lately. The town is agitated. I'm afraid that the Peasant Association will get into trouble one of these days. Second Brother is really an honest fellow . . . He's busy with something. Don't worry, he'll come home sooner or later."

Rumors, there were far too many rumors. Pa Chen, who was also thinking about some of those rumors, stood up and went to get his heavy lined coat. He too intended to go to the meeting.

Just as the daughter decided to join the others outside, a hand tugged lightly at her. She turned around and was delightfully surprised. She hugged her little brother, who had sneaked up behind her. The two of them sat in the doorway and stared at the many stars twinkling up above.

"Sister, I want to look at the sky and feel the breeze." Laoma leaned his head close to his sister. "That dark room scares me, and the crickets are always leaping around. It's hard for me to walk. It feels like all the blood in my body has gone into that dog bite. I can't do anything. I was just thinking about going outside like before. Isn't this the time when I should be gathering firewood on the mountain? Nighttime in the woods. Ah, all those pine needles rustling as they move, the field mice hopping around. I hear them all. And oh, the nice smell from the fungus is really more than I can bear. Sister, look, tonight the moon is rising too. When will this gash in my foot get healed? It's the Zhao's Blackie. I'll get my revenge one day. I'll quietly beat him to death. No, I'll poison him." Laoma stared out at the darkness and saw two scary dog's eyes and a big mouth with rows of sharp teeth lined up in the redness. His little heart froze as, sitting in the dark, he stubbornly nursed his revenge.

"Old man Zhao is to blame," Guijie said. "Blackie has bitten people more than once. That dog should have been killed long ago. I hear they have a medicine to heal wounds. Ma went there today but didn't see Qiqi. She's going back tomorrow. With a little medicine you'll get better."

The cool curtain of night spread silently. The dew fell. The moon was still behind the hill. The massed pines on the hilltop waved against the bright sky. Upon the distant fields there was an endless pale whiteness that looked like water. Laoma looked attentively in that direction, toward the hill that would soon have the wheel-like moon rising above it. Suddenly he thought of something.

"What of the Peasant Association? If Second Brother isn't over on that hill, you can have my head. There's something only I know about. Only, I'm afraid. I can't talk about it. If anyone found out they might kill Second Brother . . ."

2

Over on the hillside, the moonlight filtered through the openings in the dense forest in a silvery light that shone on the soft earth, the short tangled grass, and some broken boulders. The boulders were very large and, because they had been there for so long, seemed to have pine-needle blossoms sketched on them. There were also darkish traces of bird droppings. On one large rock up against the roots of a tree sat a solitary man. Laoma had guessed right. It was indeed Second Brother. That evening Chen Delu had fled from everyone's sight and hearing and had stealthily hidden himself on the hillside. It was because he knew that his mother intended to go to the Zhao house that very day that he had decided to go there. Why? He didn't even know himself, but in any case, he wasn't going to leave. He wanted to linger here in peace all alone, just as he had in the past when he had waited here. Besides, he wanted to look down at that large house sleeping safely down below; that walled, tile-roofed house, partly encircled by the blue-green hills. It looked like such a delightful place. The wide threshing ground sleeping beside a line of willows was like a mirror, or a deep lake. Suddenly, he saw spots of light shimmering like the lights on a fisherman's boat. Then, just as suddenly, they went out. His heart fluttered with the lights as he told himself that down there within that house was someone he could never forget.

He sat there surrounded by the leaves on the trees, rustling softly above his head. It seemed to him that she would again come bursting out of the trees and lean against a pine, moonbeams shining on her face and on the tears gushing from her brilliant eyes. She hadn't let him get close to her. She had cursed him, cursed his mother and father, blamed Heaven, blamed Guanyin Boddhisatva, and finally, when she had finished, she had let him hug her, cried his name, and reached out to embrace him. But then her thoughts had jumped to another, a bearded man who had possessed her. It was that same Old Zhao. Delu had jumped to his feet, kicked her, trampled on her viciously. Her clothes were torn, her hair covered her neck. She had fled in tears down the mountain, and he had run after her to tell her when they must meet again. She wouldn't dare disobey him.

But she did. In April he'd seen her, and he had heard that after she went back that time she had gotten a flogging. Mama went to see her, and said that all she did was cry, curse him, and say that one day she'd hang or drown herself. When he heard this, he felt terrible. He wanted to rush over there. He kept hoping she'd come to the forest again. It would be fine with him if she cursed him or bit him. Let her bite; that way he'd feel a little better. But she didn't come again, and it wasn't even possible to hear her voice. He thought about her fine figure and felt his own flesh ache. Gradually he began to hate.

It was in mid July that he had gone to Zhao's house wanting to bring Qiqi home to pay reverence to the ancestors. Zhao merely looked up coldly and said, "All right. I don't think she's worth much. Even though they say that she's as sturdy as an ox, she certainly can't do an oxen's work. All you have to do is give me the money and you can have her."

Delu thought of the times that Old Zhao had treated her worse than he would an ox. How he regretted he didn't have a hoe to chop Zhao into pieces. Now when he came to this hillside his hatred was often greater than his hope. When would he ever be able to spit out the gloom that filled his breast? He contemplated crimes. One day he'd see that old louse bleed. The blood would splash all over the ground and Zhao would perish at his feet, just like a dog. Then he would run away. The police couldn't catch him, and he'd go live somewhere else. He also thought that secretly poisoning Zhao would do nicely. He wouldn't let anyone find out, and that way he could still live at home. Qiqi would surely come home one day. Only he couldn't decide when to do it. He was afraid to tell anyone, especially now when, as usual, and even in a year of good harvest, the crop wasn't large enough. This made him think of doing something big. Although his resentment and hatred were concentrated on Old Zhao, he certainly did not have this matter settled in his mind. So this evening, when he finished thinking things over, instead of going down to the valley where that big house was, he went instead back around the hill to his own home. By now the moon had risen over the hill to cast its beams on hilly places and separate the light places from the dark.

3

Last autumn, at almost this same time, Chen Delu had seemed much younger. His shaved head made his low forehead look broader, and his long, slightly rising eyebrows and eyes contributed to his pleasant demeanor and made him look quite handsome. But it was just about then that those eyebrows began to frown. Sometimes he looked morose. At other times he became fidgety and tense. He made frequent trips to town along the main road with the power line running alongside it. He went to Wuping, where the inhabitants, old and young, would hasten to ask him about things. He went to Fenglinkou too, where people welcomed him with sympathetic expressions. Even in distant villages on the side roads, when people recognized him as the second Chen son, they discussed in low voices the terrible thing that had happened to him. Recently, because he had been seen so frequently going back and forth, even people in places where no one knew him were left with the impression that he was careworn. Their speculation about his personal circumstances was quite accurate. The guesses made by a peasant about the troubles of another peasant are not likely to be far from the truth.

Chen Delu's father, Pa Chen, was at that time being held in jail in Locheng because of a debt piled up over many years, amounting to nearly one hundred piculs of grain. The landlord, Old Zhao, had accused him of obstinacy and had him put in jail. Naturally Pa Chen was locked up with plenty of other prisoners like himself. Less than ten days after being jailed, he became depressed and fell ill. This meant that Chen Defu, who worked as a tailor in town, and his wife would have insufficient food. Delu's family, who lived in Zhao Village, and Qiqi also found themselves in a precarious position. Qiqi, who had been taken into the family as a future daughter-in-law, was now fifteen, and as soon as she had some money, she was to put up her hair and marry Delu. But the two of them had apparently already hoodwinked others and indulged their feelings in bamboo groves and stacks of rice straw.[1] They had gone to Old Zhao about old man Chen and kowtowed servilely, but to no avail. The magistrate at the *yamen* in town told them that only when the original accusation of indebtedness was withdrawn and the complaint retracted would the case be dropped. Old Zhao was as unresponsive to pleas as any clay Guanyin Boddhisatva. This situation made the family more and more pessimistic every day.

One evening a frustrated Delu was tramping slowly home from town. He had just come to a turn in the path where, once he had gone round the corner and passed some tangerine trees, he would be home. Suddenly a voice came out of the tangerine trees: "Delu, how's your father doing?"

He looked and saw Old Zhao's henchman, Li Baye. Delu felt something rise up in his heart and he grew hot under the collar. But he didn't want to offend; it was best to answer him. Of course his tone of voice was rather dispirited.

Li Baye, who was wearing a lined black robe, walked up and patted Delu on the shoulder: "Well, young fellow," he said, "you'll find a solution if you think hard enough. As I see it, Elder Zhao is not being inconsiderate. The truth is, there are too many tenants, which makes things hard on the landlord. You should give some thought to him, what kind of man he is, what his position is. Do you think it's easy for him to recover his honor? I have an idea worth considering. If you are willing to listen to what I have to say, we can get this case dismissed, have your father released, and avoid having him die in jail, thereby saddling you with a reputation for being unfilial." Greenish light glinted from between his narrow eyelids. He looked at Delu and smiled, waiting for him to take the bait.

"Really? Elder Zhao will let us off? Only . . ." Delu's expression immediately gave Li some satisfaction.

"Why not? If you provide him with some collateral, I'll guarantee that your father will be released. Except . . ." Like an old hunter, he quietly watched his snare.

Collateral. Where would they ever get hold of some collateral? Twenty-nine *mu* in fields, a bit of land, even the land the thatched house stood on, didn't they all belong to Old Zhao? Except for themselves, the family had no resources. Li Baye suggested no strategy, he merely promised to help.

After this news arrived home with Delu, the grass shack seemed a bit brighter. They didn't really think about it, but without realizing it, they changed their thoughts along Li Baye's outline. And so, the next day, as soon as it was light, Delu, pressured by his mother and Third Aunt, went to call on Li Baye.

The family sat chatting in the autumn sun, awaiting his report. "Ugh, that dog! I've got nothing to say. I'll let you all go ahead and believe him." Third Uncle, who had just recovered from malaria, lay in the grass soaking up the sun.

Third Aunt sat on a stool nursing three-year-old Xiao Zhen. She didn't have much milk to offer, but since Xiao Zhen didn't have anything else to nibble on, if she could get a few mouthfuls that was all right.

"Sister, you can't ignore him. What's most important now is to get Father back home. Li Baye is nothing but a bastard, but he can talk straight and everyone knows he's Old Zhao's right-hand man. We can't be too cautious, and we have to call a spade a spade. If—ouch! You wretch! You bit me! I should spank you!" She shoved Xiao Zhen away, buttoned up her dress, and kept right on talking in her staccato way. She could see Qiqi and her niece out among the scissor-shaped leaves in the taro field. They were pulling up the soft roots; very tasty, but they needed a lot of care.

Laoma went off with the ox. He enjoyed going to very distant places. He was the only one in the family who didn't understand sadness. He loved that ox, loved it very much. Once the two of them had followed the grass north as far as the foot of Crow Hill without knowing where they were going, and three wolves had come leaping down the slope. Luckily the ox fought them. Laoma lay on top of the ox and shouted as loud as he could until two woodcutters came and rescued them. After that time the two of them, ox and boy, had become even closer. This ox was already very old and couldn't do much work in the fields, but because it had saved Laoma's life, no one in the family could bear to kill or sell it. Actually, they couldn't have found a buyer for the old thing anyway.

When Delu returned, what was on his face only added to their worries. He didn't say a word, but just sat beside his mother, glowering and staring toward the east where the hill held a man he hated.

"Dummy! Speak up. You can talk about it. Say something." They pressed him. He looked toward the kerchiefed heads moving around out in the taro fields. Rage stopped up his throat. He sighed and spoke slowly.

"That old bastard has got his eye on Qiqi. I can't stand it."

All Li Baye had to say was that Qiqi could be used for collateral. Send her to Zhao's to work, and there wasn't any reason why she couldn't return sometime in the future. But Li hadn't realized that this young man thought so highly of the young girl. He showed signs of regret, and thought that he ought not to have thought up this plan. As he saw it, there were difficulties with the deal, so he had better just call it off.

But the deal went through after all.

When Qiqi learned that Ma Chen, Third Aunt, and everyone in the family were all prepared to send her to Old Zhao to work, she wept.

"You must realize that Pa Chen . . . Oh, if the harvest is good next year, we'll certainly bail you out. We'll all save our money for the rest of the year. Laoma will have to go out to find work as a laborer. Daughter will have to pick up odd jobs, like rolling lamp wicks . . . You came to live with us when you were three years old. When did I ever treat you as if you weren't born into this family? And Delu . . . if we are able to bring you home next year, you'll be sixteen too, and I'll see to it that you are married. Now you must go to rescue Pa Chen. It's just a short trip around the hill and the round trip isn't that long either, so there's no reason we can't see you." Ma Chen wept copiously along with Qiqi.

That night, when everyone was asleep, Qiqi sneaked out to the front yard. She looked at the hill that would soon separate her from her family. She was frightened. She didn't want to go. She had seen Old Zhao and heard many things about him. If . . . Her only defense was a young girl's will to resist. An overwhelming dread grew inside her, and she began to hate the people in this family. Again she cried.

Sometimes, when there was no one around to see, Delu would come running up to console her. She would merely stare at him, spit, and curse him. "May you die young! You should drop dead! Heartless wretch!"

When the day decided on arrived, Qiqi followed First Aunt out of the house and began to climb the hill, crying as she went. She cursed Delu as a weakling and the most useless man on earth. Everyone tried to calm her down. Delu, enraged by her curses, had already left in anger. Qiqi seemed to remember something and said to Ma Chen, "That pair of socks is all mended. It's underneath my pillow."

Ma Chen understood what she meant and said comfortingly, "I'll tell him. The situation left him no choice. He'll go to town tomorrow to fetch his father."

Time passed slowly. Pa Chen came back and regained his health. But Qiqi was not allowed to return. Delu went to see her several times but sometimes couldn't meet with her. The best they could manage was to agree to meet out on the hillside, but in fact, there were few times when they could do even that. Furthermore, what Delu correctly guessed, and what Qiqi constantly dreaded, finally did occur. It was not something Qiqi could be blamed for. She was only a fifteen-year-old girl, she had no strength to resist, and she was shut up inside a cage. Except for asking Qiqi about it out on the hillside, Delu could do nothing about it either. However, day by day the resentment in his heart grew. Everyone in Zhao Village, Wuping, and Fenglinkou, and nearly everyone in East Village, knew that Delu had aged a great deal this past year. Deep lines on the young man's face inscribed the history of this business and wrote out the new personality this history had created, a personality produced by a long year of great vexation and distress. Yet what would the final result of this business be?

4

Red-faced, her hair dampened by perspiration, Third Aunt came limping home, as fast as her bound feet would carry her. "There's something going on," she panted. "The road is full of people, all headed for Zhao Village. Must be trouble! Xiao Zhen, here I am! Come here! Let's go, let's all go see." She tidied her hair, wiped her brow, and rubbed her damp hand on her dress.

Pa Chen glanced at his son, who lowered his head and adjusted his straw sandals: "Was there a fight or was someone killed? Ma, I want to go!"

"You're only sugar in the medicine. They can do without you. Why ask me? It's none of my business." Ma Chen pressed an old padded jacket to her bosom, shook it, and stood up. She did not look at her daughter as she grumbled, "Humph! People like Zhao . . . if they come to a good end, then Heaven has no conscience. Those damn bastards. I'll fix them and their ancient family! Isn't Qiqi my own daughter-in-law I raised in my own house? If I go I don't want to let her see me, but how I wish I could chew him into bits. Those good-for-nothings. Let's go anyway. Those devils. Let's go see. This certainly doesn't have anything to do with Qiqi. Let's get going!" Planning to lead the way, she leaned against the doorjamb and grumbled, "They should lose their heads."

"Aunt! Uncle! Is Third Uncle here? Has Second Brother gone? Don't you all know yet?" A nephew of the family came racing up, shouting. He stood in the doorway, pummeling the air with his fists, containing his anger while his eyes searched the room. "Li Xianglin wanted me to tell you. Wang Jin has already gone." He saw Delu sitting there silently, his lusterless eyes like those of a dumb ox.

Pa Chen also looked at his son, who was chewing his lip. "What the devil business is this? What do you know about it?"

"Ah, Uncle, you mean you still don't know? There's a meeting today. Hurry up! If there's no meeting, it will cost us our harvest! People starved to death last year, and in the spring there were still people out begging for rice. Now that devil Zhao wants to press more men into his service! When the harvest is poor, there's nothing to eat. When the harvest is good, there's still nothing to eat. Doesn't the entire harvest always get taken away and end up in someone else's hands? No telling what the Peasant Association can do! Now those demons want to form a defense corps, conscript men, and take money.[2] Once they have their force organized, they'll go after us for sure! Damn them! Second Brother, get a move on! Everybody, come along! What village won't send everyone to the meeting? It will be as exciting as the lion dance at New Year's."

Chen Delu stood up with a shiver, went out, and as he fled his father's glare, the corners of his mouth curved in a cryptic little smile. He began whistling, not any tune in particular, and continued to whistle as he walked away. He could feel everyone's eyes boring into his back.

"Let's go! Husband, let's go!" Third Aunt picked up her child and limped along behind the others. Laoma's sister marched quickly behind them.

"Hey, Ma. I don't want to stay here all by myself! I want to go too!" Laoma yelled from an inner room.

Pa Chen's eyes followed his son as he hurried off and disappeared around the spur of the hill in the direction of the main road. On that stretch of road, threadlike, endless, a crowd of country people was hurrying along in the same direction, sending up a great hubbub of voices. Pa Chen's heart churned. The slow change in his son's spirits had upset him. "Damn it, there'll be troublemakers for sure." So he stood up and followed the crowd.

"The old fool wants to go make trouble, too!" Ma Chen wished she could hold her husband back, but when she saw that he wasn't saying anything, she turned angrily and went inside.

In the autumn sunlight, women wearing flowered kerchiefs crowded in among the blue-jacketed men. Along the narrow road and through the harvested paddy fields, they rushed forward like scattered soldiers in loose formation. Some people were curious. Some were talking loudly to conceal the uncertainty they felt. Others were unable to repress the violence of their emotions. They were all mixed together in one great stream impelled by a whirlwind toward a single spot.

The whirlwind blew in from all directions and crowded into Old Zhao's courtyard. People jammed themselves inside, elbow to elbow, feet stepping on feet. Curious eyes swept over this face and that. They were asking each other questions and waiting for the great upheaval that must come.

"What time is it? Why not start the meeting?"

"What's the rush? We're going to meet today no matter what."

"What'll we do if our resolution isn't accepted in town? We have to keep our courage."

A little farther off were some stone benches, on which people were sitting and squatting. Everyone was making small talk.

"Pigs have gone up in price. A couple of days ago, I took my spotted pig to market and got twenty-six strings of cash. If I had waited another month, it would have been much more. I might have gotten over thirty strings."

"My cousin had a baby girl a few days ago. Oh me, what a scary thing! She was all by herself in the room, lying on the bed watching the baby she'd put in the footpan waving her hands and feet and screaming. Eventually the sound stopped. But then, unfortunately, her brother-in-law barged in and gave out a scream. By then it was impossible to hide. My cousin had to throw away all the bedding. Others in the family came in, washed what needed washing, covered the baby with loose cotton balls, and surprisingly, the little thing lived. Cousin cried, but no one scolded her. They all knew what she wanted to do.[3] Anyway, there's nothing that can be done about it now."

Small children came to listen to stories. There was quite a crowd. Many of them were women chatting about other matters. Everyone felt they had so much to say that they couldn't hold it in, and so there was a lot of racket.

Some of the more important men went from one place to another shouting, "Oppose all taxes. The harvest is ours!" Or else they sang the songs that were spread by the Peasant Association. People kept arriving, and the peasants' self-defense corps came, too.

"Hey, hey, look at Xiaoniu! What're you up to? A platoon leader, a torn-pants platoon leader. Even your dick is hanging out!" The people stopped talking and started laughing. Xiaoniu's face was scarlet. He felt the crotch of his pants, but it was okay; nothing wrong. "Fuck your mother!" he yelled back.

But the onlookers weren't about to let him off. They looked at the crude, rusty spear he carried on his shoulder. "Why, what's that? You use that for dicking around? Wouldn't it be better to put what's in your pants on your shoulder?"

As soon as Xiaoniu lost his temper, they all hooted and walked away. Another bunch over at the side added, "Li Xiangsheng is here. Look, Xiaolong is here too. Damn. Xiaolong is going to make a speech. Wonderful, wonderful!"

Members of the squad that was to keep order showed up, with strips of red cloth tied around their forearms. The spears of the self-defense corps stood out in rows above the heads of the crowd. In the sun the red tassels looked like fires burning in the sea of people. Someone announced the beginning of the meeting. Everyone crowded in together.

Fists were raised. A man no one seemed to know jumped up onto the platform. Someone finally recognized him as Mao Jijiang from Fenglinkou. In everyone's heart there was an unsettling question, "Where's Wang Jin? Where did Wang Jin go?"

At this moment Wang Jin was in a small room in Old Zhao's west courtyard. Paintings, calligraphy, and curios were arranged all about. It was nice and secluded. Old Zhao often came here to while away the time. When there were no guests, he would lie on the *kang* and just relax.[4] If someone did come to call, they could have a chat. His servants usually didn't come here. Today Wang Jin had been invited to come to this room because he had some important matters to discuss. It was his fourth visit to this room; he'd been there before on account of Peasant Association matters.

"Please think of something. You must have some idea." Old Zhao fiddled with his tobacco pipe and spit frequently as he paced back and forth. "During these last six months, I've taken your advice on everything, right? Qian Zhongshi has more land than I do; Li Yuantai has many shops in town; Zhang Haisheng's brothers have official positions. They've all fled to the provincial capital, and now I'm the only responsible person in the district. As for the new grain, they hauled it away by boat. How much do I have? There are so many people in my household! And now . . ." His face was so red that it couldn't have taken more of his anger. He hated Wang Jin and the others. Ever since the Peasant Association had been established, he'd had nothing but trouble. He hated Qian Zhongzhi most of all. Whenever something came up, they always made him the fall guy. But he didn't want to blame them to Wang Jin's face. He knew Wang Jin was dangerous. He feared him. But he had to put on a show of amiability.

Wang Jin sat in a chair against the wall, a cigarette in his fingers. His outward appearance had the simple directness of a peasant and the dour look of a soldier. He had a cultured Confucian manner blended with shrewd capability. Wang made others love him, but he also made them fear him. They trusted him, respected him, and relied upon him, yet no one really understood him or comprehended his great ability. There was an earnest look in his eyes as he sat there with the raging Old Zhao. He inhaled deeply on his cigarette. The ash lengthened and fell onto the front of his jacket.

"You've been in East Village for some time, so you ought to understand something about the situation. What night isn't my vegetable garden robbed, and on what mountain aren't my trees cut down? These fellows—shit! Slippery and rotten through and through. If you question them or swear at them, they just put on a pretense of stupidity. Wang, you say I'm a landlord, but all I get is about three hundred piculs of grain with which to feed over a hundred people. I don't even have enough to pay my bills. If anyone wanted to buy my land, I'd sell it, pay off my debts, and become a poor peasant. Sure, you could let me join the Peasant Association." He put on a pitiable look and gnawed at the mouthpiece of his expensive pipe, translucent jade that was greener than the sea.

All these lies did not make Wang Jin forget old Zhao's evil ways. Zhao also had friends who were officials. He owned shops too, and they were pawnshops at that. His fields certainly yielded more than four hundred piculs of grain and had to amount to over three thousand *mou*. He had henchmen: the headman in East Village, the district magistrate, the police—most of them were Zhao's men. Zhao had his own gang. He beat up many tenants, and he beat his own servants. His secondary wives had been bought, so angering his wife that she had fallen ill; even though she was bedridden he ignored her. All the female servants were his concubines. Those starving women, chosen from among the tenants, were all quite attractive. Wang Jin would never forget him, and right now outside Zhao's gates, thousands of people had assembled. These people hated him to the marrow of their bones, could not forget him, and would have loved to tear him to shreds.

One of those people who could not forget appeared in the doorway. Old Zhao spun around and looked at the man's infuriating, dirty face. "Who told you could come in here?" he bellowed. "Get out!"

Chen Delu sat down on the threshold, hesitated for a moment, then said, "I came to see Qiqi. I must see her today." Sitting near Wang Jin emboldened him.

"Creep! Get the hell out of here!" Wang Jin's glance made Old Zhao feel very uneasy, as if it might be better to moderate his tone. "The person you're looking for isn't here. Go look out back."

"She isn't there. Where have you hidden her? You'd better let me take her home today, or else!" Chen Delu drummed up his courage. He didn't know why, but as soon as he entered this place his heart had felt a little empty; resentment and fear were woven together. He didn't dare look at

Old Zhao. He had feared him all his life. Behind Zhao was an invisible force that had always kept him and people like him under control.

"What's all this crap? You stupid pig . . . Come here someone! Throw this worthless piece of shit out! Where is everyone?" All the household servants had been asked to step outside. A few women were still sewing in an upstairs room.

Wang Jin quickly smoothed his hair. He met Chen Delu's eyes, which were those of a hurt, beaten dog—beseeching, ashamed, frightened. His hands dropped, and apparently losing track of where he was, he leaned against the door frame. As if there were nothing else to do, he turned his face toward the courtyard.

This was something Wang Jin had always been concerned about. He understood these people very well. They had been more pitifully oppressed than cattle and horses and had been more submissive than those beasts of burden. But should their hearts ever be set on fire, the flames could consume them too. Wang Jin couldn't help being a little hesitant, but it was best to say something quickly. His expression lost none of its calmness as he said, "I think that we'd better discuss this matter of the defense corps. It would be better if you didn't have more men than Qian Zhongzhi and his friends."

Old Zhao endured his bitter feelings, but he would have preferred to kick Chen Delu out the door. Who did he think he was, coming here and throwing around a bunch of false accusations? But he couldn't lose his dignity in front of Wang Jin. Irritably, unwillingly, he said nothing. When he heard Wang Jin speak, Zhao was aware that there was a hidden threat behind Wang Jin's words, but he was unable to improve his position.

Two *wutong* trees grew in the courtyard and spread their dense leaves aloft. They blocked out the sun completely, except in some spots where the leaves had dried and fallen to the ground. There a little sunlight leaked through to form shadows on the dark, damp ground. These trees, this earth, the courtyard walls, and their quiet atmosphere had all been transformed into something repulsive. Chen Delu was extremely nervous. All he could think about was running away, of flying over the walls. Then he felt like rushing over and sinking his teeth into this mad dog. Listening to Zhao's voice, even his breathing, gave rise to a bottomless loathing. Delu's heart pounded. Once again he turned to look at Wang Jin.

Wang Jin, who appeared unconcerned, continued speaking to Old Zhao, "You have got to understand that this is a trick. They want to deal with us right now, not just sacrifice you." Wang Jin's calm expression soothed Zhao somewhat, encouraged him a little, and he turned around once again and sat down.

"I understand this business. I understand it. I'm not afraid. Tomorrow I'll go to town. I'll go to town." Old Zhao's face was calm, but he felt that he was in a tight spot. Chen Delu, his hatred slowly catching fire, felt even more distressed as he stared at his own hands, big hands that could lift a hundred pounds. For the last six months, he had hoped that the day would come when he could strangle his enemy. Even Old Zhao's name was enough to impel Delu to think about doing this great act. But somehow or other he couldn't get up or move to kill him. Chen Delu stared at that fat, disgusting man. He felt like spitting into that glistening, oily face. All he wanted was another opportunity. Then he'd certainly do something. He assumed a courageous manner and looked at Wang Jin, who seemed not to notice him, and just kept on talking. But Delu also saw Wang Jin smoothing his hair with his hand over and over again. Suddenly Chen Delu stood up, looking ferocious, and just as suddenly, he turned pale and began to groan. He seemed to have been paralyzed on the spot by a curse.

"Gao Zhanggeng! Gao Zhanggeng! Wang Erh Sao! Wang Erh Sao!" bellowed Old Zhao, feeling extremely uneasy.

"Damnation . . . Grab him." Wang Jin abruptly confronted Old Zhao and grabbed him by the collar. "What do you think you are doing? There are thousands of people out there who want to put you on trial . . . Here, you, grab him . . . Are you dead or what? Come here!"

"Good Heavens!" Chen Delu was so happy he thought of shouting, but subconsciously he only wanted to run away. He was afraid to look at the man they had seized.

Old Zhao struggled, broke free, and shouted, "Help! Help!" He tried to make it outside and get away, but Wang Jin gripped his robe and snarled, "No you don't. This is the day you pay the reckoning."

"Hurry! Something's happened to the master." A chorus of women's voices was heard. Chen Delu saw that Old Zhao was about to get away again. His fist was already raised to strike a cruel blow at Wang Jin's head. Delu didn't think twice. With a surge of strength, he rushed over, shoved away Old Zhao's fist, and pushed him down onto the floor.

"Take the old devil alive. Down with these tyrannical oppressors!" shouted Wang Jin with all his might.

"Ah ya! We'll be killed! It's a revolution!" Several women rushed in. They crowded around, pulling, swearing, shouting, pounding on the stools, hitting the chairs. Wang Jin was surrounded.

"Hurry, Uncle, hurry. San Chengzhuang, Qi Liping, go quickly! Help!" a voice roared from the floor. Zhao, who hadn't been hurt by the fall, was waiting for a chance to escape.

A dog, getting under everyone's feet, started barking. Another group of people came pushing in, shouting excitedly, "Down with the local tyrants! Overthrow the commander of the defense corps! The harvest belongs to us!"

And so Old Zhao was shoved outside by a horde of shabby, grotesque peasants, all of whom he recognized, all of whom depended on him for their livelihood.

5

An uncountable number of fists were raised above a sea of people. Cries of hatred exploded from every nook and cranny, rushing like a great wave above the closely packed heads and off into the night. When one wave passed, another even larger one was formed. Here, out here in Zhao's forecourt, the gloom of the old days was erased. All the dark clouds that had suffocated people were rolled away by a whirlwind, and now the world had changed its color. The sun high above looked greatly agitated. The maple trees dotting the mountainside with color burned like fire in this tide of rage sinking into the whirlwind. All the wrongs suffered burst out. Premonitions of the victory to come made all hearts quiver with joy. Voices filled with emotion called to each other in an astonishing, thunderlike roar.

"Fuck your ancestors for eighteen generations. We'll see if you'll return my land. I've wanted to settle accounts with you for a long time."

"Ask him, what's the meaning of this private defense corps? Damnation, you old devil Zhao, you think you can eat people, do you?"

"Burn his house down! Leave him with no place to live . . ."

But there were some who, although they joined in the shouting, were still full of nameless fears. They did not dare hope that what they longed for would come quickly. This was especially true of the old people. Pa Chen stood among them weeping. He looked at these people, this multitude of people like himself, all red in the face, forgetting everything. One or two would jump up onto the high place at the center of all the commotion and speak. And right there, next to where people were taking turns speaking, stood his enemy, Old Zhao, looking as if he'd died. This situation moved him thoroughly, made him weep uncontrollably. He longed to run up and spit a great gob into that pale, gray face. But his hands and feet shook convulsively. He couldn't say whether it was from boundless joy or from fear. In any case, he simply couldn't bear to look at that expressionless face. He wanted to get away from this mob. These impulses were not easy to sort out.

At first Old Zhao had made excuses for himself. His intentions were obvious. He thought, "Dammit, you bunch of mongrels, how dare you lay hands on me? If you want something, I'll give it to you! A brave man doesn't eat crow . . ." But later roars of outrage drowned him out. No one could stand listening to him. All those doltish, pig faces, all those dumb ox eyes, had been transformed into something ferocious bearing down upon him, and he began to experience fear. Feeling the path before him grow dark, he shivered. He stopped thinking and stared apathetically straight ahead. Listlessly, he stood there waiting for someone to support him. He still had a ray of hope, but it was fading fast.

Suddenly, a bunch of men came rushing in from the highway to the northeast, all yelling, "They're coming, they're coming! A lot of people, a lot of them are thugs. Maybe a thousand or more! Run! Run!" The women began to scream.

"Old Mao, let's go now!"

"Get out, get out . . . Bitch! Bitch! Damn it, I don't see my own bitch!"

People were beginning to push and shove. At the same time, the power of a newly intensified rage grew even greater. "You whore, here I come to risk my life and kill a bunch of them . . . They're a bunch of reckless, stupid bedbugs!"

The chaos increased, but Wang Jin's appearance restored order: "Time is short and we have to make a decision quickly." Wang Jin looked around him and said confidently, "The path that's laid out before us has a fork in it. One fork leads to revolt, to taking back everything and managing our own land. We must overthrow everyone who extorts our goods, oppresses us, opposes us. If we choose the other fork, we go home peacefully, give up everything, dissolve the Peasant Association, disband the workers' and peasants' self-defense corps, surrender to our enemies, and become slaves forever. So which will it be?"

All together with a single voice the answer came like thunder: "We will never surrender! We'll fend for ourselves!"

"In that case," Wang Jin continued, looking around again solemnly, "we must first make a decision. And that is . . ." He stopped, fiercely grabbed Old Zhao, then continued loudly, "What shall we do with this man?" He shut his mouth and searched the crowd with his eyes.

A murmur arose. There were hesitant voices. And then, no one knew who said it: "Kill him!"

Others joined in. "KILL HIM! Kill him first and then we'll talk some more!"

More voices were added to the cry, "KILL HIM!" Their response spread out even farther, reaching even to a group of women who stood in the distance and, as if chanting an incantation, cried "KILL HIM!"

Wang Jin stood there waiting, but no one came forward. They all wanted him killed, but no one dared to strike the first blow.

"They're only four *li* away!" A shout broke the silence. "We've got to get ready fast!"

Shouts came echoing down from the mountaintop, agitating the trees, spreading the alarm. And little by little, the people started to waver.

"The defense force must go to the pass and block the road," Wang Jin ordered.

Li Xiangsheng came running up. "Comrades! Time won't wait for us. Finish him off! Down with evil landlords! Down with powerful land-owners and devils who ravish women! Down with . . ."

A roar answered him: "Down with them!"

But the rescuers were also on their way. Tenant farmers and farmhands who had all endured the same oppression and poor peasants who had been cheated all their lives and were again being deceived were coming. They wanted to rescue their overlord. If there were no landlord, no fam-ily to support them, then what fields would they have to plant? They had no land of their own. Besides, he was a powerful man. If he were to come to grief, the local authorities would certainly mete out punishment, and the villagers would end up with nothing, not even a place to be buried in. And so, led by Old Zhao's relatives, they had come running, carrying hoes, rakes, and poles, led by the rent collectors and watchmen.

The ranks of the self-defense force, armed with spears and homemade guns, stood ready to meet the enemy coming from the northeast. They were tense, feeling a weight on their shoulders that wasn't solely the weight of iron and wooden poles; but they were also happy because of that new weight. They encouraged each other by shouting, "Don't worry, don't be afraid. When they get here, we'll finish them all off!"

Old Zhao's face was a little redder, for the color of swelling hope had faded. He sat there cowering. He had already lost all awareness and great beads of sweat on his temples and face trickled downward. Even the backs of his hands were wet. He moaned, his dim wooden eyes stared in bafflement. But no one pushed him, even though many teeth had been grinding for some time.

Chen Delu, standing behind Xiaolong, was afraid to look into the eyes of those he knew. Wringing his hands, head down, he appeared to be waiting for something.

Behind everyone, from somewhere in the rear, came the call "KILL HIM! Hurry up! What stupid bastard is afraid of him? If all of you are afraid, let me at him . . ."

Then untold numbers of people pushed forward yelling and shouting, "Today is the day of reckoning! Send him to hell! Strike!" The first kick lashed out, rolling soft, mushy Old Zhao over. "Watch me do it to him!"

A frenzy, an irrepressible madness arose. Everyone lost their sense of reason. Once the barriers were down, everybody fought for a chance to act, swearing, spitting, fists and feet all concentrated on a single spot.

Women joined too, grinning, their hair flying, cursing, crying with joy. They too wanted to add a kick, a blow, wanted to see that beaten, formless thing, that old man-eating tiger.

Those rushing to aid Old Zhao were drawing nearer, but the people's anger would not be denied. They wouldn't let the body of the man who was already dead alone. Wang Jin shouted to calm them.

"Our work here is finished," he said. "Let's figure out what to do now. At this very minute a gang of armed men, almost as many as we are, are hurrying this way. Do we fight them or leave and find a meeting place? In my opinion, we ought to go to the earth god temple and gather there. They might not even follow us. Let them have their funeral! What do you say?"

Quickly, enthusiastically, the dense crowd flowed away to the other place. The self-defense force withdrew slowly at their rear.

6

That night when the moon shone down upon the pines, and the open space that had been leveled by the tempest lay quietly in the moonlight, a single shadow appeared. Chen Delu had left his comrades and crept quietly back. He looked at the house. It was very noisy inside. He had someone on his mind, and wondered if she had taken advantage of the opportunity to run away or whether she had been flogged. He looked at that flat piece of ground where a corpse with bulging, bloody eyes, bursting from their sockets, had lain. Probably the corpse was buried already, or perhaps it was still inside the house. He'd never be able to beat Zhao; he'd lost his chance. Delu clenched his fists, aching with inner regret. But all he could do was unclench his feverish hands and sigh deeply.

Later on, soldiers were sent out from town. What became of all these people is unclear, but the reverberations of the tempest spread far and wide, stirring things up for many years.

Translated by Jean James

New Faith

As the war of resistance against Japan forced the guerrillas and communities of the Communist Base Areas to greater and greater sacrifice, Party writers pared down their fiction into simple weapons of propaganda. Ding Ling specialized in stories about the power of weakness. Even in the early 1930s, she'd been attracted to this notion. "For the Children" (1932) reworked the Peter Pan story into a revolutionary fable, and one of her most popular war stories, "The Unfired Bullet" (1937), also portrayed a child as a powerful moral hero. "New Faith," written in 1939, connects the power of weakness to the politically ordained topic of rape.

The story also demonstrates her familiarity with the problems Party cadres were encountering in their work with peasant women. Ding Ling had helped to co-found the Women's National Salvation Association. She gave many signs of wanting to learn about rural women's experience, in part, one suspects, because she felt she had already had a stake in formulating women's policy. For that reason, the grandmother who is this story's heroine has a significance not immediately obvious.

The grandmother does not recognize "woman" as a universal, inhering, real social category. Her sense of self is richly kin defined, and she knows her place as mother, widow, grandmother. In fact, until the young women of the Party drop by to solicit her help at a rally, she does not think to identify herself with other women. The relation of general, social, and ideological categories to specific, immediate instances was a preoccupation, not just of Ding Ling, but of Party theory and practice in general. The evidence here suggests that Ding Ling was beginning to appreciate the role political ideology would have to play if a new notion of womanhood was to serve as the government's vehicle for mobilizing peasant women. The importance of ideology in the definition of the new woman and her role in a socialist society may help to explain the bitterness of the debate in the early 1940s.

Indeed, as the story shows very accurately, the triumph of Yan'an policy on women was that it really did convince old women like the grandmother to expand their power and reach beyond the family through the new political bond of citizen and state. Granny reaches out from exclusive concern for her sons to the object of unity in the village and finally to mystical unity with the nation; the old woman's moral power grows and with it her stature as a heroine.—TEB

I

Beyond the meager stands of trees, on the farthest reach of the plain, the village of Xiliu lay serenely.[1] Leafless branches of the willows along the embankment outside the village whipped madly in the blasting winter wind. Under the willow trees, a whitewashed, mud-brick wall glimmered in the frozen slush, the sickly ashen white augmenting the bitter, forbidding gloom. A tall pagodalike building stood alone at the village gate. It looked like a lonely old man, wrapped in black garments sheened with age, standing at dusk gazing forlornly into the distance.

It really was dusk. The village rested in an evening haze. Yet virtually none of the mist came from dinner fires.

One after another, flocks of crows circled above the village, then flew off to the jujube grove on the hillside. Little birds that had already found their roosts in the grove chirped uncertainly, startled by the new arrivals.

What really alarmed them was the looming shadow of a man walking heavily down the hillside. At each step, his old, black, wadded-cotton shoes made a crunching noise as they shattered the thin layer of ice frozen on the tufts of grass. A wild hen with beautiful plumage fled in fear toward the grove.

Like a prisoner on his way to execution, Chen Xinhan used all his strength to keep from falling down. His listless eyes stared blankly at the sky; seemingly terrified that he might catch sight of something horrible, he hardly dared glance around. His footsteps slowed still further as he rounded the bottom of the hill.

The village was no longer deadly silent, but, like a patient just waking from a coma, moaned tiredly. It was already dark. What was that tapping noise? It sounded like a hoe striking the frozen ground. He couldn't tell from the women's voices whether they were calling or sobbing, so much did they sound like choruses of doleful, starving wolves howling late at night on the empty mountaintop. Urgent, wincing terror gripped Chen Xinhan as he heard these sounds clear as a bell. He couldn't stop a shudder from running through his body. He stood stupefied. Then, mustering courage once again, and drawn by desperate hope, he walked down the hill toward a village now encompassed in an iridescent mist that left only the vague outlines of rooftops visible.

Two human shapes moved out of the village through the evening darkness, soundlessly, single file, carrying something. When Chen Xinhan realized that the object they were carrying between them was a human body, he felt stricken. His steps became increasingly hesitant. He felt a rekindled anxiety. He walked to a spot close by and watched them, carefully noting every move they made.

Digging fitfully into the earth beside the body, the two men soon rapidly, vigorously tossed loose soil back into the pit, gradually filling it up. Then they packed it down, leaving a raised earthen mound in the shape of a *mantou* bun.[2] After a few final pats, the two men turned back to the familiar path and headed for home. By mutual consent not a word had been spoken. Only as they left did one of the two sigh deeply.

"Hey, hey, tell me. Who's in that hole? Who is it?" Chen Xinhan grabbed at them. The moaning timbre of a sick animal sounded in his voice.

"It's Mister Zhang.[3] We found him in his grandson's house. He'd probably been dumped there," one of them answered.

"His granddaughter-in-law was lying stark naked right next to him," the other continued. "She was stuck to the ground by her own congealed blood. Look. She's right over there sleeping so peacefully now. The one on the right."

Chen Xinhan let them go and fell in behind them. There was something lodged in his throat that he dared not say aloud. The younger of the two men broke the silence: "Where'd you run off to the last couple of days, Uncle Chen.[4] Better get on home fast. Your brother's already back."

"Erguan?[5] When did he get back?" Chen didn't wait for the answer. His legs had found new strength, his stride lengthened; he raised his head as one scene after another ran through his mind. Though trivial, these incidents still moved him deeply.

By then they'd entered the village proper. The darkness made it impossible to tell if any major changes had occurred, so his fearfulness changed to hope. Chen Xinhan left the gravediggers behind. He rushed off toward his house.

He'd left it five days before. Around dawn he'd heard a burst of gunfire coming from just outside the village. He'd leaped out of bed. His wife was already up, and his fifteen-year-old daughter, Jingu, ashen faced, came bursting into the room.[6] Everybody knew what was happening. "Run!" he said. "Get to Granny's house by the back route on the other side of the hill."[7]

"Daddy, oh, Daddy! If we have to die, let's die together."

"Where's my sheepskin vest?"

"Don't worry about your things now! The Japs are nearly here . . ."

He'd dragged out his bound-foot wife with one hand, his pretty young daughter with the other. Jingu ran crazed with panic. Her face looked hideous, disguised with smears of soot and dirt. They ran ahead of the crowd and soon reached the top of the hill. But then his wife started sobbing. Had their second daughter and their son gotten away? And what about Chen Xinhan's fifty-seven-year-old mother? So leaving the women to flee with the crowd, he slipped off and went back toward the village. People grabbed him, saying, "Don't turn back! Run for your life!" But he didn't know the meaning of fear because his only concern was to rescue his mother. He searched the sweeping tide of people shouting her name.

His sister-in-law, Erguan's wife, limped up to him, lugging her one-year-old daughter.

"Mama? Have you seen Mama?"

"A little while ago. She got out before me. She's got Yingu and Tong-guan. Where're we going?"

"Granny's. Hurry!"

But he couldn't flee with her. Instead he headed for home. The village was in total chaos. Bullets flew around his head, people screamed for help. The outlying houses were in flames, and white smoke rolled into the village. There wasn't a soul at his house, just a few chickens darting around the courtyard screeching. He nearly walked right into a hail of bullets. With a shout, he dodged back. He could hear hoofbeats bearing down on him but couldn't risk the time to glance at his rear. The skies were falling, the earth splitting behind him. Crushed, people hadn't the time to draw their next breath; only the sounds of a sharp cry, gasps.

Nor did he find any of his family along the road back. He traded inquiries with several people from the village he came across, but nobody could give any satisfactory answers.

He walked over to look at two old crones sitting at the top of the hill whining and sobbing with grief, but neither of them was his mother. Exhausted children straggled along, none of them his Tongguan. And now he couldn't even find his wife and daughter. If only he could find

Erguan's wife, everything would be fine. But not a trace of her was to be seen. He rested and waited around a bit, as refugees streamed past, yet not one of them was a member of his family.

"It was a whole regiment!"

"They hacked farmhands to death!"

"Will our Xiliu Village be destroyed this time?"

"I kept telling you they'd come!"

"So now we're all going to get it."

"This . . . This was preordained."

Panic was more contagious standing there in a crowd, so he went off by himself. He walked to the village of Zhangjiawan, about twelve miles away. Only twenty or thirty families lived there. It had always been a very quiet place without much coming and going, and the people there had few connections with outsiders. Their existence resembled that of primitive people. His wife's parents lived there.

No one else came that evening after he arrived to join his wife and Jingu. He spent the whole next day searching and hearing nothing but bad news about the village. On the third day, he sent word to his brothers. On the fourth, he got a return message. They reported that they'd be going home before long—beyond that nothing was certain. On the fifth day, he went out again and had good news by afternoon. The guerrillas had retaken Xiliu, and people had already begun moving back. So he did too, just to see how things stood. He was very frightened. He couldn't bear thinking about what might have happened to his family there, but he had to go back. Harried and anxious, he had left for home.

Now he was already feeling better. He'd seen nothing unpropitious, perhaps because nothing bad had happened. The two gravediggers, however, had neglected to tell him one thing: that very afternoon they'd buried a boy named Tongguan. His only son.

2

"Let me go with you guys to get it." Jingu tightened her belt and looked up at her Second Uncle, Chen Zuohan, ignoring her mother's venomous gaze.

The second son after Chen Xinhan, Chen Zuohan had inherited their father's character, his boldness and his sobriety. Whenever Chen Zuohan scowled or pursed his lips, the other brothers would exchange glances and keep quiet, and his mother would shrink quietly away to the kitchen or next room to eavesdrop. But he didn't get angry often, and he was much too indulgent with the children, which always made the women grumpy.

"Better not come. Stay home. Besides, it's still snowing outside." He patted her thinly padded jacket.

"No. I want to go." Jingu turned around, pouting. "I don't want to sit around inside." She rolled her eyes, looked over at her mother and aunt, then turned back, letting her beseeching gaze stop on the face of her uncle.

Her uncle smiled as though to say, "What a child."

"Shameless bitch!" Her mother's temper had turned perverse and difficult recently. "A big girl like you," her abuse continued, "daring to go outside with all these soldiers on the rampage."

"Stay with your mother," Chen Xinhan said without looking at his daughter. He turned and went out.

"Jingu, get a fire started. Boil some water. Remember Second Uncle Zuohan might find Granny and Little Sissy. Now what are you after?" Jingu didn't answer. She covered her head with a cloth and started out the door. "Where are you going?" her mother asked sharply.

"I'm going out for coal, if that's all right with you," Jingu yelled back at her.

Uncle Zuohan grinned again. Then he glanced contemptuously around the room and went solemnly out the door.

Chen Xinhan's wife squatted at the head of the *kang* desperately racking her brains to find some way of venting her rage, someone to blame, when a new idea came to her all of a sudden. She was sure her insight was correct. Newly kindled rage gnawed at her guts. She felt a tremendous urge to bite into human flesh. Then she checked herself with effort.

"Second Sister-in-law," she said softly, "didn't you say you saw Granny with Tongguan and Yingu the day you escaped from the Japs?"

Second Sister-in-law, holding her baby and squatting at the other end of the *kang,* had grown frightened of her sister-in-law and was choosing her words carefully these last few days.

"Sure," she replied affably. "I saw them just as I was leaving."

"And when did you run into Jingu's dad?"

"Halfway down."

"Oh!"

Conversation stopped for a moment, and then she asked, "Had you ever been to Seventh Uncle's place before?"

"Never. I was running away with lots of other people. I don't know exactly how I got there. If he hadn't been out looking around, well. . . !" Second Sister-in-law recalled that terrible confusion. If she hadn't run into Seventh Uncle, what would have happened to her then?

"Well, now. Isn't that just a little too lucky to be true! I say, Second Sister-in-law, we're related, so you don't have to mince words with me.

Jingu's father took you and the baby up there. Nothing wrong with that . . . I guess . . . So why do you two think you can put one over on me?"

"Elder Sister-in-law! Don't be absurd! The whole family is in big, big trouble. Come on. Come on, cool down."

"Sure the family's in trouble, but none of it ever fell on your head. Didn't you and your son have someone to take you to a safe place? You should pity me. Ah, my Tongguan, my son. You died so hard!" Her fist pounded the *kang,* her tears flowed, and the resentment choking her coursed out like water, yet found itself magically replenished. Her teeth gnashed and she went on cursing, "They're all bastards here. Not one of them has any sympathy or sense of shame . . ." She kept searching for words that would humiliate Second Sister-in-law, hoping she could get her angry.

Second Sister-in-law felt unfairly abused and wept under the quilt. Then, startled, the baby started shrieking.

"Ma, what's the matter? What's going on?" The scene baffled Jingu, on her way back in with a sack of coal.

The sound of her daughter's voice broke Chen Xinhan's wife's heart. Now she only had one daughter, and her younger girl had been so much cuter than this Jingu, so lively and obedient, and she'd never defied her mother. And she hadn't even seen Tongguan's corpse, only visited his little grave twice. She could imagine what he must have looked like. He'd been . . . he'd probably looked like a slaughtered lamb, with green, red, and white stuff oozing out of his slit-open belly. Every time she thought about it, she wanted to vomit; she felt the same sort of unbearable pain she'd have had if her own guts had been ripped out.

"Ma! Don't cry! Second Auntie, you . . . what're you doing?" But then Jingu herself couldn't help bursting into sobs as well.

Nightfall brought snowfall, and the darkness pressed down on the snow. Thick, interminable, nebulous layers of clouds wafted slowly to the ground. The wind tore madly at the paper windows and poured in through the cracks. Inside twilight turned to darkness. People's feelings changed too, from anxious resentment to deep grief. Their sobbing subsided. They groaned as they mourned the dead.

Second Sister-in-law gingerly put the baby, who'd fallen asleep from exhaustion, down on the *kang* and groped her way around the room; she didn't want to give anyone a reason to make trouble.

Jingu felt better once someone was moving around. The flames glowed in the stove and the air above the *kang* got warmer. Steam rising out of the boiling wok obscured the forms of those seated around the stove. They chatted again, exchanging their dreams. They began to wait in hope for their pitiful white-haired granny and innocent young daughter.

3

The north wind, swirling the silent snow, swept mercilessly across the plains and the hills on a rampage. Excruciating, bitter cold and the ravening darkness ruled the universe of night. Walls and roofs were scarce in this land laid waste. People huddled together like dogs. And the dogs curled up in the ruins, tails between their legs, so worn down that even when they saw something move, they'd just close their eyes again.

Chen Xinhan's family had spent most of the night in a fervor of hope. Now only Jingu was still on her feet, feeding the fire, adding more water to the steaming wok. Again and again she asked, "Second Uncle, do you think Granny will come back?"

"No, no. Not on a night this cold. Even if they found her, Third Uncle wouldn't let her come now." Chen Zuohan reclined on the *kang* smoking. "Go to sleep, child."

"Not unless you do. Look how soundly Mommy's sleeping."

"Mmm. The ordeal's worn her out."

Jingu, however, ignored his sympathetic remark. She questioned him on and on about what was going on in the village. She also talked to him about her grandmother. They both hoped she wouldn't come back that night because it was so cold.

Then they thought they could hear cries and moans mingled with the howling of the wind. Jingu was frozen with terror, looking at her uncle and holding up her hand as if to say, don't move! Listen! Her uncle held his breath and listened closely, for nothing could be seen in the darkness outside. Even her father, half asleep on the *kang*, sat up. But there was nothing there. Still they waited in the dim lamplight until the sky turned as gray as a fish's belly and they were certain that their hopes would have to be postponed for another day. Soon it was just as silent inside as out.

A bleak day dawned. The endless blackness turned slowly to pale gray, and from the remote sky snowflakes came raining down thick and fast, whirling ever downward. No birds sang. No cocks crowed. Even the dogs did not bark. The snow covered the destruction, the tattered mess; frozen, the ordure, animal bones, and feathers all became invisible. The entire blood-soaked land disappeared under the frozen snow. The only things left were black words on a white wall: "Extirpate Communism! Support the Greater East Asia Co-Prosperity Sphere!" written over the scrubbed out, faded inscription "Drive Japanese Imperialism out of China!" Now the darker words were being disfigured too, by rivulets of melting snow running like snot and tears down a weeping face.

There was only one living thing moving about on the plain. Then it too collapsed. Covered with snow, had it not begun instinctively to crawl forward again, it would have been impossible to spot. Gradually this living thing moved into the village. It was human. But no one was around in the village, and so the figure fell on the roadside again. It struggled up once more to drive off a curious dog. Weakly it waved its arms, tried to straighten its bent back. Fearfully, listing, it staggered toward a familiar house. The dog no longer recognized this human being. Listless, yet unwilling to leave it, the dog tailed it. A simple desire had brought the thing to Chen Xinhan's yard, but once there it lay immobile, like a broken tile, on the ground. Two greedy yellow eyes gazed down; it was too weak to drive the dog away again, too weak even to cry out. It could only moan and close its dry and withered eyes. Another dog came through a hole in the courtyard wall and barked twice. The first dog leaped forward, barking back. The body on the ground groaned again.

"Father!" cried newly awakened Jingu. "I hear something outside!"

"Dogfight."

"I hate that disgusting noise. I'll go chase them off."

Jingu slipped off the *kang* and picked up a lump of coal. Both dogs barked menacingly at her as she stepped through the doorway. She threw the coal at them and they ran off barking.

"She can't even leave the dogs alone," grumbled her mother under the quilt.

"Second Uncle! Hey, there's something in the yard!"

The girl stepped closer as the dogs barked furiously. Jingu drove them off then kicked at the body. It opened its eyes a little and moaned. Then Jingu uttered a horrified, inhuman shriek like a bamboo rent in two.

Following a lot of frantic activity, the body, now dressed in dry cotton-padded garments, lay unconscious on the warm *kang*. Strands of wispy hair glued onto the sockets of her empty, sunken eyes. Second Sister-in-law fed her hot rice gruel. Jingu threw herself down next to her mommy's feet and wept. The baby, who didn't recognize the granny who'd always carried him around and kissed him all the time, sat in a corner of the *kang* afraid to make a sound. Chen Xinhan had already gone for a doctor. His wife was sobbing uncontrollably as she thought of her vanished daughter. She wanted her back!

"Ma, do you recognize us now?" Chen Zuohan asked repeatedly. But the old woman could not give him a satisfactory answer. She couldn't even gesture to him.

He watched her protectively, her terribly aged face, two dead, fishlike eyes inlaid in a piece of burnt wood. His hatred fanned into a great flame. "Ma." He directed each deliberate syllable toward that wooden face. "Ma! You can die in peace now. Your son will give his life to revenge you. I live on now only for Jap blood! I'll give my life for you, this village,

Shanxi Province, the nation of China! I want Japanese blood so I can cleanse and fertilize our land. I want Jap blood!"

Like the intoned chant at an exorcism, his spell brought her slowly back to life. The old woman on the *kang* moved. Her lips quivered. "Japs!" she cried a moment later in mortal terror. She'd recovered consciousness. She looked speechlessly at her daughters-in-law and grandchildren, as tears streamed from her eyes; then, like a duck with its throat cut, wings flapping convulsively, neck writhing, she bent her head down and sobbed like a child.

"Granny! Granny! Granny!" The room was suffused with sorrow, to be sure. Yet new buds of warmth and hope had also begun to flower.

4

The strength of her desire to live quickly restored the old woman's health. A few days later she was sitting in the yard sunning herself, surrounded by the other women in the family. She was telling a story.

"Oh, that girl screamed and yelled, pounding her legs like the sticks on a big drum, her pale white belly writhing . . ."

"Don't, Granny, don't. I'm scared!" Jingu hid her face in her hands.

"Three Japs climbed on her at the same time." She seemed to enjoy intimidating her granddaughter. "She couldn't even scream anymore; her face turned purple . . . Unh . . . unh . . . unh . . . she moaned like a cow. Even childbirth isn't as painful as that. She looked at me, so I told her, 'Bite your tongue off. Bite! Hard!' I figured she'd be better off dead."

"Oh, Granny, Granny!" The women's faces blanched.

"She died too. But not from biting off her tongue," the old woman continued smugly. "Her naked carcass lay in a big pool of blood; more than if she'd had a baby. Her chest was all bloody too, blood running down her midriff, down her shoulders. They'd chewed off her little nipples." With demonic eyes she stared like a witch at her granddaughter's face. "Nipples no bigger than yours! Her sweet little face was all chewed up as well, like a maggoty apple. And she still kept looking at me with those big round eyes."

The old lady had changed. Didn't she love her own family anymore? Why was she always terrorizing them? When they sighed or cried, she'd become incensed and shout, "Go right ahead, cry your eyes out! Nothing but a pot of worthless piss. Just wait. The Japs will be back . . ." And if she saw their faces blaze red with anger, she'd feel quite satisfied at the fire she'd started.

At first she'd stop telling her stories when she saw her sons. She was afraid of their searching glances, and besides, the personal shame and sorrow she felt kept her from going on when they were around. She described how her other granddaughter had died. The thirteen-year-old child had served as a "comfort girl." Half dead of terror from being crushed under the heavy soldiers' bodies, she kept screaming for her mommy and grandma. She only "comforted" two soldiers before they threw her into a corner. She lived a day longer, tears visible on her ashen face. Just before the old lady was sent to the "Home of Respect for the Aged," they dragged Yingu off, still alive.[8] Her grandmother said that they probably threw her to the dogs alive.

She'd also witnessed Tongguan's death. She described it in detail without a thought to the unbearable grief it would cause her daughter-in-law. She said Tongguan was a good child because he wouldn't obey them. He kept on even with a bayonet pointed at him; when he tried to get away, the Jap skewered him and even then he didn't cry. He died well.

She'd seen too much. In the last ten days, she'd seen more evil than she'd witnessed before in her whole life. When the neighbors came to ask about their relatives she would tell them truthfully how their parents, wives, and children had been sacrificed under the butcher's knife and how, while alive, they had suffered endless pain.

The old lady had never been much of a talker, but now, seeing the effect her stories had, she felt a lot more comfortable. She got sympathy and understanding from telling stories, and it made her realize that other people shared the hatred she felt. For that reason, she just forgot to be timid. At first she tended to stutter and hesitate, and then she'd cry. But by watching her listeners' faces, she'd learned how to phrase her tales most effectively.

She told them about her own humiliations too, about what she'd had to do at the "Home." She'd washed their clothes, stitched their little Japanese flags, endured their whippings. Whenever she reached that point, she'd pull back her sleeves and unbutton her collar to show where her scars were. She'd also had to sleep with a man. An old Chinese man had been forced to do it to her while the Japs all stood around watching. "Please don't hate me," the old man had sobbed, as his tears fell on her face.

She began touring the entire village, crowds following behind her, pointing out all the places where specific atrocities had taken place.

"You're not going to forget this now, are you?" she'd shout at them belligerently.

Soon she was doing this every day, and if there was only a handful of people out in the street, she'd burst into somebody's house and, gesticulating wildly, harangue them there. Her listeners invariably forgot what they were supposed to be doing and, caught up by her emotions, would begin talking. The whole village knew her, particularly the children, who called on her frequently.

Her sons and daughters-in-law talked the situation over. "We've got a maniac in the family!" The eldest daughter-in-law was always the first to speak up. "Why, she isn't eating, and doesn't take care of her hair. Now she just won't stay home!"

"Granny sure has changed. When she talks about Tongguan and Yingu, she doesn't shed a single tear. I really don't understand what's going on in her mind." The second daughter-in-law peeked at her husband. Lost in thought, he only frowned.

Chen Xinhan was thinking about the day before, when he'd gone over to listen to the old woman as she preached her stories in front of a crowd. When she got to the parts about what had happened to her personally, Xinhan had felt as though he were the one losing his mind. A son's blood coursed through his body, yet he didn't know whether to shout or go over and hug his mother or just run away. He shuddered violently, speechless all of a sudden, just as his mother caught sight of him and stopped telling her story to stare at him numbly. The audience turned around, but nobody laughed. He felt more misery than he'd ever experienced before. He walked over to her, put out his hand, and said, "I promise I'll get revenge!" Her face split with joy and she reached toward him as well, then suddenly shrank away. She shriveled up like a cornered animal, slipped through the crowd, and ran away. No one spoke. Heads bowed as though heavily weighted, people in the crowd moved away slowly, with dragging steps. He alone remained in the deserted street. He felt empty and, at the same time, as though he were being choked.

"The way I see it," Eldest Daughter-in-law started up again angrily, "the whole family's gone crazy. Why don't you say something to her? All this going on, and you act as if you're above it all."

"Say something? What do you want me to say? I know what she's suffering."

"So who isn't suffering?"

Chen Xinhan did not want to prolong this conversation. He did not want to quarrel with his mother just for the sake of argument. He looked at his brother.

His brother agreed with him. He asked the women if he should get a rope and tie the old lady up to keep her from going out. He said he thought that everything would be all right so long as Jingu went along to keep an eye on her and stop her from offending anybody.

5

When her third son, Chen Lihan—her youngest and best loved—got back, he stroked his mother's white hair and stammered, "I apologize,

Ma. You wouldn't have fallen into Jap hands if I'd been home that day. But you can't always have things your own way once you join the army."

"And what good would you be to me if you hadn't enlisted?" She looked her son over. He was a young man of twenty or so, wearing a short jacket, a pistol strapped to his waist. The sight of him seemed to satisfy her. "It's a world of guns now, Sanguan. Just tell me, how many Japs have you killed?"

She didn't need to complain to him about how she'd suffered, because he didn't need to be told. She vastly preferred listening to stories about fighting the Japanese, feeling more comfort from that.

"Well," her son said, "since you are not afraid of hearing about such things, I'll tell you."

Chen Lihan's face lit up immediately. He stood straight and tall and launched into his story: how they'd counterattacked and occupied this village, Xiliu, killing more than twenty Japs, and then moved on to retake Dongliu Village and Li Village; how they'd breached the Jap line at Sanyang Village, had had to retreat, but now held it once again. It was impossible to remember for sure how many Japs they'd killed. They had captured a lot of war materiel, including rifles, bullets, and rations. He went on to say that among his group of men was the famous hero Zhang Dachuan, who'd gone to town on his own, with a light machine gun hidden under his jacket. There were too many Jap soldiers around, so he didn't use it there. But later, on his way out of town, he'd run into a dozen of the bastards, all just begging to die; so he'd shot the hell out of them. Chen Lihan also told about the time they'd caught a Jap soldier and how he and a bunch of the locals were carrying him between them on a pole. But this Jap was really fat. Somehow he'd gotten away from them along the way, and even with half a dozen of them trailing him, they never did get him back.

The old lady stuffed herself full of these stories and couldn't wait to find someone to retell them to. She'd gotten even more uninhibited lately because her oldest son, a member of the farmer's co-op, was off buying seed for the spring planting. Her second son had been drafted, and her third was gone four nights out of five. Besides, she wasn't the least bit afraid of her third son. So one night when she saw two big trucks parked in the courtyard, she asked Chen Lihan, "Are they our trucks?"

"Yeah, they're ours. They're our transport trucks."

"Well, I don't care what they haul, even if it's pigs or dogs. So long as they're ours, I know what I'm going to do with them. Tomorrow I'm going to Wangjia Village."

They all turned and stared at her.

"What do you mean there's no room on them, that they're for hauling food?" She cut their objections short. "I don't care, I'm going. I want to see my brother and sister-in-law."

So the next day, she and Jingu rode a grain transport truck to Wangjia Village. She found her brother and his wife and told them all about the atrocities. Again she watched the falling tears, the belligerence that listening to her stories evoked in people. Then to soothe their wounded spirits, she acted out all the exciting, hortatory stories she'd just heard from her son, adding her own flourishes and making people smile again. She used the moment to urge everyone there to join the guerrillas.

"You cowards!" she bawled, seeing them hesitate. "Afraid to die! Well, just wait 'til the Japs get here and butcher you all. I've seen them wipe out lots of powder puffs, just like you!"

Actually, many who heard her stories did join the guerrillas. Sometimes she'd lead a small group back home and hand them over to her son. "Take them," she'd say. "They all want to be like you. They all want guns."

After getting back from Wangjia, it was even harder for her to sit quietly at home, or even, for that matter, in Xiliu Village. So, taking Jingu along with her, she went to other villages. When there was no ride handy, she walked. "Why don't you talk too," she'd shout at Jingu.

Jingu was among the first to stand up for her grandma. She loved her and basked in the daily devotion she got from her. Each time Granny hustled her off on another trip, Jingu would gaze at her raptly in total understanding. Then Granny would embrace her, hugging her tightly, and heave a sigh of relief. It made Jingu feel warm inside again, but it was a happiness mixed with pain. Truth be told, Jingu was her grandmother's biggest supporter. Any time she talked privately with people, she'd use, with some embarrassment, phrases she'd picked up from her grandmother.

The love the old woman felt for her sons had also altered. Earlier, a great deal earlier, actually, she had thought of them as obedient little kittens. Later on, she'd only been concerned that they hurry up and grow into adults. She longed for the time when they'd be able to take over some of her burdens, things pressing down on her from society and in the family. Her sons grew up strong as bears and alert as eagles, but they never paid any attention to her. Her only recourse was to love them in silence, sadly, fearful of losing them. Later still, when they reached full maturity and things grew more difficult, her nature hardened. Since they obviously had no consideration for her at all, she hated them sometimes. Yet she became even more dependent upon their love, and that weakened her. Her fear of them had increased because all it took was a sign, a word, the sight of them, to dissolve her heart. But now she'd lost that fear. It no longer was crucial to her how they regarded her; their feelings were just not that important anymore. But didn't she love them now? Did she despise them? No, not a bit. She just saw them from a heightened perspective. When her sons talked to her about fighting Japs, she actually felt her love rekindle and was intensely pleased that the hardships she'd suffered rearing them had been worthwhile.

Slowly her daughters-in-law also stopped looking at her askance. Painful recollections and hopes for the future brought the women closer each day, harmonizing their relationships. When the women were alone, they always returned to the same topic of conversation. The frequent bickering that had afflicted the family before disappeared now, replaced by a new love founded on a common idea. The family found a closeness and unity it had never known before. And none of them ever realized that it was all the doing of the old lady.

6

The sons came home with unusual news. Some people wanted to talk to her. More than likely it was because of her conduct. Little Jingu held her Granny's hand tightly as her Granny reassured her.

"Don't be scared, Granddaughter. Who could treat me worse than the Japs already did? I've taken the worst a body could. If I'm not even afraid of Hell anymore, what's there to be afraid of?"

"What the hell business is it of theirs?" Eldest Daughter-in-law said angrily. "Do you mean we can't even talk? No one ever said 'Chinese are lousy; Japs are great.' Shoot! They can take it and shove it!"

But why did they want to see her? Her son couldn't say for sure. All he said was that someone had come from the Association looking for him, asking if she were his mother and what their address was, but that's all anyone knew about it. He wasn't real clear on what was going on, but he was pretty sure it was nothing to worry about.

The news made them rather uneasy. No stranger had ever come to call on her in her entire life. But she didn't lose any sleep over it that night. She really didn't care much about that sort of thing anymore.

The next day two women came over, one wearing a short jacket like the old woman's, the other, hair bobbed, in a uniform. They were both quite young. Without even a nod to conventional politeness, the old woman asked them in. They spoke first.

"Well, Mother," one of them addressed her in terms of special respect, "you may not know me, but I've known you for a long time. Twice I've heard you giving speeches."

"Speech." She didn't understand the word "speech" and just grunted glumly.[9]

"When I heard you speak, really, I couldn't help crying. Mother, since the Japs got hold of you, you must have seen everything you talk about with your own eyes, right?"

Her expression got friendlier. She thought, "Aha! They've finally come for news." And she began talking in an unending flood of words. They listened patiently to the greater part of the story. "Oh yes, Mother, we're with you on everything," they said when they were able to get a word in edgewise. "We too hate Japs with everything we've got. We try like mad to get people to join up and avenge the Chinese people, but we simply can't speak the way you can. Join our Association, Mother. Our Association tries to tell people these things in order to strike a blow against the Japs . . ."

"Jingu." Without waiting for them to finish, the old lady called her granddaughter, "Jingu, they've come to invite us to join their 'Association.' What do you say to that?" Without waiting for Jingu's reply, she turned back to her visitors. "I don't understand all that stuff," she said. "If you want me, I'll join. I'm not afraid you're just playing tricks on me, either. Two of my three sons joined the guerrillas and the other's in the Peasant Association. So it's all right if I join an association too. I won't lose anything by it, no matter what. Only if I join, my granddaughter has to join too."

They gave Jingu an enthusiastic welcome on the spot and offered the same to the two daughters-in-law.

The Women's Association expanded its membership rapidly after the old woman joined it. She went around every day recruiting, and once the women learned she was a member herself, they all wanted in. And so the women began to do quite a lot of work. Because of this, the old lady felt happier and seemed younger physically and in spirit. One day they decided to hold a big meeting in honor of the victories won by the guerrillas during the last three months. The meeting would take place at the same time as the celebration of International Women's Day on the eighth of March, and women's groups from nearby villages were invited to participate.

On the day of the rally, the old lady led several dozen women from Xiliu Village. Some carried their children; others led them by the hand. But they had not gathered to chat about children. They talked about their work responsibilities. A large number whose feet were bound had walked all the way, only barely aware of their pain and fatigue.

Quite a few had already arrived at the meeting place. The old woman's sons had come too, and many of her acquaintances waved to her from here and there. Gradually all the attention gave her a new feeling, a kind of uneasiness. It resembled shyness but was, in fact, the pride of accomplishment. After a little while, she felt calm again.

Slowly the crowd swelled. To the old woman it looked like a wave rolling in, and she was filled with happiness. So! They've got this many people!

The meeting began. Someone was speaking from the platform. The old woman listened raptly. It seemed to her that the speaker didn't waste a word. Who, listening to this speech, would not be moved by it? How could anyone listening fail to be concerned about the nation? Then they wanted her up on the platform.

When she heard their invitation, she was seized with unspeakable shyness and embarrassment. But her courage returned at once, and tottering a little, she walked to the podium on a wave of applause. Standing on high gazing downward, all she could see was a great mass of densely packed heads stretching out as far as the distant village wall, each with a face looking up at her. She felt rather stunned and giddy: What should I say, she thought. So she began by talking about herself.

"I am an old woman who was molested by the Japanese Imperialist troops. Look, all of you . . ." And she rolled up her sleeves to show her scars. "What are you scared of?" she said, hearing a murmur of sympathy from below. "This? This is nothing . . ." Then she described the circumstances of her humiliation in plain, cold language, not trying to save her own face or hide her pain or spare their sensitivities. Her gaze roamed over their faces. They looked miserable! So she shouted, "Don't pity me! You should really pity yourselves! And protect yourselves! Today you think that I am the only one to be pitied. But, today, if you don't rise up, stand up to the Japs . . . Ha! Heaven! I really don't want to see you suffer the way I did . . . I'm old, after all. A little more suffering is nothing to me: when I die, that's that, and so what. But look at you, how young you are! You should go on living. You haven't enjoyed what life has to offer. Can you have been born just to suffer, just to get pushed around by Japs?"

"We want to live!" Hundreds of voices shouted in anguish, "We weren't put here for the Japs to degrade and humiliate!"

She took over the burden of pain from those voices. She felt overwhelmed by something. At that instant she had only one desire: to sacrifice herself for their gratification. "I love all of you the same as I love my own sons," she shouted, "I'd die for you; but the Japs would never be satisfied with just me. They want you. They want every place, everywhere. Even a million me's wouldn't be enough to save you. You've got to save yourselves. If you want to stay alive, you'd better find a way to do it . . . Before, I wasn't even willing to let my sons go out the door, much less fight. Now they're all guerrillas. They might get killed one day, but if they hadn't joined up, they would die even sooner. As long as there are those who can drive away Japs for everyone's sake, I wouldn't mind even if my own sons got killed. And if one of them dies, I'll remember him, you'll remember him, because he did it for all of us!"

Words gushed out of her like a wellspring. She couldn't think of how to stop them even when her excitement began flagging, and she couldn't stand straight any longer; her voice hoarsened, making it hard to shout. But the roar of applause went on and on. They wanted more.

At each shout the sea of heads broke into billows, like waves on the shore. Finally the old woman gathered all her remaining strength: "We must fight to the end!" An enormous roar answered her, the sound of a tidal wave crashing on the beach in a storm.

Leaning against arms that had come to prop her up, she gazed at the seething mass below. She felt an intimate awareness of something very powerful. Slowly she raised her eyes and looked above their heads to the vast open space, the endless blue sky. She saw the collapse of the old, the radiance of the new, and though tears blurred her vision, it was a radiance that sprang from her own steadfast faith.

Translated by Jean James and Tani E. Barlow

When I Was in Xia Village

Ding Ling published two pieces in the early 1940s that had a profound effect on everyone who read them. One was "In the Hospital" (1940) and the other was "When I Was in Xia Village," written in late 1940 and published in 1941. Both stories criticize either a specific social policy or restrictive publication policies. Hostile reviews pointed to the sophisticated confusion between the storyteller of "Xia Village" and Ding Ling's own alleged views. Years later, after enduring much criticism, Ding Ling published an account of how she came to write the story. She had never met anyone like Zhenzhen, had never been to a village that resembled Xia. The incident came to her through a friend's story.

"When I Was in Xia Village" upset literary policy enforcers because it reverted back to Ding Ling's earlier preoccupation with sex and justice. It also placed a woman seeking social redress at the center of the plot. This had the effect of making Zhenzhen the agent of her own self-naming. Zhenzhen, for her part, wants to be free of relationships and pressures that reduce her to victimhood, the subject of sexual assault, the raped. Her family and state would make her a symbol. All around her people try to assign meaning to her tragedy. No one except the narrator allows Zhenzhen the liberty to say for herself what the experience has done to her and how she will let it shape her life "as a woman."

The narrator of the story complicates our interpretation. She has little interest in village life except for her friendship with Zhenzhen. Village pressure to gossip repels her, and she won't even interrogate the sick girl. Her sole concern is Zhenzhen's moral recuperation, and to that effect she seems to offer a radical, even "Maoist" moral practice, though she has a greater sense of the personal than, say, the comrade who tells the story of Chen Man in a later story, "People Who Will Live Forever in My

Heart." In "Xia Village" the mysterious Party comrade and the sexually compromised heroine stand in a sororal relation to each other. Perhaps Ding Ling was attempting to reverse, at least metaphorically, an association she found intolerable in Communist Party practice between a woman's political loyalty and her sexual chastity.—TEB

Because of the turmoil in the Political Department, Comrade Mo Yü decided to send me to stay temporarily in a neighboring village. Actually, I was already completely well, but the opportunity to rest for a while in a quiet environment and arrange my notes from the past three months did have its attractions. So I agreed to spend two weeks in Xia Village, a place about ten miles from the Political Department.

A female comrade from the Propaganda Department, who was apparently on a work assignment, went with me. Since she wasn't a person who enjoyed conversation, however, the journey was rather lonely. Also, because her feet had once been bound and my own spirits were low, we traveled slowly. We set out in the morning, but it was nearly sunset by the time we reached our destination.

The village looked much like any other from a distance, but I knew it contained a very beautiful Catholic church that had escaped destruction and a small grove of pine trees. The place where I would be staying was in the midst of these trees, which clung to the hillside. From that spot it would be possible to look straight across to the church. By now I could see orderly rows of cave dwellings and the green trees above them. I felt content with the village.

My traveling companion had given me the impression that the village was very busy, but when we entered it, not even a single child or dog was to be seen. The only movement was dry leaves twirling about lightly in the wind. They would fly a short distance, then drop to earth again.

"This used to be an elementary school, but last year the Jap devils destroyed it. Look at those steps over there. That used to be a big classroom," my companion, Agui, told me. She was somewhat excited now, not so reserved as she had been during the day. Pointing to a large empty courtyard, she continued: "A year and a half ago, this area was full of life. Every evening after supper, the comrades gathered here to play soccer or basketball." Becoming more agitated, she asked, "Why isn't anyone here? Should we go to the assembly hall or head up the hill? We don't know where they've taken our luggage either. We have to straighten that out first."

On the wall next to the gate of the village assembly hall, many white paper slips had been pasted. They read "Office of the [Communist] Association," "Xia Village Branch of the [Communist] Association," and so on. But when we went inside, we couldn't find a soul. It was completely quiet, with only a few tables set about. We were both standing there dumbly when suddenly a man rushed in. He looked at us for a moment, seemed about to ask us something, but swallowed his words and prepared to dash away. We called to him to stop, however, and made him answer our questions.

"The people of the village? They've all gone to the west door. Baggage? Hmm. Yes, there was baggage. It was carried up the hill some time ago to Liu Erma's home." As he talked, he sized us up.

Learning that he was a member of the Peasant's Salvation Association, we asked him to accompany us up the hill and also asked him to deliver a note to one of the local comrades. He agreed to take the note, but he wouldn't go with us. He seemed impatient and ran off by himself.

The street too was very quiet. The doors of several shops were closed. Others were still open, exposing pitch-black interiors. We still couldn't find anyone. Fortunately, Agui was familiar with the village and led me up the hill. It was already dark. The winter sun sets very quickly.

The hill was not high, and a large number of stone cave dwellings were scattered here and there from the bottom to the top. In a few places, people were standing out in front peering into the distance. Agui knew very well that we had not yet reached our destination, but whenever we met someone she asked, "Is this the way to Liu Erma's house?" "How far is it to Liu Erma's house?" "Could you please tell me the way to Liu Erma's house?" Or, she would ask, "Did you notice any baggage being sent to Liu Erma's house? Is Liu Erma home?"

The answers we received always satisfied us, and this continued right up to the most distant and highest house, which was the Liu family's. Two small dogs were the first to greet us. Then a woman came out and asked who we were. As soon as they heard it was me, two more women came out. Holding a lantern, they escorted us into the courtyard and then into a cave on the side toward the east. The cave was virtually empty. On the *kang* under the window were piled my bedroll, my small leather carrying case, and Agui's quilt.

Some of the people there knew Agui. They took her hand and asked her many questions, and after a while they led her out, leaving me alone in the room. I arranged my bed and was about to lie down when suddenly they all crowded back in again. One of Liu Erma's daughters-in-law was carrying a bowl of noodles. Agui, Liu Erma, and a young girl were holding bowls, chopsticks, and a dish of onions and pepper. The young girl also brought in a brazier of burning coal.

Attentively, they urged me to eat some noodles and touched my hands and arms. Liu Erma and her daughter-in-law also sat down on the *kang*. There was an air of mystery about them as they continued the conversation interrupted by their entry into the room.

At first I thought I had caused their amazement, but gradually I realized that this wasn't the case. They were interested in only one thing— the topic of their conversation. Since all I heard were a few fragmentary sentences, I couldn't understand what they were talking about. This was especially true of what Liu Erma said because she frequently lowered her voice, as if afraid that someone might overhear her. Agui had changed completely. She now appeared quite capable and was very talkative. She listened closely to what the others were saying and seemed able to grasp the essence of their words. The daughter-in-law and the young girl said little. At times they added a word or two, but for the most part they just listened intently to what Agui and Liu Erma were saying. They seemed afraid to miss a single word.

Suddenly the courtyard was filled with noise. A large number of people had rushed in, and they all seemed to be talking at once. Liu Erma and the others climbed nervously off the *kang* and hurried outside. Without thinking, I followed along behind them to see what was happening.

By this time the courtyard was in complete darkness. Two red paper lanterns bobbed and weaved above the crowd. I worked my way into the throng and looked around. I couldn't see anything. The others also were squeezing in for no apparent reason. They seemed to want to say more, but they did not. I heard only simple exchanges that confused me even more.

"Yüwa, are you here too?"

"Have you seen her yet?"

"Yes, I've seen her. I was a little afraid."

"What is there to be afraid of? She's just a human being, and prettier than ever too."

At first I was sure that they were talking about a new bride, but people said that wasn't so. Then I thought there was a prisoner present, but that was wrong too. I followed the crowd to the doorway of the central cave, but all there was to see was more people packed tightly together. Thick smoke obscured my vision, so I had no choice but to back away. Others were also leaving by now, and the courtyard was much less crowded.

Since I couldn't sleep, I set about rearranging my carrying case by the lantern light. I paged through several notebooks, looked at photographs, and sharpened some pencils. I was obviously tired, but I also felt the kind of excitement that comes just before a new life begins. I prepared a time schedule for myself and was determined to adhere to it, beginning the very next day.

At that moment there was a man's voice at the door. "Are you asleep, comrade?" Before I could reply, the fellow entered the room. He was about twenty years old, a rather refined-looking country youth. "I received Director Mo's letter some time ago," he said. "This area is relatively quiet. Don't worry about a thing. That's my job. If you need something, don't hesitate to ask Liu Erma. Director Mo said you wanted to stay here for two weeks. Fine. If you enjoy your visit, we'd be happy to have you stay longer. I live in a neighboring cave, just below these. If you need me, just send someone to find me."

He declined to come up on the *kang*, and since there was no bench on the floor to sit on, I jumped down and said, "Ah! You must be Comrade Ma. Did you receive the note I sent you? Please sit down and talk for a while."

I knew that he held a position of some responsibility in the village. As a student he had not yet finished junior high school.

"They tell me you've written a lot of books," he responded. "It's too bad we haven't seen a single one." As he spoke he looked at my open carrying case that was lying on the *kang*. Our conversation turned to the subject of the local level of study. Then he said, "After you've rested for a few days, we'll definitely invite you to give a talk. It can be to a mass meeting or to a training class. In any case, you'll certainly be able to help us. Our most difficult task here is 'cultural recreation.'"

I had seen many young men like him at the Front. When I first met them, I was always amazed. I felt that these youth, who were somewhat remote from me, were really changing fast. Changing the subject, I asked him, "What was going on just now?"

"Zhenzhen, the daughter of Liu Dama, has returned," he answered. "I never thought she could be so great." I immediately sensed a joyful, radiant twinkle in his eyes. As I was about to ask another question, he added, "She's come back from the Japanese area. She's been working there for over a year."

"Oh my!" I gasped.

He was about to tell me more when someone outside called for him. All he could say was that he'd be sure to have Zhenzhen call on me the next day. As if to provoke my interest further, he added that Zhenzhen must certainly have a lot of material for stories.

It was very late when Agui came back. She lay down on the *kang* but could not sleep. She tossed and turned and sighed continuously. I was very tired, but I still wished that she would tell me something about the events of the evening.

"No, comrade," she said. "I can't talk about it now. I'm too upset. I'll tell you tomorrow. Ahh . . . How miserable it is to be a woman." After this she covered her head with her quilt and lay completely still, no longer sighing. I didn't know when she finally fell asleep.

Early the next morning I stepped outside for a stroll, and before I knew it I had walked down to the village. I went into a general store to rest and buy red dates for Liu Erma to put in the rice porridge. As soon as the owner learned that I was living with Liu Erma, his small eyes narrowed and he asked me in a low, excited voice, "Did you get a look at her niece? I hear her disease has even taken her nose. That's because she was abused by the Jap devils." Turning his head, he called to his wife, who was standing in the inner doorway, "She has nerve, coming home! It's revenge against her father, Liu Fusheng."

"That girl was always frivolous. You saw the way she used to roam around the streets. Wasn't she Xia Dabao's old flame? If he hadn't been poor, wouldn't she have married him a long time ago?" As she finished speaking, the old woman lifted her skirts and came into the store.

The owner turned his face back toward me and said, "There are so many rumors." His eyes stopped blinking and his expression became very serious. "It's said that she has slept with at least a hundred men. Humph! I've heard that she even became the wife of a Japanese officer. Such a shameful woman should not be allowed to return."

Not wanting to argue with him, I held back my anger and left. I didn't look back, but I felt that he had again narrowed his small eyes and was feeling smug as he watched me walk away. As I neared the corner by the Catholic church, I overheard a conversation by two women who were drawing water at the well. One said, "She sought out Father Lu and told him she definitely wanted to be a nun. When Father Lu asked her for a reason, she didn't say a word, just cried. Who knows what she did there? Now she's worse than a prostitute . . ."

"Yesterday they told me she walks with a limp. Achh! How can she face people?"

"Someone said she's even wearing a gold ring that a Jap devil gave her!"

"I understand she's been as far away as Datong and has seen many things. She can even speak Japanese."

My walk was making me unhappy, so I returned home. Since Agui had already gone out, I sat alone in my room and read a small pamphlet. After a while, I raised my eyes and noticed two large baskets for storing grain sitting near the wall. They must have had a long history, because they were as black as the wall itself. Opening the movable portion of the paper window, I peered out at the gray sky. The weather had changed completely from what it had been when I arrived the day before. The hard ground of the courtyard had been swept clean, and at the far edge a tree with a few withered branches stood out starkly against the leaden sky. There wasn't a single person to be seen.

I opened my carrying case, took out pen and paper, and wrote two letters. I wondered why Agui had not yet returned. I had forgotten that she had work to do. I was somehow thinking that she had come to be my companion. The days of winter are very short, but right then I was feeling that they were even longer than summer days.

Some time later, the young girl who had been in my room the night before came out into the courtyard. I immediately jumped down off the *kang*, stepped out the door, and called to her, but she just looked at me and smiled before rushing into another cave. I walked around the courtyard twice and then stopped to watch a hawk fly into the grove of trees by the church. The courtyard there had many large trees. I started walking again and, on the right side of the courtyard, picked up the sound of a woman crying. She was trying to stop, frequently blowing her nose.

I tried hard to control myself. I thought about why I was here and about all my plans. I had to rest and live according to the time schedule I had made. I returned to my room, but I couldn't sleep and had no interest in writing in my notebook.

Fortunately, a short while later Liu Erma came to see me. The young girl was with her, and her daughter-in-law arrived soon after. The three of them climbed up on the *kang* and took seats around the small brazier. The young girl looked closely at my things, which were laid out on the little square *kang* table.

"At that time no one could take care of anyone else," Liu Erma said, talking about the Japanese attack on Xia Village a year and a half before. "Those of us who lived on the hilltop were luckier. We could run away quickly. Many who lived in the village could not escape. Apparently it was all fate. Just then, on that day, our family's Zhenzhen had run over to the Catholic church. Only later did we learn that her unhappiness about what was happening had caused her to go to talk to the foreign priest about becoming a nun. Her father was in the midst of negotiating a marriage for her with the young proprietor of a rice store in Xiliu Village. He was almost thirty, a widower, and his family was well respected. We all said he would be a good match, but Zhenzhen said no and broke into tears before her father. In other matters, her father had always deferred to her wishes, but in this case the old man was adamant. He had no son and had always wanted to betroth his daughter to a good man. Who would have thought that Zhenzhen would turn around in anger and run off to the Catholic church. It was at that moment that the Japs caught her. How could her mother and father help grieving?"

"Was that her mother crying?"

"Yes."

"And your niece?"

"Well, she's really just a child. When she came back yesterday, she cried for a long time, but today she went to the assembly in high spirits. She's only eighteen."

"I heard she was the wife of a Japanese. Is that true?"

"It's hard to say. We haven't been able to find out for sure. There are many rumors, of course. She's contracted a disease, but how could anyone keep clean in such a place? The possibility of her marrying the merchant seems to be over. Who would want a woman who was abused by the Jap devils? She definitely has the disease. Last night she said so herself. This time she's changed a lot. When she talks about those devils, she shows no more emotion than if she were talking about an ordinary meal at home. She's only eighteen, but she has no sense of embarrassment at all."

"Xia Dabao came again today," the daughter-in-law said quietly, her questioning eyes fixed on Erma.

"Who is Xia Dabao?" I asked.

"He's a young man who works in the village flour mill," replied Liu Erma. "When he was young, he and Zhenzhen were classmates for a year. They liked each other very much, but his family was poor, even poorer than ours. He didn't dare do anything, but our Zhenzhen was head over heels in love with him and kept clinging to him. Then she was upset when he didn't respond. Isn't it because of him that she wanted to be a nun? After Zhenzhen fell into the hands of the Jap devils, he often came to see her parents. At first just the sight of him made Zhenzhen's father angry. At times he cursed him, but Xia Dabao would say nothing. After a scolding he would leave and then come back another day. Dabao is really a good boy. Now he's even a squad leader in the self-defense corps. Today he came once again, apparently to talk with Zhenzhen's mother about marrying Zhenzhen. All I could hear was her crying. Later he left in tears himself."

"Does he know about your niece's situation?"

"How could he help knowing? There is no one in this village who doesn't know everything. They all know more than we do ourselves."

"Mother, everyone says that Xia Dabao is foolish," the young girl interjected.

"Humph! The boy has a good conscience. I approve of this match. Since the Jap devils came, who has any money? Judging from the words of Zhenzhen's parents, I think they approve too. If not him, who? Even without mentioning her disease, her reputation is enough to deter anyone."

"He was the one wearing the dark blue jacket and the copper-colored felt hat with the turned-up brim," the young girl said. Her eyes were sparkling with curiosity, and she seemed to understand this matter very well.

His figure began to take shape in my memory. When I went out for my walk earlier that morning, I had seen an alert, honest-looking young man who fit this description. He had been standing outside my courtyard, but had not shown any intention of coming in. On my way home, I had seen him again, this time emerging from the pine woods beyond the cave dwellings. I had thought he was someone from my courtyard or from a neighboring one and hadn't paid much attention to him. As I recalled him now, I felt that he was a rather capable man, not a bad young man at all.

I now feared that my plan for rest and recuperation could not be realized. Why were my thoughts so confused? I wasn't particularly anxious to meet anybody, and yet my mind still couldn't rest. Agui had come in during the conversation, and now she seemed to sense my feelings. As she went out with the others, she gave me a knowing smile. I understood her meaning and busied myself with arranging the *kang*. My bedroll, the lamp, and the fire all seemed much brighter. I had just placed the tea kettle on the fire when Agui returned. Behind her I heard another person.

"We have a guest, comrade!" Agui called. Even before she finished speaking, I heard someone giggling.

Standing in the doorway, I grasped the hands of this person whom I had not seen before. They were burning hot, and I couldn't help being a bit startled. She followed Agui up onto the *kang* and sat down. A single long braid hung down her back.

In the eyes of the new arrival, the cave that depressed me seemed to be something new and fresh. She looked around at everything with an excited glint in her eyes. She sat opposite me, her body tilted back slightly and her two hands spread apart on the bedroll for support. She didn't seem to want to say anything. Her eyes finally came to rest on my face.

The shadows lengthened her eyes and made her chin quite pointed. But even though her eyes were in deep shadow, her pupils shone brightly in the light of the lamp and the fire. They were like two open windows in a summer home in the country, clear and clean.

I didn't know how to begin a conversation without touching an open wound and hurting her self-respect. So my first move was to pour her a cup of hot tea.

It was Zhenzhen who spoke first: "Are you a Southerner? I think so. You aren't like the people from this province."

"Have you seen many Southerners?" I asked, thinking it best to talk about what she wanted to talk about.

"No," she said, shaking her head. Her eyes still fixed on me, she added, "I've only seen a few. They always seem a little different. I like you people from the South. Southern women, unlike us, can all read many, many books. I want to study with you. Will you teach me?"

I expressed my willingness to do so, and she quickly continued, "Japanese women also can read a lot of books. All those devil soldiers carried a few well-written letters, some from wives, some from girlfriends. Some were written by girls they didn't even know. They would include a photograph and use syrupy language. I don't know if those girls were sincere or not, but they always made the devils hold their letters to their hearts like precious treasures."

"I understand that you can speak Japanese," I said. "Is that true?"

Her face flushed slightly before she replied, in a very open manner, "I was there for such a long time. I went around and around for over a year. I can speak a fair amount. Being able to understand their language had many advantages."

"Did you go to a lot of different places with them?"

"I wasn't always with the same unit. People think that because I was the wife of a Jap officer I enjoyed luxury. Actually, I came back here twice before. Altogether, this is my third time. I was ordered to go on this last mission. There was no choice. I was familiar with the area, the work was important, and it was impossible to find anyone else in a short time. I won't be sent back anymore. They're going to treat my disease. That's fine with me because I've missed my dad and mom, and I'm glad to be able to come back to see them. My mother, though, is really hopeless. When I'm not home, she cries. When I'm here, she still cries."

"You must have known many hardships."

"She has endured unthinkable suffering," Agui interrupted, her face twisted in a pained expression. In a voice breaking with emotion, she added, "It's a real tragedy to be a woman, isn't it, Zhenzhen?" She slid over to be next to her.

"Suffering?" Zhenzhen asked, her thoughts apparently far, far away. "Right now I can't say for certain. Some things were hard to endure at the time, but when I recall them now they don't seem like much. Other things were no problem to do when I did them, but when I think about them now I'm very sad. More than a year . . . It's all past. Since I came back this time, a great many people have looked at me strangely. As far as the people of this village are concerned, I'm an outsider. Some are very friendly to me. Others avoid me. The members of my family are just the same. They all like to steal looks at me. Nobody treats me the way they used to. Have I changed? I've thought about this a great deal, and I don't think I've changed at all. If I have changed, maybe it's that my heart has become somewhat harder. But could anyone spend time in such a place and not become hardhearted? People have no choice. They're forced to be like that!"

There was no outward sign of her disease. Her complexion was ruddy. Her voice was clear. She showed no signs of inhibition or rudeness. She did not exaggerate. She gave the impression that she had never had any complaints or sad thoughts. Finally, I could restrain myself no longer and asked her about her disease.

"People are always like that, even if they find themselves in worse situations. They brace themselves and see it through. Can you just give up and die? Later, after I made contact with our own people, I became less afraid. As I watched the Jap devils suffer defeat in battle and the guerrillas take action on all sides as a result of the tricks I was playing, I felt better by the day. I felt that even though my life was hard, I could still manage. Somehow I had to find a way to survive, and if at all possible, to live a life that was meaningful. That's why I'm pleased that they intend to treat my disease. It will be better to be cured. Actually, these past few days I haven't felt too bad. On the way home, I stayed in Zhangjiayi for two days and was given two shots and some medicine to take orally. The worst time was in the fall. I was told that my insides were rotting away, and then, because of some important information and the fact that no one could be found to take my place, I had to go back. That night I walked alone in the dark for ten miles. Every single step was painful. My mind was filled with the desire to sit down and rest. If the work hadn't been so important, I definitely wouldn't have gone back. But I had to. Ahh! I was afraid I might be recognized by the Jap devils, and I was also worried about missing my rendezvous. After it was over, I slept for a full week before I could pull myself together. It really isn't all that easy to die, is it?"

Without waiting for me to respond, she continued on with her story. At times she stopped talking and looked at us. Perhaps she was searching for reactions on our faces. Or maybe she was only thinking of something else. I could see that Agui was more troubled than Zhenzhen. For the most part she sat in silence, and when she did speak, it was only for a sentence or two. Her words gave voice to a limitless sympathy for Zhenzhen, but her expression when silent revealed even more clearly how moved she was by what Zhenzhen was saying. Her soul was being crushed. She herself was feeling the suffering that Zhenzhen had known before.

It was my impression that Zhenzhen had no intention whatever of trying to elicit sympathy from others. Even as others took upon themselves part of the misfortune that she had suffered, she seemed unaware of it. But that very fact made others feel even more sympathetic. It would have been better if, instead of listening to her recount the events of this period with a calmness that almost made you think she was talking about someone else, you could have heard her cry. Probably you would have cried with her, but you would have felt better.

After a while Agui began to cry, and Zhenzhen turned to comfort her. There were many things that I had wanted to discuss with Zhenzhen, but I couldn't bring myself to say anything. I wished to remain silent. After Zhenzhen left, I forced myself to read by the lamp for an hour. Not once did I look at Agui or ask her a question, even though she was lying very close to me, even though she tossed and turned and sighed all the time, unable to fall asleep.

After this Zhenzhen came to talk with me every day. She did not talk about herself alone. She very often showed great curiosity about many aspects of my life that were beyond her own experiences. At times, when my words were far removed from her life, it was obvious that she was struggling to understand, but nevertheless she listened intently. The two of us also took walks together down to the village. The youth were very good to her. Naturally, they were all activists. People like the owner of the general store, however, always gave us cold, steely stares. They disliked and despised Zhenzhen. They even treated me as someone not of their kind. This was especially true of the women, who, all because of Zhenzhen, became extremely self-righteous, perceiving themselves as saintly and pure. They were proud about never having been raped.

After Agui left the village, I grew even closer to Zhenzhen. It seemed that neither of us could be without the other. As soon as we were apart, we thought of each other. I like people who are enthusiastic and lively, who can be really happy or sad, and at the same time are straightforward and candid. Zhenzhen was just such a person. Our conversations took up a great deal of time, but I always felt that they were beneficial to my studies and to my personal growth. As the days went by, however, I discovered that Zhenzhen was not being completely open about something. I did not resent this. Moreover, I was determined not to touch upon this secret of hers. All people have things buried deeply in their hearts that they don't want to tell others. This secret was a matter of private emotions. It had nothing to do with other people or with Zhenzhen's own morality.

A few days before my departure, Zhenzhen suddenly began to appear very agitated. Nothing special seemed to have happened, and she showed no desire to talk to me about anything new. Yet she frequently came to my room looking disturbed and restless, and after sitting for a few minutes, she would get up and leave. I knew she had not eaten well for several days and was often passing up meals. I had asked her about her disease and knew that the cause of her uneasiness was not simply physical. Sometimes, after coming to my room, she would make a few disjointed remarks. At other times, she put on an attentive expression, as if asking me to talk. But I could see that her thoughts were elsewhere, on things that she didn't want others to know. She was trying to conceal her emotions by acting as if nothing was wrong.

Twice I saw that capable young man come out of Zhenzhen's home. I had already compared my impression of him with Zhenzhen, and I sympathized with him deeply. Zhenzhen had been abused by many men, and had contracted a stigmatized, hard-to-cure disease, but he still patiently came to see her and still sought the approval of her parents to marry her. He didn't look down on her. He did not fear the derision or the rebukes of others. He must have felt she needed him more than ever. He understood what kind of attitude a man should have toward the woman of his choice at such a time and what his responsibilities were.

But what of Zhenzhen? Although naturally there were many aspects of her emotions and her sorrows that I had not learned during this short period, she had never expressed any hope that a man would marry her or, if you will, comfort her. I thought she had become so hard because she had been hurt so badly. She seemed not to want anything from anyone. It would be good if love, some extraordinarily sympathetic commiseration, could warm her soul. I wanted her to find a place where she could cry this out. I was hoping for a chance to attend a wedding in this family. At the very least, I wanted to hear of an agreement to marry before I left.

"What is Zhenzhen thinking of?" I asked myself. "This can't be delayed indefinitely, and it shouldn't be turned into a big problem."

One day Liu Erma, her daughter-in-law, and her young daughter all came to see me. I was sure they intended to give me a report on something, but when they started to speak, I didn't allow them the opportunity to tell me anything. If my friend wouldn't confide in me, and I wouldn't ask her about it directly, then I felt it would be harmful to her, to myself, and to our friendship to ask others about it.

That same evening at dusk, the courtyard was again filled with people milling about. All the neighbors were there, whispering to one another. Some looked sad, but there were also those who appeared to find it all exciting. The weather was frigid, but curiosity warmed their hearts. In the severe cold, they drew in their shoulders, hunched their backs, thrust their hands into their sleeves, puffed out their breath, and looked at each other as if they were investigating something very interesting.

At first all I heard was the sound of quarreling coming from Liu Dama's dwelling. Then I heard Liu Dama crying. This was followed by the sound of a man crying. As far as I could tell, it was Zhenzhen's father. Next came a crash of dishes breaking. Unable to bear it any longer, I pushed my way through the curious onlookers and rushed inside.

"You've come at just the right time," Liu Erma said as she pulled me inside. "You talk to our Zhenzhen."

Zhenzhen's face was hidden by her long disheveled hair, but two wild eyes could still be seen peering out at the people gathered there. I walked over to her and stood beside her, but she seemed completely oblivious to my presence. Perhaps she took me as one of the enemy and not worth a moment's concern. Her appearance had changed so completely that I could hardly remember the liveliness, the bright pleasantness I had found in her before. She was like a cornered animal. She was like an evening goddess. Whom did she hate? Why was her expression so fierce?

"You're so heartless. You don't think about your mother and father at all. You don't care how much I've suffered because of you in the last year." Liu Dama pounded on the *kang* as she scolded her daughter, tears like raindrops dropping to the *kang* or the floor and flowing down the contours of her face. Several women had surrounded her and were preventing her from coming down off the *kang*. It was frightening to see a person lose her self-respect and allow all her feelings to come out in a blind rage. I thought of telling her that such crying was useless, but at the same time, I realized that nothing I could say now would make any difference.

Zhenzhen's father looked very weak and old. His hands hung down limply. He was sighing deeply. Xia Dabao was seated beside him. There was a helpless look in his eyes as he stared at the old couple.

"You must say something. Don't you feel sorry for your mother?"

"When the end of a road is reached, one must turn. After water has flowed as far as it can, it must change direction. Aren't you going to change at all? Why make yourself suffer?" The women were trying to persuade Zhenzhen with such words.

I could see that this affair could not turn out the way that everyone was hoping. Zhenzhen had shown me much earlier that she didn't want anyone's sympathy. She, in turn, had no sympathy for anyone else. She had made her decision long ago and would not change. If people wanted to call her stubborn, then so be it. With teeth tightly clenched, she looked ready to stand up to all of them.

At last the others agreed to listen to me, and I asked Zhenzhen to come to my room and rest. I told them that everything could be discussed later that night. But when I led Zhenzhen out of the house, she did not follow me to my room. Instead, she ran off up the hillside.

"That girl has big ideas."

"Humph! She looks down on us country folk."

"She's such a cheap little hussy and yet she puts on such airs. Xia Dabao deserves it . . ."

These were some of the comments being made by the crowd in the courtyard. Then, when they realized that there was no longer anything of interest to see, the crowd drifted away.

I hesitated for a while in the courtyard before deciding to go up the hillside myself. On the top of the hill were numerous graves set among the pine trees. Broken stone tablets stood before them. No one was there. Not even the sound of a falling leaf broke the stillness. I ran back and forth calling Zhenzhen's name. What sounded like a response temporarily comforted my loneliness, but in an instant the vast silence of the hills became even deeper. The colors of sunset had completely faded. All around me a thin, smokelike mist rose silently and spread out to the middle slopes of the hills, both nearby and in the distance. I was worried and sat down weakly on a tombstone. Over and over I asked myself, "Should I go on up the hill or wait for her here?" I was hoping that I could relieve Zhenzhen of some of her distress.

At that moment I saw a shadow moving toward me from below. I quickly saw that it was Xia Dabao. I remained silent, hoping that he wouldn't see me and would continue on up the hill, but he came straight at me. At last I felt that I had to greet him and called, "Have you found her? I still haven't seen her."

He walked over to me and sat down on the dry grass. He said nothing, only stared into the distance. I felt a little uneasy. He really was very young. His eyebrows were long and thin. His eyes were quite large, but now they looked dull and lifeless. His small mouth was tightly drawn. Perhaps before it had been appealing, but now it was full of anguish, as if trying to hold in his pain. He had an honest-looking nose, but of what use was it to him now?

"Don't be sad," I said. "Maybe tomorrow everything will be all right. I'll talk to her this evening."

"Tomorrow, tomorrow—she'll always hate me. I know that she hates me." He spoke in a sad low voice that was slightly hoarse.

"No," I replied, searching my memory. "She has never shown me that she hates anyone." This was not a lie.

"She wouldn't tell you. She wouldn't tell anyone. She won't forgive me as long as she lives."

"Why should she hate you?"

"Of course—" he began. Suddenly he turned his face toward me and looked at me intently. "Tell me," he said, "at that time I had nothing. Should I have encouraged her to run away with me? Is all of this my fault? Is it?"

He didn't wait for my answer. As if speaking to himself, he went on, "It is my fault. Could anyone say that I did the right thing? Didn't I bring this harm to her? If I had been as brave as she, she never would have—I know her character. She'll always hate me. Tell me, what should I do? What would she want me to do? How can I make her happy? My life is worthless. Am I of even the slightest use to her? Can you tell me? I simply don't know what I should do. Ahhh! How miserable things are! This is worse than being captured by the Jap devils." Without a break, he continued to mumble on and on.

When I asked him to go back home with me, he stood up and we took several steps together. Then he stopped and said that he had heard a sound coming from the very top of the hill. There was nothing to do but encourage him to go on up, and I watched until he had disappeared into the thick pines. Then I started back. By now it was almost completely dark. It was very late when I went to bed that night, but I still hadn't received any news. I didn't know what had happened to them.

Even before I ate breakfast the next morning, I finished packing my suitcase. Comrade Ma had promised that he would be coming this day to help me move, and I was all prepared to return to the Political Department and then go on to [my next assignment]. The enemy was about to start another "mopping-up campaign," and my health would not permit me to remain in this area. Director Mo had said that the ill definitely had to be moved out first, but I felt uneasy. Should I try to stay? If I did, I could be a burden to others. What about leaving? If I went, would I ever be able to return? As I was sitting on my bedroll pondering these questions, I sensed someone slipping quietly into my room.

With a single thrust of her body, Zhenzhen jumped up onto the *kang* and took a seat opposite me. I could see that her face was slightly swollen, and when I grasped her hands as she spread them over the fire, the heat that had made such an impression on me before once again distressed me. Then and there I realized how serious her disease was.

"Zhenzhen," I said, "I'm about to leave. I don't know when we'll meet again. I hope you'll listen to your mother—"

"I have come to tell you," she interrupted, "that I'll be leaving tomorrow too. I want to leave home as soon as possible."

"Really?" I asked.

"Yes," she said, her face again revealing that special vibrancy. "They've told me to go in for medical treatment."

"Ah," I sighed, thinking that perhaps we could travel together. "Does your mother know?"

"No, she doesn't know yet. But if I say that I'm going for medical treatment and that after my disease is cured I'll come back, she'll be sure to let me go. Just staying at home doesn't have anything to offer, does it?"

At this moment I felt that she had a rare serenity about her. I recalled the words that Xia Dabao had spoken to me the previous evening and asked her directly, "Has the problem of your marriage been resolved?"

"Resolved? Oh, well, it's all the same."

"Did you heed your mother's advice?" I still didn't dare express my hopes for her. I didn't want to think of the image left in my mind by that young man. I was hoping that someday he would be happy.

"Why should I listen to what they say? Did they ever listen to me?"

"Well, are you really angry with them?"

There was no response.

"Well, then, do you really hate Xia Dabao?"

For a long time she did not reply. Then, in a very calm voice, she said, "I can't say that I hate him. I just feel now that I'm someone who's diseased. It's a fact that I was abused by a large number of Jap devils. I don't remember the exact number. In any case, I'm unclean, and with such a black mark I don't expect any good fortune to come my way. I feel that living among strangers and keeping busy would be better than living at home where people know me. Now that they've approved sending me to [Yan'an] for treatment, I've been thinking about staying there and doing some studying. I hear it's a big place with lots of schools and that anyone can attend. It's better for each of us to go our own separate ways than it is to have everyone stay together in one place. I'm doing this for myself, but I'm also doing it for the others. I don't feel that I owe anyone an apology. Neither do I feel especially happy. What I do feel is that after I go to [Yan'an], I'll be in a new situation. I will be able to start life fresh. A person's life is not just for one's father and mother, or even for oneself. Some have called me young, inexperienced, and bad-tempered. I don't dispute it. There are some things that I just have to keep to myself."

I was amazed. Something new was coming out of her. I felt that what she had said was really worth examining. There was nothing for me to do but express approval of her plan.

When I took my departure, Zhenzhen's family was there to see me off. She, however, had gone to the village office. I didn't see Xia Dabao before I left either.

I wasn't sad as I went away. I seemed to see the bright future that Zhenzhen had before her. The next day I would be seeing her again. That had been decided. And we would still be together for some time. As soon as Comrade Ma and I walked out the door of Zhenzhen's home, he told me of her decision and confirmed that what she had told me that morning would quickly come to pass.

Translated by Gary J. Bjorge

Thoughts on March 8

This famous 1942 essay—the title refers to International Women's Day—talks thoughtfully but very bluntly about inconsistent sexual politics in the Communist Party. It also offers insight into how the concept "woman" became formalized in political theory and bureaucratic practice after 1942. Ding Ling made a lot of charges in "Thoughts on March 8." But she also hung onto a sense, shared inside the Party women's department, that the construction of "woman" in political terms had to come before any Chinese woman of any class would be liberated. "Woman," Ding Ling argues strenuously here, is a social and political category just as "proletariat" is. Like workers, women should identify their interests in relation to Party requirements; but when this works against their immediate needs, women have no alternative but to define themselves against the set parameters of theory, against the current line. Ding Ling was claiming "woman" as a legitimate point of theoretical struggle.

Interestingly, Ding Ling began this essay with an analysis of "woman" as an essential entity. The feminine qualities of irrationality, willfulness, regret, romanticism, and love of illusion are indeed associated with women, but they are not, she points out, enduring or necessarily inherent flaws. The habits of discipline, reflection, and rationality, which she outlines in the second part of the essay, can counter weak practices. "Thoughts on March 8" includes a great deal of self-criticism.

Ding Ling's extraordinary claim in the essay is that she could speak for herself "as a woman" and for women generally. She claimed to write the truth. Her faculties for truth telling were her revolutionary credentials, her life as a Communist, and her gender. She actually wrote the essay on August 3, 1941, but held it back until March of the following year. Though later she was to claim surprise at how much uproar it caused, this fact suggests she had at least a suspicion of its power to embarrass.

"Thoughts on March 8" ushered in an unprecedented round of public criticism and Party struggle. Ding Ling apologized for speaking so strongly; she even criticized other outspoken Party writers. But her self-criticism, published in the *Liberation Daily,* did not retract the charges she had initially made, and she always refused the charge that her views were an expression of "narrow feminism."

There was something to offend everybody in this essay. Political theorists resented her implication that the Party had an internal class system. War planners were angry because they had yet to find a policy for mobilizing women that served both family interests and the aims of the state. In fact, it seems quite certain that Ding Ling's criticisms in "Thoughts on March 8" played a part in reforming women's policy and thus, indirectly, in Maoism's victory.—TEB

When will it no longer be necessary to attach special weight to the word "woman" and raise it specially?

Each year this day comes round. Every year on this day, meetings are held all over the world where women muster their forces. Even though things have not been as lively these last two years in Yan'an as they were in previous years, it appears that at least a few people are busy at work here. And there will certainly be a congress, speeches, circular telegrams, and articles.

Women in Yan'an are happier than women elsewhere in China. So much so that many people ask enviously: "How come the women comrades get so rosy and fat on millet?" It doesn't seem to surprise anyone that women make up a big proportion of the staff in the hospitals, sanatoria, and clinics, but they are inevitably the subject of conversation, as a fascinating problem, on every conceivable occasion.

Moreover, all kinds of women comrades are often the target of deserved criticism. In my view these reproaches are serious and justifiable.

People are always interested when women comrades get married, but that is not enough for them. It is virtually impossible for women comrades to get onto friendly terms with a man comrade, and even less likely for them to become friendly with more than one. Cartoonists ridicule them: "A departmental head getting married too?" The poets say, "All the leaders in Yan'an are horsemen, and none of them are artists. In Yan'an it's impossible for an artist to find a pretty sweetheart." But in other situations, they are lectured: "Damn it, you look down on us old cadres and say we're country bumpkins. But if it weren't for us country bumpkins, you wouldn't be coming to Yan'an to eat millet!" But women invariably want to get married. (It's even more of a sin not to be married, and single women are even more of a target for rumors and slanderous gossip.) So they can't afford to be choosy, anyone will do: whether he rides horses or wears straw sandals, whether he's an artist or a supervisor. They inevitably have children. The fate of such children is various. Some are wrapped in soft baby wool and patterned felt and looked after by governesses. Others are wrapped in soiled cloth and left crying in their parents' beds, while their parents consume much of the child allowance. But for this allowance (twenty-five yuan a month, or just over three pounds of pork), many of them would probably never get a taste of meat. Whoever they marry, the fact is that those women who are compelled to bear children will probably be publicly derided as "Noras who have returned home." Those women comrades in a position to employ governesses can go out once a week to a prim get-together and dance. Behind their backs there will also be the most incredible gossip and whispering campaigns, but as soon as they go somewhere, they cause a great stir and all eyes are glued to them. This has nothing to do with our theories, our doctrines, and the speeches we make at meetings. We all know this to be a fact, a fact that is right before our eyes, but it is never mentioned.

It is the same with divorce. In general there are three conditions to pay attention to when getting married: (1) political purity; (2) both parties should be more or less the same age and comparable in looks; (3) mutual help. Even though everyone is said to fulfill these conditions—as for point 1, there are no open traitors in Yan'an; as for point 3, you can call anything "mutual help," including darning socks, patching shoes, and even feminine comfort—everyone nevertheless makes a great show of giving thoughtful attention to them. And yet the pretext for divorce is invariably the wife's political backwardness. I am the first to admit that it is a shame when a man's wife is not progressive and retards his progress. But let us consider to what degree they are backward. Before marrying, they were inspired by the desire to soar in the heavenly heights and lead a life of bitter struggle. They got married partly because of physiological necessity and partly as a response to sweet talk about "mutual help." Thereupon they are forced to toil away and become "Noras returned home." Afraid of being thought "backward," those who are a bit more daring rush around begging nurseries to take their children. They ask for abortions and risk punishment and even death by secretly swallowing potions to produce abortions. But the answer comes back:

"Isn't giving birth to children also work? You're just after an easy life; you want to be in the limelight. After all, what indispensable political work have you performed? Since you are so frightened of having children and are not willing to take responsibility once you have had them, why did you get married in the first place? No one forced you to." Under these conditions, it is impossible for women to escape this destiny of "backwardness." When women capable of working sacrifice their careers for the joys of motherhood, people always sing their praises.[1] But after ten years or so, they have no way of escaping the tragedy of "backwardness."[2] Even from my point of view, as a woman, there is nothing attractive about such "backward" elements. Their skin is beginning to wrinkle, their hair is growing thin, and fatigue is robbing them of their last traces of attractiveness. It should be self-evident that they are in a tragic situation. But whereas in the old society they would probably have been pitied and considered unfortunate, nowadays their tragedy is seen as something self-inflicted, as their just deserts. Is it not so that there is a discussion going on in legal circles as to whether divorces should be granted simply on the petition of one party or on the basis of mutual agreement? In the great majority of cases, it is the husband who petitions for divorce.[3] For the wife to do so, she must be leading an immoral life, and then of course she deserves to be cursed.

I myself am a woman, and I therefore understand the failings of women better than others.[4] But I also have a deeper understanding of what they suffer. Women are incapable of transcending the age they live in, of being perfect, or of being hard as steel. They are incapable of resisting all the temptations of society or all the silent oppression they suffer here in Yan'an. They each have their own past written in blood and tears; they have experienced great emotions—in elation as in depression, whether engaged in the lone battle of life or drawn into the humdrum stream of life. This is even truer of the women comrades who come to Yan'an, and I therefore have much sympathy for those fallen and classified as criminals. What is more, I hope that men, especially those in top positions, as well as women themselves, will consider the mistakes women commit in their social context. It would be better if there were less empty theorizing and more talk about real problems, so that theory and practice would not be divorced, and better if all Communist Party members were more responsible for their own moral conduct.[5] But we must also hope for a little more from our women comrades, especially those in Yan'an. We must urge ourselves on and develop our comradely feeling.

People without ability have never been in a position to seize everything. Therefore, if women want equality, they must first strengthen themselves. There is no need to stress this point, since we all understand it. Today there are certain to be people who make fine speeches bragging about the need to acquire political power first. I would simply mention a few things that any frontliner, whether a proletarian, a fighter in the war of resistance, or a woman, should pay attention to in his or her everyday life:

1. Don't allow yourself to fall ill. A wild life can at times appear romantic, poetic, and attractive, but in today's conditions it is inappropriate. You are the best keeper of your life. There is nothing more unfortunate nowadays than to lose your health. It is closest to your heart. The only thing to do is keep a close watch on it, pay careful attention to it, and cherish it.

2. Make sure you are happy. Only when you are happy can you be youthful, active, fulfilled in your life, and steadfast in the face of all difficulties; only then will you see a future ahead of you and know how to enjoy yourself. This sort of happiness is not a life of contentment, but a life of struggle and of advance. Therefore we should all do some meaningful work each day and some reading, so that each of us is in a position to give something to others. Loafing about simply encourages the feeling that life is hollow, feeble, and in decay.

3. Use your brain, and make a habit of doing so. Correct any tendency not to think and ponder, or to swim with the current. Before you say or do anything, think whether what you are saying is right, whether that is the most suitable way of dealing with the problem, whether it goes against your own principles, whether you feel you can take responsibility for it. Then you will have no cause to regret your actions later.[6] This is what is known as acting rationally. It is the best way of avoiding the pitfalls of sweet words and honeyed phrases, of being sidetracked by petty gains, of wasting our emotions and wasting our lives.

4. Resolution in hardship, perseverance to the end. Aware, modern women should identify and cast off all their rosy illusions. Happiness is to take up the struggle in the midst of the raging storm and not to pluck the lute in the moonlight or recite poetry among the blossoms. In the absence of the greatest resolution, it is very easy to falter in mid-path. Not to suffer is to become degenerate. The strength to carry on should be nurtured through the quality of "perseverance." People without great aims and ambitions rarely have the firmness of purpose that does not covet petty advantages or seek a comfortable existence. But only those who have aims and ambitions for the benefit, not of the individual, but of humankind as a whole can persevere to the end.

August 3, dawn

Postscript. On rereading this article, it seems to me that there is much room for improvement in the passage on what we should expect from women, but because I have to meet a deadline with the manuscript, I have no time to revise it. But I also feel that there are some things that, if said by a leader before a big audience, would probably evoke satisfaction. But when they are written by a woman, they are more than likely to be demolished. But since I have written it, I offer it as I always intended, for the perusal of those people who have similar views.

Translated by Gregor Benton

People Who Will Live Forever in My Heart: Remembering Chen Man

Ding Ling wrote this short piece in what could be called manual prose since it claims the power to represent objective reality so truthfully that the text is a veritable instruction booklet for land reform workers. One of the most important points the 1949 essay seeks to teach is that the impulse to unite as women might feel right initially but easily leads nowhere. A visiting cadre may have personal feelings about individual villagers, yet hard as it seems, these have no place in political struggle, in socialist transformation. The cadre's job is to decide what conditions prevail and how male supremacy can be broken in a world cramped and organized by lineage, family, landlords, secret rivals, and feudal habits of thought.

The narrator of this story speaks with the full authority of the Chinese Communist Party behind her. She has an agenda for this village that Chen Man cannot grasp in full. The official voice sees womanhood as a state-created mechanism for political liberation. Chen Man sees only the local causes of her oppression, and she can see no further than her eccentric position in proper feudal relations between husband and wife, outsider and insider, mother and daughter. The story emphasizes that while Chen Man is among the most oppressed of the villagers and thus deserves tutelage in liberation politics, she is not the villager's choice and thus the outside cadres must look elsewhere to fill their quota of women in the new government. The official politics of womanhood will not directly address Chen Man's particular experience of oppression. Nor does the simple fact of Chen Man's gender entitle her to self-representation. History, not women individually or collectively, vested in dictatorship of the proletariat is the agent of women's liberation.—TEB

Chen Man was among my best friends in Song Village. We will remember each other always. She was an old woman in her fifties, and when she recollected her past, pleasant events did not spring to mind. Her destiny was no different than that of her grandmother, her mother, and her daughter. Chen Man did not know why they had to suffer so much.

"Ah, the road is so very, very long," she said to me. "The days endless. The suffering of the mother's generation hasn't ended before the daughter's generation begins theirs. I've done a mountain of work and shed a river of tears."

Certainly her life could not be described in one sitting, nor could it ever be completely committed to writing. All I can do now is record how we met each other and how we came to be friends.[1]

The second day after our arrival in Song Village, we called a meeting of the Poor Peasant's Association in the area. We didn't have any close contacts there (at the time Song was a newly liberated district). The general idea was that in meetings and in separate interviews and the like there would be opportunities to get to know various people and discover some reliable activists.[2] But the first day, half the people wouldn't say a word. What a small number of them had to say wasn't all that bad, but they didn't dare speak in public. And the few who were willing to appear turned out to be sneaky and undependable. Later on, when we formed small groups to elect group leaders, there was one group that simply couldn't elect anybody. When we went to see what was going on, everybody was declining in favor of someone else, and some just sat there with their heads down, never making a sound.

We tried to explain to them about elections, but they were convinced. Just then a poorly dressed old woman stood up. "Look at all of you," she cried heatedly. "What a bunch of deadbeats! Never in a million years could you have anticipated a day like this! The People's Liberation Army has made us poor people our own masters, called on us to 'turn over' our lives, and you're still scared of this, scared of that.[3] You'll spend the rest of your lives suffering like dumb plow animals. Gentlemen! Lift those stupid heads up!"

The small group of people stared at her silently. Then someone, I don't know who, said softly, "You do it. You be it."

"I'll do it. If you elect me, I'll do it."

Then most of them said, "We elect you! We elect you. You do it!"

"That's fine," someone commented to us. "She's the one. She's from Li Laodong's household.[4] Her name is Chen Man."

We asked them all again and they said unanimously, "She's it. She'll do fine."

"So I'm it," Chen Man said. "I'm not afraid of anything. Anything comes up, just ask me, all right? Comrades, write my name down. It's Chen Man." So that's how she became the group head.

The next day at the general meeting of the village Poor Peasant's Association to elect a representative to the Mass Organization, she was among those nominated to run for chairperson. She was extraordinarily brave, and asked me, "Can womenfolk manage too?" I told her that both men and women were expected to "turn over." Anyone who wanted to work for their fellow villagers could serve as chairperson. Delighted, she smiled and said, "If you say it'll be okay, then I'll do it. What you've said is right. I am not afraid of them. I'll do as you say."

During the meeting, I encouraged her. "Auntie," I said, "tell everybody here about your plans and ideas, so they can all be like you, unafraid. Okay?" [5]

"Well, how can a woman short on knowledge and experience say anything persuasive," she said tentatively. "Since gentlemen are supposed to direct ladies, how are they ever going to let an old woman be leader?" [6]

I told her that was a bunch of old nonsense and that she needn't pay any attention to it. So she strode up to the table in front of the chair's platform, where, without hesitation, as though she'd rehearsed her speech in advance, she spoke out forthrightly: "I'm an old woman. I don't know what I ought to say. Or whether what I'm going to say is right or wrong. But I say that, starting today, our village can change and we can be masters of our own fate. We have Chairman Mao, so we don't have to be scared of anybody. All the poor people in the world belong to one family, united in spirit and all of one mind. With Chairman Mao as our leader and the People's Liberation Army to support us, the despotic landlords are all finished. Their militia will be destroyed very soon. So what do we have to be scared of? We must all thank Chairman Mao from the bottom of our hearts; we must turn ourselves over, and be our own masters to make Chairman Mao happy."

Some of her listeners smiled. Others did not. In the end, she missed being elected to serve as a representative to the Poor Peasant's Mass Organization by just a few votes. Two other women, real rabble rousers, were elected. We felt very strongly that there must have been a reason for this. But as we'd just arrived in the village and did not really understand the general situation, we felt it better not to jump to any hasty conclusions.

Later on, several people told me that Chen Man was an impoverished seamstress who had come here from another village, bringing her un-

married daughter with her, and that they lived with Li Laodong. Li Laodong was seventy-five years old this year. He'd been seventy when he
took her on.

I went to see her that afternoon because I wanted her at least to do her
job as leader of the small group. The following day, some people told me
that her small group had elected another head. Everyone had opposed
her on the grounds that she was an outsider. As it turned out, all the
others belonged to the same clan, all surnamed Li. Other people said that
Li Laodong would not let her leave the house.

Still others told me that she had a bad reputation. I asked if she had
been someone's concubine. The answer was no. I asked if her daughter
had misbehaved, and was told that she was a good girl. It was all because
her late husband had been a female impersonator in a Beijing opera
troupe!

I considered this problem for some time and decided that since they
did not want her to be the head of the small group, I would not go see
her either. That evening I sent someone to check up on her. He returned
and reported that everyone said she was sick. The next day I sent someone else around. The report came back that she seemed to be ill, was
lying in bed, and hadn't eaten for two days. I felt anxious for her and
was upset all day. I thought about the many embarrassments and all the
persecution she had endured; but because I wanted to understand matters more clearly, I had to sit by patiently without interfering and observe
how other people treated her.

By the morning of the fourth day, I couldn't stand it any longer and
headed for her house. I hadn't taken more than a few steps when I saw
her. Chen Man, hair unkempt, clothes disheveled, came up and clutched
my arm. "I've come to see you," she said. "I have something to say to
you. Everyone says I'm sick, but it's nothing of the sort. Don't believe
them."

We walked back together. The hand clutching mine felt scorching hot.
As we entered my house, she said, "The reason I haven't been able to eat
is that for many days and nights I've been groping for a truth. Now that
I have it cleared up, I can eat and comb my hair."

I didn't dare ask her what that something was. I urged her to relax on
my *kang* and poured her a cup of boiled water. I figured that when she
had something to say, she'd say it.

"I used to be a nobody in this village," she began. "And I was humiliated wherever I went. People called me a whore; some of them even hit
me and my daughter. That was because they didn't respect us, despised
us. Now, of course, people hate and fear me. I don't dare go to sleep at
night because I'm afraid someone will come kill me. Comrade! You must

know that since I've gained your support, I've become a real person. Did you think that after I had turned over no one would hate me or be afraid of me? Hah! You're smiling. Well, you'd better believe it. Only you probably don't think I'm afraid of them. Really, I can't sleep at night. I tell old Li and my daughter to take turns guarding the window, scared somebody might break in. My old man's no good. He's got the 'bones of a beggar, heart of a scrooge.' He's not on your side. He makes big plans but has little to show for them. When he took me, he was seventy and I was fifty. You tell me what we could possibly have in common. He wanted me to serve him, and all I wanted was a safe place to bring my daughter up right. The old guy's barely human. He won't bring his grain home for fear that when he kicks off one day, it will all come to me. If he really were to die, we wouldn't even be allowed to mourn for him or kowtow in front of his tablet before we'd be driven off.[7] I shouldn't talk about these things. But I'm not afraid of them anymore; now they're afraid of me. Even though I'm an outsider, I've still lived here five years. I'm not stupid. I know who's good and who's bad. In actual fact, though, you newcomers won't ever figure out what's what in this village, not in a day, or even in two. I'm really of the same mind as you folks. You and I haven't said much to each other, but I understand everything. I haven't slept or eaten for days trying to discover what's on your minds. I say something, I do something, and then I consider whether or not it agrees with your views. That's because your mind is the mind of Chairman Mao, and Chairman Mao's mind is a mind that's for us all. Before, the more I thought the more mixed up I got. I want my daughter, Erni, to sing and do the *yangge* rice-sprout dance.[8] Everyone says I'm crazy. But I tell Erni that singing is the way to thank Chairman Mao, and dancing the *yangge* is for our liberation. Last night I got this all figured out. I'm so happy. Comrade, listen. I feel that everything in the past that was right is wrong today, and that everything that was wrong in the past is now right. If I want to do something, I must do as I've just said. Tell me, isn't that so?"

I was simply astonished. I felt that she had opened my mind. This old woman had such insight. If people really want to "turn over" and be free, if they want to "turn over" their way of thinking, certainly they have to suffer a lot and think a great deal. I didn't have anything to ask her. I knew that she would tell me everything. So I just encouraged and comforted her. Later she sat up, crossed her legs, brushed back the disheveled hair from her forehead. It seemed as though something very important had occurred to her. Solemnly she said, "Comrade, I'm not afraid that you'll laugh at me. I have made up a song, and I'd like to sing it for you to express what I feel."

Naturally, I was afraid she might not sing it, so I was as considerate of her feelings as I could be. Then she began to sing:

> The sun rises red, so red
> The sun is like Mao Zedong
> Crops without sun will ne'er grow tall
> Poor folk without Mao will e'er lack all.

It seemed to me that I had read this song somewhere, but Chen Man was illiterate, so it was impossible for her to have plagiarized it. Furthermore, this was a newly liberated area. Perhaps she had heard someone else singing it, and it had left an impression on her. On the other hand, maybe it was just a coincidence, people with the same emotions singing the same song. I asked her to explain, and she said, "Why is it that when there is no sun the crops don't grow? It's because the big trees cover them. The big trees are just like the landlords. Only after the trees have been chopped down can the crops see the sun. If we can't overthrow the landlords, then we will never be free. Comrade, tell me if that's right or not."

(I thought of saying here that Chen Man was a poet, but perhaps others would say I exaggerate. However, she really did sing for me for many hours, putting her whole life into song. There was no doubt that her story had the capacity to move people. All of this, of course, happened at a later time.)

I also asked her if she had composed the songs. She said yes, and I said, "Auntie, you're pretty good at it. You must do some more. When you do, I'll write them down for you and send them to Chairman Mao."

She seemed to fly up off the *kang*. "I'm well," she said to me. "My head is clear. I've thought everything through, so I'm not sick anymore. Don't worry, we can take care of things in this village. There are lots of good people here. Li Manchuan is in our westside group, and he's very good. He comes across kind of crudely and he's a bit gruff, but he's an honest, upright person who's doesn't scare easily. I'll tell you more about it later. I'm going home now to let you eat. I'll be back when I have something else to say. My old man is no good. I scold him all day long, trying to force him to change his ways."

I grasped her hand firmly and courteously took her to the door. "Auntie," I said, "you're a fine person. You're one of us, and we're your people. Be calm. Eat and sleep in peace. No one will dare harm you. The two of us old aunties will have to talk this all over. Tell me everything you know, and I'll tell you what I understand to be the reasons things are the way they are. We will rely on you, and you can rely on us. We're of

one mind, and we all want Song Village to turn over entirely. We want
every poor person in Song Village to be like you—crystal clear in understanding, masters of the village."

She left, her hair falling down over her neck. Her stride was vigorous.
I saw clearly her strong, resolute, and wise heart. I saw clearly our mutual unquestioned trust. I loved her. I had discovered a new world in her.
Her figure moved slowly into the distance, and as it did so, my happiness
grew. There was no way I could conceal my delight. I almost burst out
laughing as I returned to my room. I sought out my comrades. With an
even more optimistic feeling of ability and confidence, we began to arrange our new tasks.

This was only the beginning of my acquaintance with Chen Man. Naturally, our friendship grew by the day. Because the struggle in Song Village deepened, becoming increasingly detailed, our accord strengthened
and put our relationship on a sturdier, more harmonious basis. Now,
whenever there is nothing on my mind, or perhaps when I need some
affection, I recall many people, and Chen Man is one of them. It is sad
that at this time all I can do is write down this simple memoir. However,
I hope that by doing so, the people who live forever in my heart will also
live forever in the hearts of others.

Translated by Jean James

Du Wanxiang

This allegory of Du Wanxiang who "served the people heart and soul," is Ding Ling's final, haunting glance back to the problem that in the end was her most sustained concern in a long and eventful life. The 1978 parable memorializes the author's own history in the Chinese revolution. It is clearly meant to provide a correct interpretation of, if nothing else, the writer's unimpeachable motives. Du Wanxiang is Ding Ling's final laying to rest of Sophia's desires. Du Wanxiang makes concrete Ding Ling's own measure of the socialist woman, that abstract mythic category, struggled over and chronically disputed; shaped, like a papier-mâché figure, through the application of layer after layer of Party directives and labor quotas; raddled by old kinship relationships. The concept is sometimes inconsistent, often contradictory, but the fruit, even so, of a sixty-year political struggle.

Ding Ling wrote the first draft of the story on the eve of the Cultural Revolution. Fifteen tormented years later, she reconstructed that long lost utopian vision. At the edge of the civilized world live the unspoiled people of China in a Daoist-Communist utopia, engaged in the struggles that secure life on earth—against the soil, the wind, the animals, and the snow. In the determined effort of one good woman, who would rather light a candle than curse in the dark, the modern Everywoman of People's China shapes herself. This ungendered, politically redemptive woman comes into existence because of Ding Ling's willingness to recuperate, to open up to new uses despite their unmistakable injustices, conventions of daily life that felt so familiar.

This parable recovers older meaning at two levels. First, "Du Wanxiang" restores the womanly virtues Ding Ling had watched her mother's generation revile. Tractable, silent, loyal, gentle, stern, hardworking, and utterly selfless Wanxiang embodies a series of popular stereotypes—the suffering daughter-in-law, the orphaned stepdaughter, loyal wife, nurturing mother. Her love for Chairman Mao and her very conformist adaptation of inherited female roles allow her to squeeze her way into the world of legitimate authority. She claims her limited power without ever challenging male supremacy. Wanxiang governs through virtue, albeit Maoist virtue. She only rules because her power source is not the family but the nation, not woman-hating custom, "culture," but Communist aphorisms and ethical practices. Du Wanxiang is liberated and powerful only when she serves the state and its people.

"Du Wanxiang" also made the case that the Yan'an ethics of suffering, frugality, and equality should be reconsidered even in light of their links to Mao's Cultural Revolution. This story selectively reaffirms a simple revolutionary ethic while, at the same time, pulling to its center a story about women's triumph. Politics, Du Wanxiang's efforts appear to argue, is still central to women's liberation, even in a disenchanted and post-revolutionary world.

Du Wanxiang speaks with a popular voice that has no reference to texts or canons, not even the written "classics" of the Chairman's own *Little Red Book*. She speaks always in her own voice, as a female cadre, a politician, but she does not speak "for women." She uses her motherhood strategically in the interest of community, and only tangentially do her feminine virtues work to her individual benefit. She is what she works so hard to be, a self-less person.

In this text, Ding Ling conjoined her history as a daughter of revolution to her history as a woman, in the person of an obscure, strong-willed village Communist. The language of the story reinforces the point. It juxtaposes old-fashioned four-character idioms and assorted bits and pieces of "Maospeak." The world of red tractors and smoke-belching trains, of loudspeakers and brilliantly lighted culture palaces, of normal family tyrannies, marketplace and class conflicts, of model workers and ordinary political rhetoric is compellingly evoked in a romantic official-style narrative. The story does not completely mask the many tragedies of the Chinese socialist revolution. Indeed, it alludes to them constantly. It is therefore not clear, as always in Ding Ling's best fiction, whether or not this shade obscures the socialist glory of Du Wanxiang's achievements.—TEB

Red Apricot Tree

Spring came. Dust-burdened spring wind whipped over the loess plain. The parched air sucked dry all moisture. The ground cracked open. People stared at the sky, sighing. Even so, the grass still made its way out of each crevice, soundlessly, until patch by patch, it had stained the ground green. Leaves on the trees unfurled slowly. The lapping sound of water carried out of the gray, mud-colored hollow as a small mountain creek gurgled to itself in solitude. A steep mountain path, across which cattle and flocks of sheep wandered occasionally, twisted its precipitous way up and down. Over the low wall built of scattered rampart stones stretched a dazzling bramble of red apricot blossoms, delighting everyone up and down the hollow. So! It was spring. Irrepressible, unfreezable, drought-resisting spring. Everything alive lifted its head stubbornly to the sunlight, pulled upright in a display of vitality.

The little eight-year-old girl, Wanxiang, from the Du family, had already suffered three years of harsh scolding and sudden ear-boxings under her stepmother's baleful gaze. By this time she already shouldered a lot of household labor, and got pleasure from it. She could go down for water to the deep, deep gully and return with two half-buckets on her shoulder pole, so her dad didn't have to do that at all anymore. And every noon, she'd climb a mile up the high steppe to where her father was working, carrying his meager lunch. Her father loved her. Nonetheless, he could do little more than gaze in silent sympathy at his lovely daughter. Wanxiang herself paid little attention to such things, preferring instead the wide blue sky and drifting white clouds. How vast the steppe was. The high steppes all around were dotted with poor peasants, just like her father, bent over their far-flung plots, and scattered flocks of sheep grazed the fallow pastures. So wholesome! Wanxiang's long, narrow, single-lidded eyes, so like those in old paintings, looked around searchingly. Those huge hawks circling the sky, now overhead, now slipped from sight, where did they fly off to? Were they looking for their mothers? One day Mama would come home. Mama's eyes were so soft, her hands so warm, her voice so intimate, and sleeping in her embrace was so sweet.

Over the three years Wanxiang had been motherless, she'd longed for Mama by day and dreamt of her at night. When would she come back? Wanxiang had long ago developed a way of explaining away her mother's loss: Mama had gone to her mother's place on an errand and one day she'd come back. Along the vast expanse of the steppes, Wanxiang's desire for her mother glided freely, like the hawks above, comforting the tender young heart.

Wanxiang was just like the red apricot tree. Unmindful of the ruthless weather, the driving, yellow loess sandstorms, the splendid beauty of the apricot's burgeoning young shoots behind the jaggedy old stone wall, just like Wanxiang's own beauty, roused the impoverished people of the hollow, comforted their suffering, and inspired their wildest dreams of a bright future.

Conduct of a Daughter-in-law

One year followed the next until, all told, five had passed. Wanxiang turned thirteen. So her stepmother went ahead and gave her to a family named Li in the neighboring steppe to be their daughter-in-law.[1] The day of her wedding, Wanxiang made a little bundle with an old tunic, a pair of worn trousers, a pair of raggedy shoes, a snaggle-toothed comb, and a looking glass no larger than the palm of her hand, put it all on her back, and left home in the company of her father. It was the dead of winter. The people of the mountain hollow had all shut their doors against the cold. Only one village elder stood at the threshold of his house on the edge of town to see them off.

"Wanxiang! Little girl," he said to her. "When you get to the Li family be obedient. Do everything you're supposed to do and pay attention to proper manners.[2] Never make anybody angry at you."

The old man and his advice made the resolute Wanxiang's eyes smart. Though she never saw him again, his voice and face were engraved forever in her memory. It was the single farewell gesture she got from that remote, miserably poor village where she had passed the first thirteen years of her life.

Snow started drifting down. Her father plodded along in front of her, wordless. He could not bear the thought of giving up his little girl to be somebody's daughter-in-law. He was also thinking how he'd failed his dead wife by not watching as carefully over her daughter as she had wished. But then, figuring that nothing ever turned out the way he wanted, he had no recourse. Leave her to her own fate!

Wanxiang knew, as she walked the long road through the steppe with such effort, straining against the north wind, treading tracks through the snow that her dad cleared in front of her, that she was entering a new world. She had no illusions about it. But she wasn't frightened either. She figured she was pretty well grown already and could stand just about anything. Wanxiang knew what it took to be a daughter-in-law. No matter what kind of situation she ended up in, she'd always be able to cope, because she knew how to labor and how to endure hardship. She was a young sapling bred in adversity, a shoot of spring-blooming apricot, an orphan, in any case, who had lost her mother and whose new parents-in-law and family could certainly be no worse than her stepmother had been.

There were lots of people in the Li family. The two old folks had four sons and four grandsons, Wanxiang being the wife of the youngest son. They were still poor folk, but a good sight better off than Wanxiang's people. The twenty *mu* of land they owned was enough to keep them all fed, and they'd built a nice new little brick *kang* in the family house for their son and his new wife. It dawned on Wanxiang, as she fingered the short coarse pile of her very first new blanket, how warm wool felt really is.

Her three sisters-in-law felt their hearts sink as they eyed her skinny frame. "Useless little girl," they sighed. "We could have gotten a donkey colt with the fifty dollars we paid for her."

Wanxiang was quiet and observant. By listening to the family members talk, she had them all figured out. Her Popo told her to get to work and showed her how they did the household chores.[3] So Wanxiang calmly rolled up her sleeves and started fetching water, firing the stove, cooking, feeding the chickens, and slopping the hogs. Before long she was taking her shift at cooking along with the other daughters-in-law. When it got to be her turn, she would stand up on a stool to reach the stove so she could turn out dishes for the whole enormous family. She was just as competent at fetching water and carrying the rice soup and lunch dishes up and down the steppe gullies. She learned how to farm from working in the fields and always managed to keep pace alongside the others. Exacting as her highly skilled Gonggong was, he never found fault with her work.[4] Even the pitiless sisters-in-law had no cause for complaint. And so Wanxiang put down roots in this little mountain hollow, laboring tirelessly year round for the immense Li family.

The small mountain hollow she'd just entered formed her entire world now. The earth-shattering, world-shaking events commencing elsewhere had yet to rumble through her remote little hollow. Sometimes Gonggong brought home snippets of news he'd heard in the village, but it meant as little to an ignorant young woman like Du Wanxiang as wind on the steppes or water in the gullies. That did not stop the growing force of the wind and rising water from finally reaching into every remote mountainous hollow, however. In the end, Lijia Hollow could not avoid being sucked in. Their hollow had no landlords or rich peasants, since most of the land they tilled didn't even belong to them but was leased out from other villages. One day the Liberation Army, the Communist Party, and work teams suddenly arrived. Abruptly land was turned over to the tillers. Wanxiang's family got a lot because they had so many people, and Gonggong and Popo kept going around, agog, clambering from parcel to parcel, gaping at the vivid green and yellow crops, and babbling about what a fantastic thing had just occurred! For a while Wanxiang didn't really grasp what had excited the old folks so, but the joy everybody felt at getting land and the exhilarating pandemonium finally got to her too. Shortly afterward, the Liberation Army started recruiting volunteers and everybody was saying that it was to "resist America and aid Korea." Before Wanxiang had a chance to even learn what the words "resist America and aid Korea" really meant, the youngest Li son had already been inducted into the army. The parents said they thought it only right since their family had four. In a flash, Wanxiang's husband, Li Gui, had left the mountain hollow, a red badge pinned to his chest. It happened in 1951. Wanxiang was seventeen years old.

Mama Comes Home

Around this time, a work team showed up to review the land reform effort. Among them was a middle-aged woman comrade who lodged at the Li's place and slept with Wanxiang on the little *kang*. During the day, she went up the steppes to work the land with the farmers, or cooked, or slopped the hogs. At night she taught the village women how to read. Of all the women in the village, Wanxiang was most inspired to learn, so the comrade favored the seventeen-year-old daughter-in-law and stayed up half the night to talk with her. Wanxiang was entranced. As she listened, enraptured, her horizons expanded and she started seeing farther, aspiring to greater heights. She realized how much more happiness she could derive from serving people beyond her immediate family. At the woman comrade's urging, Gonggong and Popo finally let Wanxiang go to the county seat for a three-month training program. She came back even more solid and resolute than before. Superficially she seemed as docile and tractable as she had in childhood, perhaps more so; but now, in addition, a mild, enigmatic smile played around her mouth as though she harbored pleasant thoughts about everyone she met, all she did, life itself. Of course they all noticed, and everyone wanted to know what was making her so happy.

Wanxiang felt delivered back to her mother's arms, and that was the simple fact of the matter. Concerned people were watching out for her, had aspirations for her. Conscious of their encouragement and support, like a child learning to walk at her mother's side, she took a step, stopped, looked about, and felt their gazes around her. She wasn't an orphan anymore. She was no longer a friendless, pathetic woman who only knew how to toil and how to avoid vicious, brutal scolding and abuse. A gentle wind blew over the steppe. White clouds wafted through the azure sky. The little mountain path felt like a broad boulevard. Wanxiang spent her days working the land behind her brothers- and sisters-in-law, carrying her loaded poles up and down the slopes, but at night she walked from household to household propagating the Party and government policies the way she'd learned from the work team. The programs she understood, she sought to teach by example. Those she didn't quite get, she read out loud and tried to adapt according to what she had heard. She was made the head of the women's team, then the chairwoman of the Women's Association. Two dozen families lived in the village, and she had to know what fully half of those people desired. Subsequently she was recruited into the Communist Party. She had found her real mother. Slowly she matured in this village, living as freely and comfortably there as a fish lives in water. Not a soul expressed contempt, or ever disrespected her.

In 1954 the volunteers who had fought in the Anti-American War came home. The men in the village from the oldest uncle to the youngest nephew spent every night listening as Wanxiang's husband told fantastic war stories. This quickly earned him their respect. When Wanxiang discovered that he was a Party member too, she nearly died of happiness. She no longer thought of him just as her helpmate, because now their relationship was made sacrosanct by the common language, the common ideals the two of them would share for the rest of their days. Li Gui hadn't been back more than a few days when he left for Sichuan Province to study culture, politics, and military affairs. The Party wanted to cultivate the brave, loyal Korean veterans, toughened by real experience of war, for later service as military officers.

Du Wanxiang remained in the isolated mountain hollow as she had the other time he'd gone off. She worked hard for everyone in the family. Her responsibilities for women's work kept her constantly on the run. Years passed. Would she move along slowly with this mountain hollow as it underwent social reconstruction and developed toward socialism, toward a communist society?

Soaring to the Great North Wasteland

Everybody in Lijia Hollow was talking about a new development in the spring of 1958. Li Gui and his whole group from the Sichuan Military Affairs Academy were being sent off to somewhere called the Great

Northern Wasteland. The entire village was alive with speculation! The
Great Northern Wasteland referred to a really terrible area along China's
enormously long border, far, far away, where, in the old days, criminals
had been banished or exiled. How could they send Li Gui all the way out
there when he was such a nice boy who had seen service in Korea? He
had endured so much. He deserved more than that. It just wasn't right.
They couldn't make much out of Li Gui's letter, either, other than that
he was going to support the socialist construction of the frontier and had
sent instructions for his wife to join him. How could she go? Just where
the hell was this Great Northern Wasteland, anyway?

Rumor claimed that it was a frigid place where snow fell even in June,
and where, during the winter, people froze to death or got blown away
by the wind. If you touched your nose, it fell right off. Ears too. The
sisters-in-law looked sympathetically at Wanxiang and were against her
going. Gonggong and Popo said their daughter-in-law's leaving made it
that much harder to get their son back, so they wanted to contact higher
authorities and insist he be demobilized back home. Her comrades at the
Party branch said she should think it over since life would be tedious way
out there as a dependent and she would probably be better off staying to
continue her work in the village.

"Ma, Dad," Du Wanxiang finally said after listening quietly to all
manner of such speculation and advice, the half-smile playing about her
mouth. "Let me go take a look. I promise I'll let you know exactly what
the real situation is. Anyway, if Li Gui can go, why shouldn't I? Li Gui
is part of a population transfer that involves, not just him, but a whole
lot of people. If they can live out there, why can't I? Improving the border
region will require lots of work. Anyway, I'd never sit around and let
other people feed me. Plenty of people in the village can do my work.
I'm dispensable. That's how I see it. I'm determined to go."

Everyone, including Gonggong and Popo, had to acquiesce when they
realized how strongly she'd set her will to this. Not long after that, shoul-
dering a knapsack packed with a fresh change of clothes, a comb and
wash things, a couple of maize cakes, and the money Li Gui had sent,
she said goodbye to the beloved familiar place in which she'd spent the
first twenty years of her life. Gonggong took her all the way to the Tian-
shui railway station and instructed her to write them a long, detailed
letter as soon as she arrived.

The train sped east with a roar, flashing through the rows of distant
mountain ranges. On either side of the track, open fields spread out before them, only to drop back as they rushed along. Against the unbelievable blue of the sky, banks of white clouds amassed, dissipated like gos-
samer, then suddenly mushroomed into new formations. Although

Wanxiang had often gazed at the broad vaults of the sky and at the distant horizon, she had never before now seen such an endlessly mutable landscape of open field and forest. Gusts of wind blew through the open window, gently raising her short bangs, and caressing her deeply flushed face.

A ruby sun floated in the western sky as the train veered northward. Crimson light from a sky in flames poured through the window, filling the carriage with a transparent misty radiance. The sun, a fireball bolting golden light, slowly set. The sky seemed like a far-flung net, and as the purple haze rose, the dusk gathered, and its somber blues became manifest, night fell.

Station after station, town after town, the train continued onward. Crowds of every kind—people dragging children, supporting old folks, carrying loads of various sizes—rushed onto the platform and crowded into the compartment, settling into seats only just barely emptied. There were other long lines of people in the stations, as well, walking through the ticket taker's gate amidst songs sung in praise of the great nation. Harsh lights illuminated the depot. The train pulled out again. The galaxies of flashing lights through which the train glanced along its way glinted more brightly than the sweep of stars dotting the overcast sky. Oh, China, China! How boundless, how magnificent, how mysteriously entrancing this great nation was! Du Wanxiang had left the tiny mountain gully for a new universe that had never existed even in her wildest dreams. She was so tense with excitement that she couldn't focus or think straight; all that kept her from collapsing with fatigue was her indomitable spirit. And so, eyes wide, she sat in her seat as though her strength would never give out. That is how she remained, nibbling on her maize cakes, sipping boiled water. In and out of the stations, she followed the others, boarding and debarking trains, for three days and three nights, until the other passengers told her that they had reached the Great Northern Wasteland. So! She had arrived!

What Is This Place?

The train stopped. On the snowy ground by the train station and the platform stood rows of all kinds of red, green, blue, and black machines, some of them so big—bigger than a house—that Wanxiang did not know what to call them. Over the machines stretched green, yellow, and gray tarpaulins covered with heavy drifts of snow. Everywhere crowds of people milled around in greatcoats and padded jackets, eyes flashing beneath leather hats, mouths roaring with laughter, as though they knew one another well.

"What farm are you from?" one asked.

"Hey! Look! These East-Is-Red tractors from Luoyang are for our farm," someone said.

"Hey," somebody off in the distance shouted, "what kind of machine is this; where was it made? We want ones made in China."

"When you go back," yet another was saying, "take the bean seeds and the tractor spare parts back with you. Everybody's waiting for them."

All over, groups of people were shouting work chants as they picked over and hauled things to be loaded onto the trucks. Stuffed to bursting, the brand new Liberation-model trucks set off, convoy after convoy, on their snow chains. The truck lot outside the train station was enormous and packed entirely with ten-wheel trucks crammed in like boxes in a chest. It turned out that the trucks all belonged to state farms, though it was hard to say which was whose since there were so many farms out here. Standing, looking down the slope, the road spread out like a spider web in every conceivable direction. Where did all these roads lead to? To state farms! The town was a matter of just a few streets, nothing much in the way of shops, but all along the roads, on both sides of the street, ran sewage drains and newly planted, orderly rows of white birch trees. The streets were crowded with people as though it were market-fair day. The locals were really odd, though. Everyone buying seemed to choose the very same few things: thermos bottles, lunch boxes, mosquito coils, colorful cotton towels. And the buyers seemed to know the sellers well. Not infrequently, shop clerks could be overheard saying things to customers like "Spring planting in or not? We just got some mosquito repellant from Guangzhou; it's great." Or a customer might ask, "Have you got any sickles? Come rainy season and the grain harvest, we'll really need sickles."

The hottest spot in town was the bean-curd-soup-and-fritters shop. Everybody who got on or off the train or a truck and people staying at the guest houses all loved to come by for a bowl of hot bean curd soup and a couple of fritters fresh from the fat. It was also a great place to exchange news, news that centered on one front—the state farms. Things like "I hear you people have got some army officers, heroes of the Battle of Sangkumryung Ridge" or "Heard the secretary is back and has gone off to [that] farm." [5]

"Yeah, he's back! He's out at our place. Once the secretary arrived, he didn't go to headquarters or back to the office. In the spirit of the year we reclaimed Nanniwan, he got right in his jeep and went out to the fields to test the quality of the soil and grain.[6] Then he dropped into the tractor yard and came out driving a tractor, inspected our machines, tested our farm technology, all the while laughing and cutting up with our tractor hands and farm tool workers."

"When I first got to the state farm, my thinking was kind of unstable. I don't know how, but somehow the secretary found out. He came around to the old hut where I was living. 'Last year you fought a war to victory,' he said to me. 'Now you're stationed out here so you can develop this region, fight the earth itself, hand to hand combat against Nature to build a communist society. It's a fantastic enterprise. It demands a lofty spirit and soaring ambition, the effort of a lifetime. Your children and grandchildren, all generations after them, will remember you and thank you from the bottom of their hearts.' As soon as I heard the secretary say that," he concluded with a chuckle, "I brought my wife and kids over and we put roots down for good."

"Last year during grain harvest, it rained a whole month. Our whole team—man, beast, machine—all hit the battlefield. In our team there was a demobilized platoon leader who got his sickle but went off to sit under a tree and read. Soon an old geezer came wandering by, sickle in hand, wearing PLA shoes, his trousers rolled. He sees this guy.

" 'What are you doing out here reading,' he asks him. 'How come you're not out working in the field.'

" 'Don't let me stop you,' he answers. 'Just count me out.'

" 'The fat's in the fire,' the old geezer says, stopping midstride. 'Everybody's out there doing their part to salvage the harvest. What's your story?'

" 'I just don't feel like it,' he says.

" 'If you don't get the hell out there,' the old geezer screams, flying into a perfect rage, 'I'm going to throw you in the brig.'

" 'I'd like to see you try it, you old fart.'

" 'What if this old fart is Wang Zhen,' the old geezer says with a snort. 'Then nothing would stand between you and the brig.'

"That scared the platoon leader out of his mind, and snatching his sickle, he ran off down the road, totally mortified, until he saw some people in a field. He rushed over to tell them all about what the secretary had done . . . That day he set the record for harvesting three *mu* five *fen*."

When Du Wanxiang heard this story, she laughed along with the rest of them, and this initial impression was deeply carved onto her memory. From four o'clock in the morning until eight at night, customers flowed in and out of the shop. How could there be customers at four o'clock in the morning? Sunrise comes early in the Great Northern Wasteland.

Later on, it would be light as early as three o'clock. Once day breaks, who wants to wait for the sun to climb out of bed? At this time of year, morning was the best time of the day. At four—later it would be three, and even two o'clock—a fine line of light would form against the east horizon, then bathe the sky in translucent white light. The breeze bore the comforting chill of melting snow, the fragrant musk of the awakening forest, as it assailed the people's nostrils and penetrated deeply to the core of their hearts. The translucent white gradually turned scarlet, the stars went out in the heavens, and everywhere tiny birds began calling. Narrow bands of golden red lit up the borders of the clouds. "Here comes the sun," people couldn't help saying. All creation was manifest in its boundless vitality. Life resurgent.

Wanxiang was put up at a guest house. The place was packed with people milling around the dorms, hallways, dining hall, the courtyard, so without much formality they felt comfortable asking each other "Which farm do you belong to? Where have you been assigned? What kind of work do you do? Does your farm have houses yet, or are you still living in tents?"

There were two other female comrades and a little boy sharing Du Wanxiang's room. The one in her late teens looked like a student. She was light on her feet, spoke unhesitatingly, and had a habit of holding her head up high to glance at people out of the corner of her eye. When she heard that someone in the neighboring rooms had said that there were lots of wolves in the Great Northern Wastelands, she curled her lips in a sneer, exposing a row of nice white teeth. "Wolves," she snorted. "What's the big deal? It's the stupid bears that come rushing over when they see the tractor, won't let you through, and attack your headlights." She'd been a tractor hand on a state farm for a year and had opened so much wasteland she couldn't keep count. Du Wanxiang admired her lavishly from afar. The other woman was the wife of a demobilized naval officer and had brought their six-month-old baby boy along with her. She was an extraordinarily warm, kindly woman.[7] She subjected Du Wanxiang to careful, loving interrogations about her hometown and personal history, and she heartened her by saying, "There's nothing about the Great Northern Wasteland that should scare you. You'll be used to it in a few days. I'm a Southerner, and I grew up in the city, where we ate and dressed well and had a wonderfully comfortable way of life. When I first heard we were coming here I thought, Whatever am I going to do in such a frozen place? It was February when I got here. It was frozen solid and the wind cut to the bone. There was nowhere to stay, and all we had to eat was sorghum and soybeans. We had to start from scratch leveling land to build houses. I won't kid you and say it was easy. After a real busy spell, strange to say, we ended up liking it and decided we'd stick with it for the long haul. It's like the secretary says, we'll settle in and make a go of it. I've lost the taste for living a custom-made life and eating other people's scraps. Now I'm sending the baby back to his granny's. In two years, when we have a kindergarten, I'll bring him back. All a person really needs is total dedication to the Party, the Revolution, and the impoverished; then no hardship is insurmountable, no job beyond your strength. It is only in love and dedication to these things that you can know the real meaning of life and happiness."[8] As the woman, who'd nearly talked herself into a frenzy, looked steadily at Wanxiang, she felt she might have said too much, too fast.

"A person like you who can endure and toil, a Party member whose husband was a volunteer soldier," she said mildly with a tinge of remorse, "you'll love it here. You'll do just fine. I really hope you find a good life and work here!"

Her husband, the former naval officer, a man of dignified demeanor, bushy eyebrows, and glinting eyes, who was amiable and humble, walked into the room and greeted Du Wanxiang with great courtesy. Then he happily bundled up their son and went out for a walk with his wife. What sort of people were these? Just what sort of place was this?

This Is Home

The guest house official handed Du Wanxiang over to a driver who was taking his transport truck up to one of the other state farms and could drop her there. Two other female dependents and their children and three administrative cadres were also hitching a ride. The weather was light that day and the ground hard, dotted with scattered patches of unmelted snow that made a crunch as the big wheels rolled over them. The sun shone over the distant mountains and on the land to either side of the road, where blinding white light reflected back at them. Elsewhere, up higher, the sun had burned off the snow, opening an expanse of moist, black mud. For someone from the loess steppes like Du Wanxiang, trucking through the rich black soil steaming with evaporating water was a fabulous new experience. "People from Heilongjiang say," one of the others told her, "that if you poke a chopstick in the ground here, it'll sprout."

Their truck chugged along, mountains in the distance, plains close by, villages few and far between, few signs of human habitation; all they saw were more trucks. Others might have found it boring. These riders could not tear their eyes off the sights, gloating over every little thing as though it were one of the world's great wonders.

The wind gusted without warning. A light blanket of mist fell on the horizon, thickening rapidly overhead to the consistency of dingy cotton wool. As growing apprehension prompted lots of startled looks, tiny feathery white flakes began drifting down from the sky like flower petals, meagerly at first, then in profuse whirling clusters. The children in the cab jabbered with excitement. "Isn't that something," the adults chuckled. "All of a sudden it snows, just like that."

The truck picked up speed and plowed through the flurries. As the snow fell faster, the flakes got larger, piled in drifts, swept crossways, and settled quietly on the passengers' clothing and their headkerchiefs, and stuck onto their lashes and brows. Fresh accumulations replaced what melted. More settled where they'd rubbed spots free. The sky was a shapeless blank except for sheet upon sheet of falling shredded cotton. It was as though the entire world had been incorporated into the blossom of a white peach or plum, or perhaps a hydrangea flower. The truck was forced to a crawl. It inched forward. Steaming sweat poured from the driver's body despite the chill of the spring snowstorm. The state farm wasn't far, and he wanted to get there as fast as he could.

Shortly they heard voices through the cottony fog, and the truck came to a halt. First one person, then the whole group descended on them to unload the truck, helping people up, and carrying the children and baggage off. "Is the road still passable?" they asked, concerned. "We were really worried. Rush inside and warm up."

They'd put down at the farm bus stop, but where was Li Gui in all this crowd? Hadn't Li Gui come to meet her? No, she guessed not. Du Wanxiang let herself be bustled into a large room made warm and cheerful by an oil-drum fire, its flue running up into crudely hewn beams. There wasn't much in the room except a white timber table and some stools. People gathered around the newly arrived dependents to find out how they were feeling and whether they needed anything.

"Being on the road is trying," they said. "Let's take you to the farm guest house first for a few days to rest up. By all means, if you need anything, or if there's a problem, let us know. This is your home now." Du Wanxiang had never met these people before, but she felt as if she were being greeted by her own kin, as though she'd come back home after a long absence. It all felt so new yet so comfortably familiar. So, just as she had always done, she started looking after people. She poured boiled water someone had brought over into bowls and served it. She got the broom from the corner and swept up when she noticed mud and cigarette butts on the floor. At first the people were stiffly polite. Gradually they lost sight of the fact that she was a newly arrived guest from thousands of miles away and treated her like an old-timer. One of the cadres she'd ridden in with admired Du Wanxiang's complacency and pleasant expression.

"You're home now," he told her. "We've all settled in here to raise families and prosper. Actually, we ended up here because our company commander brought the whole lot of us in on orders. He told us we were going to a state farm. Two days we spent on transport trucks. At dusk on the second day, the trucks just stopped at a piece of wasteland at the bottom of the mountain.

" 'Fall out,' the company commander said, 'you're home.' Home? There was a stretch of virgin forest, and untouched grassland, but where was home? We looked at each other incredulously and didn't move.

" 'Out, all of you,' the commander said. 'What are you waiting for.' Finally he said, 'Look sharp! Out now! There are trees to chop down and lots of grass and vines to cut if you mean to get a shed built against the weather tonight.' The commander debarked first, the rest of us followed. That was our first step toward the comfortable lives we live today. Things are different now. Take a look at our company command post tomorrow, and you'll see. It's a high-rise building complete with electricity and telephones. It's astonishing when I think back to how we started."

Life as a Dependent

Production Team Thirteen, thirty *li* from the company command post, was a new unit. Li Gui was a tractor hand on this team. He was new to the job but meticulous and hardworking and not ashamed to ask his instructor when he ran into problems. All the drivers in this group had undertaken the high-prestige work of tractor driving without previous experience; they were learning on the job and were consequently tremendously busy. His wife's arrival made him very happy.[9] He was now allowed to move from the collective dorm directly into a brand-new, mud-brick, thatched-roof cottage, where they set up housekeeping. He handed over all the responsibilities for getting things in order to Wanxiang. He felt enormously pleased that his wife of eleven years, who'd worked her fingers to the bone for his family, could live comfortably and serenely on the paycheck he brought home.

It only took Du Wanxiang a couple of hectic days to get the place fixed up. Everything about their basic existence seemed just fine. Yet she just could not stem the surges of excitement all the new things she'd seen along the way had stirred in her. She decided, since her brain was bulging with new ideas, that she should find somebody to talk to, or some job to do. But Li Gui was almost never home. And when he was, he'd only make household small talk with her. "Get settled in first," he'd say, off-handedly, "then we'll talk about something for you to do. Anyway, what are you suited for except working your plough and hoe in the field. That's all been mechanized on big model farms like this. What's wrong with just keeping house?"

May was the busiest planting season here. Crimson tractors plowed the enormous well-harrowed fields, moving far, far away, almost out of sight before turning and laboring back again. Du Wanxiang had been standing beneath a row of newly planted poplars in front of the dormitory for the longest time. She was not the sort of person who expressed herself well. Also, coming out of the little mountain gully, she figured everybody else must be more proficient than she. Now even Li Gui had become a big man. He'd been abroad, fought the American devils in Korea; years of study had raised his level of knowledge to the point where now he was a tractor hand operating a huge, forty-horsepower truck. Dawn to dusk, dusk to dawn, he plowed his way through that vast, flat, black sea. He was quite gregarious around the drivers and the other people in his unit. Still, after work, he'd wait for her to serve him dinner, wolf down his food, and then go out looking for people he could socialize with or a poker game or chess partner. He never talked to her. He treated her just the way Gonggong treated Popo. Li Gui had never actually treated her any differently, and she'd never held it against him or made any special demands. But now she was thinking, "Did he drag me all the way out here just to cook and keep house for him?" Even when this thought entered her mind, she still felt no animosity toward him. Rather, inadvertently, her respect and longing to be like him increased in direct proportion to her growing disdain of her own inadequacies. When she could no longer control her feelings, she went looking for the team leader.

"Please, sir," she said to him, "give me an assignment. I'm so wretched with nothing to do."

The team leader was an old-timer. He was a demobilized soldier who had lots of contact with dependents from all over the country, and he knew how difficult the women found their initial adjustment. As part of his ideological work with them, he'd been wracking his brains for some kind of solution. Still he hadn't quite grasped what it was that the woman before him making anxious demands for work really wanted, nor why she was so passionate about getting involved in hard labor.

"Well, that's just terrific," he said. "A new production unit is always looking for good people. Go on, do whatever you think needs doing, whatever you think you can manage. Placing you in the organization would be a different matter, of course, since for the life of me, I don't know where I could put you." [10]

Wanxiang said nothing. But each subsequent day, the hastily thrown-together facilities housing the thirty dependent families started to change. The filthy latrine no one had ever bothered with before was suddenly immaculate, swept out daily, spread with a surface layer of lime so that people no longer gagged on the stench when they used it. Thresholds sparkled without the coal chips, garbage, and cigarette butts. At first no one paid any attention or questioned the change, assuming it had happened naturally. Some of the women who had lots of kids and found buying grain and oil bothersome, seeing that Wanxiang had no children, prevailed on her to lug things around for them or to mind their children. Gradually more and more people sought her help. At first they thanked her profusely, but later they just took her for granted. When she proved so obliging, they looked to her for help on matters they could easily have done themselves. They asked her to make a few pairs of cloth shoes for their children when they caught her making some for herself. Or seeing that she was doing her mending, they'd drag their husbands' things out and bring them over to her. Some even borrowed grain coupons or a few coins, which they never repaid. Wanxiang never faulted them. All in all, everybody felt quite satisfied having a person like her in their midst. And the team leader had no time to spare looking after wives. On the surface, life flowed along like a placid pool of water. Li Gui noticed his wife was not agitating to go to work anymore and seemed to live quite peacefully. Like a tiny wind-tossed boat, this orphan woman who had struggled so hard for so long deserved to find a safe harbor out of reach of the gale, where she could live in peace a little while.

Joyous Summer

The July sky over the Great Northern Wasteland was a livid blue. Breezes played gently at people's clothing. A riot of colored blossoms covered the luxuriant meadow, perfuming the air. Pink asters, pale red wild lilies, slender tiger lilies, corpulent peonies, and a profusion of unnamed varietals embellished the vast plain in velvet tapestry. Butterflies, bees, and dragonflies hovered, color glinting off their wings. Pheasants, wild duck, egrets, and waterbirds frolicked in the marshes; deer and stag bolted through the hills. The old masters of the Great Northern Wasteland, the black bear, wild boar, wolves, and foxes, having withdrawn disconsolate to bordering regions, hankered for those luxuriant hills and the underbrush of the grasslands, and sneaked back through the crops in search of food, to attack, without warning, the new masters of the place. This fertile land that looked so peaceful from afar was in fact a battlefield of living things all struggling to ensure their own survival.

In such beautiful surroundings, the farm landscape formed an even grander sight. The corn was green, the wheat yellow; it fell before the screaming-red tractors and combine harvesters as they mowed forward through the golden waves of grain like ships through an ocean. Black earth appeared in their wake. Pyramids of straw lined the cleared-over fields. The sun shone brilliantly on high. One after another, trucks sped down the road. The sound of human voices came rolling out of the grain-drying yard. A soprano horn blared martial tunes and melodies. Voices, sometimes a tenor, at other times a soprano, sang enchanting melodies from all over the world, modulating the mood of the people laboring there. Some moments they felt as though they were staring down from the highest mountain peak; at others it was as though they were floating in a tempestuous, surging ocean, dragged uncomplaining through a raging current; sometimes they seemed to be strolling over a little river. But what provoked people's attention most was when headquarters command sounded roll call or reported the size or quality of the yield.

Du Wanxiang in the lead, a group of dependents fed wheat into a smoke-belching winnower and then swept the ground around the enormous mounds of grain with big brooms. When had anybody ever seen so much wheat! The gang of young women in brightly colored clothes lined up in the drying yard, their heads bent to the task of drying wheat. Du Wanxiang felt the beauty and solemn majesty of the universe at that moment. Rejuvenated, she raised her head and gazed about at the zealous faces of the women singing and laboring beside her. Then she lowered her eyes to look at the grain rolling like precious gemstones beneath their feet. The radiant, tumbling grains cut playfully into their bare soles. She trod back and forth across it, turning it over and over to dry. She felt like dancing about and hooting as she had when she was a seven- or eight-year-old child. But it was a return to a vastly more joyous childhood than the one she'd spent hauling half-filled buckets of water, scaling the high steppes all alone, and plodding back alone, eaten up with anxiety and dread. With generous abandon, she threw back her head and sang her childhood mountain songs. The songs drew everyone's attention. They cocked their heads to listen to those indomitable, lusciously vibrant, sensuous shepherd songs from across the Northwest steppes. They gaped, astonished, at the ordinarily silent, smiling woman. Then others, moved by her ballads, sang with passionate abandon songs from where they'd come. The whole drying yard reverberated with the purity of their music as songs and laughter floated vibrantly everywhere. How great and glorious life was!

Du Wanxiang labored with intense joy absolved of fatigue and hunger. She worked as the others rested, persevering even when they broke for meals. Some of the dependents laboring on the drying ground got paid by the hour, some by the piece. Only she worked for no pay at all. Everyone on the drying ground stared with astonishment at the short, fragile young woman, the smile playing constantly around her mouth; how extraordinary her apparently bottomless source of energy was, how peculiar that so lofty, solemn, and virginal a glow radiated from her ordinary face. It was impossible to keep one's eyes off her.

Gold in Dross

Winter came. The north wind howled. A characteristic Great Northern Wasteland blizzard covered the land with snow and sand and raged on all day, shrouding everything in such darkness it was impossible to know where you were. Even exerting your utmost strength, it was still hard to stay upright. The frigid cold of the Great Northern Wasteland spared no one. Still the people of the Great Northern Wasteland took pride and pleasure in their victories. At thirty degrees below zero, brows and beards were matted with snowflakes, eyelashes froze together in tiny ice wands; yet the sweat still poured down through their bangs and froze onto their foreheads. Their shirts were drenched with perspiration even as the woolen jumpers and felt jackets they wore as outer garments were criss-crossed with a thick layer of snowy frost. Only younger men in top physical condition, with strength enough for a struggle to the death, were selected to fell timber up on the mountain, cut grass for tinder, or fetch the rocks needed for the canal. But Du Wanxiang shattered the sex barrier, braving her own way, joining the back-breaking toil as though she were one of those select young men.

Thus winter gave way to summer, years followed one another, and Du Wanxiang achieved extraordinary things from her very ordinary station in life. She moved slowly, yet always outstripped her co-workers. The number of those who admitted her superiority grew, while those who refused to submit tried hard to keep up with her. Relying on her inexhaustible strength, Du Wanxiang swept through the rapid current. She handled everyone she encountered and every affair she managed with the same broad-minded equanimity, always doing little things on the sly for some person she felt was in need. At the annual year's end appraisal, acclaim for her efforts came flowing in like spring water from people

everywhere. The kinds of things they reported always seemed quite ordinary until they added it up. Then everybody realized how hard it must
have been for one person to do so much. So in spite of her self-effacing
manner, the collective always promoted her. First she was the standard
bearer of the squad, then of the state farm, and then of the whole district.

Du Wanxiang seemed to be sailing forward like a boat on a favorable
wind when, in fact, like the Yangzi River itself, her way was strewn with
hidden dangers. When she ran aground on unforeseen trouble, she for-
tified herself against it. By nature she was a warm person who never
quarreled or had differences of opinion with others. But the dependents
were not easy to lead. Once she encountered someone stealing public
property. Wanxiang talked and talked, trying to dissuade her, when unexpectedly, the woman turned on her in a rage and told her to stop med-
dling. Wanxiang trembled with emotion. She flushed bright red and,
grasping the thief's hand, gravely reprimanded her: "How can you act
like this?" she said. "This is public property. No one can take it. Give it
back right now!"

Her righteousness overwhelmed her opponent, who returned the property and fled, ashen-faced. During a year of below-average yields, when
their grain allotment had dropped, Li Gui's parents came to stay at just
the time the baby girl was born, so all of a sudden life got very tough.[11]
After the autumn harvest, lots of people went to the fields to glean grain.
That year, because of excessive rain, the machine harvest hadn't been too
efficient. So there was lots of grain around to pick up. Li Gui's father
went out gleaning too. In the end, farm employees gleaned through their
noon rest hour and all evening after work, filling hemp sacks of all sizes
and lugging them home. Du Wanxiang also gleaned, and since she had
quick eyes and fast hands, she rapidly outstripped the others. But she
took her bags of soy beans and wheat, sack after sack, to the collective
drying ground. Pointing to her lean, solitary back, some people mocked
her for being such a fool. Others reviled her for making such a show of
herself. The tension showed its face in the family as well: Popo refused
to cook. Where in the world, she asked rhetorically, did a mother-in-law
cook for the daughter-in-law? Then Gonggong wouldn't eat, saying the
food should go to the young people. Li Gui aligned himself with his
parents.

"There's nothing wrong with people gleaning a little grain for themselves out of what the government left behind," he nagged. "Why don't
you just stay home. Why do you have to bust your ass gleaning for the
government? People just run you down behind your back."

Du Wanxiang paid no attention to the laughter and scolding. She used
every gentle argument she could to persuade her family, but went on
gleaning, as before, and turning her gleanings over to the government.

"This grain belongs to the state," was what she said. "As workers on a state farm, we should watch out for the state's entire populace. The standard grain ration for an employee of our farm is already much higher than almost anywhere else." Her wasted body making her eyes seem even larger, Du Wanxiang impressed quite a few people. Primary school students organized themselves to glean for the state.

One year a group of educated youth from the city arrived at the farm. Most were middle-school graduates. They knew a lot of big words, could hold forth on any subject, sang and danced effortlessly, and were basically lively, naive kids. Team Thirteen got two dozen of these blessed darlings, and Du Wanxiang was assigned to be their group leader, taking charge of their labor and studies and generally looking after them. The girls were astonished when they met Du Wanxiang. How could this rustic, totally unremarkable, dumpy little woman be a Communist Party member and the standard bearer of the entire district? She sure didn't look it. How had she made such a name for herself!

The changeable young girls spent their first few days having a terrific time. But then some of them got homesick, and others started humming that old folk tune, "Who Doesn't Treasure Their Precious Youth . . . "

They also got along with their group leader just fine for the first couple of days and appreciated her cordial, controlled amiability and how meticulous her work was. But gradually they got bored with her patched blue clothes and her obnoxiously unfashionable haircut. And she was so completely humorless! Patiently Du Wanxiang told them all that had gone into the founding of this farm, told about Secretary Wang Zhen, and about the old Red Army man who was farm commander. They were all stories she'd heard about the experiences of noble people, and they'd moved her. Some of the girls liked these stories and were determined to learn from the old Red Army man. Others resented her for being garrulous, and they pouted.

"Really!" they sniffed, "How can this semiliterate, hayseed commune dependent teach us anything about politics? We're doing her the courtesy of letting her handle us. Why doesn't she take a good look at herself!"

But Du Wanxiang, seemingly oblivious to their slighting looks, fastidiously redoubled her commitment, kept guiding and vigorously monitoring them. She loved the girls steadfastly. They had left their warm families. They had abandoned their elegant urban lives and, following Chairman Mao's directive, come down to this hard border region to learn about labor. They were full of budding ambition. Her zealous love for Chairman Mao and the Party obligated her to care for them. She felt there were things she should learn from them, as well. For that reason, when they needed sympathy she was maternal, but she also provided the strictness of a teacher when necessary. She understood that they needed both latitude and discipline. In time she became indispensable to the girls, who sought her out when they ran into trouble, never forgot her when they were happy; when they got back from visiting relatives, they always had a memento for their "sister" Dujie from Mommy and Daddy. Those who had initially held her in contempt saw their own mistake. Gradually they changed their attitude toward her.

One time Du Wanxiang took them all out to a forest about ten *li* away to collect firewood. When they left in the morning, the creek was still frozen solid, but on the way back it had melted into a river six or seven inches deep and three meters wide. One of the girls halted on reaching the bank of the creek. "Dujie!" she cried. "The water's too cold. How am I going to get across?" Without missing a stride, Du Wanxiang removed her snow shoes. Then another girl shouted for her. "Get on," said Du Wanxiang, in a crouched over position. "Go on. I'll carry you."

Back and forth Wanxiang carried the girls on her back. The last one could not wait, and shucking off her shoes, gnawing her lip, she waded into the frigid water. Her feet were so unbearably cold she burst into tears. Wanxiang immediately sat down on the ground with the girl and put the frozen feet inside her warm padded jacket, inside her underwear, right up against her own breast, as she massaged her legs.

"Dujie, oh, Dujie," the girls surrounding them cried in shock when they discovered that Du Wanxiang's feet were frozen purple. That night as they lay on the *kang,* they could not sleep. "I conceded her superiority when I realized that none of us could have done what she did," one of them said.

"We middle-school students talk a good line," said another, "all about how we're going to revolutionize our thoughts by learning from the workers, peasants, and soldiers. But when it comes to practice . . . we're not so great."

"As I see it," interjected a third, "there are those among us who still exploit the devotion of our peasant and worker comrades for their own benefit and then call them all fools."

"Don't try to put anything over on Dujie," came the retort. "She's nobody's fool. They don't make fools into Party standard bearers. Du Wanxiang has earned the prestige that a Communist Party member ought to be accorded. We should study her and learn from her."

Deep Roots, Many Leaves

Every day, starting in January 1964, Du Wanxiang went to work in the Trade Union office on the second floor of the magnificent Culture Palace.

The chairman of the Trade Union was an old comrade from the Resistance War against Japan. Several of the managers and secretaries had been demobilized and sent down to the farm after the victorious War of Liberation in 1949. The youngest person in the office was a female accountant who had been part of a cultural troop in the volunteer militia during the war in Korea. Du Wanxiang felt enormous respect for them all. In fact she looked on them as her teachers, and they cherished her too. They all wanted to help her improve her work, so they guided her in reading directives and pamphlets, in drafting work plans, revising study objectives, and in preparing the various drafts of speeches; this last because more and more, Du Wanxiang was being asked to speak at model worker convocations, to give talks about her own experience and her appreciation of the works of Chairman Mao. Sometimes she was required to attend provincial-level Conferences of Model Workers for the Exchange of Experiences. Additionally, there were visiting reporters to meet and leading comrades touring the farm to entertain. Fame touched her, gently bathed her, like the spring breeze or the flowing water. It did not intoxicate her. She went on rushing from the Cultural Palace to the headquarters for management of farm dependents, to various enterprises and local production units. Then off she'd go to outlying units where she'd stay a few days working with local dependents, carefully working out matters with the cadre, and holding conferences. The material she wrote on what she'd seen and grasped gave her a vehicle for posing various problems. And she was quite dogged about night school, where for the past two years she had been studying culture. The people at school marveled over her rapid progress. The various ranking managers and branch secretaries at the office, who'd initially considered her nothing more than an ordinary female cadre promoted by the Party, realized their mistake. Each passing day brought more comprehension. Yet what gave her that increasingly evident principled nobility?

Du Wanxiang was going to give another talk about her personal experience. Her comrades at work launched into a frenzy of preparation. They were inspired to help her make this speech better and even more moving than usual. After talking with her for some time, they flipped through stacks of reports, magazines and directives, rifled the collected works of Marx, Lenin, and Chairman Mao, searching for quotations, and in the end, they produced a draft that was mellifluous yet to the point. But as Du Wanxiang studied the text, finding it an adequate speech in every respect, an old feeling of bitterness assailed her once again. She would not endure it again. Many times before after she had read her speech aloud from the platform under the gaze of an audience of thousands, she'd felt anxious and bogus when the people applauded her. The text of this speech was excellent. It drew on newspaper editorials. It evidenced real appreciation of Chairman Mao's works. It relied heavily on the experiences of outstanding revolutionary figures. Yet, Du Wanxiang thought, these beautiful words are not what I speak. Mouthing the words of others is cheating. She felt she couldn't go on like this anymore. She'd be able to stand the loss of her status as a standard bearer, and never give another speech or see her name in print again, but she was going to have to be honest. She still could not write a proper essay, but she could—no, she absolutely had to—speak her own truth. As she thought, so she would speak. She decided to start fresh. She would extract points from her own ideas and then work with the words she really grasped to speak directly from her heart. First she blocked out a draft which she delivered to some of her comrades at the union and to her night-school teacher, looking to them for criticism. At a general meeting of workers, she finally delivered a speech she had written herself in her own language. This was around the end of 1965.[12]

On the night of her speech the sky, burnished like a mirror, glittered with a million stars. There wasn't a breath of wind. The cypresses in the square in front of the Culture Palace seemed severe and exceptional under their fresh layer of thick snow. A pale, watery white light refracted over roads stretching far and near. It was a cold, quiet night. But a dazzlingly brilliant light gleamed out from inside the Culture Palace, punctuated by bursts of laughter and applause. It was Du Wanxiang reporting on her work and her thoughts to a packed audience of all the farm's employees assembled in the warmth of the Great Assembly Hall of the Culture Palace.

She started by talking about her childhood in that miserable little mountain gully, the endless, grinding toil of countless generations who had endured brutal oppression; about the troubled seasons of the ignorant, uneducated people who lived there. From the grinding depths of that bitter life, she had imagined some other world, some other life, and some other kind of relationship between people! Those listening felt they were entering that dark despondent time with Du Wanxiang, straight into the soul of the travailing people. It made them recall themselves how generations of their ancestors had been whipped by vicious wind and storms, and how those generations had doggedly produced the will and resolve to struggle. And in the end, the working people had demonstrated their power against the three great mountains that had afflicted old China from the start.[13] Du Wanxiang pushed out of that interminably drought-stricken steppe: the tentative shoot braved the wind and sand and grew proudly into a red apricot tree.

Then Du Wanxiang's report turned to the glorious new universe that the revolutionary victory had brought. A breath of spring wind blew through the Great Audience Hall of the Culture Palace, and the audience's delight in this brand new life broke through Du Wanxiang's plain, simple prose as though in broad, rolling, brilliant billows: China! People's China! Length and breadth, a land of plenty. Your spacious skies of blue, your soft, silky grasslands, far-flung villages, dense green forests, your sweet flowing waters, your great ancient cities, and your brocade sash of flourishing new towns—they embraced all of this in their hearts, and each was intoxicated, overwhelmed with good fortune, feeling that it would be possible to ride out a tempest, sit astride great ocean waves, and fly over hill and dale to vanquish every sweated task.

Of all these places, which did they love most? The Great Northern Wasteland! And what venture was the loftiest? Reclamation and reconstruction of the Great Northern Waste! And who commanded their greatest admiration? The people of the Great Northern Wasteland who had blazed trails with unsurpassed hardship, daunting strength, and had wrestled victory and great pleasure from struggle.[14] They had left their homes far, far behind to reclaim the marsh and wasteland for China, to guarantee the safety of China's northern borders. They had cast off their traditional consciousness and with unbounded fervor and full hearts, had established a modernized socialist agricultural base, tempering themselves to become new model workers of the highest moral qualities. They had produced great wealth and created a new proletarian culture. Although these were China's border regions, they were still linked tightly to the heart of the nation. An enormous wave of emotion welled from the hearts of those listening to Du Wanxiang at this point; they all felt like shouting: "Communist Party! Brilliant and great Communist Party! You've cast such light on humankind! Given such hope, such warmth! Such good fortune! We will struggle forever for you, for the great enterprise of Communism. We all belong to you!"

"I am an ordinary person," Du Wanxiang said in closing. "I have done nothing more than what ordinary people do. The little I've understood, the reason why we're all here today, is because of you. You, my hardworking comrades, you people with ideals, you've prompted my mental development, encouraged me. We've all been educated and nurtured by the Party. All I want is to stay under the Party's leadership forever, acting with practical wisdom, honestly carrying out the Party's directives, and struggling for our Communist enterprise for the rest of my life."

Then Du Wanxiang stood, a smile on her lips, at the front of the platform, looking self-effacingly at the people in the Great Audience Hall. There wasn't a sound. Everyone waited. They were waiting for her talk, beautiful as flowing water, seductive as harp music, to continue. Her speech helped them see, hear, and feel things they had never seen or heard or been moved by before. It was as if she had transformed those ordinary things and made them suddenly more significant. Du Wanxiang had not recited the classics like a pedant. The maxims and wisdom of those classical works were diffused throughout her simple speech. Just as crops absorb sunlight, rain, and dew, good people, good works, and good precepts had slowly saturated her very soul, worked into her blood, and made her a living thing deeply rooted, with abundant foliage, able to resist all contagion. Du Wanxiang did not have a lofty, bigger-than-life spirit. She was simple and affectionate. No matter how much people looked up to her and were guided by her, in the end she remained the same amiable, straightforward, simple and honest, modest, incandescently fervent Du Wanxiang so comfortably familiar to all of them.

The Party secretary walked over and grasped her hand tightly. "Comrade Wanxiang," he said with joyous sincerity, "you've taught us a wonderful lesson. I want to thank you on behalf of all of us from the bottom of my heart."

Suddenly a thunderous clap of applause broke through the Great Audience Hall. Waked from their reflection, the farm employees, as though discovering a ray of light in the dead of night, felt a surge of unbridled hope in their hearts. They approved of Du Wanxiang completely. Du Wanxiang is our frontline soldier. We must learn from her. We must go forward with her.

Translated by Tani E. Barlow

Introduction

1. See Chad Hansen, "Individualism in Chinese Thought," in *Individualism and Holism: Studies in Confucian and Taoist Values,* ed. Donald Munro (Ann Arbor: University of Michigan Center for Chinese Studies, 1985).
2. See Charlotte Furth, "Androgynous Males and Deficient Females: Biology and Gender Boundaries in Sixteenth- and Seventeenth-Century China," *Late Imperial China* 9, no. 2 (December 1988). I am reading somewhat against the grain. Professor Furth supplies the evidence but does not draw the same conclusions that I do.
3. Kang Yuwei (1858–1927) was the leader of the 1895 reform movement and a key figure in the appropriation of political philosophy, institutions, and practices. Liang Qichao (1873–1929) was his student. Liang became a major intellectual figure. Both men were active in early formulations of the woman problem.

Miss Sophia's Diary

1. A reference to masturbation.
2. The literal translation would be "Little Brother Wei." The use of this pseudo-kin address indicates her intimacy with Wei. Note that she calls Ling Jishi, her lover, by his formal name.
3. Translation from Joseph, Joseph S. M. Lau, "Diary of Miss Sophia," *Tamkang Review* 5, no.1 (1974).
4. *Dianxin* are small dumplings stuffed with meat or shrimp and steamed, fried, or baked.
5. This is from Joseph Lau's translation.
6. The late Ming collection of short stories known as the *Liaozhai zhiyi* contains many bizarre stories, many of erotic encounters between ghosts and human beings.
7. Literally "Elder Sister Yun." The text makes reference both to people who

appear to be Sophia's blood sisters and a variety of women honorifically called sisters. Elder Sister Yun is a close friend, most likely an old lover.

8. The English transliteration of "Miss" is in the original text.

9. Common home place or dialect would have given Sophia and Ling Jishi an adequate pretext for knowing each other. The only other reason, the nurse implies, must be lust.

10. Translation after Joseph Lau.

11. Translation from Joseph Lau.

12. After W. F. Jenner's translation *Miss Sophia's Diary* (Beijing: Panda Books, 1985).

13. Here the text makes the Versailles Treaty a sign of post–May Fourth ambivalence about Western cultural offerings. It conjoins Ling Jishi and Western promises of democracy and may be read as a metaphor for all that seems beautiful on the outside but is revealed to harbor, in Sophia's words, "a cheap soul."

14. The reference is to a late-sixteenth-century opera in which a woman dies of romantic longing and is restored to life by the power of love. The opera is an anatomy of female passion.

15. Ding Ling refers here to boys who share the girls' commitment to women's liberation and sexual equality, boys "in the movement." Ling Jishi comes from what by definition is a conservative, immigrant community and has thus not been exposed to the idealism of the May Fourth movement.

16. Translation after Lau.

17. Translation after Jenner.

18. This name, possibly an error in transcription, may refer to Jianru from the theater date. If so, what Mengru/Jianru has to say about the relationship between sexuality and emotion mocks Sophia, reminding her of her old homoerotic attachments.

19. The word Ding Ling uses for character, *renge,* was a hotly disputed philosophic issue in a post-Confucian world. *Renge* was the mark of the individualistic person.

20. Since the family system was the primary target of the liberation movement, Ling's tempting Sophia with retreat into the autocratic family is a savage irony. She wants to consummate her passion; he wants another marriage.

A Woman and a Man

1. In light of Japanese aggression, this affectation makes Ouwai an even worse sycophant. Ding Ling also connects deracinated male literary figures with interest in Japanese culture in part 1 of *Shanghai, Spring 1930.*

2. "Little" or "Young" Wang.

3. Lao Zhang is, literally, "Old" Zhang.

4. The word in the text is *quehan,* a compound that along with *quedian,* Ding Ling uses frequently to denote women's weaknesses and faults. For other examples, see *Shanghai, Spring 1930* and "Thoughts on March 8."

Yecao

1. This is one of the bluntest expressions of Ding Ling's belief in the inherent flaws of female nature. She repeated it constantly in the thirties, and even

touches upon it in "Thoughts on March 8." In this context it is linked with the reconsideration of the male/reason and female/emotions opposition.
2. An amah is a maidservant, cook, or children's nanny. She would often be an elderly woman.

Shanghai, Spring 1930

1. Censorship made it necessary to cross out references to the Communist Party. Some of the references can be supplied from later editions. Others are conjecture. Bracketed terms have been added for those deleted in the original.
2. The first is an unleavened, round, baked bread and the other a long thin stick of dough fried in deep fat. These foods are the conventional breakfast of the un-Westernized Chinese person.
3. *Qipao* was the fashion current in urban areas in the twenties and thirties. In the U.S.A. it is sometimes known as the Suzie Wong dress. Cut to emphasize the bosom, figure molding, with a high collar, the dress was a Chinese adaptation of Manchu fashion along Western lines.
4. In the original, the date is censored. Labor Day is used in other editions.
5. These are the terms used in later editions.
6. When the capital of China under the Guomindang government moved south to Nanjing, the "southern capital," the "northern capital," Beijing, became "Northern Peace," or Beiping.
7. The term is *quedian*.

Net of Law

1. The *yamen* was the imperial government offices and court where the local magistrate served.

Mother

1. The Guanyin Boddhisatva is the patron goddess of mercy.
2. Widows since Mencius's time had acted as tutors for their children.
3. Ding Ling has forgotten that Yao Ma has large—only partially or loosely bound—feet. Footbinding was almost universal in China by the early twentieth century. Working women had their feet bound loosely. The women of gentry and urban bourgeois families had their feet bound tightly to produce a tiny, uniform, salable foot. Only minority and Hakka women eschewed the practice altogether.
4. The county magistrate was the local representative of the throne. This man would have held an examination degree and come from the same sort of family as the Yu family.
5. Since the Manchus had imposed the convention, cutting the queue signified the end of the Manchu reign.
6. Academies of various kinds flourished in the late Qing dynasty at the village, county, and urban levels. A large lineage like the Jiangs had enough property to support their own school where they sent all talented boys in the surname group. Should one succeed in the examinations or, later, government office, the entire lineage association benefited.

7. The term is *shoujie,* a woman who remains a chaste widow and who could, under the dynasty, petition for a commemorative arch.
8. Her shoes are simple, in contrast to the highly colored and ornamentally embroidered satin shoes women of her class generally wore.
9. Each woman speaks Hunan dialect and reads the common literary heritage. The revolutionary movement initiated the notion of a common "national" tongue.
10. In this discussion Manzhen refers to both the *guiju* and the *lishu,* the ritual conventions governing people's behavior.
11. The word for "will," *zhiqi,* may also be translated as "determination."
12. This would make Third Mistress Yu Xiao Han's mother-in-law. Many families preferred to raise their own daughters-in-law because it gave the son's mother a larger degree of control over her son's affairs after the marriage.
13. Taken from the stone tablets of the Northern Wei period and noted for very vigorous, "masculine," strokes.
14. People learned calligraphy by making copies of famous pieces that had been carved in rock. The stone around the ideograph would be inked, and the paper impression left the characters outlined in white. These copies were easy to take and distribute as models.
15. The Four Books and the Five Classics were the basic texts of Neo-Confucianism.
16. In Chinese the titles were *Bishenghua* and *Menglizhun.* Wu Dingguang's wife has pedestrian taste in romances.
17. Most of the older women are opium addicts and need their fix.
18. The term is *xianhui* and it defines the stereotyped "virtuous wife, good mother."
19. The Four Books are *The Great Learning,* the *Analects of Confucius,* the *Doctrine of the Mean,* and the book of *Mencius.* The *History* is another part of the Confucian canon. Manzhen is, in other words, quite literate even to be able to begin reading these books and using the tools of scholarship like the compendia and dictionaries.
20. *Yi taitai* is either ego's wife's married sisters, ego's maternal married aunts, or formal concubines.
21. These lanterns were given by the throne and signified high rank.
22. Official families kept to the "Confucian" convention of gender segregation. Thus there were only two ways for elite women to have relationships with men. First, since *lishu* and *guiju* prevented meetings with "strangers" of the opposite sex, women socialized only with male kin. Second, they met husbands, strangers, on their wedding night and expanded their range of male kin. The female academy introduced a modern "public" space. The elite women in this scene are seeing men they've known through gossip and news but possibly never laid eyes on.
23. Manzhen's Third Sister, Sangu Taitai (Mrs. Third Aunt) and Third Master's Wife (This Mistress Yu), Manzhen's sister-in-law.
24. *Jinghuayuan* was a famous novel about the triumph of female virtue. One hundred female spirits come to earth as talented and beautiful women who go through the examination system and become officials.
25. The description of Xia Zhenren is a portrait of Xiang Jingyu, a revolutionary feminist.
26. The child's name means large or great.

27. The Xinchou treaty refers to the Boxer Protocol of 1901. Lin Zexu was a hero of the Opium War of the 1840s who burned British opium in defense of Chinese sovereignty.
28. Lamps were part of the opium paraphernalia.
29. Qiu Jin was a revolutionary figure martyred by decapitation in 1907. She is considered to be the first major "feminist" figure of the twentieth century and a major player in the revolutionary movement preceding 1911. She actively sought martyrdom. The Xia Zhenren/Xiang Jingyu figure in this novel, who represents the emergence of a socialist-feminist theory, criticizes this course. Her attack on old-fashioned literary style (literally, "eight-legged essays," originally the examination format, later slang for outdated, bureaucratic writing) prefigures the events of language reform and anti-Confucianism in 1919.
30. Guan Zhong was a successful official in the feudal state of Qi. He died in 645 B.C.
31. The Zhongxing or "Revive China" Society, one of many gentry-elite anti-Manchu political organizations.
32. Manzhen refers here to the Boxer Rebellion of 1900.
33. Home may also be translated family. Thus Manzhen is meditating on the meaning of the *jia* to her, and she decides that she and her children constitute a nuclear unit.
34. "Long Hairs" is the slang term for the Taiping rebels, who wore their hair long and unbraided.
35. The name, "Liu Family Village," suggests that it is peopled by one dominant lineage.

Affair in East Village

1. Far more commonly such marriages were difficult to consummate and maintain. Marriage partners saw each other as siblings. Ding Ling seems to be romanticizing out of ignorance of the peasants' lives.
2. It was common practice for the ruling rural elite to form self-defense militia under their own lieutenants. This allowed them to maintain the status quo, to impose quasi-legitimate surcharges on tenants, to cream off strong young men, to pay bribes extorted by superiors, and to supply labor for whatever government held power in the area.
3. Female infanticide.
4. The *kang* is an adobe platform, built about two feet off the ground. Heated air circulates from the stove through the hollow space inside the *kang*. It is cool in summer and warm in winter and is, as Ding Ling's stories make clear, the center of social life for the inhabitants of the communities of the north.

New Faith

1. The village of West Willow. Other names that transmit meaning include those of the three Chen brothers: Chen Xinhan or "Renew Han China" Chen, Chen Zuohan or "Aid the Han Chinese" Chen, and Chen Lihan or "Establish the Han Chinese" Chen.
2. A *mantou* is a steamed roll made of wheat and eaten in the North as daily bread.

3. The men refer to him as Zhang Laoyeh, a title that is both familiar and respectful.
4. The name in Chinese is Chen Dashu, the second term signifying that Chen belongs to (but is substantially younger than) the generation of the speaker's father.
5. In Northern dialect, this means "Second Brother."
6. Jingu means "Gold Daughter."
7. Laolao, "Granny," is the familiar term for one's maternal grandmother.
8. "Home of Respect for the Aged" is a euphemism for a labor camp.
9. The cadres, including art workers like Ding Ling, introduced the vocabulary of political propaganda and empowerment into village life. Among these words and behaviors was "speechifying."

Thoughts on March 8

1. The more literal rendering of this line is as follows: "When a woman capable of work sacrifices her career and becomes a 'virtuous wife, good mother' [*xianchi liangmu*] everybody sings her praises." This of course was the hated stereotype of domestic femininity that May Fourth radicals attacked so violently.
2. The "tragedy of backwardness" is, of course, divorce.
3. This was simply not true among peasants. Outside the revolutionary elite, divorce was the daughter-in-law's tool against an abusive mother-in-law and the wife's second greatest threat against her husband. The first was suicide.
4. The word in the text is, once again, *quedian*. For other uses of this word to describe women's failings see *Shanghai, Spring 1930* and "Yecao."
5. This passage has been edited to achieve sex neutrality. The version of this translation published earlier read, "if each Communist Party member were more responsible for his own moral conduct." Since Chinese does not give pronouns a gender, my revision is in fact truer to the text.
6. The important term is *houwu*, "regret," a constant theme in the writer's earliest fiction.

People Who Will Live Forever in My Heart

1. The Chinese term is *jizai*, meaning to record or to take a record. Ding Ling thus distinguishes this account from other narratives that may be described as "literature." Her emphatic statement that it takes time to "know" a person (politically, that is) is also framed in the relationship of the land reform official and the villager. The parallel with "When I Was in Xia Village" should be obvious. What has changed is the function of the narrator.
2. According to established practice, this was the first step in initiating land reform: to find "active elements" and carry out a rough class analysis.
3. The term is *fanshen*, which means to reverse or turn over, to go from rags to riches. *Fanshen* became a slogan for what peasants sought out of the process of political empowerment and seizure of land.
4. Literally, "Endless Winter" Li.
5. Daniang, or "Auntie," is a respectful as well as an affectionate address.
6. Chen Man is not using the May Fourth terms *nanxing* and *nüxing*, which indicate male and female sex, but rather the terms *yemen* and *niangmen*,

which signify gender by invoking kinlike relations. The ideograph *ye* (to which the pluralizer *men* has been added) means father, master, or sir. *Niang* means both mother and women or girls.

7. Such mourning rituals were the prerogatives of the wife.
8. The Chinese Communist Party reintroduced this transformed folk dance as a public celebration on days of political significance. Along with agit-prop, revolutionary opera, and story-telling, it used conventional practices to signify revolutionary commitments.

Du Wanxiang

1. The term for a daughter-in-law, *xifu,* is also used colloquially to mean wife.
2. The word is *guiju,* "protocol," which Ding Ling had attacked as a May Fourth activist and written about in *Mother.*
3. *Popo* is the colloquial term for mother-in-law.
4. Father-in-law in colloquial speech is rendered *gonggong.*
5. *Buzhang* is a secretary of a local department.
6. Nanniwan was a great event of the Sino-Japanese War. This is a reference to the Yan'an spirit that Ding Ling had so thoroughly embraced.
7. Note the use of *nuxing,* a neologism from the May Fourth period meaning "female sex." Ding Ling rarely uses this term.
8. This sentence echoes the point Ding Ling had made over three decades earlier in "Thoughts on March 8."
9. *Qizi,* the term Ding Ling uses here, is the old-fashioned word for wife. The more ideologically charged, egalitarian term would be *airen,* which means spouse but is literally translated as "lover."
10. He would also have to pay her.
11. This is a reference to the famine years of 1958–62, which followed upon the Great Leap Forward in 1957.
12. The beginning of the Great Proletarian Cultural Revolution. Here Ding Ling's reference can only be interpreted as a statement of her own dilemma, the paradox of the Communist literary figure.
13. The three mountains being feudalism, imperialism, and bureaucratic capitalism.
14. This rhetoric echoes the 1942 theme that pleasure and happiness are the product of struggle.

NOTES ON THE TRANSLATORS

TANI E. BARLOW is assistant professor of history at the University of Missouri-Columbia. Her book-length manuscript on Ding Ling, fiction, and sexual difference is in the final stages of completion.

GREGOR BENTON teaches in the Department of South and Southeast Asian Studies at the Anthropology-Sociology Center of the University of Amsterdam.

GARY J. BJORGE wrote the first English-language doctoral study of Ding Ling's fiction. His degree is in Chinese from the University of Wisconsin–Madison, and he now teaches history at the United States Army Command and General Staff College, Fort Leavenworth, Kansas.

CHARLOTTE CALHOUN is a San Francisco Bay Area translator. She earned a B.A. in Far Eastern history from Stanford University and an M.A. in Chinese from San Francisco State University.

DONALD HOLOCH is professor of Chinese language and literature at York University in Ontario. He is a literary critic, the author of numerous scholarly articles, and a translator.

JEAN JAMES is an art historian of the Han period whose avocation is translating modern Chinese fiction. Her work includes translations of Lao She's *Rickshaw* and *Ma and Son*.

RUTH KEEN is the editor for modern Chinese literature at Eugen Diederichs Verlag in Cologne. She took her master's degree in Chinese language at the Free University of Berlin and has edited, translated, and written articles on modern Chinese women's fiction.

KATHERINE TIANTUNG LO received a B.A. in English language and literature from Zhongshan University in Canton and an M.A. in library science from the University of Denver. She was professor of English language at Zhongshan and came to the United States in 1979. She is currently working in information management, particularly on data base development and computer networks.

HAL POLLARD did his post-graduate study at the Free University in Berlin during the early 1980s. His present whereabouts are unknown to the editor.

SHU-YING TS'AO teaches language and literature at York University in Ontario. She is a well-known translator of modern Chinese fiction and has written a number of influential articles on selected topics in modern fiction.